Black Patriots and Loyalists

Black Patriots and Loyalists

FIGHTING FOR
EMANCIPATION
IN THE WAR FOR
INDEPENDENCE

Alan Gilbert

THE UNIVERSITY OF CHICAGO PRESS

Chicago and London

ALAN GILBERT is the John Evans Professor in the Josef Korbel School of International Studies at the University of Denver. He is the author of *Marx's Politics: Communists and Citizens*, *Democratic Individuality*, and *Must Global Politics Constrain Democracy?*

The University of Chicago Press, Chicago 60637
The University of Chicago Press, Ltd., London
© 2012 by The University of Chicago
All rights reserved. Published 2012.
Printed in the United States of America

21 20 19 18 17 16 15 14 13 12   1 2 3 4 5

ISBN-13: 978-0-226-29307-3 (cloth)
ISBN-10: 0-226-29307-6 (cloth)

Library of Congress Cataloging-in-Publiation Data

Gilbert, Alan.
  Black patriots and loyalists: fighting for emancipation in the war for independence / Alan Gilbert.
     p. cm.
  Includes bibliographical references and index.
  ISBN-13: 978-0-226-29307-3 (hardcover : alkaline paper)
  ISBN-10: 0-226-29307-6 (hardcover : alkaline paper)   1. United States—History—Revolution, 1775–1783—Participation, African American.   2. African American soliders—United States—History—18th century.   3. Antislavery movements—United States—History—18th century.   I. Title.
  E269.N3G55 2012
  973.3′460896073—dc23

2011035577

Contents

Preface

Fifty years ago, historians often celebrated the American Revolution as the first independence movement that created free political institutions. In seceding from Britain, America's revolution was political, not social. It was thus distinguished from the French Revolution, which served as a model social uprising. In the French Revolution, sans-culottes stormed the Bastille and fought for equality; peasants torched the chateaux. In the American Revolution, by way of contrast, George Washington mobilized Patriot soldiers to defeat the British, culminating in the victory at Yorktown. Patriots became the rulers, but the social structure, so it seemed, was largely unaffected.

Although some historians, such as R. R. Palmer in his *Age of the Democratic Revolution*, emphasized the reach of the American Revolution, its role in inspiring French, Italian, and Polish uprisings, such an account is both Eurocentric and myopic. For one thing, the great insurrections in the Americas also followed, particularly the insurrections of the slaves in Saint Domingue who fought French, British, and Spanish colonialisms for thirteen years and who forged Haiti in 1804, and the rebellion of the colonized Latinos and *pardos* (blacks) who freed Venezuela in 1819 and gradually emancipated the slaves there.[1] It is true that after the American Revolution, the seeds of freedom blossomed around the world, especially in areas colonized by the great European powers. However, this was not so much a harvest of what the American Revolution had sowed as the gradual and fitful spread of an international movement for liberty and equality to diverse corners of the globe. The movement spread not like a hothouse flower, cultivated by the European elites, but like a weed, often uprooted but never contained. It was spread by people of all sorts within and by those empires, as well as in and by revolts against them, such as the rebellion of the thirteen American colonies.

The American Revolution may have been a political revolution, not a social one, but both the ideas of the Revolution and the concrete military necessities occasioned by it had immediate and lasting social ramifications. Not least of these was the relationship between the struggle for independence from Britain and the struggle to end chattel slavery in the thirteen American colonies and the British Empire as a whole.[2]

Emancipation and independence were linked in a number of ways, from the conceptual heritage of the American revolt in British Whig political thought, Enlightenment philosophy, and Protestant individualism to the egalitarian struggles of sailors, artisans, and free blacks in the cities of the empire. The American Revolution, it was often claimed, was necessary because the imperial administration wished to "enslave" the free English settlers of the thirteen colonies and deprive them of their fundamental human rights. As both Tories and Americans of honor and conscience pointed out, to the chagrin of slave-owning Patriots, the existence of chattel slavery in the colonies—and indeed, in some states, rebellion actually undertaken to preserve it—stood totally at odds with Patriot claims to be fighting for "freedom."

Struggles to abolish slavery, like the struggles for colonial independence, were international—or perhaps it might be better in this case to say "prenational"—because the democratic independence movements of the eighteenth century were to give impetus to the great age of nationalisms in the nineteenth and twentieth centuries. In the British Empire, abolitionist sentiments had made considerable headway by the time of the American Revolution, as we will see. As we will see as well, reaction against abolitionism was one of the spurs that drove some Patriots to revolt, especially in the American South.

During the American Revolution, the worldwide movement for greater democracy thus in fact occurred as two revolutions, one undertaken to achieve political independence and the other to achieve social equality, and as the American rebellion developed, while the two revolutions sometimes ran together, in parallel, they more often were at odds. Those who fought for independence sometimes did so to oppose emancipation. Conversely, in what may at first seem like a paradox, some of those who fought to crush the incipient rebellion for American "freedom" did so to further their own freedom from slavery, embracing British offers of emancipation in return for their service in the imperial cause.

Freed black slaves fought on both sides in the American Revolution for their freedom, but only belatedly did that emancipation become part of the policy of the American independence movement. It was thus the British, not the American Patriots, who most advanced the cause of the revolution for social equality, even while opposing the revolution for political independence. What follows is the story of the role played by black freedom fighters in those two revolutions.

When the full story of the two revolutions is told, we see that the story of the fight for social equality by America's black slaves extends beyond the time of the American Revolution itself and beyond the boundaries of the thirteen colonies—to Nova Scotia and ultimately to Africa, to Sierra

Leone, where blacks emancipated by fighting for the British during the Revolution immigrated and settled. Telling that story thus places the strivings of blacks for freedom during the American Revolution in their proper context, the context of the ongoing struggles for liberty and self-determination that characterized not just the late eighteenth century but subsequent centuries as well.

The account that follows has its own history. After the civil rights movement and especially since the early 1990s, various historians, led by Gary Nash, Peter Wood, Sylvia Frey, Marcus Rediker, Graham Russell Hodges, Woody Holton, Simon Schama, and Cassandra Pybus, have begun to explore the role of African American soldiers on both sides of the conflict. They advanced important earlier accounts, for instance Herbert Aptheker's *American Negro Slave Revolts* (1943) and Benjamin Quarles's *The Negro in the American Revolution* (1961). They raised the issue of bondage—the profound social issue of the revolution—to prominence. They also traced the international role of sailors and artisans, black and white, in promoting abolition. Theirs is a tale, increasingly, of social revolution, one that deserves to shine in the intellectual firmament along with others.

In 1996, as part of a manuscript titled *Friendless Aliens, Friendless Citizens*, I wrote an essay on democratic institutional design in the *Federalist Papers* in the context of the Alien and Sedition Acts. I had taken Barrington Moore's course on comparative revolutions—the basis for *Social Origins of Dictatorship and Democracy*—at Harvard in 1965 and had joined the Students for a Democratic Society the next year. As an antiracist long interested in revolutions, I found myself reluctant to probe racism in the American Revolution, for this event pitted the independence of slave owners against the biggest slave-trading empire in the world. As an emblem of human freedom, I thought, there would have been a few black revolts, but little else.

But Nash's *Race and Revolution* (1993) offered a more interesting tale than I had imagined, one in which during the American Revolution slaves fled to freedom on the British side, not to the standard of liberty raised by the Patriots:

In the North and South, thousands of slaves fled whenever the British forces were within reach. Although the number can never be exactly calculated, it was very large. Jefferson reported that 30,000 slaves had fled their masters during the Invasion of Virginia in 1781. Knowing that more than half of Virginia's blacks were in situations that would have made flight nearly unthinkable—because they were children under 15, physically depleted men and women over 45, women with young children, or men whose flight would have left their families at the mercy of revengeful masters—this is a gigantic number. . . . In South Carolina, a similar proportion of adult males—about half—probably fled to the British during the Southern campaigns from 1779 to 1781.[3]

It was thus possible that, had things turned out differently, the emancipation of American slaves might have occurred during or immediately after the Revolution. Nash gives several reasons why: (1) many leaders, including slave owners in the middle South, recognized the inconsistency of bondage and American freedom; (2) the Saint Dominguen revolution reinforced this sentiment;[4] (3) an environmental, rather than a biological, theory of slave "inferiority" held sway; (4) the federal government could have sold unsettled territory in the West to compensate owners for emancipating slaves; (5) the government could have compelled South Carolina and Georgia, in exchange for protection against the Creek Indians, to give up bondage; and (6) the cotton gin was not invented until after the Revolution, and bondage, compared with what it later became, was not exceptionally profitable.[5] But Nash does not see the mainspring of emancipation within the Revolution itself: the competition of British and American forces for recruits who were often freed in exchange for soldiering. Both emancipation and independence thus could have been possible in the new United States at the end of the eighteenth century.[6]

Yet the American Revolution did not lead to emancipation. Instead, it was English abolition that legitimized and helped constitute this second revolution and that undercut the legitimacy of the revolution for independence. Independence proved to be about liberty only for white colonists, and the gravest defect of this revolution proved to be its denial of freedom to bondspersons. As the English essayist Samuel Johnson quipped, "How is it that we hear the loudest *yelps* for liberty among the drivers of negroes?"[7] In contrast, led by the abolitionist Granville Sharp, British thinking about the justice of American independence, but the injustice of American bondage, helped consolidate a new English movement for abolition.[8]

Emancipation by the imperialists has profound implications for how we think about the American Revolution. That thinking is inevitably shaped by the sort of nationalist mythology that is part of every culture—in the American case, by a narrative of the Revolutionary War in which the heroes are always the freedom-loving Patriots, and the villains are always the aristocratic British and their hired mercenaries. But as is usually the case, the reality was more complicated. Viewed in light of the long struggle for equal rights for all, we see enough casual racism and social and racial condescension on both sides to subvert any claims to absolute "good" or "bad." However, one of the issues with which any reader of the narratives that follow must contend is the way in which, more often than otherwise, it is the British who are in the right and the Patriots who are in the wrong on the issue of human rights. In comparative terms, imagine if peasants and sans-culottes in the French Revolution had fought for the aristocrats, rather than destroying their power. Imagine if Napoleon had freed most slaves in Saint Domingue to fight Toussaint L'Ouverture as the representative of the comparatively less oppressed, "the colored." Imagine if Lenin had opposed workers and represented only intellectuals, but the czar had relied on strikes to combat the Russian Revolution. Imagine if the United States, and not the Vietnamese National Liberation Front, had mobilized peasant radicalism and overturned landlords.

Exploring the work of other social historians on the role of blacks during the American Revolution, for instance, Peter Wood, Sylvia Frey, Graham Hodges, Woody Holton, Douglas Egerton, Christopher Brown, and Simon Schama, I found lineaments of a broad picture.[9] Nevertheless, the emphasis, as in Gary Nash's recent *The Forgotten Fifth* (2006), is on blacks as important participants in the Revolution, rather than on their decisive role, glimpsed, but not emphasized, in the larger international struggle for freedom—a freedom that the Revolution denied them.[10]

My approach therefore differs from some previous histories of the Revolution. First, historians sometimes reimagine and rephrase the words of those distant from them in time and situation. A style like that often goes down easily with the reader and makes a book attractive. But it can also risk superimposing the historian's musings over the authentic voices of the period.

In this book, the original voices have been emphasized so that the conversations of these great public movements will be audible to the reader. This style allows the reader to hear an enormous, multivocal demonstration of the centrality of blacks in the Revolution, the imperial/Patriot dynamic of recruitment and emancipation, and the seeds of liberty that these movements spread. It enables the reader to feel the texture of documents, to recover buried evidences of a second revolution.

This project, begun in 1996, is based on material I found in thirteen research libraries in the United States, London, Paris, and Spain, as well as documents from the online South Carolinian and Canadian archives. Some historians have concentrated on particular stories, say of black Loyalists in South Carolina, and thus have circumscribed the archival evidence they consult. Although surviving documents do indeed mostly tell particular stories, such documents often do not tell a full tale. In what follows, I have tried to place the stories of individuals and the actions of various figures—some well known, others not—within the larger story of the international struggle for freedom and self-determination.

However, I have not smoothed over the storytelling with imagined detail. Rather than compose a seamless tale, I want to acquaint the reader with fragmentary sources and show how the many fragments— Dunmore's Royal Ethiopian Regiment, the Patriot First Rhode Island Regiment, Colonel Tye and the imperial "Black Dragoons," the observations of the Germans Flohr and von Closen on black Patriots at Yorktown, and the like—come together.

The story is set, for the most part, chronologically. Because much of the evidence is fragmentary, no single tale unfolds in the broad pattern of two revolutions emerging before the outbreak of war, competitive royal and Patriot emancipations during the Revolution itself, and the seeds of freedom spread after independence. But when all the strands are woven together, the centrality of the second revolution in the international democratic movement for social equality, self-determination, and self-government becomes clear.

The participants in that revolution heretofore have largely remained nameless. Where possible, I have analyzed lists, and I name names and tally numbers. Two kinds of numbers circulate widely in the literature on blacks in the American Revolution. One estimates how many blacks escaped to the British. As Gary Nash says, this is a "gigantic number," but one that will never be known exactly. Estimates range between twenty thousand and one hundred thousand. By analyzing rosters of British troops, I show that the number of blacks is large. If one adds in the thousands of not yet organized blacks who trailed all the major British forces and provided a continuing source of economic support and military replacement, the number of black redcoats indeed takes on dimensions accurately called "gigantic."

Historians have offered wildly conflicting estimates of the blacks who emigrated with the British after their defeat, as well as the number freed, as opposed to those still enslaved. Detailed lists survive of blacks who left New York on ships with the Crown as well as of black settlers in Canadian settlements. In breaking these lists down, I show that many more free blacks left with the British for Canada than earlier estimates suggest. This larger emigration reflects both the scale of the movement of blacks to fight against the slave owners and the Crown's role, even in defeat, in liberating them. I also analyze the number of free blacks who emigrated from southern ports.

In a second set of numbers, historians surmise how many blacks fought for the Patriots in different states. Here, the counts tend to be small, an estimated five thousand. But many more blacks fought for the Patriots than historians have heretofore imagined. For instance, until Henry Wiencek's *The Imperfect God* (2003), the First Rhode Island Regiment, made up of freed slaves and indigenous people, was not well known beyond specialists. Even that regiment highlighted soldiers whose freedom the Patriots had purchased. Yet at the Rhode Island Historical Society, I found a relatively complete list of blacks and Narragansett Indians who fought for Rhode Island, compiled by the historian Louis Wilson. Analyzing the numbers, I discovered that in 1778, the state purchased the freedom of only 11 percent of black and Native American recruits. As I will show, many more joined throughout the war. Again, I name names and tally numbers.

Until recently, Thomas Jefferson's horror at the slave uprising in Haiti has led to silence among historians.[11] Until Douglas Egerton's *Gabriel's Revolt* (1994), historians spoke of Gabriel's "Conspiracy," although, of course, no one outside of England would speak of George Washington as merely a "conspirator." Historians have spoken of blacks who fought for democracy in Sierra Leone as "nationalists." They have regarded abolitionist, but patronizing, whites who have left a written record, including Benjamin Franklin, as noble and treated blacks as silent and diminished. The accounts that follow revise and correct these misinterpretations.

I have no sympathy for racist cant. I have often questioned the language of those active in the events at the time, as well as that of subsequent historians. This history of two revolutions honors the efforts of blacks to free themselves and of antiracist whites, such as James Otis and John Laurens, to make American liberty genuine. The actions of many tens of thousands of blacks who escaped and fought are also eloquent. Most could not write and have left no other tale. Luckily, some direct accounts from contemporaries such as Murphy Steele, Boston King, Elleanor Eldridge, and Thomas Peters survive. They do not speak for all, but they describe unforgettably common oppressions and heroic efforts to overturn them. Hegel envisioned all history as the working out, in the social and political institutions of a state and internationally, of the insight that all humans are free. These struggles illuminate his insight.

Acknowledgments

Jack Womack, a wonderful historian of Zapata and the Mexican Revolution, has encouraged this book, through difficult times, for a new light it may cast on emancipatory revolutions in North America and to the south.

Mike Goldfield recommended that I seek out John Tryneski at Chicago—a brilliant suggestion—and has asked pointed questions about whether gradual emancipation was possible in the Revolution. His *The Color of Politics* is a paradigm for revealing in American history racism's fundamental thread.

I discussed this book, particularly the early use of an original position by many thinking about the injustice of slaveholding during the Revolution, with John Rawls. Noam Chomsky looked at an early draft and made suggestions. I have benefited from Vincent Harding's wisdom about this period in American history and its connection—the river—to our own.

I gave the University Lecture on this topic at the University of Denver in 1999 and was greatly encouraged by Bill Zaranka, Dan Ritchie, and Tom Farer, my dean and friend. It had force then, and much more in this form.

Sage, Whitney, and my wife, Paula Bard, attended that lecture; they and Brendan and Claire have all supported this project.

I have also spoken on this topic to colleagues at the seminar organized by Martin Rhodes at the University of Denver and to the political science departments at the Universities of Michigan and Washington. I am grateful to Arlene Saxonhouse and Jamie Mayerfeld for inviting me to the latter two occasions. Tapes of the Denver and Washington talks can be found on my blog—democratic-individuality—at http://democratic-individuality .blogspot.com/2011/02/video-of-my-talk-on-emancipation-and.html and http://democratic-individuality.blogspot.com/2009/09/videolecture-on-emancipation-and.html.

I have benefited from an American Council of Learned Societies grant to do research on this project during 1999–2000 in Rhode Island, Massachusetts, Virginia, Washington, DC, and Seville, Spain.

I organized a panel for the Organization of American Historians meeting in 2008 in New York with Gary Nash, Graham Russell Gao Hodges, and Mike Goldfield. I am grateful to them and other historians there, particularly Doug Egerton, for lively discussions.

As a political theorist writing as a historian in an area where the telling of stories often assumes the shape of a novel, I have benefited from the help of a number of editors. I would like specially to thank Bud Bynack, whose sympathy with and startling insight into the manuscript helped me to shape its final form; Michael Parrish; and the poet Ever Saskya.

I am especially grateful to John Tryneski for the editing at the University of Chicago Press, a conversational experience unlike—richer and subtler than—any I have had before.

Among friends and research assistants, Lisa Burke, Rich Rockwell, Matt Weinert, Reggie Rivers, Doug Vaughan, Jeremy Dadah, Jim Cole, Jill Henry, and Sasha Breger contributed suggestions to this manuscript.

Long ago, as a student at Walden School in Manhattan from first to fourth grade, I was friends with Andrew Goodman, who went with the Student Nonviolent Coordinating Committee Freedom Summer project in 1964 to Philadelphia, Mississippi. There his journey in support of equality ended, with those of James Cheney and Michael Schwerner. They shared in and extended the long journeys for freedom and equality that make American and global history. I dedicate this book to them.

Introduction
Fear, Hope, and the Two Revolutions in America

My declaration that I would arm and set free such slaves as should
assist me if I was attacked has stirred up fears in them which cannot
easily subside as they know how vulnerable they are in that particular,
and therefore they have cause in this complaint of which their others
are totally unsupported.
— *Lord Dunmore to the Earl of Dartmouth, June 1775*

s Aristotle once said of the helots in Sparta, slaves were "lurking in ambush" for their American masters in the early eighteenth century.[1] On September 9, 1739, launching what became known as the Stono Rebellion, blacks in South Carolina marched along the Stono River with banners that proclaimed "Liberty!" Led by "Jemmy," they killed the two owners of a gun shop and armed themselves. By evening, they numbered nearly one hundred. The rebels killed twenty-five whites before Lieutenant Governor William Bull rallied the better-armed whites to kill half of the blacks and eventually to arrest the others.[2] Similar uprisings in Manhattan in 1712, where the black slave population rivaled that of free whites,[3] and in Maryland in 1740, where authorities suppressed a plot to seize Annapolis,[4] reveal an ongoing black resistance to bondage.[5]

But legends of revolt terrified whites as much as real violence, and even accounts of actual acts of rebellion reveal as much or more about white anxieties concerning the possibility of slave revolts as they do about the black resistance to slavery itself. In 1741, for example, ten fires broke out in New York, and Cuffee, a black man, was seen running from one. Powerful New Yorkers, particularly Daniel Horsmanden, a judge and member of the governor's executive council, suspected a conspiracy. They charged and hanged a group that included both blacks and poor whites, some of whom had congregated at John Hughson's tavern. Curiously, all other "legal" records have perished; only Horsmanden's account of the trials survives.

After some confessed, under torture, the authorities charged a wider circle, and in prison some of the accused heard that naming others was the only way to avoid hanging. They later recanted.[6] The evidence for the revolt was thus dubious, but Horsmanden argued that torture ascertained "the appearance of truth"—that is, what the torturer already knew—despite blacks' "great deal of craft," "unintelligible jargon," "broken hints," and the assumption that "it will be chiefly found in the examinations and confessions of negroes" that they "are seldom found to hold twice in the same story."[7] Nearly one hundred executions stemmed from Horsmanden's suspicions.[8] But ostensible colonial justice paid little attention to the rule of law.

Even for a white "Englishman," if poor, there was no habeas corpus. For instance, the Hughsons, who owned the tavern, Mary Kerry, and other poor whites were swept up in the hysteria and hanged. In 1737 Hughson had organized gatherings parodying the secretive stuffiness of well-to-do Masons, which also appear to have been taken for "a conspiracy."[9] In confessing a desire to burn "white New York," some poor whites identified with blacks.

Working-class taverns or "grog-shops," with their joining of black and white artisan republicanism, indeed would continue to play a significant role in egalitarian agitation through Gabriel's Rebellion in Virginia in 1800.[10] But the reason that the prosecution of the "conspiracy" of 1741 was carried out in the racist terms that characterize Horsmanden's discourse was that the events occurred against a background of fear about the possibility of impending black slave revolts and rebellion.

As historian Jill Lepore notes, as early as the 1730s, "from the depths of cargo holds, Caribbean slaves sold in New York brought stories of [West Indian] uprisings with them. . . . Dozens of black Caribbeans traveled to New York in ships owned by New York merchants whose slaves would be accused of conspiracy in 1741. . . . In all 39 of the black New Yorkers accused in 1741 were owned by men who directly participated in the Caribbean slave trade."[11]

In 1702 New York had passed the most draconian legislation against slaves in the British Empire:[12] "The body of legislation that constituted New York's 'Negro Law' is a brutal testament to the difficulty of enslaving human beings, especially in cities. New York's slave codes were almost entirely concerned with curtailing the ability of enslaved people to move at will, and to gather for fear that they might decide, especially when drunk, that slavery was not to be borne and one way to end it would be to burn the city down."[13] New York's "Act for Regulating Slaves" called for castrating black men accused of raping or "fornicating with" white women.

In 1712, in response to the uprising of that year, New York had carried out a wave of executions: authorities arrested seventy slaves and four free blacks, tried forty-three, convicted twenty-five, hanged twenty, and burned three at the stake. In a June 23 letter to the Lords of Trade in London, a frightened Governor Robert Hunter recounted: "In that court were twenty seven condemned, whereof twenty one were executed, one being a woman with child, her execution by that means suspended. Some were burnt, others hanged, one broke on the wheel, and one hung alive in chains in the town, so that there has been the most exemplary punishment inflicted that could be possibly thought of." Pointing to the small number of executions following Caribbean revolts, he reported to the lords: "I am informed that in the West Indies where their laws against their slaves are most severe, that in case of a conspiracy in which many are engaged a few only are executed for an example."[14]

Like the accounts of Caribbean slave revolts in New York, the accounts of events such as the Stono Rebellion and the New York revolts of 1712 and 1741 rippled through the colonies, and like them, they propagated further fears and anxieties. During the American Revolution, a Hessian captain, Johann Hinrichs, wrote fearfully of the Stono Rebellion, but got the date wrong by three years: "In the month of August, 1736, each was told whom he was to kill" by some mysterious other. Males were to be slain, women used "to gratify [the rebels'] desires," children to be "sacrifices."[15] And naming his fears, on April 11, 1756, James Glen, the royal governor of South Carolina, warned of "dangerous Enemies, [our] own Negroes, who are ready to revolt on the first Opportunity, and are Eight times as many in Number as there are white Men able to bear Arms."[16] Assemblyman Henry Laurens of South Carolina, of whose son John we will hear much in the chapters that follow, feared "domestic broils . . . more awful and more distressing than Fire, Pestilence, or Foreign Wars."[17]

The anxiety about the possibility of slave rebellions thus formed a common bond among many white settlers in both the North and the South. In 1733 Andrew Bradford, editor of Philadelphia's *American Weekly Mercury*, warned of a slave rebellion by recalling the "villainous attempt" in New York in 1712, which, but for the local garrison, might have "reduced [the Town] to Ashes . . . the greatest part of the Inhabitants murdered." The editor also invoked a recent "massacre on the Island of St. Johns" in the Caribbean. In language that Loyalist strategist Joseph Galloway would echo in 1775, Bradford alerted "communities not to be too careless of their Safety, with respect to those intestine and inhuman Enemies who are in some Colonies but too much indulged, and by some particular Persons rather encouraged in their Vices, than put under a due and necessary Subjection."[18]

Anxieties about the threat of slave revolts also merged with the threats posed by other others: "So soon as the Season was advanced that they could lay in the Woods, one certain Night was agreed on, that every Negro and Negress in every Family was to rise at Midnight, cut the Throats of their Masters and Sons, but not meddle with the Women, whom they intended to plunder and ravish the Day following, and then set all their Houses and Barns on Fiore [sic], kill the draught Horses, and secure the best Saddle Horses for their flight immediately towards the Indians in the French Interest."[19] Similar fears of black–Native American unity haunted elites in Virginia, North Carolina, South Carolina, and Georgia.

In 1739, as well as during the French and Indian War of 1755, Maryland owners also feared insurrections of blacks in alliance with Catholics transferred by the Crown from Canada.[20] In Maryland the slave and servant population, added to the despised Catholics, nearly equaled free Protestant whites. In 1755 Maryland jailed William Stratton, a white "servant," and "two slaves" for poisoning Jeremiah Chase, a member of the House of Delegates. Because slaves were considered less than human, their names went unreported. Governor Horatio Sharp put the militia on alert.[21]

As a restless, ever-present "enemy," the "witches," Loyalist Quakers, and "Papists" threatened narrow, Protestant communities in the South. Thus, the Maryland House of Delegates denounced Governor Sharp for encouraging "Popery" because "the constant and unwearied Application of the Jesuits to proselyte, and consequently to corrupt and alienate, the Affections of our Slaves from us, and to hold them in Readiness to arm at a proper Time for our Destruction, together with every Consideration of Danger from a powerful Foreign Enemy, are circumstances truly Alarming."[22]

White fears were strengthened by slave revolts that continued throughout the Atlantic colonies in the latter half of the eighteenth century, especially in the Caribbean. In 1760 Tacky's Rebellion burst out in Jamaica. Named for an enslaved Coromantee chief from Africa who gathered fellow Coromantee bondsmen, the rebellion started in St. Mary's Parish on Easter Monday. According to Edward Long, the sugar planter and historian, this uprising was "more formidable than any hitherto known in the West Indies."[23] In April, blacks burned the cane fields. As a symbol of allegiance with a revolt that would dominate Jamaica for several months, slaves shaved their heads. Freedom fighters killed sixty soldiers. The British army shot three hundred to four hundred blacks. Some took their own lives rather than submit.[24] Rebellions occurred in Bermuda (1761), Dutch Guyana (1762, 1763, and 1772), Jamaica (1765, 1766, and 1776), British Honduras (1765, 1768, and 1773), Grenada (1765), Montserrat (1768), St. Vincent (1769–73), Tobago (1770, 1771, and 1774), and St. Croix and St. Thomas (1770 and after).[25]

Faced with the reports of past black revolts and the possibility of future slave rebellions, "only the blind could be free from fear," the historian Winthrop Jordan notes—"a chilling fear which even the rhythmic tedium of daily life could never entirely smother."[26] But as the tensions between the American colonies and the metropolitan British government grew in the years before the American Revolution, the fears of slave revolts that gripped the white colonists and slaveholders in the British colonies in America were exacerbated by the unmistakable movement on the part of the British government toward the abolition of slavery. That movement did not come to fruition in the British Empire until the abolition of the slave trade in 1807 and the abolition of slavery itself in 1833. Its early manifestations, however, appeared at the same time that the tensions between the colonies and the metropolis were coming to a head, and indeed, for some white colonists, the specter of abolition seemed to be among the many impositions on the colonies, North and South alike, that the movement for freedom and independence sought to redress. Thus, the issues of emancipation and independence—the movement for the emancipation of the slaves held across the British Empire and the movement for independence from it in the thirteen North American colonies—were inextricably linked.

EMANCIPATION AND INDEPENDENCE

What exacerbated the fears of white colonists instead appeared to the slaves of the American colonies a source of hope. Fears of the consequences that an imperial policy of freeing the slaves might hold helped motivate many white colonists to join the Patriot cause as the Revolution unfolded. At the same time, hope that the British were recognizing the inhumanity and immorality of slavery and were willing to contemplate freeing the slaves motivated many black slaves to side with the Loyalist cause.

As it did for many Patriots, for whom the king, in accord with a long political tradition, literally embodied the nation, for black slaves in the American colonies, hope for redress of their condition sometimes centered on belief in a "good king" misled by nefarious ministers of state. According to Bradford, "Hall's Negro," supposedly drunk, had told a white man named Rennalds that "the Englishmen were in generall a pack of Villains, and that they kept the Negroes as Slaves contrary to a positive Order from King George, sent to the Governor of New-York, to let them all free, which the said Governor did intend to do, but was prevented by his C . . . [word abridged in text: Council] and A . . . [Army], and that was the Reason there subsisted now so great a difference between the Governor and the People of both Provinces."[27] And in 1774 in St. Bartholomew's County, South Carolina, a black man known only as George foretold that a good king would free the slaves.[28]

Ironically, in the rhetoric of the Old Whigs that framed the discourses of the American Revolution, what the Patriots were claiming in a just war for independence fought to achieve their own rights as free men and women was freedom from "slavery."[29] What black American slaves who embraced the Loyalist cause were claiming was the same thing—not as a hyperbolic term for the effects of taxation without representation or mercantilist economics, but as freedom from being treated as mere chattels and property. In this context the words "independence" or "sovereignty" took on a resonance among southern Patriots not of "no taxation without representation" but of the preservation of bondage from the threat of emancipation.[30] As the British abolitionist Granville Sharp pointed out in an acute way to the Philadelphia physician Benjamin Rush, "*American liberty cannot be firmly established* without some scheme of general Enfranchisement" because "the toleration of domestic slavery in the colonies greatly weakens the claim of *natural Right* of our American Brethren to Liberty." Sharp added: "Let [the Americans] put away *the accursed thing* (that horrid *Oppression*) from among them, before they presume to implore the imposition of *divine Justice*."[31] But among many white Patriots, the cry "liberty" in Patrick Henry's famous phrase "Give me Liberty or give me Death!" became a perverse call for the "freedom" to hold others as slaves.

Thus, two revolutions were actually under way in the 1770s and 1780s in Britain's American colonies, and the victory achieved in one with the signing of the Treaty of Paris in 1783 both delayed and made imperative victory in the second, a victory not achieved until fourscore years later. The struggle for the independence of the American colonies from Great Britain stood in a complex relationship with the struggle for the emancipation of the black slaves in those colonies. The prospect of an emancipation promised by the colonial British administration was actually one of the factors that drove the white slave-owning colonists toward rebellion and independence. At the same time, both the pragmatic tactical advantages of employing freed slaves in the struggle for freedom and the logic of a revolt against a colonial administration perceived as attempting to "enslave" free Englishmen and to deprive them of their fundamental human rights helped move the Patriots toward a recognition of the contradictions in their own thought and behavior and the eventual necessity of a further revolution in which emancipation, not just independence, would be the result.

SOMERSETT, THE DUNMORE PROCLAMATION, AND THE PROSPECT OF FREEDOM

As the American Revolution approached, the hopes of black American slaves were raised by William Murray, chief justice of Britain and the first Earl of Mansfield. His 1772 decision in *R v Knowles, ex parte Somersett*, held slavery to be illegal in Great Britain, although not elsewhere in the British Empire, declaring that "the state of slavery is of such a nature, that it is incapable of now being introduced on any reasons, moral or political; but only positive law, which preserves its force long after the reasons, occasion, and time itself from whence it was created, is erased from memory. It is so odious that nothing can be suffered to support it but positive law. Whatever inconveniences, therefore, may follow from the decision, I cannot say this case is allowed or approved by the law of England; and therefore the black must be discharged."[32]

The origins of the case lay in the late 1760s, when Charles Stewart, a slave owner, returned to London from a job as paymaster in Boston. He brought with him James Somersett. Two years later, Somersett escaped. Captain John Knowles recaptured Somersett, imprisoned him on the slave ship *Ann and Mary* bound for Jamaica, and attempted to sell him. Making a test case of bondage, Granville Sharp, one of the first and fiercest English campaigners for abolition and a great democratic theorist, sued on Somersett's behalf. On June 22, 1772, Lord Mansfield emancipated Somersett.[33]

No British law, Mansfield argued, sanctioned "so high an act of dominion"—the seizure of Somersett by Knowles on English soil. The opinion also did not return Somersett to Stewart. Thus, the verdict appeared to mean that Justice Mansfield granted the freedom of blacks in Britain— James Somersett had made himself free there.

Yet imperial rulings about slavery were characteristically a patchwork. This decision could have had only a narrow legal scope. Mansfield certainly did not manumit all blacks in the British Isles. As Benjamin Franklin, a visitor in London, put it acidly, "Pharisaical Britain! To pride thyself in setting free a single slave that happens to land on thy coasts, while thy merchants in all thy ports are encouraged by thy laws to continue a commerce whereby so many hundreds of thousands are dragged into a slavery that can scarce be said to end with their lives since it is entailed on their posterity!"[34] In other such cases, Mansfield's rulings reject cruelty, but do not abolish bondage. Even in the report of the *Somersett* case, Mansfield hesitated: "The setting of 14,000 or 15,000 men at once loose by a solemn opinion is very disagreeable in the effects it threatens."[35] Despite his triumph in *Somersett*, Granville Sharp rightly indicted the chief justice's willingness to prefer "pecuniary or sordid property, as that of a master in a horse or a dog, to inestimable liberty."[36]

But the *Somersett* verdict brought hope to blacks. On June 27, 1772, the *Public Advertizer*, a London newspaper, noted, "On Monday near two hundred blacks with their ladies had an entertainment at a public-house in Westminster, to celebrate the triumph which their brother Somerset [*sic*] had obtained over Mr. Stuart, his master. Lord Mansfield's health was echoed round the room; and the evening was concluded with a ball."[37] Most ordinary people interpreted the *Somersett* decision to emancipate all slaves on English soil.

Blacks then made their way to freedom in London. Often, even the masters shared their belief about *Somersett* or could not stop them. On July 10, 1772, John Riddell of Bristol Wells angrily wrote to Charles Stewart, "I am disappointed by Mr. Dublin who has run away. He told the servants that he had rec'd a letter from his Uncle Sommerset [*sic*] acquainting him that Lord Mansfield had given them their freedom & he was determined to leave me as soon as I returned from London which he did without even speaking to me. I don't find that he has gone off with anything of mine. Only carried off all his own cloths which I don't know that he had any right so to do. I believe that I shall not give my self any trouble to look after this ungrateful villain."[38] In America, twenty-one newspapers published forty-three stories about the *Somersett* decision. For slave owners, that verdict sounded a death knell. They could no longer bring their property to the "Mother Country" because it was illegitimate.

In the black underground, word of *Somersett* spread like lightning. In 1773, for instance, an advertisement warned that a "runaway" couple had fled for Britain, "where they imagine they will be free (a Notion now too prevalent among Negroes, greatly to the vexation and prejudice of their masters)."[39] A different advertisement related the story of Bacchus: "About 30 Years of Age, five feet six or seven inches high, strong and well made. . . . He was seen a few Days before he went off with a Purse of Dollars, and had just before changed a five Pound Bill; Most, or all of which, I suppose he must have robbed me of, which he might easily have done, I having trusted him much after what I thought had proved his Fidelity He will probably endeavour to pass for a Freeman by the Name of John Christian and attempt to get on Board some Vessel bound for Great Britain, from the Knowledge he has of the late Determination of Somerset's [*sic*] Case. Whoever takes up the said Slave shall have 5 £ Reward, on his Delivery to Gabriel Jones."[40]

Among blacks kept illiterate by their masters and without access to judicial documents, the public meaning of the decision alone held sway, and they acted on what they had learned, asking to be emancipated by the British authorities. Between 1773 and 1777, three groups of Boston blacks petitioned for freedom to Massachusetts royal governor Thomas Gage and later to the revolutionary authorities. They appealed to natural rights, as would the Declaration of Independence. In 1777 "a Great Number of Blackes" wrote to the Massachusetts legislature or General Court, denouncing the owners' hypocritical Christianity: "Your Petitioners apprehend that they have in Common with all other men a Natural and Unaliable [*sic*] Right to the freedom which the Grat Parent of the Unavers hath Bestowed equalley on all menkind and which they have Never forfeited by any Compact or agreement whatever."[41] In 1774, if the royal governor would emancipate them, according to a third petition, another "grat Number of blacks" volunteered to fight for the British under General Gage.

Anticipating the arrival of English troops in November 1774, Virginia slaves planned an insurrection. Colonists, however, got wind of the rebellion. In a November 1776 letter to Philadelphia editor William Bradford, James Madison urged hiding the truth that it was the British who seemed to colonial slaves to be the defenders of liberty: "If america and Britain should come to an hostile rupture I am afraid an Insurrection among the slaves may and will be promoted. In one of our Countries lately a few of those unhappy wretches met together and chose a leader who was to conduct them when the English Troops should arrive—which they foolishly thought would be very soon and that by revolting to them they should be rewarded with their freedom Their Intentions were soon discovered and proper precautions taken to prevent the Infection. It is prudent such things should be concealed as well as suppressed."[42]

Madison was the one being foolish here. On November 7, 1775, in a proclamation that would echo though the colonies, John Murray, the fourth Earl of Dunmore and the royal governor of the colony of Virginia, would indeed offer slaves their freedom:

I do require every Person capable of bearing Arms, to [resort] to His MAJESTY'S STANDARD, or be looked upon as Traitors to His MAJESTY'S Crown and Government, and thereby become liable to the Penalty the

Law inflicts upon such Offences; such as forfeiture of Life, confiscation of Lands, &c. &c. And I do hereby further declare all indentured Servants, Negroes, or others, (appertaining to Rebels,) free that are able and willing to bear Arms, they joining His MAJESTY'S Troops as soon as may be, for the more speedily reducing this Colony to a proper Sense of their Duty, to His MAJESTY'S Liege Subjects, to retain their Quitrents, or any other Taxes due or that may become due, in their own Custody, till such Time as Peace may be again restored to this at present most unhappy Country, or demanded of them for their former salutary Purposes, by Officers properly authorised to receive the same.[43]

The Dunmore Proclamation was a response to a particular situation in Virginia, as we will see, but the strategy that it exemplified and the rise of abolitionist sentiment in the mother country made what had seemed unthinkable as an official policy of the British administration in London—emancipation throughout the empire—suddenly the subject of speculation in the American colonies. Replying to Madison on January 4, 1777, Bradford recognized Parliament's instigation of slave revolt: "Your fear with regard to an insurrection being excited among the slaves seems too wellfounded." According to Bradford, "A letter from a Gentleman in England was read yesterday in the Coffee-house, which mentioned the design of [the] administration to pass an act (in case of rupture) declaring all Slaves & Servants free that would take arms against the Americans. By this, you see such a scheme is thought on and talked of; but I cannot believe the Spirit of the English would ever allow them publically to adopt so slavish a way of Conquering."[44]

As independence neared, the *Somersett* decision helped ignite a wildfire of egalitarian unrest.[45] As we noted in the New York riots of 1741, class and race forged ties of solidarity in opposition to both the slaveholders and the colonial elites. This was particularly evident in the resistance to press gangs, one of the abuses that continued into the nineteenth century and that led to the War of 1812. In the Knowles riot in Boston of 1747, "armed Seamen, Servants, Negroes and others" fought press gangs that forced civilians into the British navy. In 1765 "Sailores, boys, and Negroes to the number of above Five Hundred" rebelled against press gangs in Newport, Rhode Island. In 1767 in Norfolk, Virginia, "Whites & Blacks all arm'd" attacked Captain Jeremiah Morgan. In 1768 a "mob" of "sturdy boys & negroes" staged a riot in Boston—royal revenue collectors had seized John Hancock's sloop, the *Liberty*, provoking a series of uprisings. As historian

Jesse Lemisch notes, after 1763 "armed mobs of whites and Negroes repeatedly manhandled captains, officers, and crews, threatened their lives, and held them hostage for the men they pressed.'"[46] Rebels met imperial force with force.

Revolts thus often occurred in ports. As historian Markus Rediker stresses, "With their promise of anonymity and an impersonal wage in the maritime sector, [ports] served as a magnet to runaway slaves and free blacks throughout the colonial period and well into the nineteenth century. Most found work as laborers and seamen. Slaves too were employed in the maritime sector, some with ship masters as owners, others hired out by the voyage. By the middle of the eighteenth century, slaves dominated Charleston's maritime and riverine traffic, in which some 20 per cent of the city's adult male slaves labored."[47] Thus, slaves, free blacks, and impressed and free whites worked together.[48]

With commerce and the tides, sailors spread news of liberty, and in the second revolution, the revolution for freedom and equality for all, the emancipatory idioms of sailors played a role. In London, North American, and Caribbean ports, sailors denounced impressment as "slavery plain and simple," governed by the lash and an absence of rights.[49] In 1773 John Allen's "Oration on the Beauties of Liberty" condemned the corruption of gangs, which "ought ever to be held in the most hateful contempt, the same as you would a banditti of slave-makers on the coast of Africa."[50] Black sailors, free and slave, carried these words among bondsmen. They brought their knowledge to a subterranean network proceeding from slave to slave, house to field, and plantation to plantation across hundreds of miles.[51]

In 1772 slaves rebelled against bondage in Perth Amboy, New Jersey; in 1774 a joint African-Irish movement arose in Boston, again uniting blacks and poor whites. In December 1774, in St. Andrews Parish, according to the *Savannah (GA) Gazette*, "six negro fellows and four wenches" killed a master and an overseer and attacked neighboring plantations.[52] British authorities burned two of the leaders alive. At a meeting the next year, St. Andrews's residents expressed "abhorrence" of slavery, but did not free blacks.[53]

In 1775, in Ulster County, New York, Dorchester County, Maryland, and Norfolk, Virginia, blacks demonstrated. According to the Dorchester Committee of Inspection, "The insolence of the Negroes in this county is come to such a height, that we are under a necessity of disarming them which we affected on Saturday last. We took about eighty guns, some bayonets, swords, etc. The malicious and imprudent speeches of some among the lower classes of whites have induced them to believe that their freedom depended on the success of the Kings troops. We cannot therefore be too vigilant nor too rigorous with those who promote and encourage this disposition in our slaves."[54]

In Wilmington and Tar River, North Carolina, owners suppressed "conspiracies." In Tar River, Merrick plotted with a white sailor to obtain arms.[55] In June, also in North Carolina, the Wilmington Committee of Public Safety instituted "patrols to search & take from Negroes all kinds of Arms whatsoever." As Janet Schaw, a "Lady of Quality," records in her journal, the committee aimed to force each black to return home by nine at night. Schaw adds that a Whig "killed"—we would now say murdered— one of these blacks. No insurrection took place because, she thought, slaves did not possess guns. Nevertheless, she noted, when a posse jailed forty blacks, torturers gave them each "a hundred lashes" and "cropped their ears."[56]

Patriot protests about British denials of law and liberty were thus fundamentally compromised by persistent, despotic Patriot violence toward blacks. From St. Bartholomew Parish in South Carolina, Thomas Hutchinson wrote to Henry Laurens that a certain Jemmy denounced a leader named George for stirring revolt: "Prince and Patience belonging to Francis Smith, Jack, hector & daphney, belonging to William Smith, Shifnal, Quashey & Jupiter, belonging to his Master,[57] Ben & Pearce, belonging to James Parson's Esqr. & Ben, belongg to Jno. E. Hutchinson are Preachers, & have (many of them) been preaching for two Years past to Great crowds of Negroes in the Neighborhood of Chyhaw, very frequently, which [Jemmy] himself attended . . . that at these assemblies he had heard of an Insurrection intended & to take the Country by Killing the Whites."[58] On the testimony of one witness, citing words, not acts, a South Carolina "court" murdered George.

We can turn to none other than John Adams as the voice of opposition to the second American revolution. In 1770 Crispus Attucks led a demonstration in Boston against the forcible quartering of troops with civilians and the English redcoat competition with American journeymen for jobs. (British soldiers also took civilian employment.) Of African and Native American ancestry, Attucks had escaped bondage and became a sailor.[59] In the "Boston Massacre," redcoats murdered him and five others. In a shining moment, John Adams would fiercely advocate the Declaration of Independence.[60] Yet his speeches and writings were often sublimely reactionary. As the Crown's lawyer, Adams demonized Attucks: "This Attucks . . . appears to have undertaken to be the hero of the night; and to lead this army with banners, to form them in the first place in Dock square, and march them up to King street with their clubs. . . . This man with his party cried, do not be afraid of them. . . . To have this reinforcement coming down under the command of a stout Molatto fellow, whose very looks was enough to terrify any person, what had not the soldiers then to fear? He had hardiness enough to fall in upon them, and with one hand took hold of a bayonet and with the other knocked the man down."[61] Adams spoke for the elite who feared the revolutionary activism of blacks and poor whites. If they struck against the British, might they not also strike at American slave owners?

The Declaration of Independence maintains that each of us is "endowed by our Creator with certain inalienable rights" and that among these are "life, liberty and the pursuit of happiness." But at the time, this founding document restricted these liberties to whites. Thus, Jefferson suspected that George III could use blacks and Indians—those most oppressed by the colonists—against the American cause. As the Declaration avowed: "He [the King] has excited domestic insurrections amongst us, and has endeavored to bring on the inhabitants of our frontiers, the merciless Indian Savages, whose known rule of warfare is an indistinguished destruction of all ages, sexes and conditions."[62]

Perhaps out of shame, Jefferson did not name blacks.[63] And in drafting the Constitution, William Paterson, a New Jersey representative, stated flatly that Congress "had been ashamed to use the term 'Slaves' and had substituted a description." According to another New Jersey delegate, the Constitution's authors sought by omission to avoid any "stain" on the new government. Nevertheless, the practice of bondage betrayed the American Revolution more deeply than a word.[64]

Faced with rebellions in North Carolina, South Carolina, and Virginia and the menace of newly freed black redcoats, owners experienced ceaseless "dread of instigated insurrections," in the common phrase. Paralleling the Declaration of Independence in a 1776 book, North Carolinian James Iredell denounced Britain's "diabolical purpose of exciting our own Domestics (Domestics they forced upon us) to cut our throats, and involve Men, Women and children in one universal massacre."[65]

The two revolutions in eighteenth-century America—the revolution for independence to escape from the "slavery" imposed on the colonies by the imperial British administration and the revolution for freedom and emancipation from the slavery imposed by many of those who sought to achieve independence from Great Britain—thus proceeded together, often at odds with each other and always in a complicated relationship in which both the highest principles of the Enlightenment and of Christianity and the basest motives of human prejudice, fear, and greed contended, sometimes in the same person, to shape the future of the new United States and the world beyond.

chapter 1 ¶ Lord Dunmore, Black Insurrection, and the Independence Movement in Virginia and South Carolina

[Dunmore's proclamation tends] more effectively to work an
external separation between Great Britain and the Colonies,
than any other expedient, which could possibly be thought of.
—*Edward Rutledge, South Carolina signer of the*
Declaration of Independence, December 1776

n Virginia, in a fraught atmosphere in which white Patriots believed themselves threatened alike by the oppressions of the colonial administration and the prospects of slave revolts, not just the Dunmore Proclamation but a whole series of actions by Governor Dunmore exacerbated the hostility between the Patriots and the Crown, simultaneously hastening the advent of the American Revolution and helping to put in motion the revolution that paralleled it, the revolution in the status of America's black slaves. A similar situation prevailed in South Carolina, where advocates of the revolution for American independence were both motivated by and opposed to the revolution in the status of black slaves. The specter of slave revolts incited by Dunmore's actions seemed to many Patriots in both colonies to be of a piece with other deliberate acts by the colonial administration contrary to the interests of the colonial settlers.

Attracted by British freedom, blacks thronged to Dunmore's standard. One result was the central role of the Royal Ethiopian Regiment on the British side in the first battles of the Revolution in Virginia. Another was a continuing ferment, for instance by Loyalists William Dalrymple and Joseph Galloway, to enlist and emancipate slaves while Patriot elites, zealous to preserve bondage, seceded.[1]

Already in 1772, Governor Dunmore, contemplating the emancipation of colonial slaves, had written to Colonial Secretary William Legge, the Earl of Dartmouth, that Patriot slave owners, "with great reason, trembled at the facility that [their] enemy, would find in Such a body of men, attached by no tye to their Master nor to the Country. . . . It was natural to Suppose that their Condition must inspire them with an aversion to both, and [that they] therefore are ready to join the first that would encourage them to revenge themselves, by which means a Conquest of this Country would inevitably be effected in a very short time."[2]

Initially paralyzed by the interests of British commerce and the fact that some slaves were Tory "property," the Crown hesitated to adopt Dunmore's strategy. London did not free blacks for joining the British army. Instead, Prime Minister North awaited events in the field. Nonetheless, hopes for freedom from an idealized king, the *Somersett* decision, and Dunmore's threats encouraged blacks to escape to the Crown in massive numbers even before Dunmore's official proclamation on November 7, 1775.

Virginia's Patriot slave owners' fears of a black insurrection incited by royal policies coalesced with their growing resistance—armed resistance—to the agents of the British Crown.[3] On the morning of April 20, 1775, the day after the Battle of Lexington in Massachusetts marked the outbreak of armed hostilities between the Patriots and the British, Governor Dunmore transferred twenty barrels of gunpowder from the public magazine in Williamsburg to an imperial ship, the *Magdalen*.[4] This had a double effect. It denied the gunpowder both to the Patriots at a time when armed rebellion against the Crown was breaking out and to the white community at a time when rumors of slave rebellions once again exacerbated white fears. At this crucial juncture, the two revolutions, for independence and emancipation, came together—and came in conflict.

With both the thwarted 1774 black insurrection in Virginia, news of which Madison wanted to suppress, and word of other uprisings fresh in people's minds, as *Dixon and Hunter's Virginia Gazette* reported on April 22, the people of Williamsburg assembled, led by the mayor, and sent a note to Dunmore citing the possible imminent slave rebellion—and his administration's apparent encouragement of it—as the reason why they needed access to the gunpowder: "We have too much reason to believe that some wicked and designing persons have distilled the most diabolical notions into the minds of our slaves and therefore the utmost attention to our internal security has become the more necessary."[5] The phrase "some wicked and designing persons" refers elliptically to Dunmore's own repeated threats. Later, on May 1, 1775, Dunmore reported to the Earl of Dartmouth, the secretary of state for the colonies, that the mayor had delivered an address that had stressed "the alarm into which the people had been thrown at the taking away of the powder in a private manner by an armed force, particularly at a time when they are apprehensive of insurrections among their slaves, (some reports having prevailed to this effect)" and had concluded "with a peremptory demand that the powder be delivered up immediately to them."[6]

It was the prospect of the gunpowder falling into the hand of rebelling slaves, Dunmore told the mayor, that had caused him to secure it on the ship for safekeeping. "Hearing of an insurrection in a neighboring county," Dunmore had responded; he had removed the powder. If a slave revolt were to occur in Williamsburg, he said, he would swiftly return it. Yet "he was surprised to hear that the people were under arms on this occasion and that he should not think it were prudent to put powder into their hands in such a situation."[7]

Patriots marched on the *Magdalen*. Armed with grapeshot, the ship's log reports, sailors opposed "the inhabitants of Williamsburgh [who] were under arms and threatened to attack the Schooner."[8] And Patriots Alexander Spottsswood, G. Weedon, Jonathan Willis, and Hugh Mercer, officers of the Fredericksburg militia, wrote to Commander William Grayson of the Prince William County militia that they had indeed gathered troops to march on Williamsburg. They sought his support: "In these sentiments this Compny could but determine that a number of public spirited gentn should embrace this opportunity of showing their Zeal in the Grand Cause by marching to Wmsbrg to enquire into this Affair and there to take such steps as may best answer the purpose of recovering the powder & securing the Arms now in the Magazine."[9]

The "Grand Cause" of the revolt of the American colonies against British oppression here became one with fear of slave uprising as the motive for pursuing Virginia's independence. In response to the Dunmore Proclamation, Virginian "Patriots" strove to preserve bondage. To recruit slave owners for the militia, Patrick Henry circulated the proclamation. Patriot gazettes alluded to the governor's "black banditti." To Thomas Jefferson on June 3, 1776, Francis Eppes, a Virginia plantation owner, referred to "Lord Dunmore & his motley crew."[10] In the backcountry, according to Patriot Phillip Fithian of southwestern New Jersey, the Dunmore Proclamation "quicken[ed] all in Revolution." Too glibly, Richard Henry Lee announced that "Lord Dunmore's unparalleled conduct in Virginia has, a few Scotch excepted, united every Man in that large Colony."[11]

On April 27, 1775, to prevent further escalation of the incident, however, Peyton Randolph, soon to be first president of the Continental Congress, wrote to Mann Page, Lewis Willis, and Benjamin Grymes that the taking up of arms had "incensed the Governor a good deal and from every thing we can learn was the principal Reason why his Answer was not more explicit and favorable. His Excellency has repeatedly assured several Respectable Gentlemen that his only motive in Removing the Powder was to secure it, as there had been an alarm from the County of Surry which at first seem'd too well founded, 'tho it afterwards proved groundless."[12]

By explaining the sequestration of the gunpowder in terms of the threat of a revolution among black slaves, the governor had aimed to secure the submission of white Virginians inclined to their own kind of revolt. On May 1, 1775, the governor reported to Dartmouth, he had thought it prudent to seize the gunpowder at Williamsburg to thwart "the raising of a body of armed men in all the counties."[13] As Randolph's April 27 letter underlines, however, the raising of Patriot soldiers occurred outside Williamsburg only as a response to Dunmore's removal of the powder.[14] And while Dunmore claimed to Dartmouth that he took the arms to protect owners against black insurrection, no elite Virginian believed this.

If Dunmore's flamboyant stance had been more honorable, he might have taken credit for attempting to undo bondage. Instead, imperial emancipation was, for him, a means to maintain the empire. In contrast, American insights would eventually generate a novel contractarian vision of black and white equality. Still, if freedom is the measure of the American Revolution, ironically, it was not an American Patriot, but a British royal governor, "Dunmore the Liberator," in historian Benjamin Quarles's phrase, who, despite the colonial administrator's equivocations, initially took action for the relief of the most oppressed.[15]

LORD DUNMORE, EMANCIPATION, AND THE PATRIOT REBELLION

But Dunmore had danced a tightrope between inciting the menace of black insurrection to achieve the submission of slave owners and at the same time provoking them by infringing on their right to bear arms. And the colonists weren't his only problem. Despite his incendiary words, Dunmore needed to persuade London that he somehow proceeded with caution. As he explained to the secretary for the colonies, "I thought proper in the defenceless state in which I find myself, to endeavour to soothe them verbally to the effect that I had removed the powder, lest the Negroes might have seized upon it, to a place of security from whence when I saw occasion I would at any time deliver it to the people; but in the ferment in which they then appeared it would be highly improper to put it into their hands."[16]

However, to promise salvation from the threat of black rebellion to those to whom he depicted the horrors of a slave uprising that he himself would instigate could only inspire indignation. To seize powder at the rumor of black insurrection, prompting Patriots to take up arms against him, and then to tell them that he did it "in their defense" further incensed them. Such paradoxes reveal Dunmore's contempt for the acuity of both the colonists and his London superiors.

He soothed no elite Virginians, and their armed revolt proceeded apace. To Dartmouth, Dunmore wrote: "Parties of armed men were continually coming into town from the adjacent counties the following days, offering fresh insults." Once again, Dunmore threatened to reduce the colonists' "houses to ashes" and to arm their slaves against them: "And I have already signified to the magistrates of Williamsburg that I expect them on their allegiance to put . . . a stop to the march of the people now on their way before they enter this city, that otherwise . . . it is my fixed purpose to arm all my own Negroes and receive all others that will come to me whom I shall declare free; that I do enjoin the magistrates and all others professing to be loyal subjects to repair to my assistance or that I shall consider the whole country in an actual state of rebellion and myself at liberty to annoy it by every means possible, and that I shall not hesitate at reducing their houses to ashes and spreading devastation wherever I can reach."[17]

On May 15, Lieutenant General Thomas Gage alerted Dartmouth to Dunmore's "very alarming" situation. Gage feared that "the assistance in my power to give him will avail but little." He ordered the Fourteenth Regiment at Providence Island and St. Augustine to Virginia. In addition, Gage had heard "by a private letter that a declaration his lordship had made of proclaiming all the Negroes free who should join him had startled the immigrants."[18] Long before Dunmore issued his famous proclamation, everyone—white and black, Patriot and Tory—knew that the governor bid blacks to free themselves by joining the Crown.

In a June 19 "Address to the Earl of Dunmore," the House of Burgesses suggested disingenuously that "the county was in a perfect state of tranquility till they received an account of your lordship's removal of the gunpowder from the public magazine to one of His Majesty's ships of war and of your irritating and most unjustifiable threats."[19] Imagining conspiracy, the burgesses described Dunmore's act as part of a pattern designed from London: "The inhabitants of this country, my lord, could not be strangers to the many attempts in the Northern Colonies to disarm the people and thereby deprive them of the only means of defending their lives and property. . . . The like measures were generally recommended by the ministry and the export of powder from Great Britain had been prohibited. Judge then how very alarming a removal of the small stock which remained in the public magazine for the defense of the country and the stripping the guns of their locks must have been to any people who had the smallest regard for their security."[20]

The burgesses pointed out the irrationality of Dunmore's "reassurances." White Virginians hardly stood in the way of suppressing black revolt: "The reason assigned by your lordship for taking this step we should have thought the most likely at any other time to have dictated a very different conduct. We should have supposed that a well-grounded apprehension of an insurrection of the slaves ought to have called forth the utmost exertion to suppress it."[21]

According to the governor, an imperial ship had originally owned the powder. The burgesses replied: "We have made inquiry into that matter and cannot find that there ever was any powder brought either from the *Rippon* or any other man-of-war, so that we presume your lordship must have been misinformed."[22]

They insisted that a tax on the colonists for self-defense had paid for the powder. By their first demonstration with guns on April 20, the burgesses suggested disingenuously, they had intended no insult to Dunmore. On the governor's promise to return the powder in case of a revolt, however, they asserted diplomatically, but not credibly, that "everything [would be] perfectly quiet."[23]

Dunmore's posturings were grandiose, his temper hair-trigger. The burgesses recalled, "Your lordship sent a message into the city by one of the Magistrates which you delivered with the most solemn asseverations that if any insult was offered to Captain Foy or Captain Collins you would declare freedom to the slaves and lay the town in ashes and that you could easily depopulate the whole country."[24]

On May 15, Dunmore informed Dartmouth that "the commotion in this colony . . . has obliged me to shut myself in and make a garrison of my house, expecting every moment to be attacked."[25] In fact, Dunmore fled from the governor's palace to the frigate *Foley* at Yorktown. On June 24, Virginians sacked his residence. According to Dunmore, "A considerable body of men violently forced into the governor's house bursting open a window by which one part entered who then forced the principal door by which the rest entered, and they carried off all the arms they could find to the number of between two and three hundred stand which had been always kept in the hall of this house, and [a] considerable number of muskets and other arms, my own property."[26]

Dunmore's threats to free and arm black slaves had helped precipitate the rebellion of the Patriots, yet to London, Dunmore denied his provocations. He was within "his rights" as royal governor, he averred, to seize the powder. In a June letter to Dartmouth, however, Dunmore at last acknowledged that slave owners had reason to dread black revolt. His threat to arm and liberate slaves "has stirred up fears in them which cannot easily subside."[27]

A torrent of rumor quickly surged through the colonies about the monarch arming slaves. A 1775 story suggested that William Campbell, the new governor of South Carolina, had brought with him "14,000 stand of arms" for blacks.[28] On April 25, James Kenny, a Philadelphia Quaker, wrote to Humphrey Marshall, a botanist and fellow Quaker, that "a great Woman in London who had been lately in conversation with the King" had revealed terrifying royal secrets. He reported, "Arms is to be given to all of ye. Negroes to act against ye. Colonies."[29]

Since the French and Indian War in the 1750s, Britain had enlisted blacks. An imperial commander during that war, George Washington, knew what could be done by the Crown. For instance, the British had impressed Sip Wood, a black man from Windham, Connecticut, into the navy. On May 20, 1772, Wood petitioned the Connecticut colony that he "went into the Campaign in the Company under the Command of John Slap and Served this Colony during all the season from the 2nd day of April to the 27th of October." He requested "Eleven pounds, Eighteen Shillings & ten pence."[30] Patriots had ample reason to fear that the Crown would massively extend black recruitment.

Where blacks imagined the king as liberator, whites saw only a tyrant. According to an April 1775 rumor, George III threatened to arrest the Continental Congress and end the rule of law. James Kenny wrote to Humphrey Marshall: "That all of ye Laws are to be Vigorously put in force. . . . Ye Congress are to be taken Prisoners and Try'd by ye chief Judge of ye Admiralty where no evidence shall be admitted but their own Writings to convict & hang them." Taxation without representation, in the form of the Stamp Act, was also oppressive. But many white colonists equated freeing blacks—an imperial act defying the colonists' despotism toward slaves—with the tyrannical denial of habeas corpus or representation. In Kenny's words, "All of ye Colonies is deemed rebels which all such as are taken in that case are to be tried by said Judge & all such as are convicted, thier [sic] Lands are to be confiscated by the King."[31]

In their hubris, Dunmore and London underestimated the Patriots. On June 12, 1775, General Gage in Boston reported the armed rebellion's fury to Lord Barrington: "People would not believe that the Americans would seriously resist if put to the test, but their Rage and Enthusiasm, appeared so plainly in the month of August last" that Gage could not have acted with the peremptoriness that "very many here, and with you, thought I ought to have acted."[32]

In this, as in many moments of crisis that were to follow, military necessity overcame pride and distaste, and pragmatism trumped racism. Gage suggested recruiting Native Americans and, following Dunmore, blacks: "You may be tender of using Indians, but the Rebels have shown us the example, and brought all they could down upon us here. Things are now come to that Crisis, that we must avail ourselves of every Resource, even to raise the Negroes, in our cause."[33]

British public opinion also favored black enlistment. William Henry Lyttleton, a former governor of South Carolina and member of the House of Commons, proposed that Parliament "encourage the negroes in that part of America [the South] to rise against their masters." He likened the United States to a chain, the commercial North of which was strong, the southern states subject to internal rebellion "on account of the number of negroes in them."[34] If Britain were to attack the South, Lyttleton surmised, "the negroes would rise and embrue their hands with the blood of their masters." This call for slave insurrection, however, was "most severely reprehended from the other side . . . as being too black, horrid and wicked, to be heard of, much less adopted by any civilized people."[35] The debate in the House of Commons raged until 4:30 in the morning. Lyttleton's motion was defeated by a vote of 278 to 108. Still, to crush the rebellion, more than a quarter of Parliament thought blacks should be freed and mobilized.

Thus it was that a radical emancipatory pragmatism won the day, and following his proclamation in November 1775, Dunmore officially formed the Royal Ethiopian Regiment. In November and December, hundreds of escapees joined Dunmore aboard the *William*.[36] To the soldiers' delight, when Dunmore formed the regiment, he inscribed on their uniforms the incendiary words "*Liberty to Slaves*." He also gave each recruit freedom and one pound, one guinea. In a week, some five hundred blacks, mainly from Virginia, enlisted, even though Dunmore had only a navy, and to escape, get out on the river, and reach him, blacks needed determination.[37] According to the Northampton Committee of Public Safety, two hundred "immediately joined him." On November 19, Andrew Sprouwel, a Loyalist shipyard owner in Virginia, estimated that three hundred had escaped to Dunmore. On November 24, John Page, a Patriot plantation owner, raged to Thomas Jefferson, "Numbers of Negroes and Cowardly Scoundrels flock to his Standard." On November 27, Edmund Pendleton, a lawyer, notified

Richard Henry Lee, proposer of independence to the Second Continental Congress, that "slaves flock to him in abundance." The *Virginia Gazette* insisted that there were "boatloads."[38] In June 1776, a Huntington, Long Island, demonstration hung "an effigy of [Dunmore] . . . with its face black like his Virginia Regiment."[39]

Fruitlessly, Patriots in Maryland sought to bar "all correspondence with Virginia by land or water."[40] Nevertheless, news spread swiftly among blacks. On December 13, 1775, the *Maryland Gazette* reported from Virginia: "Since lord Dunmore's proclamation made its appearance here, it is said he has recruited his army, in the counties of Princess Anne and Norfolk, to the amount of about 2000 men including his black regiment, which is thought to be a considerable part, with this inscription on their breasts:—'Liberty to slaves.'—However, as the rivers will henceforth be strictly watched and every possible precaution taken, it is hoped others will be effectually prevented from joining those his lordship has already collected."[41]

The *Maryland Gazette* reported clashes between Dunmore's force and Patriots in Norfolk: "Dunmore's party has demolished several houses back of the town, and fortified themselves; also . . . col. Hutchings and some other gentlemen, their prisoners, had been removed to the ships on account of the gaol having been set on fire."[42] On December 15, 1775, the Virginia General Assembly warned against Dunmore's "seduction." Playing God by excommunicating Loyalist blacks from religion, the assembly issued a counterproclamation that declared "all Negro or other slaves, conspiring to rebel or make insurrection, shall suffer death, and be excluded from all benefit of clergy."[43]

Blacks disregarded the assembly's imprecations.[44] In the *Virginia Gazette* on November 16, 1775, Patriot Robert Brent denounced the escaped slave "Charles," a "shrewd, sensible fellow who may prove desperate and resolute, if endeavoured to be taken." "His elopement," Brent reported, "was from no cause of complaint, or dread of a whipping (for he has always been remarkably indulged, indeed too much so) but from a determined resolution to get liberty, as he conceived, by flying to lord Dunmore." Furthermore, Charles had taken an unspecified "variety of clothes." In addition, Robert Brent begged the return of "two mares, one a darkish, the other a light bay, with a blaze and white feet, and about 3 years old." He offered a reward of "Five Pounds" for Charles and especially "the mares, so that I get them again."[45]

Likewise, Landon Carter, a Virginia plantation owner, recorded in his diary: "Last night after going to bed, Moses, my son's man, Hoe, Billy, Postillion, John, Mullatto Peter, Tom, Panticove, Manuel & Lancaster Sam, ran away, to be sure, to Ld. Dunmore, for they got privately into Beale's room before dark & took out my son's gun & one I had there, took out of his drawer in my passage all his ammunition furniture, Landon's bag of bullets and all the Powder and went off. . . . Those accursed villains have stolen Landon's silver buckles, George's shirts, Tom Parker's new waist-coat & breeches."[46] Robert Carter, Landon's grandson, gathered his slaves together and lectured them on Dunmore's "treachery." His lecture, he glibly concluded, persuaded them. But slaves do not tell oppressors the truth. They also soon escaped to the Crown.[47]

A partial record of Dunmore's forces lists none of these escapees. All eighty-seven blacks belonging to Virginia farmer John Willoughby Jr. left.[48] Yet only fourteen enlisted.[49] More may have reached a haven. Still, we have no record of what happened to most of them (seventy-three—more than five times the number who joined Dunmore). They might also have been killed or died of smallpox during the attempt to reach imperial lines.

Surviving lists dramatically understate the number of blacks who flocked to the British side, and no writing survives of the blacks who joined Dunmore, either before the Dunmore Proclamation or in the Royal Ethiopian Regiment. Letters of their American enemies, however, contain tales of the exploits and fate of some of them. Joseph Harris, a "small mu-latto man" "owned" by Henry King of Hampton Roads, was a ship's pi-lot. In July 1775, Harris escaped to Dunmore, who gave him command of the *Liberty*, a pilot boat. During a hurricane on September 5, Harris ran the boat aground. He and an Englishman, Captain Matthew Squires, es-caped in a canoe.[50] Americans looted the ship and set it afire "in return for [Squires's] harbouring gentlemen's negroes and suffering his sailors to steal poultry, hogs, &c." Captain Squires demanded the return of the goods from the Hampton Roads Committee of Public Safety. It would do so, the latter responded, only when Squires sent Joseph Harris back into bondage.[51]

On October 26, Squires attacked Hampton Roads with six small vessels, one commanded by Harris. The Patriots defeated Squires and captured a boat. In a standard racial distinction, they recorded "3 wounded Men 6 sailors and 2 Negroes." Though blacks sailed the boats, somehow the men were not "sailors." American citizens treated white imperial captives "with great humanity." The same citizens tried blacks for their lives.[52]

In a second case, a painter, whose name is not mentioned but who had belonged to George Washington, escaped to Dunmore in the sum-mer of 1775. Desiring vengeance, Lund Washington, George Washington's cousin and manager, wrote: "I suppose there is very little Chance of getg the painter from Lord Dunmore, if he comes up here and indeavors to Land at mt Vernon[,] Raising the rest, I will shoot him, that will be some Satisfaction."[53] In battle, Patriots wounded and captured the painter.

In a November 12, 1775, letter to his brother Michael, William Brown Wallace, a Patriot soldier, records a third incident, a "small brush near James River with Dunmore's forces." Wallace describes the severe punishment of blacks: "Afterwards [Patriots were] Boarding one of the Vessels out of which they took 5 white & 2 black prisoners who are now in the Guard House in this City [Williamsburg]. The Negroes are in Close Jail and is to stand a Tryal for Life. But the white men are used very well."[54] In the quasi-amity of the early war, combatants treated white rebel and royal prisoners alike. But a Patriot vision of "enemies" and "betrayers" shows the special terror created by Lord Dunmore's black troops and the risks that black slaves seeking freedom took to join them.

Epidemics of smallpox were yet another hazard that escaped slaves had to confront. Because of smallpox, the active members of the Royal Ethiopian Regiment averaged only some three hundred soldiers. According to John Dent of the Patriot Maryland militia, the shore at St. Mary's, Virginia, was "full of Dead Bodies, chiefly negroes. We are poisoned with the stench."[55] Still, recruitment, the governor reported to the secretary of state, went "very well, [except] a fever crept in amongst them which carried off a great many Very fine fellows." Without smallpox, he estimated, the regiment might have enlisted two thousand men.[56]

Despite Dunmore's actions in the spring, summer, and fall of 1775, not until February 18, 1776, did he tell Dartmouth that he had issued his proclamation. Offering on his own initiative to emancipate slaves who would fight on the Loyalist side and then actually forming a regiment composed of them was not exactly proceeding with caution or working to prevent the incipient rebellion, and to protect himself from Dartmouth's criticism, Dunmore harped grandiloquently on how he had been forced to act "Alone," because London had abandoned him.[57] Reporting the Patriots' firing on British ships near Hampton Roads and parrying potential charges that he had acted rashly, Dunmore stressed to Dartmouth that

these overt acts of Rebellion determined me to issue the enclosed *Proclamation*, which, however, I postponed as long as possible in hopes of having instructions from your Lordship for my conduct in this as well as in the many other matters I have so often prayed to be instructed in for many months past, but not one line have I had the honour to receive from your Lordship since yours of the 30th of May. God only knows what I have suffered since my first embarking from my anxiety of mind, not knowing how to act in innumerable instances that occur every day, being one moment diffident of my own judgment (and not having one living soul to advise with) and then on the other hand fearing, if I remained a tame spectator and permitted the rebels to proceed without any interruption, that they would by persuasion, threats, and every other art in their power, delude many of His Majesty's well-disposed subjects to their party.[58]

The governor had heard that "a hundred and twenty or thirty North Carolina rebels" marched into Virginia to Great Bridge, about nine miles from Norfolk. Leading the Fourteenth Regiment (109 redcoats and 22 Norfolk volunteers), Dunmore embarked by boat, and the Patriots fled. Dunmore then heard that "between three and four hundred of our Rebels assembled at a place called Kemp's Landing," nine miles from Great Bridge. In the first battle of the new war in the South, on November 15, 1775, Dunmore reported to Dartmouth, he routed the Americans: "We accordingly marched thither immediately, and about a mile from the place our advanced party were fired upon by the Rebels from a thicket before our people discovered them. I immediately ordered the main body, who were within two or three hundred paces, to advance and then detached a party with the volunteers to outflank them. At the same time the advanced guard with the grenadiers rushed into the woods. The Rebels fled on all quarters; we pursued them above a mile, four or five were killed, a good many wounded, and eighteen taken prisoners on that and the following day."[59]

The presence of these imperial forces, he told Dartmouth, inspired Loyalists to flock to the Crown: "The good effects of this most trifling success was manifested strongly by the zeal which the people showed on this occasion to His Majesty's service when unawed by the opposite party. . . . The next day I suppose not less than a hundred of those very men who were forced into the field against me the day before came and took the enclosed oath. Your lordship may observe that about three thousand have taken that oath."[60] On Dunmore's return to Norfolk, two hundred more made the pledge.[61]

A few weeks later, on December 9, 1775, however, the Patriots' Second Virginia Regiment under Colonel Woodford defeated Dunmore's Loyalist troops at Great Bridge. To his brother William, Patriot colonel George Johnston reported the battle's ferocity: "Their brave Capt Fordyce (now lying dead in our Church) at every hazard rallied & brought them up to the very Muzzles of our Guns. . . . The officer [Ens.—unclear] Holmes who carried the flag of Truce was on the Bridge, he says that the dragging of the dead over has made a bloody path."[62]

As Johnston reported, a defector had misinformed Lord Dunmore about the strength of Patriot forces: "Return thanks for this to a little villain who deserted from us a few nights ago. He informed L. D. that we had not more than 300 here, upon which it was determined to attack us with fixed bayonets."[63] A much larger group of Patriots, armed with muskets, surprised the attackers. Johnston stressed the major role of black Loyalists: "At two other times, we have . . . killed 6 or 7 Negroes 1 white has been taken & 4 negroes prisoners."[64]

On December 17, 1775, Lund Washington wrote to George Washington: "We have only jest come to hand of a Party of Lord Dunmore[s] men Attackg one hundred of our men that were intrenchd on this Side the Great Bridge, Dunmores Party were repulsd with the loss of 50 men kill'd and tak'n." Lund Washington exaggerated. The Americans killed thirteen Loyalists—the majority black—and wounded or captured seventeen.[65] Nevertheless, Lund railed against liberation: "Lord Dunmore's Negroes Soldiers are, it is said, commanded by Scotchmen—proper Officers for Slaves, for they themselves Possess Slavish Principles."[66]

But using freed black slaves as a military force was not something that either the British colonial administration or the British army had contemplated, and what role emancipated blacks should or could play in countering the incipient Patriot revolt was a matter of some debate. Dunmore was a visionary strategist, but a weak commander. At the Battle of Great Bridge, the Royal Ethiopian Regiment contained half of Dunmore's force of six hundred, but he committed a grave tactical error by stationing the blacks at the rear. And although Dunmore's proclamation and recruitment of slaves to the Loyalist cause could have set an example for the Crown, the prime minister, Lord North, did not command other governors to emulate Dunmore and recruit all-black units of soldiers. Still, Black Loyalists fought determinedly to end bondage, and even without orders from London, Dunmore's example and massive black escape—thousands of still-to-be-organized escapees trailed every British force—inspired other imperial commanders to enlist many blacks. They even formed separate companies of "Black Pioneers," artillerymen, and others. But the Crown did not recognize the explosive resource it had attracted.

The decision not to exploit the strategic innovation that Dunmore had discovered—or into which his reaction to events had pushed him—cost

Crown much of its initial advantage over the Americans. If Britain had
bilized blacks mainly as soldiers, the Revolution would have sunk like
one unless it, too, enlisted and liberated them. Even so, as we will see
in subsequent chapters, the Patriots would form regiments of black soldiers in Rhode Island, Connecticut, and Massachusetts, and as the American First Rhode Island Regiment would show, emancipated blacks fought
harder and served longer in the cause of freedom than other soldiers on
the Patriot side. The Continental army also recruited many blacks in Pennsylvania and Maryland and made repeated efforts to forge black units in
South Carolina and Georgia.

Eventually, the Crown enlisted substantial numbers of black soldiers
and organized segregated units that sometimes fought. But other commanders failed to form blacks primarily into redcoat companies. Because
smallpox thinned his ranks and because Dunmore was not an aggressive
commander, the Royal Ethiopian Regiment did not win stunning victories. Still, many black soldiers continued to fight on the British side.

In terms of recruitment, Dunmore's Ethiopian Regiment did result
in proposals to and occasional formation of similar regiments by other
imperial commanders. At the end of 1775, Captain William Dalrymple of
the Twentieth Regiment of Foot proposed "strengthening General Howe's
Operation in the North by a diversion in the South, without taking off
the Troops." He relied on the governor's example and, Dalrymple prayed,
direct leadership: "Lord Dunmore's Name is Half an Army in the Bay of
Chesapeake; and therefore it is of the last Consequence that this Body of
Men should act under him."[67]

Like Dunmore, Dalrymple called for freeing indentured servants and
added his own suggestion: prisoners. In a proposal to William Howe,
commander in chief of British forces, Dalrymple wrote: "His Lordship can
raise a very large Body of indented servants & convicts at Baltimore Annapolis Alexandria & Fredericksburg or rather to make the operation more
simple and prevent the Division of this Amount he may limit these Levies
to Baltimore & Annapolis & the Countries round them. To these He may
& indeed should add the bravest and most ingenious of the black Slaves
whom He may find all over the Bay of Chesapeake."[68]

Dalrymple disparaged West Indian blacks, probably because their wave
of rebellions had threatened British domination. Yet he praised North
Americans: "People in England are apt to confound an African-born Black
in the West Indies with a Virginia or Maryland Black born in those Provinces. The first is the Meanest of Mankind, the others are full of Intelligence, Fidelity & Courage, as will be found upon Enquiry."[69]

Dalrymple believed that any maneuver in the Chesapeake area would sow consternation among American slave owners. Patriots would drive blacks into the interior, creating the diversion Dalrymple recommended to Howe: "The Project in Chesapeake Bay alone would at least have the Effect to Throw the Estates on the Delaware waste, because the Masters will carry off the Servants from their Estates upon hearing what is passing in Chesapeake Bay."[70]

In place of soldiers imported from Britain, Dalrymple stressed using blacks and indentured servants as "irregulars"—guerillas who did not wear red coats. His strategy presaged the recruitment of black and multiracial groups in New Jersey and South Carolina. To Howe, Dalrymple stressed the signal benefits of black troops: "Considering that such capital Important Advantages may be obtained without any Diminution of the Regular Troops destined for other purposes, without any Expense except the Temporary support and Transport of the Provisional Corps without any Inconvenience to the Army present or future, the Proposer humbly conceives that under the Name of a Project, it has a chance for all the Advantages of One, without a Possibility of Disadvantage, the Risk of which is Generally the Objection to Projects."[71]

Others in the imperial camp conveyed the same advice as Dalrymple. Writing to Secretary of State George Germain, Joseph Galloway, a Loyalist delegate from Philadelphia to the First Continental Congress, contrasted the northern colonies as "compact," "thicker settled," with "few Slaves" and "more dissatisfied," compared with their counterparts in the South. He named blacks "intestine enemies" of the Patriots: "The Middle and Southern Colonies are by far the Weakest in Military Force, and of course, the Easiest to Conquer. In four of them, the Labouring Class of People, from whence the Soldiers can only be procured is chiefly composed of Negroes, whom the new States justly esteem so many intestine Enemies and therefore will not trust them in arms."[72]

Blacks would provide the reserve, Galloway suggested to Germain, from which the Crown could draw recruits: "In the class of Fighting Men among the Negroes, there are no men of property; none whose attachment of Interest would render them averse to the bearing of Arms against the Rebellion, and that more fighting men would be raised for this reason among them than among the whites although they [the whites] amount to three times the number of slaves."[73]

The Crown would send repeated military expeditions into the Chesapeake area and Virginia, notably those led by Generals Howe, Arnold, and Cornwallis and Colonel Tarleton. In a brief New England campaign following Dalrymple's proposal, Howe formed a "Company of Negroes." On the evacuation from Boston in 1776, emancipated blacks accompanied him to Halifax.[74] In Philadelphia the Crown mustered a "Company of Black Pioneers."[75]

The Dunmore Proclamation triggered more than just a debate about British recruitment policies and military tactics in the colonies, however. Throughout the South, it set in motion the second revolution among blacks themselves, who did not wait for official invitations to join in a fight for their liberty. As early as 1775, much greater numbers of escapees trailed imperial troops than officers could assimilate into the army. Enemies to all slave masters, these "irregulars" were themselves a fighting force. For instance, William Bull, the last Loyalist lieutenant governor of South Carolina, retired to his Ashley Hall plantation in St. Andrew's Parish. His political sympathies, however, did not shield the area, which was "plundered and greatly damaged by the irregular and great swarm of Negroes that followed . . . the [British] Army."[76] Having no subsistence from the Crown, the unorganized took what food they could gather. Because blacks had produced the crops, they reappropriated stolen resources.

In addition, even slaves who remained on plantations no longer worked for the masters. Instead, they cultivated their own plots. As the war progressed, black and other Loyalist troops seized the remaining southern produce. A common stereotype about camp followers in war stigmatizes such people as prostitutes. These legions were a radically different phenomenon. Often, as in sacking Ashley Hall, they acted on their own. Moreover, to survive, individuals provided needed services to the British, for example, attending to horses or selling food. Throughout the rebellion, the empire would continually mobilize black soldiers either as regulars or for guerilla war.

Dunmore's example thus might have triggered British mobilization of freed slaves as warriors, and unless the Patriots recruited and emancipated an even larger number of blacks, the advent of the second revolution might have suppressed the first. Instead, the British dithered while the colonies burned and smallpox decimated Dunmore's black supporters.

In Virginia, after the defeat at Great Bridge on December 9, 1775, Dunmore retreated to a flotilla of one hundred ships. His forces fired cannons at Patriot snipers and burned nineteen buildings in Norfolk. Under Colonel William Woodford, the Americans then set two fires that ravaged the fifth-largest city in North America. They imputed Norfolk's destruction to the British,[77] and with no buildings to obstruct their vision, the Patriots could easily trace the movement of ships to reequip Dunmore's forces.[78]

On February 1, 1776, the governor took his supporters to Hampton Roads, the largest American port south of New York. At the mouth of Chesapeake Bay, Hampton Roads provided access to Virginia, Maryland, Delaware, and Pennsylvania. Dunmore hoped to send Loyalist privateers to capture enemy vessels, secure supplies, and bar Patriot commerce. Unlike previous imperial authorities, Dunmore arrested merchants who traded with the rebels.[79]

Partial records for Dunmore's flotilla, compiled by historian Peter J. Wrike, show the presence of 155 blacks, including 88 men in the Royal Ethiopian Regiment,[80] 45 wives, and 4 children. In addition, 11 free black men, 3 women, and 4 children were on board.[81] Slave owners routinely broke up families. Yet despite the horrors of the military camps, escapees brought their children to the imperial side.

Blacks who fled the same plantation knew and trusted each other. Sometimes they shared a common surname, that of the owner. Some were brothers, sisters, and spouses, perhaps led by a parent or elder sibling.[82] For example, a list of Dunmore's sailors includes fourteen Willoughbys of the eighty-seven who fled the Willoughby plantation.[83] One peculiar fact is that few children accompanied them. Only four appear on this list, the same number as for a much smaller contingent of already free African Americans. The regiment had two corporals, Crouch and Curry, recorded by their last names, which was unusual, as well as two sergeants, Britain and John P. Royal. Only Mingo Peeding had an African first name.

Whether Wrike's separate list of already free African Americans is accurate is unclear. Joseph Harris, a pilot, had gained liberty under the Dunmore Proclamation. But Moses Stephens, Matthew Tucker, George Mills, John King, and Edward Johnson were free seamen. In response to the repeated promises of the governor to emancipate others, they, too, joined with the Crown.[84]

Captain Andrew Snape Hamond commanded HMS *Roebuck*. With forty-four guns, 100 marines, and 260 sailors, the ship dwarfed any vessel in the rival Continental navy. In mid-February 1776, Hamond's arrival at Norfolk deterred a Patriot attack on Dunmore's flotilla.[85] With the impatience of Hotspur, Hamond chafed to fight. Instead, he protected the governor's retreat: "I received such an account of Lord Dunmore's Situation, as obliged me to look in upon him, when I found I had just arrived in Time to save him out of the hands of the Rebels."[86]

Initially, it appeared that Hamond and Dunmore would have substantial, combined forces capable of aggression against the enemy. The *Roebuck*, however, engaged in but a few skirmishes. Writing to his friend Hans Stanley, Hamond despaired: "You hear seldom from me . . . because I have nothing material to acquaint you with the history of a defensive kind of war, which has been my misfortune for some time past to have been engaged in, is painful for me to relate, and would give you no pleasure to read. . . . In short, the support & protection that I have been under the absolute necessity of giving to Lord Dunmore & his floating Town, consisting of a Fleet of upwards of 90 Sail, destitute of almost every material to Navigate them as well as Seamen, has given full employment for three ships for these three months past . . . and had we to deal with People the least enterprizing, we should not have been able to have done it so long."[87]

By uniting the *Roebuck* with an army of redcoats and Loyalists at the mouths of the Delaware River and Chesapeake Bay, Hamond hoped to attack Philadelphia in late 1776. Vice Admiral Molyneux Schuldham, commander of the British navy, encouraged him. But, Hamond lamented, given "the distress of the Army which had obliged them to evacuate Boston, no troops could be sent to assist me." The Crown would delay an attack on Philadelphia for nearly two years. Hamond commented on "being myself most heartily tired of carrying on a sort of Piratical war that tended in no degree to benefit his Majestys Service."[88]

Generals Clinton and Cornwallis came to Hampton Roads. Dunmore was aghast that, following the advice of Clinton, a former governor of North Carolina, the Crown chose to invade there instead of fighting for Virginia, "the first Colony of the Continent, both for Riches and Power."[89] In Virginia, Dunmore thought, they might have grasped the rebellion's seriousness. He might then have won them to rely on black soldiering, and with his usual outspokenness, Dunmore notified London of these officers' lack of strategic sense.

Clinton would lose, even in North Carolina. Fighting was no easier for inexperienced redcoats than for inexperienced Patriots. On June 15, 1776, Patriot colonel George Johnston reported scornfully that "Genl Lee with our 8th Regiment is moving to So Carolina in search of Clinton who has not been heard of since he left Cape Fear the 1st instant."[90] On June 21, Johnston surmised: "Clinton is certainly lying off Charles Town with his whole Force."[91] Clinton, however, did not fight.

Smallpox continued to plague the populations of escaped slaves, including Dunmore's Ethiopian Regiment. A form of inoculation was known, but it caused agony and prevented the illness only in some.[92] Inoculation mimicked the disease, and though it seldom ended in death, in Norfolk in

1768, Virginians had rioted against the injections.[93] In the closed quarters of Dunmore's flotilla, however, no remedy could curb the disease's spread, and in May 1776, after Dunmore had settled briefly at Tucker's Mills in Portsmouth, the epidemic grew. On May 16, 1776, Hamond glimpsed how difficult his situation would become: "A small pox made its appearance among the Black troops and in order to save them, the Surgeons recommended that the whole be inoculated. This was likely to be a great reduction of our force. Therefore . . . we thought it most advisable to move the Fleet immediately; for had we waited until the Enemy had planted cannon at certain places on the Riverside . . . it would scarce have been possible to have got the Vessels down the River, and they must have fallen into the hands of the Rebels." On May 27, Hamond feared that the remains "of the Squadron did not amount to more than 200 effective men so great had been the mortality among the Negroes while at Tuckers Mills."[94]

Yet intelligence obtained by the Patriots from deserters often proved inaccurate. For instance, Johnston mistakenly predicted that the governor "will bend his Course to North Carolina."[95] On May 27, 1776, Francis Eppes guessed that Dunmore might flee to Canada: "On May 22, Lord Dunmore & his fleet left Norfolk. Where he is destined God & himself only know. It is given out that they intend for Cape Fear or Halifax tho Colonel Woodford seems to think they intend making an attack on some other part of this country. This I think hardly probable as they are in great distress for every kind of provisions."[96]

Eppes also knew of the smallpox. News of the epidemic among blacks restored Patriot nerve. He surmised that the governor's forces would have to make camp as soon as possible "without being molested" by American attack.[97]

On June 1, Dunmore decided to occupy Gwinn's Island in Chesapeake Bay. Hamond still expected to fight. But Dunmore's retreat weighed down Hamond with a flotilla dying from the inside.

On June 10, Hamond applauded black fortitude. Furthermore, a continual flow of black recruits arrived; escape to the British in Virginia persisted throughout the war. Still, Hamond had no illusions about "the Fever's" intensification: "The Negro Troops, which had been inoculated before they left Norfolk, got thro' this disorder with great success, but the Fever which had been so fatal to them there, followed them also to the island; so that notwithstanding the Corps was recruited with six or eight fresh men every day, yet the mortality among them was so great, that they did not now amount to above 150 effective men."[98]

Hamond's forces had become a shell. On July 9, Hamond reported, he had to flee Virginia: "An attack was to be made upon the Island, and being too weak to resist any considerable force (the Army being reduced by the small Pox and an epidemic fever) my Lord Dunmore and the land officers were of opinion that their Post on the Island was no longer tenable and accordingly determined on evacuating it immediately."[99]

On July 14, Hamond still hoped for an offensive. Angrily, he reported to Stanley that he had advised Dunmore "in the strongest terms to use his endeavours to persuade the People that had put themselves under his protection, to sail with their Vessels to some place of Security, on account of the great inconvenience that arose to his Majesty's Service by keeping two ships to guard them." Hamond weeded out those of the governor's ships incapable of sailing. On August 5, he notified Stanley, "I am sending all that is able & in a condition to go to Sea to St. Augustine, after having destroyed about twenty sail, and put the people that inhabited them into other vessels. We shall then be much more at liberty to act offensively against the Enemy than we hitherto have been, which if we had a sufficient force to do might be done to great advantage, as on account of the Navigable Rivers of this Country, there is no part of the continent where ships can assist land operations more than in this."[100]

Meanwhile, however, the smallpox epidemic became overwhelming. On July 24, Hamond reported that "the *Fowey* had 35 men sick, and Lord Dunmore's Army was reduced to about 150 Rank and File, one third of which was incapable of Duty." They decided to make their way, "in our weak situation," to New York. On August 5, Hamond thought fleetingly of St. Augustine and hoped vainly for battle. He also chronicled the Royal Ethiopian Regiment's fate: "Unfortunately my Lord Dunmore's Troops have been so few in number, such a motley set and so full of disease that it has been totally impossible to do or attempt any thing of consequence; and our whole exploits have amounted to nothing more than burning and destroying Houses on the Banks of the Rivers, and taking the Cattle off the Farms, which decides nothing. Whenever a Thousand men can be spared, properly equipt, for the service of this Colony, with eight or 10 sail of small Ships to act with them, they may distress the Colonys of Maryland & Virginia to the great[est] degree, and employ more than ten times their numbers to watch them."[101] Yet in the future, not English ships, as Hamond imagined, but black irregulars would tie down the Patriot militias of New Jersey and South Carolina.

While Dunmore dithered and disease riddled the Royal Ethiopian Regiment, the Patriots of Virginia were still reeling from the prospects that the Dunmore Proclamation held for slave owners and their own revolt for "liberty." They were often as much concerned with forestalling a slave revolt in favor of the Loyalist cause as they were with defeating the British. On April 5, 1776, American general Charles Lee informed George Washington that the British, reinforced by black troops, might seize Virginia's capital: "I cannot help perswading [*sic*] myself that their object will be to take possession of Williamsburg—not only from its tempting advantageous situation commanding in great measure two fine rivers and a Country abundant in all the necessaries for an army; but the possession of the Capital would give an air of dignity and decided superiority to their arms, which in this Slave Country where dominion is founded on opinion [mutilated] a circumstance of the utmost importance."[102]

On May 10, 1776, Lee forwarded Washington a Council of Officers' report that recommended abandoning the American post at Kemp's Landing. At the same time, to stem flight to the Crown, the report requested the Virginia Convention to order the evacuation of blacks from Prince Anne and Norfolk Counties.[103] American legislation to force blacks away from Loyalist territory mirrored Hamond's reports of black recruitment at Gwinn's Island. Thus far, the Patriots had extended no offers of freedom. Instead, American soldiers were employed mainly to prevent black escapes. Counterrevolution against the second revolution undermined the first.[104]

Preoccupied with the dangers of bondage, George Washington wrote presciently of the imperial threat to the South to his brother, John Augustine Washington: "Surely Administration must intend more than 5000 Men for the Southern district, otherwise they must have a very contemptable opinion of those Colonies, or have great expectation of assistance from the Indians, Slaves & Tories."[105]

During May, American general Andrew Lewis occupied part of Gwinn's Island. But he, too, fought more to isolate slaves from Dunmore than to defeat the British. On May 22, 1776, Colonel George Johnston defined his assignment as deterring black escape. As he wrote to his brother William, his mission was "to harass the enemy & prevent any persons [especially slaves] from going on board that might be induced to take that step by the late Resolution of the Convention to remove all the Inhabitants from this part of the Country." With his band of "20 men," Johnston proudly noted the presence of guards on every shore and told of skirmishes "every day." Of Dunmore's forces, he crowed that "they hazard their Lives to procure Wood & Water."[106]

On the preceding Sunday, Johnston reported, a force of seventy tried to "drive us off," but the Patriots defeated them.[107] The whole effort "has distressed his Ldship to such a degree that added to his former disagreeable Situation, his Life is become so miserable, he is removing his whole Fleet to the [Hampton] Roads; whither he will then proceed is uncertain." Johnston was right that Dunmore would leave Gwinn's Island but wrong about the destination. Johnston raged at Dunmore's black troops, his "*Effects and black friends.*" And the disease that was laying waste to Dunmore's troops heartened the Patriots. According to Johnston, "It is said by Deserters that the Small Pox is on board & that they are inoculating. The Negroes continue to die by half dozens daily."[108]

On June 15, 1776, from Williamsburg, Johnston fantasized an easy victory over Dunmore: "This morning a part of the Artillery Company marched for Gwinn's Island with 2 brass fixed pieces, 'tis said they will take 10 or 12 larger pieces on the road, & about the 20th the Public is to be entertained with the sight of Ld D & his whole Fleet dancing in the air; the *Roebuck* and *Fowey* are to be refitted (if not too much bored by Cap. Arundel) & sent immediately in search of the *Liverpool*, who being deceived by his former friendly [unclear] is to be taken without the loss of a grain of Powder, and so on to the whole of them."[109] But no battle took place.

Johnston also recounted attempts to surround Dunmore: "Our men are at Gwyn's [*sic*] Island erecting Batteries & exchanging a few Shot daily. If not the Enemy be reinforced, they may perhaps be routed in a Month, not less."[110] On August 9, Peter Minor, an American soldier, envisioned the passing of Lord Dunmore's ships as an aesthetic spectacle: "I've nothing worthwhile relating save only that Dunmore has gone to New York with his fleet. They came down the Bay Sunday last and anchored opposite to the Pleasure House. Being fifty-two sails a most Beautiful Sight."[111] Patriot officers and soldiers enthusiastically "wish[ed] only for an opportunity to try themselves." On Monday morning, Colonel Edward Stevens of the Culpeper County Minutemen led a brief skirmish. But Dunmore and Hamond departed. The Americans guessed, according to Peter Minor, "35 sail gone to the West Indies, the others to New York."[112] Actually, the whole fleet had gone to Manhattan.

Minor concluded, "We [have] nothing to do." Still, he participated in a brief action against three who had disembarked from the ship. He reported, "We took one prisoner who came ashore with Two Negroes." The idea that all were free did not occur to him. But the Americans did not keep careful watch: "The Negroes made their Escape." From the remaining prisoner, Minor reported, "we can get nothing . . . that is of Consequence. We learned from him that the Fleet is gone."[113]

On exploring Gwinn's Island, horror struck the Patriots. They discovered dead bodies, including those of infants, and, according to one soldier, 130 mass graves. From the ships, desperate survivors of the smallpox epidemic had dumped corpses overboard.[114]

The remnants of the Royal Ethiopian Regiment retreated to New York. On August 21, 1776, these black soldiers fought in the Battle of Brooklyn Heights. The Americans captured "Major Cudjo of Lord Dunmore's Black Regiment," a leader with an African name.[115] Blacks with immediate and second-generation ties to Africa and memories of freedom, either their own or their families', often fought fiercely. Again suggesting Dunmore's innovativeness, Cudjo held a high rank.

On September 16, 1776, the Crown captured New York. No further record exists of the Royal Ethiopian Regiment as a whole. Yet as we will see later, its surviving members fought throughout the war.

THE TWO REVOLUTIONS IN THE SOUTH: SOUTH CAROLINA

In South Carolina, as in Virginia, although imperial oppression played a role in the revolution undertaken by Patriots, fear of a slave insurrection was a dominant motive. Fearing black revolt, South Carolina's slave owners were initially loyal to Britain; Dunmore's threats, however, provoked South Carolina's declaration of independence. On the eve of the Revolution, two events prompted Patriot hysteria: Charlestown leaders lynched Thomas Jeremiah, a free black sea captain, and other elite South Carolinians plotted with Georgians to massacre maroons—escaped slaves—at Tybee Island in Georgia. In both cases, Henry Laurens, a future president of the Continental Congress, played a leading role. In principle, Laurens opposed bondage; his actions, however, often betrayed his principles. In contrast, John Laurens, his son, of whom we will hear much more in subsequent chapters, would become an influential abolitionist in the Patriot elite, the author of the Continental Congress's 1779 proposal to free and recruit several thousand blacks in South Carolina and Georgia.

In 1764, eleven years before the Revolution, prominent South Carolinians had complained against the Stamp Act to imperial agent Charles Garth. Their petition named taxation without representation a violation of a "British man's" rights: "The first, and in our opinion the principal reason, against such a measure, is its inconsistency with that inherent right of every British subject, not to be taxed but by his own consent, or that of his representative. For, though we shall submit most dutifully at all times to acts of Parliament, yet, we think it incumbent on us humbly to remonstrate against such as appear oppressive, hoping that when that august body come to consider this matter they will view it in a more favorable light."[116] Their vow to obey Parliament "at all times" in fact threatens the opposite. They already protested.

The signatories also stressed South Carolina's greater willingness than the other colonies to supply troops for the French and Indian War and warned of the threat from Creek Indians: "It is absolutely necessary for the preservation of a people, in such a situation that they may be suddenly attacked by savage enemies, that they should not be so exhausted and impoverished by taxes as to be disabled from raising the necessary extraordinary supplies."[117] Because they were stealing land from and murdering indigenous people, the settlers had reason to fear.

But among their other concerns, the signers' anxiety about the existence and growth of a black majority is clear. They proposed to ban the slave trade for three years, a law that, however, would take effect only in 1776, twelve years from the date of the letter: "This law is thought so absolutely necessary to the safety and welfare of the province, as well to guard against the danger to be apprehended from too great a disproportion of slaves to white inhabitants, as also to give the planters an opportunity of discharging their debts."[118]

Historian Sylvia Frey points out how this anxiety about the growing black majority led to fear among South Carolina Patriots of a black insurrection. With antislavery sentiment gaining ground in London,

> in May [1775] a report that slaves would be set free on the arrival of the new governor, Lord William Campbell, and that the sloop of war carrying Campbell was also bearing fourteen thousand stand of weapons became "common talk" among slaves throughout the province and "occasioned impertinent behavior in many of them." The discovery of an insurrection plot, planned to coincide with the British arrival, threw the white citizenry of Charleston into panic. "The newspapers were full of Publications calculated to excite the fears of the People—Massacres and Instigated Insurrections, were words in the mouth of every Child," recalled [British Indian agent] John Stuart.[119]

Written in response to the Stono Rebellion, article 17 of South Carolina's Negro Act of 1740 weakly tried to prevent the winds of freedom gusting from colonized to enslaved, to eradicate servants' notions of liberty. Just prior to the Revolution, the threat of insurrection panicked South Carolinian slave owners. As Georgia's governor Sir James Wright reported to the Earl of Dartmouth on May 25, 1775, "Hearing of the engagement or skirmish between the King's troops and the provincials near Boston and a report . . . that the administration have it in view to send over troops to

Carolina and at the same time to attempt to liberate the slaves and encourage them to attack their masters have thrown the people in Carolina and in this province into a ferment."[120] The myth of a liberatory king and the reality of the Dunmore Proclamation spread fear among whites—and especially among slave-holding Patriots.

On August 31, 1775, William Campbell reported rumors of British-inspired slave insurrection to Dartmouth: "During the sitting of the Provincial Congress, a very little before my arrival here, a letter is produced from a Mr. Lee in London to a leading man in this place in which he boldly asserted the ministry had in agitation not only to bring down the Indians on the inhabitants of this province but also to instigate and encourage an insurrection amongst their slaves."[121]

Dunmore's threats in Virginia simultaneously inspired blacks and terrified South Carolina's slave owners, driving a previously Loyalist southern elite toward the Patriots and prompting aspirations of mass escape among blacks. Just arrived, Campbell did not understand the impact of Dunmore's proclamation throughout the South. Instead, this "infernal falsehood" about freeing blacks, as he called it, and the loathing of many slave owners for the Crown, appalled him. "It was also reported and universally believed," Campbell told the Earl of Dartmouth, "that to effect this plan 14,000 stand of arms were actually on board the *Scorpion*, the sloop of war I came out in. Words, I am told, cannot express the flame that this occasioned amongst all ranks and degrees."[122]

The trial of Thomas Jeremiah was both prompted by and inflamed such fears. It pitted white Patriots against the royal government, with the royal government, not the Patriots and slave owners, on the side of freedom and justice. The royal governor ineffectually opposed the efforts of fearful local slave owners to convict and hang a free black as a scapegoat to their fears of imperial abolitionism and black insurrection. On August 11, 1775, a colonial court indicted Jeremiah, a free black fisherman, for allegedly planning to help the Royal Navy enter Charlestown harbor. Composed of two justices of the peace and five freeholders, the court relied on hearsay, elicited under duress, from "Jerry's friends and acquaintances."[123] Jeremiah had, however, committed no act. At most, he had an intention—which was no crime. But even this the court failed to establish.

According to the testimony of a slave named Sambo, Jeremiah had said, "There was a great war coming soon" and had conspired to take over a ship. "What shall we poor Negroes do in a schooner?" Sambo had asked. We will "set the schooner on fire, jump on shore and join the soldiers," Jeremiah allegedly responded, because "the War was come to help the poor

Negroes." But this testimony did not even fit the charge of showing the British into the harbor. Alternately, Jeremiah's brother-in-law, Jemmy, testified that Jeremiah already had stores of powder and sought guns.[124]

Remarkably, widespread sympathy for Jeremiah existed among whites, both Tory and Whig. For instance, Campbell praised "Jerry" as "one of the most valuable & useful men in his way in the Province."[125] "Uncommon pains," Henry Laurens wrote to his son John, "had been taken to Save him. . . . Tis remarkable that both of the Clergymen of our Church [the Anglican Church of Charlestown] visited him frequently and became Solicitous for him."[126]

Then Jemmy retracted his testimony. He "declared Jerry was Innocent, this declaration was made in a variety of Answers by Jemmy to the Revd Mr. Smith's questions."[127] Smith, one of the Anglicans mentioned by Henry Laurens, was a Patriot, but not a member of the court. He reported the recantation to the royal governor, who, in turn, conveyed this information to Laurens, head of the Committee of Public Safety.[128] The committee, however, ignored Campbell.

The court also consulted the colonial "Judges & Attorney General" for their opinions. "For a while," Henry Laurens reported, "those Sages were pleased to aver that a Free Negro was not amenable to that Act [the Negro Act of 1740], & one of them threw Magna Charta [sic] in the faces of the people." A free man in South Carolina supposedly had rights, guaranteed to all "English men" by the Magna Carta. What was the American Revolution about if not the protection of such rights against imperial tyranny? Yet writing to his son, Laurens ignored these ideas, ones vital to sustaining individual freedom and the rule of law. Instead, he blustered, "the Gentlemen dared not Subscribe to a declaration which must have called Something more valuable than their Law knowledge into question."[129] He meant their lives: if the judges upheld Jeremiah's rights, Laurens implied, the Patriots—at least the slave owners—would have hanged them.

In Laurens's interpretation, "the retraction by Jemmy could have no weight with Men who would give themselves time to consider that his first Evidence was corroborated by two other Witnesses, that a Sambo who was the main Witness would not retract."[130] As stated, of two main witnesses, only one stuck to his "evidence." In book 11 of *De l'esprit des lois* [Spirit of the Laws], Montesquieu, one of the favorite political philosophers of the American revolutionaries, insisted that for conviction, a nontyrannical criminal law requires two witnesses to an act. This "trial" had only one witness, contradicted by another, and testimony to an intention, not to an act, at that. And again, the law that the court wrongly applied covered slaves, not free men.

Laurens also reviled the man who had changed his testimony: "With regard to Jemmy I know not his person but he is certainly a liar of the most abominable order of Liars."[131] If so, however, why did the court favor his anti-Jeremiah testimony at first? In any case, Laurens admitted, he "knew not his person." In addition, he suggested that Jemmy had been bought off. On August 18, a shocked Alexander Innes, secretary to Campbell, noted "how cruel . . . the Suggestion in Mr. Laurens Letter of last night, that either pardon or reward was offered to procure [Jemmy's] recantation. Mr. Smith can satisfy Mr. Laurens in that point if doubt remains in his breast." Innes, who also didn't know Jemmy, simply agreed that "cordially . . . Jemmy is the most abominable of Liars."[132]

To his son, Henry Laurens condemned "Jerry's" fear. No innocent man, he insisted, need feel dread. A Huguenot, Laurens believed in a religion that had been persecuted in France. Yet he apparently had no thought that a member of a detested race, dragged by hysterical whites to jail, his life at stake, might have reason to fear. The Negro Act permitted Jeremiah no lawyer. Reverend Smith, a Whig and Patriot, but no member of the court, was as near to a representative as Jeremiah would find. Henry Laurens continued to lash out: "Jerry when he was first confronted by Jemmy positively denied that he knew his person that he knew the Man although upon enquiry it clearly appeared that they were old acquaintances & nearly allied by Jerry's connection as a husband to the other Man's Sister."[133]

Although the evidence was flimsy and the law doubtfully applied to what was at worst not a crime, nevertheless, the court found Jeremiah guilty as charged and sentenced him to be hanged.[134]

Laurens praised the sentence in a letter to his son. He wrote, "I am now fully Satisfied that Jerry was guilty of a design & attempt to enurage [encourage] our Negroes to Rebellion & joining the King's troops if any had been sent here."[135] Laurens also raised the specter of a mob slaying the royal governor: "Although I know nothing of the out of Door Secrets of the people, & carefully avoid Such knowledge, yet I had heard enough to fill me with horror from a prospect of what might be done by Men enraged as Men would have been if a pardon had been Issued."[136] Here Laurens deceived his son. He did not participate in the revolutionary movement, at least in the movement of sailors and artisans ten years earlier. But unlike Laurens, most sailors were abolitionists. Despite anti-English sentiment, they would probably not have murdered the governor over pardoning a black seaman. In contrast, Laurens was apprised of the Patriot "out of Door," that is, revolutionary, movement among slave owners. He instigated the lynching of Jeremiah and halted efforts to spare him.

Under the 1740 Slave Act, the local court could try blacks without appeal. Only if petitioned by the court could the royal governor intervene. Consequently, Lord William Campbell wrote to Henry Laurens, "In a Case of Blood I wave *Ceremony*, I would even give up *Dignity* to Save the Life of an Innocent Man. . . . I take every Holy Power to witness I am innocent of this Mans death, upon your Heads be it, for without your interposition, I find I cannot Save him."[137]

A supporter of the slave trade, Campbell nonetheless wrote to Lord Dartmouth of "the accursed politics of this country." Campbell did not believe in a royal conspiracy to stir black insurrection. His affection for justice led him to condemn the trial and to compare it to the putative actions of New England rebels: "The leaders of the faction in this province have not come short of their brethren to the northward in the most diabolical system, and I think have improved upon them in some respects by the matchless cruelty they have exercised in the prosecution of their infamous plan."[138]

He briefly appraised the case: "After sitting a week and taking uncommon pains to get evidence no proof of any kind could be produced to convict [Jeremiah] or give sufficient grounds to believe any attempt of the kind they pretended to fear was ever intended." Yet the South Carolina court condemned Jeremiah. Campbell wrote angrily: "I assure you my Lord, my blood run [*sic*] cold when I read on what grounds they had doomed a fellow creature to death. I easily saw that without a petition from his judges I should not be able to save him. I therefore expressed to the justices in the strongest terms my sense of the weakness of the evidence, and entreated that for his own sake and that of his fellows he would get a petition signed by them."[139]

But the judges defied the governor's "interference." Apparently Campbell considered extralegal action on Jeremiah's behalf. If Campbell had tried to pardon Jeremiah, he wrote, he would be considered by white South Carolinians to be fomenting slave rebellion—"they would hang him at my door." Henry Laurens's letter to Campbell had concluded "with the remarkable expression, that [the pardon] would raise a flame all the water in the Cooper River would not extinguish."[140] Laurens thus threatened the royal governor with insurrection.

Meanwhile, the colonial chief justice and attorney general issued opinions exculpating the "unhappy prisoner." But "his death was determined on" by a court. With a horror unusual for an English official, Lord Campbell informed Dartmouth, "I leave your lordship to conceive the poignancy of my agony and distress on this occasion, I was almost distracted and wished to have been able to fly to the remotest corner of the earth from a set of barbarians who are worse than the most cruel savages any history has described."[141] He had heard, Campbell added, that Jeremiah had confessed to Reverend Smith. Despite Smith's "violence in their cause," that is, despite his Patriot sympathies, the governor had sought him out. As Campbell explained to Dartmouth, Smith

> candidly told me that he attended this black as much from a desire to ascertain the reality of an instigated insurrection as from motives of humanity, that he had used every argument, every art, to draw him to confession, endeavouring to make him contradict himself in the many conversations he had with him, but in vain. His behavior was modest, his conversation sensible to a degree that astonished him, and at the same time, he was perfectly resigned to his unhappy, his undeserved fate. He declared he wished not for life, he was in a happy frame of mind and prepared for death. Mr. Smith concluded this affecting story with acquainting me that the wretch, one of the evidences against Jerry and condemned with him, retracted what he had said against him and voluntarily declared his perfect innocence.[142]

The stock phrase "instigated insurrection" used by Smith shows how intensely white Patriot southerners feared royal emancipation. On August 18, the colony hanged Thomas Jeremiah and burned his body.[143] "To conclude this heartrending story," Campbell wrote to Dartmouth, "the man was murdered."[144]

Writing to his son after Jeremiah's death, as if to soothe a bad conscience, Henry Laurens contemptuously evaluated Jeremiah's character: "Jerry was a forward fellow, puffed up by prosperity, ruined by Luxury & debauchery & grown to an amazing pitch of vanity & ambition & withal a very Silly Coxcomb[.] Such characters are found in all Countries, & Men may be ruined by prosperity when perhaps their whole Estate real & personal would not yield an hundred Guineas[.] Riches are great or Small comparatively as a Negro Fisher Man Jerry was comparatively as Rich as a Vannuk, in the Circle of Stockholders."[145]

In London, John Laurens dutifully accepted his father's assignment to interpret the execution of Thomas Jeremiah "not to the prejudice of the poor Carolinians."[146] "The affair of the negro man Jerry has been quite differently represented here," John wrote to Henry on October 4. "I shall set a proper light whenever it occurs here in conversation, for according he prevailing story, the character of our countrymen for justice and ...manity would suffer very much."[147] In fact, Thomas Jeremiah was one of South Carolina's earliest heroes and martyrs of freedom.[148]

The fear of black insurrection that prevailed among South Carolinians opposed to the authority and actions of the royal government and that led to the trial and murder of Thomas Jeremiah was endemic across the South. Slaves had long escaped to the Great Dismal Swamp between North Carolina and Virginia and to wildernesses in South Carolina, Georgia, and what later became Louisiana and Florida. They formed free "maroon" colonies.[149] The Dismal Swamp settlement included roughly two thousand members. Between 1672 and 1864, some fifty communities traded with nearby settlers and struck at enemies.[150]

During the American Revolution, however, such refuges—though the blacks who lived there made no plans to join the Crown—appeared threatening to many southern colonists, and the actions that their fears of black insurrection—of a second revolution—motivated placed them in opposition to the very freedom from slavery that they felt compelled to claim for themselves from their British oppressors. Colonel Steven Bull of the Georgia militia recommended to Henry Laurens, president of the Charlestown Council of Safety, that with the advent of the American Revolution, "it is far better for the Public and the owners for the deserted negroes [some two hundred] who are on Tybee island to be shot if they cannot be taken." The empire might use them to fight, Bull warned. Bull also suggested that blacks might be "converted into money, which is the Sinews of War, it will only enable our Enemy to fight us with our own money or property."[151] This thought was but an owner's fantasy. The Patriots, not the Crown, trafficked in captured blacks.

In the South, blacks and indigenous people together outnumbered whites. Fearing their alliance, the colonies—and later the new American states—nurtured hostilities between them.[152] In 1763 George Milligan Johnston, a South Carolina doctor, alleged a "Natural Dislike and Antipathy, that subsists between [blacks] and our *Indian* neighbors."[153] In 1775 British Indian agent John Stuart explained, "Nothing can be more alarming to Carolinians than the idea of an attack from Indians and Negroes."[154]

During the Revolution, this fear played out in efforts that were in effect the trial and hanging of Thomas Jeremiah writ large. To persuade Laurens, Bull invoked the tactic of divide and rule: "Therefore all who cannot be taken had better be shot by the Creek Indians, as it perhaps may deter other Negroes from deserting, and will establish a hatred or Aversion between the Indians and Negroes."[155] But Bull knew Laurens had doubts. Regardless of whether Laurens approved, he suggested, the Creeks would go at the order of the Georgia Council of Public Safety. He urged Laurens to keep this plan "a profound Secret, lest the Negroes should move off, or they should ask for Arms, and so lay an Ambuscade for the Indians."[156] Bull planned a stealth slaughter.

"Now for the grand we may say the awful business contained in your letter [material crossed out]," Laurens wrote back, fretting, "it is an awful business notwithstanding it has the sanction of Law to put even fugitive & Rebellious Slaves to death, the prospect is horrible."[157] Laurens worried, however, that the "loss of Georgia seconded by the loss of Carolina" might endanger the American Revolution and jeopardize "the happiness of ages unborn." That maroons *might* join with the British appeared to him to justify a massacre.[158] Laurens cursed this "inglorious Picaroon Warr" and bellowed that "every inglorious unavoidable act of necessity which we may be driven to commit for our self-preservation, [should] be imputed" to the Crown.[159] He took no responsibility for his own cruelties. Finally, Laurens came to his decision. "We think," he wrote to Bull, "the Council of Public Safety in Georgia ought to give that encouragement which is necessary to seize & if nothing else will do to destroy all those Rebellious Negroes upon Tybee Island or wherever they may be found."[160]

Laurens seconded Bull's recommendation for the use of Indians and urged inclusion of "some discreet white Men." The word "discreet" here means "stealthy" or "secretive." Again, the Patriots would take no responsibility for the massacre. But a letter of Archibald Bullock, the Georgian who led the raid, indicates that, despite murders of innocent maroons, the planned massacre did not succeed.[161] In what was a pathetic suggestion, Laurens recommended that "the Public" make good to owners their hypothetical loss, since such an attack would not bring maroons back into bondage.[162]

Three months after Jeremiah's execution, five hundred blacks—nearly a tenth of the black population of Charlestown—had escaped to Sullivan's Island to join the forces of the Crown. Black and white Tories began to raid outlying plantations.[163] And across the South the actions of slave owners similarly drove blacks to embrace the cause of liberty, but under the standard of the British Empire, not under the flag of the Patriots.

chapter 2 ¶ Emancipation and Revolution
The Conjunction of Pragmatism and Principle

It is impossible for us to suppose these creatures to be men, because allowing them to be men, a suspicion would arise that we ourselves are not Christians.
—*Montesquieu,* De l'esprit des lois

lthough many Patriots were motivated to rebel against the Crown out of anxieties concerning the emancipation of slaves in the colonies and the retributions this could incite, in the end Dunmore's actions inspired Patriot as well as Loyalist efforts to rely on blacks in the conflicts of the Revolution. The Dunmore Proclamation and the events following it made the issue of liberty in the American Revolution much more complex. Along with instigating slave revolt, his proclamation gave Patriots a chance to make a revolution for universal freedom, not just for the freedom of white colonists from British rule. It was an opportunity in part because the groundwork for a more consistent and enlightened view of slavery had been laid within the revolutionary movement itself, but it was still an opportunity that only the exigencies of the war itself could prompt some to seize.

Several elements combined to foster a movement toward abolition in the colonies. The egalitarian claims made by black and white sailors and artisans and revolutionary crowds in American cities, as well as throughout the Caribbean and in London, resonated in many ways with the political conceptions and inclinations of some elites and Christian churches; in turn, American sailors and artisans took up their program for emancipation, which ultimately shaped the independence movement. The claims of freedom for all made sense in terms of the logic of post-1688 British political thought and the revolutionary elite's tradition of classical republicanism, and they especially resonated within the New Light Protestant and Quaker communities in the North. Patriot leaders, including George Mason of Virginia, imagined independent citizen-farmers as the social basis of a decent regime, but in America they saw only bondsmen and the hapless parasites who preyed off them. With the threat of royal emancipation, pressure from all these influences on the Patriots to recruit and free blacks increased, and the economic interests of slave owners and the endemic racism of the colonies to the contrary, there were principled as well as pragmatic reasons why Patriots were impelled to do so.

One example of the mutual influence of egalitarian agitation and intellectual responses to the problem of slavery is J. Philmore's *Two Dialogues on the Man-Trade* (1760). As we have seen, sailors circulated word of freedom internationally. In London, after talking with sailors from slave ships on the route to Guinea, Philmore published this argument, attacking "the man-trade," as his title named it, a series of claims that were to echo in the discourses of revolution in the colonies. A dialogue form enabled Philmore to address his interlocutor—Mr. Allcraft—and his proslavery arguments directly. Extending John Locke's argument that tyrants must be overthrown by revolution, Philmore justified black uprisings in the Caribbean. Locke had mistakenly seen slavery as punishment for fighting in an unjust war, but Philmore argued that such a claim could not sanction the British and Portuguese commerce in Africa or North Carolina.[1] Philmore wrote, "A rational animal is a good definition of man: and this takes in the black-skin'd as well as the white-skin'd. They have the same rational powers, as we have. They are free moral agents as we are, and many of them have as good a natural genius, as good sense, and as brave a spirit, as any of those to whom they are made slaves. To trade in the blacks then is to trade in men."[2]

In a state of nature, Philmore argued, black, white, and red are equal: "The black-skin'd and the white-skin'd, being all of the same species, all of the human race, are, by nature, upon an equality, one man in a state of nature, as we are with respect to the inhabitants of Guinea and they with respect to us, is not superior to another man, nor has any authority or dominion over him, any right to lay his commands upon him."[3]

Philmore adapted Montesquieu, arguing, "Unjustly to deprive a man of his property, is theft, or of his life, is murder, whatever colour he is of, and the murder of a man, that has a black skin, or black hair, is as great a sin, as that of a man that has a white skin, or white hair."[4] Being a Christian, Philmore added, "does not give us any worldly superiority, or any authority whatever over those, who are not Christians."[5] Each individual has obligations to "Jews, Mahometans, or even black-skin'd heathens, which the law of nature lays us under."[6]

Some Africans, Philmore noted, hunt others and sell them. But this aggression contradicts Locke's notion that a victor in a defensive war may justly enslave an aggressor's soldiers: "It is very common in the countries, where the Europeans carry on this trade, for the petty kings and princes, of which there are a great many, to go to war with their neighbors, not . . . to repair any damages they have unjustly suffered, by those neighbours, but purely to get prisoners, against the time the ships from Europe arrive upon their coast, that with them they may be able to purchase of captains of those ships, the goods they have on board. . . . Those who are engag'd in an unjust war, can have no right to any captures they make in that war."[7]

But, the interlocutor Allcraft asks, what about enslaving soldiers who "were the first invaders or aggressors"?[8] Contra Philmore's response, soldiers are perfectly capable of judging the merits of the cause. Nonetheless, they are coerced. As Philmore correctly insists, only leaders choose the cause: "You know, when one king or prince goes to war with another, the common men are not capable of judging of the merits of the cause, which party has or has not right of their side. But laying aside this consideration, they are forced to go whithersoever their king or captain leads them. They are oblig'd to obey his commands, and to desert would be death to them: therefore I think it would be unjust and cruel, in him who comes off conqueror, though he had right on his side and was engaged in a just war, to deprive those common men, who are taken prisoners of their liberty, after the war is over, or at any time to sell them for slaves for life."[9] To convert prisoners into bondsmen suggests that the soldiers are the "property" of a king and can be seized for "damages." Sale, Philmore argues, supposes soldiers "to be answerable for whatever damage or injury is done by their king, or that they are his goods or property, both of which are absurd, and the latter a supposition unworthy of human nature. . . . Consequently the buying of them for such must be altogether criminal in the Europeans."[10]

Applying the insight that humans are alike, Philmore asks how Allcraft would respond to enslaving "thirty thousand French prisoners" in war. Bondage, Allcraft answers, contradicts only "custom and the law of nations in Europe," but not Africa.[11] Concurring with the reasoning of Aristotle and Montesquieu, however, Philmore argues that slavery is unnatural: custom "makes no difference, as to the nature of the thing in itself; for as I have shown before, the man-trade in this last mentioned case, wherein the men, who are sold, are supposed to be prisoners, that were engaged in an unjust war, is in itself wicked and inhuman, contrary to the law of nature, the obligations of which are eternal and unchangeable. . . . They are the same all over the world, the same in Guinea or Jamaica, as in England."[12]

Philmore also indicts the "Guinea-trade" for killing a fifth of its human cargo:

The captain of the Guinea-man, when he has finished his marketing, when he has bought as many reasonable creatures, as he wants, and is full freighted, having on board we will say, two hundred of them, coupled in irons . . . he sets out for one of our plantations, in the West-Indies, or in North America, or of those belonging to the Spaniards, and may be two or three months on the voyage, during which time these negroes fare very hard, living upon beans, salt fish, or yams, and from the filth and stench . . . occasioned by their being . . . penn'd together in so little room, they must be in danger of being infected. It often happens, that a distemper does break out among them, and carries off a great many, a fifth or fourth, yea sometimes a third part of them.

Philmore empathizes with the kidnapped: "It is reasonable to suppose, that some of them have their hearts broke, and die with grief and anguish, to think they shall never more set foot on their native soil, and that the eye that hath seen them shall see them no more."[13] To be guilty of murder, he argues, does not require an "intention" to commit murder. Rather, by sale of survivors, traders aim to profit. In the course of the crimes of man-stealing and man-selling, they murder others:[14] "I do not think it necessary, in order to convict a man of murder, to make it appear, that he had an intention to commit murder. Whoever does, by unjust force and violence, deprive another of his liberty, and, while he has him in his power, reduces him to such a condition, and gives him such treatment, as evidently endangers his life, and in the event, do[es] actually deprive him of his life, is guilty of murder."[15]

After sale, Philmore adds, more die in the Caribbean: "In the island of Jamaica, almost half of the new imported negroes die in the seasoning [the introduction to slave labor] and that, in Barbados, it is reckoned, that a fourth part die in the seasoning; and . . . there are twice as many imported into these two islands, as into all our other islands, in the West-Indies, and all our colonies in North America." In a year, Philmore notes, "12,000 die upon the voyage, and in the seasoning" or are "properly speaking, *murdered*." Once again, if the Spaniards in Mexico and Peru "when they unjustly invaded those countries" killed so many, Europeans would think them "a very bloody, cruel, barbarous people."[16] He adds: "No legislature on earth, which is the supreme power in every civil society, can alter the nature of things, or make that to be lawful, which is contrary to the law of God."[17]

In the *Second Treatise*, Locke maintained that the oppressed may kill a tyrant who has dissolved the social contract and entered a state of nature with them, "as any lyon or tiger." The people have no earthly law to appeal to, but only rebellion: "The conquered [by an aggressor], or their children have no court, no arbitrator on earth to appeal to. Then they may *appeal as Jeptha did to Heaven*, and repeat their *appeal* till they have recovered the native right of their ancestors, which was to have such a legislative over them, as the majority should approve and freely acquiesce in. If it be objected, this would cause endless trouble; I answer, no more than justice does, where she lies open to all that appeal to her."[18]

Philmore sanctions the "frequent attempts to get 'the mastery' that is, their liberty, or deliver themselves out of the miserable slavery they are in" of blacks in the Barbados:[19] "all the black men now in our plantations, who are by unjust force deprived of their liberty and held in slavery, as they have none upon earth to appeal to, may lawfully repel that force with force, and to recover their liberty destroy their oppressors; and not only so, but it is the duty of others, white as well as black, to assist these miserable creatures, if they can."[20]

Allcraft recognizes that this reasoning could cause other nations justly to attack the English "man-traders": "Suppose that a ship belonging to any other nation should see one of our ships on the coast of Guinea, full freighted with slaves, ready to sail, and coming up to her should insist upon their being all set at liberty, without any ransom, and, upon their demand not being complied with, should make an attack upon the English ship, and, getting the mastery of her, should unbind the slaves, and turn them ashore loose, to go wherever they list, according to your way of thinking, Mr. Philmore, this would be not only a justifiable, but likewise a good deed, a brave action."[21]

Applying Locke's idea that revolution happens not for a single incident, but for a "long train of abuses, all pointing in the same direction," Philmore contends: "For in truth we are now at war (we Englishmen, we Christians, to our shame be it spoken) and have been for above a hundred years past, without any cessation at all, at war and enmity with our own species, not with this or that particular nation."[22]

In Boston, James Otis, a lawyer and Patriot leader, adapted the words of Philmore, Montesquieu, and Locke. Hearing Otis speak in 1761, John Adams likened him to the prophets "Isaiah and Ezekiel united," "a flame of fire." Otis, too, integrated into political theories of freedom and independence the idea of slave rebellion; his was "a dissertation," in Adams's words, "on the rights of man in a state of nature [as] an independent sovereign, subject to no law but the law written on his heart." "No Quaker in

Philadelphia," Adams added, "asserted the rights of negroes in stronger terms."[23]

But Adams took no delight in Otis's extension to emancipation of the ideas that were to drive the American Revolution for independence. Instead, he feared the "consequences" that could be drawn from equality: "[I] shuddered at the doctrine he taught; and I have all my lifetime shuddered, and still shudder at the consequences that may be drawn from such premises." Naming slave owners' dread, Adams insisted: "Shall we say, that the rights of masters and servants clash, and can be decided only by force? I adore the idea of gradual abolitions! But who shall decide how fast or how slowly these abolitions shall be made?"[24]

Published in 1764, Otis's *The Rights of the British Colonists Asserted and Proved* passionately invoked the character of British law, which protects the liberties of each citizen; he identified the American protests against British policies with the English Revolution of 1640, which resulted in Parliament's triumph over the tyranny of Charles I: "That the colonists, black and white, born here, are free-born British subjects, and entitled to all the essential civil rights of such, is a truth not only manifest from the provincial charters, from the principles of the common law, and acts of parliament; but from the British constitution which was reestablished at the revolution, with a professed design to secure the liberties of all the subjects to all generations."[25]

Otis repeatedly speaks of the "good, loyal and useful subjects" of the king, "black and white."[26] He links imperial theft of property—taxation without representation—to bondage: "In a state of nature, no man can take my property from me, without my consent: If he does, he deprives me of my liberty, and makes me a slave." Otis contrasts the lawlessness of Dutch plantations with laws fit for "free men"[27] and cites Montesquieu's 1748 *Esprit des lois*:

No better reasons can be given for enslaving those of any color than such as Baron Montesquieu has humorously given as the foundation of that cruel slavery exercised over the poor Ethiopians, which threatens one day to reduce both Europe and America to the ignorance and barbarity of the darkest ages. Does it follow that 'tis right to enslave a man because he is black? Will short curled hair like wool instead of Christian hair, as 'tis called by those whose hearts are hard as the nether millstone, help the argument? Can any logical inference in favor of slavery be drawn from a flat nose, a long or a short face? Nothing better can be said in favor of a trade that is the most shocking violation of the law of nature, has a direct tendency to diminish the idea of the inestimable value of liberty and makes every dealer in it a tyrant.[28]

If citizens choose revolution for themselves against emancipation, Otis foresees degradation: "It is a clear truth that those who every day barter away other men's liberty will soon care very little for their own."[29] Condemning the despotism of plantation owners, he points to Caribbean insurrections: "To this cause [that bondage corrupts the free] must be imputed that ferocity, cruelty and . . . barbarity that has long marked the general character of the sugar-islanders. They can in general form no idea of government but that which in person or by an overseer . . . is exercised over a thousand of their fellow men, born with the same right to freedom and the sweet enjoyments of liberty and life as their unrelenting taskmasters, the overseers and planters."[30]

Otis, too, refashioned Locke: "The natural liberty of man is to be free from any superior power on earth, and not to be under the will or legislative authority of man, but only to have the law of nature for his rule." The colonists, he insisted, have "all the rights of nature [of] the Europeans, and they are not to be restrained in the exercise of any of these rights but for the evident good of the whole community." He indicted the despotism over large numbers of enslaved human beings of the English trade: "Neither the riches of Jamaica nor the luxury of a metropolis should ever have weight enough to break the balance of truth and justice." Otis also referred to Locke's denunciation of tyrants—perhaps once "fathers" of their country—who become beasts in the jungle of nature: "The law of nature was not of man's making, nor is it in his power to mend it or alter its course. He can only perform and keep or disobey and break it. The last is never done with impunity, even in this life, if it is any punishment for a man to feel himself depraved, to find himself degraded by his own folly and wickedness from the rank of a virtuous and good *man* to that of a brute, or to be transformed from the friend, perhaps father, of his country to a devouring lion or tiger."[31] Otis advocated emancipation by force.

The defiance of Caribbean slaves, of sailors black and white, and the writings of Montesquieu, Philmore, and Otis disrupted what has sometimes been called by modern scholars such as Louis Hartz the "Lockean consensus."[32] Instead, their reinterpretation of Locke's ideas became central to a fourteen-year prerevolutionary debate about emancipation among the elite and, in taverns, among sailors, artisans, and farmers. In addition, it fit the paradigm of republicanism that many Americans, elite and free yeomen alike, espoused.

For example, in 1765, George Mason, himself a Virginia slave owner, wrote *A Scheme for Replevying Goods*, which derides the replacement of independent citizens with bondsmen and recalls the Roman republic's fate: "The policy of encouraging the Importation of free People & discouraging that of Slaves has never been duly considered in this Colony, or we shou'd not at this Day see one Half of our best Lands in most Parts of the Country remain unsetled & the other cultivated with Slaves; not to mention the ill effect such a Practice has upon the Morals and Manners of our People: one of the first Signs of the Decay, & perhaps the primary Cause of the Destruction of the most flourishing Government that ever existed was the Introduction of great Numbers of Slaves—an Evil very pathetically described by the Roman Historians."[33]

Mason's 1773 *Extracts from the Virginia Charters* describes slavery's destructiveness, that "slow poison," even for masters: "Every Gentlemen here is born a Petty Tyrant. Practiced in Arts of Despotism & Cruelty, we become callous to the Dictates of Humanity, & all the finer feelings of the Soul."[34] His words echo Montesquieu's 1748 *Esprit des lois*: "Slavery . . . is not good in its nature: useful neither to the master, nor to the slave; to the latter, because he can do nothing because of virtue; to the former, because he contracts with his slaves all sorts of bad habitudes, because he accustoms himself insensibly to the lack of all moral virtues, because he becomes proud, rash, hard, choleric, voluptuous, cruel."[35]

In the 1773 *Extracts*, Mason foresaw the weakness of the forthcoming revolution: "Taught to regard a part of our own Species in the most abject & contemptible Degree below us, we lose that Idea of the Dignity of Man, which the Hand of Nature implanted in us, for great & useful purposes."[36] The second revolution had advocates and sympathizers among the leaders of the first, and Mason refused to sign a constitution that extended the slave trade an additional twenty years.[37]

The advocates of the second revolution included those who believed that "the Dignity of Man" was "implanted" by the hand of God. Christianity had emerged as a prophetic religion among slaves, yet over long centuries, that prophecy had dulled; organized communities, Catholic or Protestant, had focused little indignation on this institution. Before, during, and after the Revolution, Baptists, Presbyterians, Methodists, Congregationalists, and especially Quakers suddenly awakened to the sin of enslaving another soul. For instance, in the fall of 1774, the Reverend Levi Hart, a New Light minister in Preston, Connecticut—the New Lights were a pro-phetic movement against the Presbyterian establishment—denounced bondage for violating natural law and contravening Connecticut's dem-ocratic constitution. Hart mocked the traffic's supposed justification: "What have the unhappy Africans committed against the inhabitants of the British colonies and islands in the West Indies to authorize *us* to seize them, or bribe them to seize one another, and transport them a thousand leagues into a strange land, and enslave them for life?"[38] Reminding his parishioners of Rhode Island's law against the slave trade, Hart asked, "Can this Colony want motives from reason, justice, religion, or public spirit, to follow the example?"[39] On December 30, 1774, in Fairfax, Virginia, the sermon "Reigning Abominations" by Baptist Elhanan Winchester named the slave traffic an unparalleled "national sin" that would inspire "national punishment," including military defeat.[40] In effect, he foresaw a civil war.

Black Christians were also forceful. Enslaved in Africa at age fifteen, Phyllis Wheatley, who later in Massachusetts would become a celebrated poet, analogized blacks to Jews in Egypt: "In every human Breast, God has implanted a Principle, which we call Love of Freedom; it is impatient of Oppression and pants for deliverance. And by the leave of our modern Egyptians, I will suggest the same principle lives in us."[41]

After the Revolution, white Protestants often endorsed racist politics. Nonetheless, both before and during the uprising, many saw defeats by the British in the perspective of what Samuel Hopkins would call this "sin of crimson dye," poisoning all Patriot efforts to win freedom for them-selves.[42] Flight from persecution in Europe, the wide expanse of a new country, and the freedom of settlers in a wilderness not dominated by serfdom led, for many, to a fierce sense of personal independence. In the uncanny setting of war, the fights for independence and emancipation combined. The glaring contradiction of bondage gave Christians a fiery, prophetic voice about that moment and for the future.

A series of "Great Awakenings" swept through the Protestant commu-nities in the North American colonies in the eighteenth century, a move-ment of religious revivals based on the "living spirit," as participants experienced it, that occurred outside the control of older authorities—a kindling of a new spiritual light in opposition to a religious establishment grown rationalist and elitist. Among the leaders of the New Light move-ment that resulted was Samuel Hopkins, who became a minister in New-port, Rhode Island, in 1770. In this commercial center, tales of the Middle Passage's horrors were rife. Hopkins soon identified slave owning as a cause of corruption, or lack of what he called "disinterested benevolence" in its citizens.[43]

Abolitionist arguments had an effect: although the U.S. Constitution eventually recognized the slave trade, in 1774 the Continental Congress banned it. In 1776 Hopkins's *A Dialogue Concerning the Slavery of the Africans* urged the representatives to go further and enact emancipation: "We naturally look to you on behalf of half a million of persons in these colonies, who are under such a degree of oppression and tyranny as to be wholly deprived of all civil and personal liberty, to which they have as good a right as any of their fellow-men, and are reduced to the most abject state of bondage and slavery without any just cause."[44]

In the *Dialogue* Hopkins urged the representatives to see the intimate connection between barring the slave trade and abolition: "We have the satisfaction of the best assurances that you have done this not merely from political reasons, but from a conviction of the unrighteousness and cruelty of that trade, and a regard to justice and benevolence,—deeply sensible of the inconsistence of promoting the slavery of the Africans, at the same time we are asserting our own civil liberty at the risk of our fortunes and lives. This leaves in our minds no doubt . . . of the equal unrighteousness and oppression, as well as inconsistence with ourselves, in holding so many hundreds of thousands of blacks in slavery."[45]

One of the speakers in the *Dialogue*—speaker B—later returns to this central theme: "And when they observe all this cry and struggle for liberty for ourselves and children, and see themselves and their children wholly overlooked by us, and behold the sons of liberty oppressing and tyrannizing over many thousands of poor blacks who have as good a claim to liberty as themselves, they are shocked with the glaring inconsistence and wonder they themselves do not see it."[46]

Members of the Continental Congress read the pamphlet. The New York Manumission Society reprinted it.[47] Like Philmore, the abolitionist Speaker B answers the most common objections to emancipation among those inclined to doubt the justice of bondage, such as Speaker A in the *Dialogue*, but who are unable to up give slave owning. The *Dialogue* became a central document of the first American abolitionist movement.

Emancipation, Speaker A suggests, diverts energies from the Revolution and should be considered only after the war.[48] Imperial domination over the colonies, B responds, incarnates God's wrath: "If the slavery in which we hold the blacks is wrong, it is a very great and public sin and, therefore, a sin which God is now testifying against in the calamities he has brought upon us."[49] He contrasts the corruption of capitalists and slave owners with moral impartiality: "How common it is for men who hire others to complain that the laborers do not earn the wages they give, and that they are constantly losing all the labor they hire. And if it were left wholly to him who hires what wages he should give the laborer, and he was accountable to none, how soon his hire would be reduced to little or nothing. The lordly, selfish employer would soon find out that his laborers hardly earned the food he was obliged to feed them. Let your uninterested, judicious neighbors judge between you and your servants in this matter."[50] "Disinterested" neighbors, Hopkins suggests, properly judge the fairness of the claims of owners such as A.

Speaker A suggests that bondage made Christians of "heathen" Africans. This was a common proslavery argument. John Trumbull, in *The (Connecticut) Journal and (New Haven) Post-Boy* for July 6, 1770, wrote satirically: "I ask my readers to lay their hands on their hearts and answer me to this serious question, Is not the enslaving of these people the most charitable act in the world? With no other end in view than to bring these poor creatures to Christian ground and within hearing of the gospel, we spare no expense of time or money." In reply, Speaker B recounts the horrors of an oppression worse than the Egyptians visited on the Jews: "For a century . . . many millions have been torn from their native country, their acquaintances, relations and friends, and most of them put into a state of slavery, both themselves and their children forever, if they have any posterity[,] much worse than death. . . . Commonly, not above seventy in a hundred survive their transportation; by which means about thirty thousand are murdered every year by this slave trade, which amount to three millions in a century."[51]

Considering bondage's crimes, Speaker B avers, "Words cannot utter [the nature of this oppression]. Volumes might be written, and not give a detail of a thousandth part of the shockingly cruel things they have suffered, and are constantly suffering."[52] Slavery poisons the conversion of any blacks. Enlightened and dissident forms of Christianity, "theodicies of ill-fortune," as sociologist Max Weber later termed them, inveigh against the hypocrisy of "Christian" slaveholders.[53] The spiritual insights of Christianity fit the vision of the poor, the "meek."[54]

Speaker A invokes God's curse on Ham: "A servant of servants shall he be unto his brethren." Does he, B replies, believe Pharaoh innocent because "god had foretold" he would enslave the Jews?[55] With hubris, A announces that he treats slaves admirably. Granting him this claim for the sake of argument, B tells of a "ruffian" who kidnaps and rapes a girl. He takes her to his cave and subsequently treats her with great kindness.[56] Does this absolve the rape?

Speaker A avows that he would free blacks if the public would indemnify him. Colonies penalize masters for manumitting blacks by making the owners support them afterward.[57] Invoking horses—the favored possession of eighteenth-century American males—B returns to a parable: "If your neighbor buys a horse, or any beast, of a thief who stole it from you, while he had no thought that it was stolen, would you not think you had a right to demand your horse of your neighbor, and pronounce him very unjust if he should refuse to deliver him to you till he had received the whole sum he had given for him? And have your servants not as great a right to themselves, to their liberty, as you have to your stolen horse?"[58]

With Dunmore's arming of blacks in mind, B presciently warns that most would join the Crown: "God is so ordering it in his providence, that it seems absolutely necessary something should speedily be done with respect to the slaves among us, in order to our safety, and to prevent their turning against us in our present struggle, in order to get their liberty. Our oppressors have planned to gain the blacks and induce them to take up arms against us, by promising their liberty on this condition; and this plan they are prosecuting to the utmost of their power, by which means they have persuaded numbers to join them."[59]

To try to stop slaves from seeking freedom with the imperial forces, B argues, would only enhance the Patriot reputation for cruelty: "And should we attempt to restrain them by force and severity, keeping a strict guard over them, and punishing . . . severely who shall be detected in attempting to join our oppressors, this will only be making bad worse, and serve to render our inconsistence, oppression, and cruelty more criminal, perspicuous, and shocking."[60]

"Before we can reasonably expect deliverance," says B, Americans must abolish bondage. [61] Hopkins prophesied the competitive dynamic of imperial and Patriot emancipation: "The only way . . . to prevent this threatening evil is to set blacks at liberty ourselves by some public acts and laws, and then give them proper encouragement to labor, or take arms in the defense of the American cause, as they shall choose."[62] Setting blacks free, he insisted, should allow work, not just soldiering. This path "would at once be doing [blacks] some degree of justice" and strategically "defeat . . . our enemies in the scheme they are now prosecuting."[63] By suggesting that emancipating blacks, without requiring recruitment, would cut the ground from under the Crown, Hopkins saw furthest ahead among the Patriots.

Like apostles of the New Light such as Hopkins, Quakers, with their belief in an individual's immediate relationship with God and their devotion to freedom of conscience, were especially strong opponents of slavery. A prominent antislavery advocate was New Jersey Quaker, tailor, and writer of wills John Woolman.[64] In 1742, when his "master" asked him to write a bill of sale for a black woman, Woolman's conscience was awakened by his own implication with "slave-keeping":

> My master, having a negro woman, sold her, and desired me to write the bill of sale, the man being waiting who bought her. The thing was sudden; and though I felt uneasy at the thoughts of writing an instrument of slavery for one of my fellow creatures yet I remembered that I was hired by the year, that it was my master who commanded me to do it, and that it was an elderly man, a member of our society who bought her; so through weakness I gave way and wrote it; but at the executing of it, I was so afflicted in my mind that I said before the Master and the Friend that I believed slave-keeping to be a practice inconsistent with the Christian religion. This in some degree abated my uneasiness; yet as often as I reflected seriously upon it, I thought I should have been clearer if I had desired to be excused from it as a thing against my conscience, for such it was.[65]

Subsequently, he responded to such requests by talking with each person about why bondage contradicted their deepest convictions, which eventually led them to free their slaves. For instance, Woolman reports,

> about this time an ancient man of good esteem in the neighborhood came to my house to get his will written. He had young negroes, and I asked him privately how he purposed to dispose of them. He told me; I then said "I cannot write thy will without breaking my own peace, and respectfully gave him my reasons for it. He signified he had a choice that I should have written it but as I could not consistently with my conscience, he did not desire it, and so he got it written by some other person. A few years after, there being great alterations in his family, he came to me again to get me to write his will. His negroes were yet young and his son, to whom he intended to give them, was, since he first spoke to me, from a libertine become a sober young man, and he supposed that I would have been free on that account to write it. We had much friendly talk on the subject and then deferred it. A few days after he came again and directed their freedom, and then I wrote it.[66]

In 1754 Woolman traveled through Maryland, Virginia, and North Carolina to challenge bondage. His journal reports numerous debates with Quaker slave owners. Woolman saw blacks clearly and with compassion. Moved to speak with other Quakers, he experienced, when alone, the hardship of the journey: "The sense I had of the state of the churches brought a weight of distress upon me. The gold to me appeared dim and the fine gold changed, and though this is too generally the case yet the sense of it in these parts hath in a particular manner borne heavy upon me. It appeared to me that through the prevailing of the spirit of this world the minds of many were brought to an inward desolation and instead of the spirit of meekness, gentleness and heavenly wisdom which are the necessary companions of the true sheep of Christ, a spirit of fierceness and love of dominion arose."[67]

In a Christian idiom, Woolman traces a large story here: how otherwise good people sometimes sanctify horrors for an age. The followers point to the errors of the seemingly most virtuous: "From small beginnings in error great buildings by degrees are raised and from one age to another are more and more strengthened by the general concurrence of the people and as men obtain reputation by their profession of the truth their virtues are mentioned as arguments in favor of general error; and those of less note to justify themselves say such and such good men did the like. By what other steps could the people of Judah arrive at that height in wickedness as to give just ground for the Prophet Isaiah to declare, in the name of the Lord, 'that none calleth for justice nor any pleadeth for truth' (Isaiah, 59:4)."[68] Woolman depicts a fierce clash of character in which wisdom and gentleness oppose love of dominion and hubris. He had set out on a solitary journey, yet one man initiated what would become the great change in Quakerism about slavery that would shake other Christian sects as well. Many other Quakers had an inkling of the evil of bondage; Woolman gave them voice.

By the diverse paths of slave revolt in the Caribbean, the sailors whom Philmore and Otis heard, and such Christians, many solitary journeys ultimately came together in a moral and political challenge to a seemingly all-powerful institution. According to Woolman, "In my traveling on the road, I often felt a cry rise from the center of my mind, thus: 'O Lord, I am a stranger on the earth. Hide not thy face from me!' On the 11th we crossed the Patawmack and Rapahannock and lodged at Port Royal. On the way we had the company of a colonel of the militia who appeared to be a thoughtful man. I took the occasion to remark in general on the difference between a people used to labor moderately for their living, training up their children in frugality and business, and those who live on the labor of slaves. The former in my view being the most happy."[69]

Woolman's is the first invocation of what would later become a great republican theme on the productivity and happiness of the free: "He [the colonel] concurred in my remark and mentioned the trouble arising from the untoward, slothful disposition of the Negroes, adding that one of our laborers would do as much work in a day as two of their slaves. I replied that free men whose minds were properly on their business found a satisfaction in improving, cultivating and providing for their families; but negroes laboring for others who claim them for their property and expecting nothing but slavery in their lives had not the like inducement to be industrious." The unnamed colonel agreed. Yet he then blamed the supposed disposition of the victim. Woolman broadened the perspective to the bondage of Christians by Turks—he might also have alluded to Christianity as initially the religion of slaves[70]—and to the nature of most power exercised by a few over others: "After some further conversation, I said that men having power too often misapplied it; though we made slaves of the negroes and the Turks made slaves of the Christians I believed that liberty was the natural right of all men equally."[71]

Woolman reports another person's apology for slave owning, "mentioning the wretchedness of the negroes occasioned by their intestine wars as an argument in favor of our fetching them away for slaves. To which I replied. If compassion for the Africans on account of their domestick struggles was the real motive for our purchasing them, that spirit of tenderness being attended to, would incite us to use them kindly as strangers brought out of affliction [so that] their lives might be happy among us. And as they are human creatures whose souls are as precious as ours and who may receive the same help and comfort from Holy Scriptures as we do, we could not omit suitable efforts to instruct them." Here a spiritual impulse contrasts vividly with a corrupt slave owners' "Christianity," which sanctions persecution. Especially for Quakers, encouraging such wars was hardly a moral virtue: "That while we manifest by our conduct that our views in purchasing them are to advance ourselves and while our buying captives taken in war animates those parties to push on the war and increase the desolation amongst them to say they live unhappily in Africa is far from being an argument in our favor."[72]

In addition, Woolman identifies slavery as a harm to owners, "a burdensome stone to those who burden themselves with it." He predicts that its weight will become "heavier and heavier until times change in a way disagreeable to us." His interlocutor then admits that he had seen "the treatment" of blacks in the province and thought that the "Almighty" might punish whites for it.[73]

Woolman delineates what would later be called exploitation: "These are the people by whose labor other inhabitants are in great measure supported and many of them in the luxuries of life." But, he says, blacks have not made a contract to labor as bondspersons. Here the idea of a moral or democratic contract surfaces, as it would throughout the revolutionary era. "These are the people," he wrote, "who have made no agreement to serve us and who have not forfeited their liberty that we know of." Woolman might also have questioned if even the "forfeiting" of liberty justifies enslavement. Instead, he affirms Christian egalitarianism: "These are the souls for whom Christ died and for our conduct towards them we must answer before Him who is no respector of persons."[74]

Inspired by Woolman, the September 29, 1758, yearly meeting of Friends in Philadelphia barred slave owners from future assemblies: "If after the sense and judgment of this meeting, now given against every branch of this practice, any professing with us should persist to vindicate it, and be concerned in importing, selling or purchasing slaves, the respective monthly meetings to which they belong, should manifest their disunion with such persons by refusing to permit them to sit in meeting for discipline, or to be employed in the affairs of Truth."[75] In 1760, in the town assembly at Newport, Rhode Island, Woolman excoriated bondage, but received little support.[76] Still, justice gradually appealed to many. Moses Brown, a Newport merchant, had grown rich in the West Indian traffic. In 1773, however, living up to his name, Moses emancipated his slaves and became a Quaker.[77]

Quakers saw the agony in the lives of many slaveholders who were otherwise conscientious congregants. They offered compassion toward as well as resistance to these individuals. On May 9, 1774, Anthony Benezet, a Philadelphia campaigner against bondage, wrote to Moses Brown about Samuel Nottingham, a mutual friend. Nottingham had married a woman who owned slaves in the Caribbean—married her for her money, Benezet surmised. Nottingham thus achieved compound misery: "This first misstep has been a source of many difficulties & much sorrow to him, his wife is I am persuaded a well-minded woman. She suffered much in her first husband's time which united her to friends & to Samuel; nevertheless I can't think if she had not been possessed of considerable wealth that he would have thought of her for a wife."[78] With an empathy that resonated with the former slave merchant Brown, Benezet spoke of the barbs Nottingham's conduct invited: "Indeed he is rather to be pitied than blamed. I have often conferred with him on the subject of his or rather his wife's Negroes; the many rubs he has received on that account in these parts, even in public meetings [in Philadelphia] I apprehend makes him more shy of spending as much time amongst us as he otherwise would."[79]

In 1774 the New England Quaker meeting expelled unrepentant slave owners. Under Quaker urging, the Providence, Rhode Island, town meeting decided to free several blacks who had become its property: "It is unbecoming the character of freemen to enslave the said negroes." The general assembly, it urged, should manumit at maturity all blacks born in Rhode Island. The assembly considered banning the importation of slaves: "Those who are desirous of enjoying all the advantages of liberty themselves, should be willing to extend personal liberty to others."[80] Newport, however, was the center of the New England slave trade. Rhode Island merchants pressured legislators to dilute the final bill.

In 1775 the Rhode Island legislature proposed organizing a public discussion about bondage, but no action ensued. At the Providence town meeting in August, Brown explained that a law would "materially affect the property of individuals." Citizens had backed away from their previous abolitionism.[81] Still, eroding complacency, the tides of emancipation washed again and again into this and other colonial assemblies.

Emancipation was thus an important part of the disputes over an American revolution. And in crowds, in the Continental army, aboard ships, and in escapes to the British, colonial blacks and their allies kept alive the belief in freedom for all propagated by the likes of Otis, Hopkins, and Woolman, despite slave-owning opposition.

One result was to make possible the grudging recruitment of blacks to the Patriot cause following the Dunmore Proclamation. George Washington had a lively sense of the threat the proclamation posed to that cause. As he wrote to Lieutenant Colonel Joseph Reed on December 15, 1775, "If the Virginians are wise . . . Lord Dunmore should be instantly crushd, if it takes the forces of the whole Colony to do it, otherwise, like a snow Ball in rolling, his army will get size—some through Fear—some through promises—and some from Inclination joining his Standard—But that which renders the measure indispensably necessary, is, the Negroes; for if he gets formidable, numbers of th[e]m will be tempted to join who will be affraid to do it without." But as a slave owner, Washington was reluctant to recruit blacks for the Patriot cause. He labeled Governor Dunmore an "Arch Traitor to the Rights of Humanity" and indicted the emancipator of Virginian slaves for what amounted to Washington's own crimes. True, Dunmore emancipated mainly Patriots' slaves, but this still put Washington—a defender of "freedom" only for whites—in no position to argue that point.[82]

When Washington was appointed commander in chief of the Patriot armies, blacks in fact already composed an important part of America's military force. In contrast, many whites abstained or signed up for short-term militias rather than enlisting in the Continental army. And incarnating the liberty that the American Revolution denied their brothers and sisters, blacks had contributed decisively to Patriot forces at Lexington, Concord, and Bunker Hill.[83] Washington had permitted black soldiers to remain in the Continental army but proscribed further recruitment. Meeting from October 18 to 24, 1775, representatives of the Continental Congress vowed: "Ought not Negroes to be excluded from the new Inlistment especially such as are Slaves—all were thought improper by the Council of Officers. Agreed, that they be rejected altogether."[84] On November 12, 1775, the Continental Congress declared all blacks ineligible to serve.

Washington, however, soon recognized the military advantage this policy gave the Crown. After Christmas, Washington warned Virginian Richard Henry Lee of the dangers posed by the Dunmore Proclamation in the same terms he had used in his letter to Colonel Joseph Reed: "Lord Dunmore's Letters to General Howe &ca wch very fortunately fell into my hands [captured on the sloop *Betsey*], & Inclosed by me to Congress, will let you pretty fully into his diabolical Schemes—If my Dear Sir that Man is not crushed before Spring, he will become the most formidable Enemy America has—his strength will Increase as a Snow Ball by rolling; and faster if some expedient cannot be hit upon to convince the Slaves and Servants of the Impotency of His designs."[85]

As a result of the anxieties about slave insurrections on the part of Patriot leaders and their refusal to allow blacks a place in the fight for freedom, the South was thus exposed as the Achilles heel of the Patriot cause. "You will see by his Letters what pains he is taking to invite Reinforcement at all event[s] there," Washington wrote, "& to transplant the War to the Southern Colonies." Fearful as a slave owner about the need to mobilize blacks on the American side, aware of this potentially "fatal" American weakness, as Madison termed slavery, Washington, in his December 26 letter to Lee, lashed out: "I do not think that forcing his Lordship on Ship board is sufficient; nothing less than depriving him of life or liberty will secure peace to Virginia; as motives of Resentment actuate his conduct to a degree equal to the total destruction of the Colony."[86]

Washington grasped that the royal governor's narrower motivation was to humiliate the rebels. Yet Dunmore had also introduced emancipation into a war previously conducted for the liberation of whites. His threats spurred Washington to support freedom for blacks in exchange for enlistment.

On December 30, 1775, Washington, oddly referring to himself in the third person, ordered recruiting blacks: "As the General is informed, that Numbers of Free Negroes are desirous of inlisting, he gives leave to the recruiting Officers to entertain them, and promises to lay the matter before the Congress, who he doubts not will approve of it."[87] On July 21, 1776, Patriot general Nathanael Greene warned Washington of an imperial plan to form a black regiment in New York: "A Negro belonging to one Strikser at Gravesend was taken prisoner as he says last Sunday at Coney Island. Yesterday he made his escape and was taken prisoner by the Rifle Guard. He reports Eight hundred Negroes Collected on Staten Island, this day to be formd into a Regiment."[88] Recruiting black soldiers, the Americans responded in kind.

The military situation that Washington faced was dire when he acquiesced to the recruitment of blacks. Patriot captain John Glover's regiment from Marblehead, Massachusetts, made up of one thousand sailors, including a "number of negroes," came to the rescue. At New York in 1776, Washington had but twenty thousand troops, which he mistakenly divided between Brooklyn and Manhattan, while the British had a fleet of four hundred warships and thirty-two thousand troops. Washington also lacked intelligence on imperial troop movements. On August 28, in Brooklyn, the redcoats cordoned off the Patriots, killing or wounding one thousand. Retreating to Brooklyn Heights, Washington's forces faced annihilation. As historian Mark Boatner has written, "Nine thousand disheartened soldiers, the last hope of their country, were penned up, with the sea behind them and a triumphant enemy in front, shelterless and famished on a square mile of open ground swept by a fierce and cold northeasterly gale."[89] For two days, only the storm prevented the British from destroying the Patriots.

On the night of August 30, in a "dense fog" both shielding and endangering the retreat, Glover's black and white soldiers ferried all nine thousand troops to safety. "To persons unaccustomed to such associations," a racist Pennsylvania officer commented, the sight of blacks "had a disagreeable, degrading effect."[90] Disdainful of the Patriot response to Dunmore's black troops, Ambrose Serle, Lord Howe's secretary, mocked the American forces as "the strangest that was ever collected: old men of 60, boys of 11, and blacks of all ages and ragged for the most part, compose the motley crew."[91]

Washington left on the last boat. As one soldier wrote, "I think I saw General Washington on the ferry stairs when I stepped onto one of the last boats."[92] As historian Henry Wiencek rightly comments, "Through that long night, Washington had witnessed personally the skill and courage of the black sailors of Massachusetts who rescued his army."[93]

Later, it was Glover's sailors who ferried the Patriots across the Delaware River and enabled the surprise attack on the Hessians at Trenton on Christmas Day, 1776. Emmanuel Leutze's painting *Washington Crossing the Delaware* depicts Prince Whipple, a slave of a New Hampshire officer, serving as stroke oar in the bow of the boat.[94]

These experiences gave Washington much to consider. The pragmatic dictates of military necessity could justify a new view of black slaves, a view underwritten by the principled arguments of Patriot abolitionists. The initial strategy of the American leadership, that is, refusing to liberate and recruit American blacks, had nearly doomed the movement for independence from Great Britain. Washington's acquiescence in accepting blacks as recruits to the Patriot cause brought the two simultaneous American revolutions at least somewhat more into consonance with each other, despite the dissonances that remained. Together, as happened frequently throughout the conflict on both sides, pragmatism conspired with principle to advance the causes of both independence and emancipation.

chapter 3 ¶ The Laurens Family
and Emancipation

> *These words, slavery and right, are contradictory;*
> *they are mutually exclusive.*
> —Jean Jacques Rousseau, *Du contrat social*

he relations between the effort to achieve independence for the thirteen American colonies of Great
Britain and the effort to achieve the emancipation of
American slaves were frequently vexed with conflicts,
ironies, and contradictions. Men of high honor and
exemplars of republican principles, such as Washington and Jefferson, labored in the cause of liberty even as they owned slaves, while unabashed
racists and defenders of hierarchical prerogative readily emancipated
blacks and freed slaves willingly flocked to the standard of those seeking
to crush a rebellion ostensibly premised on the belief that all men are created equal.

Psychologically, as well as politically, economically, and socially, the
consonances and dissonances between the two American revolutions of
the eighteenth century were particularly acute in their effects on many
who supported the Patriot cause. Thomas Jefferson is only the most famous example.[1] The Laurens family—Henry, the father, and John, his
son—exemplifies the ways in which the forces driving the revolution
against Great Britain and the revolution against slavery both came into
conflict and could be resolved toward a common end.

Conflating revolutionary Christians with "Quakers," slave owners
sought to isolate those who either advocated or accepted the recruitment
of blacks to the Patriot side by stigmatizing them as abolitionists and pro-
Crown. Invoking the ostensible "dangers of democracy," they also disparaged sailors, black and white, who set in motion urban crowds. But under the pressure of military necessity, pragmatism proved to be a weighty
argument in favor of abolition, especially among the elite. Such was the
case in the Laurens family. But principle played a role as well, both in the
thought and actions of the father, Henry, who nevertheless owned slaves,
feared slave rebellions, and resisted the idea of freeing the slaves in return for their fighting, and in the thought and actions of his son John,

who, though born into the South Carolina slave-owning and slave-trading elite, worked tirelessly for emancipation as an integral part of the war for American independence.

HENRY LAURENS

As members of the colonial elite in South Carolina, the Laurens family was by no means automatically in favor of the democratic and egalitarian forces that were helping drive both revolutions. In the fall of 1765, when Christopher Gadsden's Sons of Liberty, a South Carolina Patriot group that included sailors, protested the Stamp Act, and sailors and artisans sought to seize stamped paper from Henry Laurens, Laurens, though he was later to become a Patriot leader, opposed the demonstration. As historian Peter Wood relates, "In October 1765 a mob of sailors 'armed with Cutlasses and Clubs' visited the home of Charleston merchant Henry Laurens; '*Liberty, Liberty, & Stamp'ed Paper*' was their cry. Eighty strong and warm with drink and rage, the crowd had come for the stamped paper Laurens was rumored to have stored in his home. They would, as Laurens later recalled, 'admit of no "*Parleys*" no "*Palabres*"'; they 'not only menaced very loudly but now & then handled me pretty uncouthly.'"[2]

In a letter to Joseph Brown dated October 28, 1765, Laurens depicts himself as a man of honor facing a mob at his door. He shouted that he was a well-known opponent of the Stamp Act. His wife, who was pregnant, was in agony. This spurred him to stand up. Laurens insisted to the demonstrators that street protest was the wrong way to oppose the new tax. "You are very strong. You may if you please Barbecue me. I can but die, but you shall not by any force or means whatsoever compel me to renounce my friendships or speak ill of Men I think well."[3] Laurens refused to give up the paper if he had it or act against his friend, the royal governor, James Grant.

Looking down on these sailors and artisans, he even asserted that they were all nonsailors in disguise: "A brace of Cutlasses across my breast was the salutation & Lights, Lights & Search was the Cry. I presently knew several of them under their thickest disguise of Soot, Sailors habits, slouch-hats, &Ca, & to their great surprise called no less than nine of them by name & fixed my eye so attentively upon other faces as to discover at least the same number since."[4] As he remarks, the demonstrators did not harm his garden or destroy property; the mob is fairly described, in historian Pauline Meier's phrase, as "disciplined."[5] Some of this account is probably Laurens's embroidery. Nonetheless, Laurens here displayed a sense of honor that, as he aged, appeared rarely in his life.[6]

Such demonstrations from below inspired others to rebel. By 1765, black sailors and poor whites were formally free. Still, their cry against the British tax was "Liberty!" Could slaves fail to want freedom themselves? Making the link between democracy and communism, Marx's *Eighteenth Brumaire* avers, "When you play the fiddle at the top of the state, what else is to be expected but that those down below dance?"[7] At Christmas, with the cry "Liberty!" blacks, too, began to march.

But a rebellion that did not overturn bondage brought repression.[8] During the New Year's holiday, according to Henry Laurens, "all [whites] were Soldiers in Arms for more than a week." The "all" perhaps refers to owners and does not include sailors, from whom Laurens distinguished himself. Laurens was no democrat. On January 29, 1766, he wrote to John Louis Gervais,

> The disturbance that you heard of among our Negroes gave vast trouble throughout the province. Patrols were riding day & Night for 10 or 14 days in the most bitter weather & here in Town all were Soldiers in Arms for more than a Week, but there was Little or no cause for all that bustle, some Negroes had mimick'd their betters in crying out "*Liberty*" & those latter I do believe were apprehensive of an Odious Load falling upon their Shoulders & therefore some of them might probably frame & others propagate Reports to stimulate the White Men to Watchfulness in order to prevent any evil consequences but the whole seems to have terminated in the banishment of one fellow, not because he was guilty or instigator of insurrection, but because some of his judges said that in the general course of his Life he had been a sad Dog, & perhaps that it was necessary to save appearances.[9]

Laurens's casual attitude, however, was unusual. In contrast, militia officer Steven Bull reported to the state assembly on January 14 that during Christmas recess, a "general insurrection" of slaves had been barely averted. On the 109 blacks who escaped into the swamps of Colleton County, Bull proposed to "unleash" Catawba Indians. The house agreed. In addition, it voted two hundred pounds indemnity to each owner whose "slave"—now a free man—might be killed. But no record of recapture survives.[10]

However, although they were members of the colonial elite in South Carolina, the Laurens family was by no means among those who doggedly supported the institution of chattel slavery. Like Thomas Jefferson, Henry Laurens was a man of principle, and like Jefferson, he agonized over his owning of slaves. On August 14, 1776, he wrote to John of his intention to free the *children* of his slaves: "You know my Dear Son, I abhor slavery, I was born in a Country where Slavery had been established by British Kings & Parliaments as well as by the Laws of that Country Ages before my existence. . . . I am not the Man who enslaved them, they are indebted to English Men for that favour, nevertheless I am devising means for manumitting many of them and for cutting off the entail of slavery."[11]

In a Christian idiom, he stated the principle of equal liberty: "I am not one of those who dare trust in Providence for defense & security of their own Liberty while they enslave, and wish to continue in Slavery, thousands who are as well entitled to freedom as themselves."[12] But manumission at some future date was a far cry from embracing the cause of abolition, and like many of his peers, Henry Laurens feared the prospect of actual black liberation movements and endorsed repressive measures against them, as we have seen in his brutality in the Jeremiah lynching and the plot to slaughter maroons at Tybee Island.

Laurens portrayed the disincentives even to manumission: "Great powers oppose me, the Laws & Customs of my Country, my own & the avarice of my Country Men. What will my Children say if I deprive them of so much Estate?" He estimated the value of his slaves at twenty thousand pounds sterling. Laurens also feared being condemned by antiradical ideologists, those who believe that all rebellions are stirred among otherwise contented people—"dupes"—by "outside agitators": "I shall appear to many as a promoter not only of strange but of dangerous doctrines."[13] Yet he continued forthrightly: "These are difficulties but not insuperable. I will do as much as I can in my time & leave the rest to a better hand."[14] He sensed that his son might provide that hand: "I have no doubts concerning your concurrence & approbation. I most sincerely wish for your advice & assistance & hope to receive both in good time."[15]

The Laurenses were Huguenots—Calvinists. A murderous royal Catholic establishment had driven their forbears from France. Henry Laurens valued toleration. He sympathized with the Moravians, a Protestant denomination that opposed bondage. On March 19, 1763, Laurens had written to John Ettwein, the Moravian bishop for America:

Your observations upon the influence & effect of the negro slavery upon the morals & practices of young people are but too justly founded & I have often reflected with much concern on the same subject & wished that our economy & government differ'd from the present system; but alas! since our constitution is as it is, what can individuals do? . . . We see the negro trade promoted of late by our Northern neighbors who formerly censured & condemned it. The difficulties which a few who wish to deal with these servants as with brethren in a state of subordination meet with are almost insurmountable. The bad precept & worse examples daily & hourly set before them by blacks & whites surrounding them often eradicates in one day the labour that has been bestowed on them for years.

"These are discouraging circumstances," Laurens continued. "Nevertheless I am persuaded that there are some few who will not be defeated in their strife & who think that if they gain but one soul in their whole life time that they are happy instruments & as such are amply rewarded for their trouble."[16] Yet his actions often ran counter to such abstract thoughts and rare kindnesses.

Laurens empathized with families broken up by slavery. A hardened heart, he averred to Ettwein, will find no compassion in its own time of suffering: "I don't know anything that could have contrived to distress and embarrass my plantation again more than the division of fathers, mothers, husbands, wives and children who tho slaves are still human creatures, and I cannot be deaf to their cries lest a time should come when I should cry and there be none to pity me."[17] This moral equation was common during the Revolution.

But Henry Laurens had made a fortune in what he and others called the "Guinea business" (the slave trade), and writing to friends in South Carolina, he reflected on it "avariciously," to use his own term for his profiteering: "How can it be imagined that a cargo of the most mangy creatures that ever were seen should bring 24 stirling round. . . . Without vanity, we will say that none in this country could have turned them out so high."[18] Laurens had written to Bishop Ettwein in a spirit of humility, but as Benjamin Franklin noted at the beginning of his *Autobiography*, "I scarce ever heard or saw the introductory Words, *Without Vanity I may say &c.* but some vain thing immediately followed,"[19] and the phrase "without vanity" here unconsciously betrays his pride.

In contrast, James Laurens, Henry's brother and a Tory, rejected the slave trade. Appalled by the conditions of the Middle Passage, Gabriel Managuett, South Carolina's richest man, also shunned the "African traffic." In 1763, however, Henry Laurens stopped trafficking in human lives: "I quitted the profits arising from that gainful branch principally because of many acts from the masters and others concerned towards the wretched negroes from the time of purchasing to that of selling them again, some of which, though with my knowledge were uncontrollable."[20] Despite this, he still maintained large plantations worked by slaves. And the letter to his son was the first and only sign on Laurens's initiative that he might manumit those whom he named to Bishop Ettwein as his "brethren in a state of subordination."

Laurens, like many of his countrymen, was worried about the possible consequences of the Dunmore Proclamation, and at the Revolution's outset, his letters mostly tell of the Crown's "making off" with blacks. And like many Patriots, Laurens saw this act as one of the grievances that the colonists legitimately held against the British. On January 6, 1776, he lamented to James Laurens that the redcoats "encouraged Negroes to come to them & gave many protection, 30 or 40 it is said were carried away by the *Scorpion*" between November 28 and December 18, 1775. On January 20, he complained to Colonel Steven Bull: "We have received certain information that every [British ship leaving Charlestown] carried off some of our Negroes, in the whole amounting to no inconsiderable number. . . . This will be sufficient to alarm every Man in the Colony & put those on the Sea Coast & River sides more particularly on their guard."[21]

Fear and avarice inflate numbers. Historians sometimes repeat fabulous countings. On March 12, for instance, a letter from Bull indicated that "nine of Mr. Arthur Middletons Negroes & some others the whole in Number about Twenty five have gone on board the *Man of Warr*."[22] On March 13, Bull revised the number upward: "I am well Informd between forty & fifty of his have Really Deserted & above One hundred & fifty more the Property of others who are now on Tybee Island."[23] On March 14, Laurens told his daughter Martha that the ship had swept off "about 65 Negroes," seven times Bull's initial estimate, from Middleton's estate.[24] To John Laurens, on March 16, however, Bull moderated his guess to "upwards of 50 Negroes."[25] No one—least of all Bull—knew the exact number.

Throughout the Revolution, black escapees haunted Henry Laurens.[26] In an August 21, 1777, letter to John Louis Gervais, another Huguenot, Laurens wrote: "I take it for granted the British Armament which lately disappeared from the Coast of Maryland is gone to So Carolina & Georgia in order to destroy our Trade [and] to make immense plunder of Negroes."[27] As head of South Carolina's Committee of Public Safety, Laurens, the Patriot, watched over others' estates. On January 6, 1776, he wrote to James Laurens: "Your Negroes in some measure Govern themselves. Statira & Chloe act as if they had your Interest more at heart than the rest, they now & then do render some small account."[28] Repeatedly, however, blacks escaped from the estates that Henry oversaw.[29] On March 30, 1776, Henry had written to the Virginia minister Elhanan Winchester of "instigated Insurrections of Negroes and Inroads by Savage Indians."[30] Winchester condemned slavery as a mortal sin; nonetheless, Laurens hoped that black insurrection would frighten him.

To Martha, Laurens wrote on August 17, 1776: "Negro Slaves & barbarous Indians have been taught to exclaim, 'down with the Americans & their Estates will be all free plunder.'" And on September 27, 1776, to James Laurens, Henry recognized the voluntary presence of black soldiers on the imperial side, but supposed that it must humiliate the Crown to be defended by former slaves: "Among the killed in one skirmish were eleven Negroes. [S]urely your King is not apprized of all the inglorious & disgraceful measures pursued by his Servants."[31] The British, he also knew, employed blacks to retrieve guns from the field.[32]

On August 14, 1776, Henry Laurens also complained to his son of the "picaroon inglorious war"—his favorite phrase—that "the most puissant Nation in Europe [is] engaged in."[33] Overlooking his own hypocrisy, he magnified that of the English: "Negroes are brought by English Men & sold as Slaves to Americans[.] Bristol Liverpoole Manchester Birmingham &c &c live upon the Slave Trade[.] [T]he British Parliament now employ their Men of War to steal those Negroes from the Americans to whom they had sold them, pretending to set the poor wretches free but basely trepan & sell them into ten fold worse Slavery in the West Indies, where they probably will become the property of Englishmen again & of some who sit in Parliament." He perorated this attempt to shift blame: "What meanness! what complicated wickedness appears in this scene! O England, how changed! how fallen!"[34]

On September 16, writing to his son, Laurens added histrionically, "I believe I shall very soon abandon those delightful & profitable Plantations on Altamaha River & lead my Servants to Sante[.] [T]he Georgians & East Floridians have mutually practiced the Torch [set fire to each other's towns], I cannot expect long to escape the Spreading flames."[35] Despite this bombast, he was more aware than he might seem. To Gervais on September 5, 1777, Laurens spoke frankly of black hatred for an overseer: "Casper seems to be held in contempt by the Negroes & I am afraid of Some fatal accident."[36]

Laurens responded to the threat posed by the Dunmore Proclamation and the flocking of blacks to the Loyalist standard by trying to prevent his own slaves from fleeing. On March 24, 1776, Henry Laurens wrote to Colonel Lachlan McIntosh Jr. of the Georgia militia: "I intreat you to give [overseer James Bailley] . . . orders for the removal of my Negroes & all the Rice from [Broughton] Island to the Main if you think it will be proper,"[37] and on August 14, 1776, Laurens boasted to his son that none of *his* slaves would run off with the British. That same day, McIntosh reported to Henry Laurens that George Aaron, a black overseer at Laurens's New Hope plantation, had escaped to Florida along with five of Laurens's slaves.[38]

Despite being a leader in the Patriot cause, Henry Laurens was no happier when the Continental army began to employ blacks out of military necessity. To William Brisbane, a planter, Henry Laurens noted on September 6, 1776, that in an "impolitic" move, the army had enlisted two black overseers of his frontier plantation. Responding as a slave owner, he insisted: "Of two Evils I must choose the least & draw off all my Negroes as Speedily as possible."[39]

JOHN LAURENS

About manumitting his own slaves, Henry Laurens, like Shakespeare's Polonius, had been sententious and hypocritical. Except as a threatened slave owner, for instance in the lynching of Jeremiah, he did not act. As noted earlier, however, as a younger man in 1765, Laurens had displayed a sense of honor in standing up to sailors demanding stamped paper at his house. His understanding of honor probably influenced his son John.[40] And sons sometimes take up the convictions their fathers have not acted on. On October 26, 1776, John Laurens wrote "with rapture" to his father about the manumission that the elder Laurens had mentioned; he stated that "your desire of restoring the Rights of Men, to those wretched Mortals who have so long been unjustly deprived of them, coincides exactly with my feelings upon that subject."[41]

Like his father, John Laurens was a member of the South Carolina elite, but he was of a different generation and had a very different upbringing from his entrepreneurial sire. In 1771, fifteen years after Rousseau published *Du contrat social* (*The Social Contract*), John Laurens had studied law in Geneva. In courts, debate clubs, and taverns, he was surrounded by advocates, with varying levels of comprehension, of the Rousseauian view. But Laurens really did understand it. He spoke of the "great Opposition from interested Men" that his father would experience when he declared his intentions to free the children of his slaves. With greater theoretical sophistication than Henry, John mocked frivolous arguments: "I have often conversed upon the Subject and I have scarcely ever met with a Native of the Southern Provinces or the W. Indies, who did not obstinately recur to the most absurd Arguments in support of Slavery but it was easy to perceive that they considr'd only their own Advantage arising from the Fact, and embarrassed themselves about the Right[.] [I]ndeed when driven from every thing else they generally exclaim'd Without Slaves how is it possible to be rich?"[42]

John Laurens would become a leading and unusually theoretically sophisticated abolitionist. Although discussion of Rousseau's notion of right rarely occurred among Americans,[43] he took to heart Rousseau's thought that "*slavery* and *right* . . . are mutually exclusive."[44] Rousseau also drew an unfavorable contrast between an abolitionist general will, a will to support equality, and a transient, pseudodemocratic "will of all."[45]

Laurens's pitting of "the Right" against the slaveholders' "own advantage" captures this distinction and recalls Montesquieu's suggestion that those who favored slavery in Bordeaux should take their chance with others in a lottery to become slaves themselves. Montesquieu's challenge reveals slavery as "the cry of luxury and voluptuousness, not of public felicity."[46]

In addition, *Du contrat social* denounced those who accept the "security" of Odysseus and his companions in Polyphemus's cave, waiting to be devoured: "To renounce your liberty is to renounce your quality of manhood. Such a renunciation is incompatible with the nature of man." Rousseau continues: "Be it from a man to a man or from a man to a people, this discourse is always nonsense: I make a convention with you totally to your expense and my profit, that I will observe as long as it shall please me and that you will observe as long as it shall please me."[47]

John Laurens would speak as "a citizen, a soldier, and a man." This Rousseauian phrase indicates the dignity of human freedom and independence from ownership by another. Nonetheless, John Laurens retained a slave owner's perspective about the psychology of blacks at that time. In a 1776 letter to his father, he ignored manifold black acts of resistance and their hunger to be free: "There may be some Inconvenience and even Danger in advancing Men suddenly from a State of Slavery while possess'd of the manners and Principles incident to such a State . . . too suddenly to the Rights of Freedmen. [T]he Example of Rome suffering from Swarms of bad Citizens who were freedmen is a warning to us to proceed with Caution." This argument reinforced Henry Laurens's vacillation. The son insisted, however, on the principle that slavery is simply wrong, the immoral shackling of another: "The necessity for it is an Argument of the complete Mischief occasioned by our continued Usurpation."[48]

Still, writing to his father, John Laurens called for gradualism: "By what Shades and Degrees they are to be brought to the happy State which you propose for them is not to be determined in a moment."[49] Here he echoed Rousseau's metaphor from *Discours sur les origines de l'inegalite* (*Discourse on the Origins of Inequality*) of the sea god Glaucus, the divine figure hidden by a coat of barnacles. Just as Rousseau's reasoning uncovered the sea god's true shape, John Laurens saw the dignity, beneath servitude, of men and soldiers.

Though John Laurens had absorbed the principles of political equality, he promised his father further study: "Whatever I can collect from Books and the Conversation of Sensible Men shall be carefully attended to."[50] Despite differences that he may not have yet articulated to himself, he told his father, "I am glad to find that you had the same confidence in me, that I had in you."[51]

In Geneva, John Laurens had befriended another American student, Francis Kinloch. As in Laurens's later relationship with Alexander Hamilton, familiarity with republican political philosophy marks their letters. A lawyer trained in England, Kinloch would serve as aide to General William Moultrie of the Patriot militia during the Revolution; in 1780 he would become a South Carolina delegate to the Continental Congress. Before the Revolution, however, he frequently argued with Laurens, and his defense of the principle of monarchy provided a foil for Laurens's distinctive republicanism. What is clear in the arguments between them is how avidly both of these future revolutionaries read political philosophy and how militantly Laurens took up the cause of a modern, antislavery republic.[52]

On November 6, 1774, Laurens warned Kinloch of "the bloody Prospect of a Civil War" looming with the "Mother Country." He mourned the king's denunciation of the Boston Tea Party: "A most daring Spirit of Resistance and Disobedience to the Law still prevails in the Province of Massachusetts Bay[,] has in divers Parts of it broke out in fresh violence of a very criminal Nature." Given the threat of war, Laurens averred, he must soon get "away to America. I have a Father. I have Sisters. . . . I have a Country which claims the small Assistance I can give—O My Friend, Shall I see Our fertile Plains laid waste parcel'd out to new Masters." In what turned out to be prophetic, he noted that "we can die but once, and when more gloriously than in defense of our Liberties?"[53]

But Laurens persuaded Kinloch to join him temporarily in the study of law. In addition, on May 28, 1776, Laurens wrote to him on the prospects of an American revolution. The lower class must back the "men of property who were quite resolute." Great Britain could destroy only the seaports. If the people retained their "virtues," Laurens insisted, America "will abound with great characters." Trade with the mother country, and riches, however, could destroy this possibility. It would lead to what republicans called a corruption of the common good, the domination of government by the wealthy and its use against the poor: Americans "would have advanced to a corrupt state with no intermediate maturity."[54]

Emulating Rousseau, Laurens would "never regret poverty and the loss of trade if there can be established, either with or without Great Britain, a government that will conduce to the good of the whole." In the same document, Laurens condemned the implications of bondage for democracy: "I think we Americans at least in the Southern Colonies cannot contend with a good Grace for Liberty, until we shall have enfranchised our Slaves. How can we whose Jealousy has been alarm'd more at the name of oppression sometimes than at the Reality, reconcile to our spirited assertions of the Rights of Mankind, the galling abject Slavery of our Negroes?"[55]

Again following Rousseau, Laurens saw the perpetuation of bondage as the triumph of base "Interest" over liberty: "I could talk much with you, my dear friend, upon this subject, " he wrote to Kinloch, "& I know your generous soul would despise & sacrifice interest to establish the happiness of so large a part of the inhabitants of our soil."[56] Attentive to the destructive effects of wealth on equal liberty, Rousseau would inspire radicals in the French Revolution: the Jacobins, sans-culottes, Babeuf, and Mably.[57] But in John Laurens, he would also have a profound advocate of an American abolitionist republic.[58] Laurens passionately affirmed the common good at which Rousseau's general will aims. He also understood the particular, tyrannical will, the "will of all," which, for instance, the Declaration of Independence's defenses of slavery or commercial corruption reflect.

Kinloch disagreed. Republics, he averred in a letter, lead to "mediocrity": "to be confounded among Butchers is dreadful to a man of Education and Feeling." Following Montesquieu's idea of a republic, Kinloch argued, "The Desire of excelling shocks the Spirit of the Constitution."[59]

In a June 16, 1776, response, however, Laurens contrasted his convictions about citizenship with his friend's: "My ambition Kinloch is to live under a Republican Government—I hate the Name of King." A republic, Laurens insisted, involves "the continual Sacrifice of private Interest to Public Good from which kind of Conduct a Happiness which Riches cannot give results to the Individual and Strength and Grandeur are ensur'd to the State." Laurens adopted this gallant maxim as a guide to his revolutionary actions. Invoking ancient republics and insisting on a public good, he confronted Kinloch's argument that "ambition is dog'd by the Government and a Man cannot make a Figure by exerting laudable Talents": "Under a Republican Government there is the fullest scope for Ambition directed in its proper Channel in the only Channel it ought to be allowed, I mean for the Advancement of Public Good. Need I desire you for proof to turn to the Histories of Ancient Republics as your Memory will present to you Instances enough of citizens vying with each other in the glorious Service of their Country and receiving distinguished marks of Approbation from her." Altering Montesquieu's perspective, he insisted that "noble emulation" in this vein does not "shock the Spirit of Democracy."[60]

Laurens contrasted distinction in virtue in a republic with mere striving for riches under a monarchy. Montesquieu imagined the possibility of a commercial republic and named Athens as an example. In modern times, he thought that England, or a federated republic, the America of the revolutionaries' hopes, could become one. In such a regime, divisions of rich and poor would neither be extreme nor generate corruption.

Kinloch stressed a "mixed government," which he found in "Cicero, Machiavelli, and Montesquieu."[61] But Montesquieu also favored a small republic and in modern times, a federated, commercial republic. Rousseau had criticized Montesquieu's vision of such a republic, and with Rousseau, Laurens was less sanguine: "The Ambition of acquiring greater Riches than the rest of one's fellow Citizens, the establishing [of] that odious Inequality of Fortunes, Source of Luxury and Wretchedness in Society—of that of usurping more power than the Law allows—such pernicious Ambition shocks the equitable Spirit of a Republic and [is] the Selfish Enemy of his Country whose conduct it appears must fall under the wholesome Rigours of the Laws."[62]

The word "odious" was perhaps Laurens's favorite term for inequalities of rich and poor. Like him, Henry Laurens, Thomas Jefferson, George Mason, and other southerners worried about the inequalities inherent in slave owning. They thought an egalitarian community of farmers or the immigration of free whites might create a decent republic.[63]

To Kinloch's concern about being confused with "tradesmen and mean Mechanics," Laurens responded aristocratically. A "man of education and feeling," he wrote on June 16, 1776, would suffer only by neglecting his own talents, "for he has it in his power to do his Country more eminent and influential Service, and thereby entitles himself to more signal Rewards— these Rewards I grant you are not calculated to enrich the Individual and introduce all the odious and destructive consequences of Riches, but they are fully Satisfactions to a Virtuous Mind." Here, Laurens's vision of republics encompasses the sense of honor that he hoped his friend Kinloch would embrace. Laurens suggests that the "useful industrious part of the Community should have their persons and properties equally protected with those of the most enlighten'd Men." By standards of virtue and honor, they should "choose Men whom they judge worthy of the important Trust f Governing." Kinloch knew the philosophical arguments; Laurens did ot belabor them: "I will not repeat here the Maxims respecting Govern-..ient which have been established by a Sidney, a Locke, a Rousseau, and which strike Unison with the Sentiments of every manly Breast."[64]

Against Kinloch, Laurens insisted that "a monarchy was the nursery of human depravity." Often, he pointed out, "chance" places on the throne "a foolish or Knavish King." Seldom does education nurture a "wise or a virtuous" one. But better a dull king than a smart tyrant: "If the King for the Misfortune of his Country is a Man of abilities, they become the Instrument of his tyranny, and share the spoils of those whom they have assisted in ruining."[65]

In *Discours sur l'oeconomie politique* (*Discourse on Political Economy*), Rousseau remarks: "I regard the poor man as totally undone, if he has the misfortune to have an honest heart, a fine daughter, and a powerful neighbor."[66] Laurens used that insight to refute Kinloch's contention that monarchy furthers "every generous principle" and rewards men of honor and merit. "Yes if a Man have the Merit of a fair Sister and can be so abject as to play the Pander to a great Man's Lust, he shall make a conspicuous figure in Life." Far from furthering "every generous principle," Laurens continued, "if you please, every infamous germ that can disgrace Humanity is most luxuriantly developed in your admired form of Government—what Room is there for generous Emulation when men of Merit overlooked see [crowds?] who have nothing to recommend them but their having been subservient to the Vices of the Great, or at best Family Interest, advanced above their heads."[67]

He could have said it was harder in monarchies, which devalue individual conscience, to choose decently. In response, Kinloch left unfinished a sentence beginning "The hands of the King . . . ." Laurens wrote back: "I will add the Hands of a King ought to be tied—that he may do no Mischief but a better way would be to have no King at all." Finally, he hoped, Kinloch would "be a Convert to the Cause of Humanity, and no longer an advocate of Kings."[68]

Initially, Laurens naïvely affirmed the Patriot cause. He accepted his father's apology for the lynching of Thomas Jeremiah and in that case embraced a racist Patriot "will of all." In his June 16 letter to Kinloch, he reported ostensibly insidious British efforts among Native Americans: "Ministerial Emissaries have been active in stirring up the Indians. The Barbarians return'd from their Hunt carried home with them two white scalps." He did not see Native Americans as human; he also did not see American efforts to recruit indigenous people as comparably insidious.[69]

But Laurens wrote presciently to Kinloch about South Carolina's treachery embodied in the legislature's zeal to hunt the escaped rather than to enlist them in the Patriot cause: "Let us fly it as a hateful country and say *ubi libertas ibi patria* [where there is liberty, there is my country]."[70] Yet he would stay in the new United States and become a fierce Patriot for abolition and genuine freedom. Kinloch would join Laurens in serving in South Carolina, but he did not support Laurens's advocacy of emancipation.

Unsurprisingly, Kinloch took umbrage at Laurens's indictment of monarchical corruption, for it might imply that he, as a monarchist, was corrupt. In a letter dated "summer 1776," Laurens offered an explanation. He had sought to "cultivate and improve" their friendship not because they always agreed, but because of "the Qualities of your heart" of which I have a "great Opinion." Friendship for gentlemen of honor pivoted around purity of feeling: "I have no copies of what I wrote, and therefore can't be exactly sure of all the Expressions which I used in my letter. This I am persuaded of that there was nothing in it that could be construed to throw any Imputation upon the Qualities of your Heart on account of the Side you took in our political dispute which I shall not continue and which will therefore end as such Disputes generally do, each party firmly retaining the Opinion with which he set out."[71]

Laurens doubted the effectiveness of political debate, yet to state his position forcefully would remain important to him. And his letters moved Kinloch, who would join him to fight for an American republic. Nonetheless, to remove offense, he gave a subtle nod to the advantages Kinloch saw in monarchy: "When I said that a Monarchy was the Nursery of Human Depravity, I never meant to insinuate that *every* Man who should think the Advantages attending that Form of Government overbalanced its disadvantages, and who therefore prefer'd it to all others, was necessarily tinctur'd with those vices which flourish in a Monarchy—no more that I meant to say that myself must be corrupted by breathing this contagious Air."[72]

John Laurens's commitment to abolition challenged his father's hypocrisy, and the father eventually came to sympathize with his son's politics, at least to a certain extent. Sometimes John persuaded Henry to adhere to principle. And despite his father's cautions, their correspondence reveals John's growing determination to undertake an emancipatory project. Patriot leaders, particularly Washington and the Continental Congress, would also come to accept the younger Laurens's views of effective revolutionary strategy—based, however, on the pragmatic argument of military necessity, not simply on the principles of egalitarian political theory. But South Carolina and Georgia repudiated black recruitment, and the Continental Congress and Washington were unwilling, short of impending defeat by the British, to force this policy on the states. Still, driven by revolutionary crowds and fear of royal enlistment of blacks, tides of abolition washed through the Patriot ranks, even in the South.

In 1777, as aide-de-camp, John Laurens joined Washington at Valley Forge. On January 14, 1778, he wrote to his father, "I barely hinted to you my dearest father my desire to augment the Continental Forces from an untried Source."[73] John Laurens asked Henry to assign him "a number of your able bodied men Slaves, instead of leaving me a fortune." On behalf of his proposal, he invoked patriotism, his father's musings about emancipation, and friendship.

Henry feared that his son would become an outcast. Instead, John hoped to accomplish a twin service: "First, I would advance those who are unjustly deprived of the Rights of Mankind to a State which would be a proper Gradation between abject Slavery and perfect Liberty and besides I would reinforce the Defenders of Liberty with a number of gallant Soldiers." He might have added that his proposal would make the American revolutionaries genuine "Sons of Liberty." In addition, unlike many British commanders, he saw the connection between servitude and the fierce desire to become "gallant Soldiers" for liberty. Yet he also wrote, patronizingly, "Men who have the habit of Subordination almost indelibly impress'd on them, would have one very essential qualification of Soldiers."[74] Laurens hoped to train these troops himself.

On January 22, 1778, Henry Laurens manifested his love for his son, but derided the project: "There is nothing reasonable, which you can ask & I refuse[.] I will not refuse this, if after mature deliberation you will say it is reasonable." But he conjured mythical specters: "Work of this importance must be entered upon with Caution & great Circonspection [sic], otherwise, a Man will be reduced to the ridiculous state of the Fox who had lost his tail." In Aesop's fable, a trap mutilated a fox. The fox then urged an assembly of his fellows to rip off their tails as well. The others demurred.[75]

On February 2, 1778, reflecting on the "difficulties and delays which are likely to attend the completing of our Continental Regiments," John responded to Henry.[76] To "that monster, popular Prejudice open-mouthed against me," he contrasted ardent "zeal for the public Service." In the style of Rousseau and despite a patronizing beginning, one slave owner conversing with another, he indicted bondage:

I confess that the minds of this unhappy species must be debased by a Servitude from which they can hope for no relief but Death and that every motive to action but Fear must be nearly extinguished in them, but do you think they are so perfectly moulded to their State as to be insensible that a better exists[,] will the galling comparison between themselves and their masters leave them unenlighten'd in this respect[,] can their Self-Love be so totally annihilated as not frequently to induce ardent wishes for a change. . . . I am tempted to believe that this trampled people have so much human left in them, as to be capable of aspiring to the rights of man by noble exertion, if some friend of mankind would point the Road, and give them a prospect of Success.[77]

In terms such as those of the *Discours sur les origines de l'inegalite*, Laurens speaks about the gradual shifts that will allow blacks to assume full human stature: "You will ask in this view how do you consult the benefit of the Slaves[?] I answer that like other men they are the Creatures of habit[;] their Cowardly Ideas will be gradually effaced, and they will be modified anew[,] their being rescued from a state of perpetual humiliation[,] and being advanced as it were in the Scale of Being will compensate the dangers incident to the new State[;] the hope that will spring in each mans mind respecting his own estate will prevent his being miserable[;] those who fall in battle will not lose much[,] those who survive will gain the Reward."[78]

John Laurens was a practical abolitionist. Favored by nature and fortune, he chose no easy path. He could, for instance, have worked for Washington, recruited a company of white soldiers as his father urged, and still have advocated the "public good." Instead, he committed himself to the nobler course of fighting determinedly for emancipation. Unique among Patriot revolutionaries, he had an insight into the nature of a general will and the terrifying inconsistency of slavery with equal rights. His time in Geneva had transformed abstract family insights into democratic political philosophy.

Henry Laurens considered his son's "scheme" to be a fantasy, "the Chimara of a young man deceived by a false appearance of moral beauty." The son named it "a laudable sacrifice of private Interest to Justice and the public good."[79] He reminded his father: "I have long deplored the wretched State of these men and considered in their history, the bloody wars excited in Africa to furnish America with Slaves, the Groans of despairing multitudes toiling for the Luxuries of Merciless Tyrants. I have had the pleasure of conversing with you sometimes upon the means of restoring them to their rights. When can it be better done, than when their enforcement may be made conducive to the Public Good, and be so modified as not to overpower weak minds."[80]

To a citizen-soldier such as Laurens, the dedication of the South Carolina Patriot militia to slave catching must have seemed disgraceful. Denying freedom to many, this practice undermined the "Public Good" for which they were ostensibly fighting.

Henry Laurens warned that his son's band would be small and include a sizable proportion of women and children. In addition, John briefly fell into the thought patterns of a slave owner. He proposed exchanging the women and children for "able bodied men." He thought "40 might be a good foundation to begin upon." But he also had a better formulation. Recognizing his father's authority as president of the Continental Congress, John looked to future potentials: "It is a pity that some such plan as I propose could not be even more extensively executed by public Authority[;] a well chosen body of 5000 black men properly officer'd to act as light Troops in addition to our present establishment, might give us decisive Success in the next Campaign."[81]

Henry Laurens asked about Washington's opinion of a black regiment. With a slave owner's sympathy, John responded: "He is convinced that the numerous tribes of blacks in the Southern parts of the Continent offer a resource to us that should not be neglected with respect to my particular Plan, he only objects to it with the arguments of Pity, for a man who would be less rich than he might be."[82]

In 1779, however, Henry warned that an obsessive "Cloud" preoccupied his son: "You have filled six Pages on the Negro scheme without approaching towards a Plan & Estimate & . . . you have totally overlooked every other subject on which I have addressed you in several late Letters."[83] The father ignored the mass flight of slaves, including his own, to the Crown. Instead, he maintained an owner's illusion that blacks would fear losing their lives in battle more than bondage: "Nay you will not be of your own opinion after a little reflection[,] you have not digested a Plan admitting which I admit only for argument you have a right to remove a Man from one state of Slavery into another or if you please into a state of Servitude which will be estimated by him infinitely worse than Slavery." In fact, the black war for freedom on both sides in the American Revolution underscored the peculiar horrors of bondage.

With surprising logic, the father then drew attention to the son's weakest argument, his proposal to trade women and children for male soldiers: "What right have you to exchange & Barter 'Women and Children' in whom you pretend to say you have no Property?" Henry also extended this abolitionist argument to the men: "The very same observation may be made with respect to the Men for you have either property in them, or you have not[;] admitting the latter which you seem to acknowledge, upon what ground of justice will you insist upon their inlisting for Soldiers, as the condition of the infranchisement. If they are free tell them so set them at full liberty & then address them in the Language of a recruiting Officer to any other free men & if four in forty take your inlisting bounty, it will be very extraordinary, this small number will do it through ignorance & three of the four be returned as Deserters in a very short time."[84] If the father had freed his slaves as he had once envisioned doing, this argument might have seemed more plausible.[85]

Henry Laurens urged John to consult with friends about "your favorite idea." He tried to frighten him: "Your own good sense will direct you to proceed warily in opposing the opinions of whole Nations lest without effecting any good, you become a bye word, & be so transmitted, to Your Children's Children."[86] Ironically, instead, John Laurens's fight for emancipation has led to a long epoch of neglect of his and his father's role during the Revolution in history books, public celebrations, and museums among South Carolinians and others.[87] John and even Henry Laurens stood up against bondage. Hence, both had to be "forgotten." Yet in February 1778, with gentleness, Henry offered to honor his son's request: "The more I think of & the more I have consulted on your scheme, the less I approve of it. Wisdom dictates that I should rather oppose than barely not consent to it but Indulgence and friendship warranted by Wisdom bids me let you take your own counsel & draw self-conviction[;] therefore come forward Young Colonel, proceed to So Carolina[;] you shall have as full authority over all my Negroes as Justice to your Brother & Sisters & a very little consideration for my self will permit you to exercise & so far do what you please & as you please."[88]

Swayed by his father's "kindness on the subject of my black battalion," John Laurens temporarily put aside his plan.[89] Faced with British victories at Savannah and Charlestown over the next year, however, he worked for a more thoughtful and practical version.

In the meantime, at the headquarters in Valley Forge, Laurens recruited powerful supporters, particularly Alexander Hamilton and, to a lesser extent, Washington himself. He thus responded to his father's worry that proposing a black battalion would lead to ridicule.

In May 1779, Laurens returned to the decisive issue of American rivalry with the Crown over the deployment of black soldiers. "It is evident that the British have not waited for our example—to sanction novel measures[;] otherwise Dunmore would not have [freed] slaves in Virginia,"[90] he wrote to his father. In a revolution for liberty, however, the Americans could reverse their despotic course and rely on black soldiers: "Our enemies have at length discovered the vulnerable point of the confederacy and determine to avail themselves [of it]. . . . [But] there is an untried resource which if properly improved will enable us not only to expel the Enemy from our territory, but transfer the theatre of the war to his."[91] "Those blacks who have hitherto been regarded as our greatest weakness," he argued, "may be converted into our greatest strength."[92] Laurens also foresaw the danger to the Revolution of "the Enemy's having recourse to the same expedient which it is pretended from the superiority of their Resources they can do with great advantage."[93]

Henry Laurens had claimed that slaves would not make good soldiers. In a somewhat racist formulation, the son elaborated on their likely military abilities: "In fact, if implicit obedience to the commands of superiors, if bodily strength and activity, if constitution proof against fatigues . . . and the intemperateness of the Seasons are essential qualifications in Soldiers, these men are superiorly qualified for that Station."[94] Here, he overlooked the decisive element: the motivation of freedom.

Laurens reiterated his own commitment: "For my part it will be my duty and my pride to transform the timid Slave into a firm defender of Liberty and render him worthy to enjoy it himself."[95] He spoke of convening "the Levies [soldiers] at a general rendezvous from remote parts—and exchanging the unfit for service that will not be sent in the first instance."[96]

At age twenty-four, John Laurens emphasized prudence to his agitated father. He wrote, "I must confess I am anxious—for as I am engaged in a plan of this kind my reputation is at stake." But while this fear "would induce me to spend as much time as possible in disciplining and instructing my Soldiers before I introduced them to the enemy . . . a desire to render service, on the other hand, would make me solicitous to bring them into the field in the active part of the Campaign."[97]

Laurens foresaw South Carolinian resistance to his plans. On March 16, 1779, he offered a sophisticated argument to inspire his father to overcome it: "You will have perceived by my last [letter] that granting the probability of obtaining an act for raising black troops in South Carolina—no time in my opinion was to be lost in applying for it, under the sanction of a Recommendation from Congress." He noted that the "present season in that country affords very good fighting weather" and wrote, again in Rousseauian phrasing, that "as a Soldier, as a Citizen, as a Man, I am interested to engage in this work."[98]

He was not explicit about the differences in his commitments and character from those of his father. Yet John Laurens's principles also inspired his father. He even embroidered an imagined heroism for Henry Laurens as a leader in the Continental Congress: "You will have the glory of triumphing over deep-rooted national prejudices, in favor of your Country and humanity at large."[99] Recalling his father's intention eventually to free his slaves, John Laurens offered his own inheritance in slaves: "I would cheerfully sacrifice the largest portion of my future expectations to [the battalion's] success."[100]

His father objected that emancipating some blacks "would inspire the Remainder with Ideas which [can] only be pernicious." "To this I answer," John Laurens replied, "your slaves are accustomed to see their Comrades manumitted every day. This occasions no murmur or discontent. The remainder continue as useful as ever."[101] In the West Indies, with a proportionally smaller white population, the French and British had successfully pursued limited emancipation. In 1791 in Saint Domingue, however, that "success" would come to an abrupt denouement in a slave revolt.

By March 1779, the theater of war had shifted dramatically. The Crown had reconquered Georgia and threatened South Carolina. Patriot general Isaac Huger had gone to Philadelphia to seek military aid. Huger, Henry Laurens, and William Henry Drayton, a member of the Continental Congress from Charlotte, all supported John Laurens's proposal to commission black troops.[102] On March 16, shifting places with and adopting the language of his son, Henry Laurens wrote to Washington: "Had we arms for three thousand such black men as I could select in Carolina, I should have no doubt of success in driving the British out of Georgia and subduing East Florida before the end of July."[103] Given the threat of British emancipation, John Laurens's position made striking headway among leading Patriots.

On March 20, however, Washington replied evasively to Henry Laurens: "The policy of our arming slaves is in my opinion a moot point unless the enemy set the example." He warned of imperial competition for black recruits: "For, should we begin to form Battalions of them, I have not the smallest doubt, if the war is to be prosecuted, of their following us in it, and justifying the measure upon our own ground. The upshot then must be, who can arm fastest?"[104]

In the previous year, Washington had tried to sell some of his slaves. Yet wanting the profit, but not the evil, he would not allow his cousin, Lund Washington, to break up black families. Lund became increasingly agitated, and in April 1778, he wrote to the commander, "With regard to sellg the Negroes—you have put it out of my power, by saying you would not sell them, without their Consent." Bett, one of Washington's slaves, would not agree. As Lund wrote, "Her Mother appeared to be so uneasy about it, and Bett herself made such promises of amendment, that I could not force her to go with the Man."[105] Another woman "was so distressed at the thought of being sold that the Man could not get her to speak a Word of English, therefore he believed she could not speak." Of Washington's slaves, Lund added angrily, "You say again you wish to be quit of negroes. . . . Tell me in plain terms, whether I should sell your negroes at Public sale or not, & how many of them & indeed who."[106]

As modern historian Henry Wiencek suggests, the moral crime of selling slaves—and fear for his estate if gradual abolition should occur in the South—gnawed at Washington. This wrong may have influenced his response to Henry Laurens. Despite this vacillation, however, Washington eventually supported John Laurens's proposal.[107] If America could win, ultimately Washington would do whatever was necessary.

Ironically, however, in a 1779 letter to Henry, Washington echoed Laurens's onetime caution to his son: "Besides I am not clear that a discrimination will not render slavery more irksome to those who remain in it. Most of the good and evil things in this life are judged of by comparison; and I fear a comparison in this case will be productive of much discontent in those who are held in servitude."[108]

Washington lied to Henry: "As this is a subject that has never employed much of my thoughts, these are no more than the first crude Ideas that have struck me upon ye occasion."[109] Yet, he suggested in this same letter, black recruitment could decide the war.

Throughout the Revolution, Washington would be both preoccupied and remarkably shifting in his views of black enlistment. Initially horrified by Dunmore's emancipation of blacks, the general supported the creation of the black Rhode Island regiment in 1778. But when it came to a policy for the heart of the South, Washington vacillated. Freeing black soldiers in South Carolina and Georgia threatened gradual emancipation in Virginia.

John Laurens's proposal would win many converts and pass easily. Far from as forcefully as he could have, in the end, Washington, too, supported it. In March 1779, the Continental Congress resolved that "a force might be raised in [South Carolina] from among the Negroes, which would not only be formidable to the enemy from their numbers, and the discipline of which they would very readily admit, but would also lessen the danger from revolts and desertions, by detaching the most vigorous and enterprising from among the Negroes."[110] Among American leaders, Hamilton, Madison, Washington, and Nathanael Greene all invoked this competitive threat posed by the Crown in freeing black slaves and recruiting them to the Loyalist cause. So did the Continental Congress in adopting the Laurens proposal.

In the parallel development of the two revolutions, the resolution of the Continental Congress in 1779 marked the moment when the effort to achieve the colonies' freedom from the oppressions of Great Britain and the effort to achieve black slaves' freedom from the oppressions of chattel slavery were, for once, in accord. Pragmatism, as much as or more than principle, motivated the development, but whether pragmatic or principled, the effect was the same.

However, principle was what motivated John Laurens and what made him an effective advocate for the second revolution. Laurens was able to make the emancipation and recruitment of black soldiers a central war policy in the Continental Congress and among revolutionary leaders by virtue of his distinguished service as a fighter in the Patriot cause and as a result of his sense of how a man of honor, raised among the eighteenth-century colonial elites, should behave. Elite abolitionism was not uncommon in America. To fight for it, however, was rare. Laurens strove to unite the two revolutions, especially against a South Carolina that had rebelled to preserve bondage and that then had surrendered to the British sooner than recruit slaves.[111]

As a citizen-soldier, John Laurens served in every battle of Washington's, starting with Brandywine in 1777. In combat, Laurens showed the same courage that he did as an abolitionist. Serving great causes, he disregarded physical risk.[112] Throughout the Revolution, death was a near companion. At Germantown, Laurens "daringly attempted to fire the [Chew] house, but was unsuccessful." The British wounded him in the shoulder. At Monmouth the enemy killed his horse under him. In the battle of Rhode Island, he led citizen partisans. Laurens also helped heal a rift with the French. He thus combined the virtues of a diplomat—a fine sense of the views and interests of others—with those of a soldier. "It is not in my power," General Nathanael Greene informed Washington in August 1778, "to do justice to Colonel Laurens, who acted both the general and the partisan. His command of regular troops was small, but he did everything possible to be done with their numbers."[113]

In 1779 the British general Augustine Prevost nearly conquered South Carolina. At the battle of Tullifinny Hill, Laurens commanded the rear guard. On his own, he decided to lead his troops across the Coosawhatchie River. The redcoats defeated them and severely wounded Laurens. He was a daring but reckless soldier.

On May 12, 1780, the British captured Charlestown and took Laurens prisoner. Washington wrote to Laurens that he could not arrange an exchange. The Crown, however, ultimately paroled him.[114]

Though a soldier, aide to Washington, and later representative in the South Carolina legislature, John Laurens accepted no remuneration. Instead, his father supported him. On June 1, 1778, Laurens wrote gratefully, "You grant me a privilege which I wished to have, but dared not solicit. I shall serve my country with greater satisfaction, and regarding you as the source of all my happiness and the author of every laudable action of which I am capable, answer your friendship with increasing love. I have drawn no pay, and would wish never to draw any, making to my country a pure offering of disinterested services."[115] Laurens acted on a fierce sense of justice.

Others, however, continued to stress the pragmatic argument for emancipation. On March 14, 1779, from Washington's headquarters, Laurens's colleague as an aide to Washington, Alexander Hamilton, wrote a pointed antislavery letter to John Jay, the first president of the Continental Congress. Laurens conveyed the letter to Jay on his way to South Carolina after the congressional resolution to deal with the issue of black recruitment there.[116] Hamilton urged Jay "to raise two, three, or four battalions of negroes, with the assistance of that State [South Carolina], by contributions from the owners, in proportion to the number they possess." He aimed to offer three thousand blacks in South Carolina and Georgia "freedom with their muskets" and to engage these battalions "into Continental pay."[117]

Hamilton reminded Jay of the frail patriotism of the South and the looming threat of Britain. Without recruiting blacks, he said, "I hardly see how a sufficient force can be collected in that quarter . . . and the enemy's operations there are growing infinitely serious and formidable."[118] He urged American vigor: "If we do not make use of [blacks] in this way, the enemy probably will; and the best way to counteract the temptations they will hold out, will be to offer them ourselves."[119]

If South Carolina formed "black battalions," Hamilton stressed, Congress should excuse that state, "being very weak in her population of whites," from a draft. Furthermore, if North Carolina and Virginia would furnish "three thousand five hundred men," Congress should not compel them to send supplies to the Continental army. "It will require all the force and exertions of the three States I have mentioned to withstand the storm which has arisen and is increasing in the South," he wrote. "I fear this Southern business will become a very *grave* one."[120]

But Hamilton was also an eighteenth-century man of honor, and to

Jay, Hamilton offered two principled arguments similar to Laurens's.[121] First, he warned of the standard distortions of racism: "The contempt we have been taught to entertain for the blacks makes us fancy many things that are founded neither in reason nor experience; and an unwillingness to part with property of so valuable a kind will furnish a thousand arguments to show the impracticability or pernicious tendency of a scheme which requires such sacrifices."[122]

Hamilton was born out of wedlock on Nevis in the West Indies,[123] and as a recent immigrant he saw the Revolution as a way to advance honorably. As a child on Nevis, Hamilton had experienced poverty and seen the greater horror of slavery.[124] Freedom, he insisted, would, like fresh air, invigorate fighters: "An essential part of the plan is to give them freedom with their swords. This will secure their fidelity, animate their courage, and, I believe, will have a good influence upon those who remain, by opening the door to their emancipation."[125]

In addition, Hamilton specified how, under imperial pressure, abolition could have occurred during the Revolution. Liberation for thousands in South Carolina could have presaged emancipation in Virginia. Hamilton added, "The dictates of humanity and true policy equally interest me in favor of this unfortunate class of men."[126]

Like Laurens, Hamilton insisted that servitude prepared blacks to be good soldiers. If placed under "intelligent" command, he suggested jingoistically, "stupid" Russians make the best fighters: "Let officers be men of sense and sentiment; and the nearer the soldiers approach to machines, perhaps the better." He added, "I will venture to pronounce they cannot be put in better hands than those of Mr. Laurens."[127] Neither he nor Laurens understood that the hunger for freedom and longer terms of service would make blacks superior soldiers.

On May 22, 1779, Hamilton wrote Laurens that Patriot major James Monroe had set out from headquarters à la Don Quixote in "quest of adventures to the Southward." Facetiously, he likened Monroe to Laurens: "He seems to be as much of a knight errant as your worship; but as he is an honest fellow, I shall be glad he may find some employment, that will enable him to get knocked in the head in an honorable way."[128] If Laurens's project provided him an opportunity for exploits, Hamilton mused, this future president, as a man of honor, would incline to it: "He will relish your black scheme if any thing handsome can be done for him in that line."[129] In farewell, Hamilton added, "Let me know fully Yr. Southern affairs. They are interesting and critical. You are judicious and impartial. God bless you."[130]

In *De l'esprit des lois*, Montesquieu wrote acidly of honor as the principle of the French regime, the spirit that informed court life and war.[131] He argued that monarchy lacks the virtue that makes the citizens of an egalitarian republic uphold a common good. It prompts noble action not for its own sake but for the sake of standing out, of appearing brilliant. Moved by honor, individuals seek distinction. From a political point of view, Montesquieu suggested, this "false honor" has as good a result as true honor: it inspires courage. That distinction was exemplified in Hamilton's amusing remarks about Monroe's ardor for Quixote-like distinction.

But Montesquieu also envisioned rare possibilities for a true honor that unites virtue and brilliance. The St. Bartholomew's Day massacre of French Huguenots by the Catholic state in 1572 exemplified intolerance. Refusing to participate, Montesquieu reports, the Vicomte d'Orte sent a message to his king that torture was not "feasible for good citizens and brave soldiers."[132] "*Bons citoyens*," "*braves soldats*"—men of honor—could not conceivably butcher innocents or, in Laurens's case, sell humans into bondage. To be noble meant to stand up for the common good. Laurens's and Hamilton's sense of true honor resembles the vicomte's.

Still, honor was the code of monarchies, connected to dramatic inequalities, not to egalitarianism. In his exchange with Francis Kinloch, however, Laurens had mentioned something close to the sense of honor in monarchies—the striving of ambitious citizens to do great service for a common good. In saying that citizens could thus, like aristocrats, achieve distinction, Laurens fused republican abolitionism with his fierce sense of honor. He creatively modified Montesquieu.

Indicating how widespread elite support was for black recruitment, Laurens's papers include a brief note from South Carolina governor John Rutledge on May 26, 1779, advocating a "black levy."[133] This was a moment of statesmanship for Rutledge. Like Washington, many other American leaders saw the necessity for such recruitment, though some, particularly in the North, advocated it more fiercely than Rutledge. Although the Continental Congress passed Laurens's resolution, both in 1779 and again in 1782, the South Carolina legislature rejected it, and after this failure, Rutledge defended the interests of slave owners, including his own.

In November 1779, Benjamin Lincoln, the Patriot southern commander, warned Washington that South Carolina had only about 750 soldiers.[134] He urged Washington and the South Carolina legislature to recruit blacks. In March 1780, Lincoln insisted to Rutledge: "My own mind suggested the utility and importance of the measure as the safety of . . . [Charlestown] makes it necessary."[135] On May 12, for want of such recruits, Lincoln would lose the battle of Charlestown. The wisdom and boldness of Laurens's project impressed others with his principle and capacity.

In 1779, the Continental Congress not only had passed the Laurens resolution but also had appointed a committee of five, including Laurens, to address the problem "that . . . South Carolina . . . is unable to make any effectual efforts with militia, by reason of the great proportion of citizens necessary to remain at home to prevent insurrections among the negroes, and to prevent the desertion of them to the enemy."[136] Once again, imperial and American competition about emancipation inspired the report, which exhibited worry that "the state of the country, and the great numbers of those people among them, expose the inhabitants to great danger from the endeavors of the enemy to excite [Negroes] either to revolt or desert."[137]

Raising black troops in exchange for American freedom, the resolution argued, would siphon off the most militant and check their revolt for their own independence and against the revolt of the colonies. In the resolution's words, black brigades would "be formidable to the enemy from their numbers and discipline" and invigorate the effort to defeat Britain. Congress offered to pay each owner "a rate not exceeding one thousand dollars for each active, able-bodied negro man of standard size, not exceeding thirty-five years of age, who shall be so enlisted."[138]

However, that proposal stirred resentment in Rhode Island, where the Continental Congress had forced the state to compensate slave owners. Nevertheless, Congress saw the comparative weakness of patriotism in South Carolina and the need for black soldiers there who would be enthusiastic about winning their freedom. The delegates sensed that such a proposal foreshadowed gradual emancipation. While they offered to pay slave owners compensation for slaves recruited to the Patriot cause, however, Congress offered "no pay or bounty" to the blacks themselves, pleading lack of funds, but promised that at war's end, each would "be emancipated and receive the sum of fifty dollars."[139]

The Continental Congress recommended this proposal to South Carolina and Georgia. But South Carolina had allocated slaves as a "bounty"—a form of recruitment pay—to white enlistees: one adult for privates, three adults and a child for colonels. The legislature did not recruit blacks even as substitutes for whites. Instead, South Carolina's first "revolution" used bondage—including child slaves—to inspire its "Patriot" officers to patrol for escapees.

As we have noted, South Carolina thus rejected a "black levy." In what amounted to treachery, the governor's council considered sending a flag of truce to British general Augustine Prevost, whose troops threatened Charlestown.[140] "The howlings of a triple-headed monster that shed the baneful influence of Avarice, Prejudice and Pusillanimity defeated this plan," Laurens wrote grandiloquently to Washington.[141]

On September 1, 1779, David Ramsay described the lack of Patriot zeal to William Henry Drayton, a fellow delegate to the Continental Congress: "Money will not procure soldiers. The militia will not submit to a draught. . . . The patriotism of many people is vox et praeterea nihil [a voice and nothing more]. The measure for embodying the Negroes had about twelve votes; it was received with horror by the planters, who figured to themselves terrible consequences."[142] Georgia's legislature voted down a similar proposal.[143]

Hamilton's affection for the centralization of the government in the new republic, particularly for a national bank, is famous. He and John Laurens learned the need for central leadership from South Carolina's rejection of their abolitionism, a motive heretofore underestimated by historians.[144] A centralized regime may, perhaps rarely, promote equal rights—for instance, each individual's right not to be owned.

Of the rejection of black recruitment by South Carolina, Henry Laurens wrote to his son, "Your black regiment is blown up with contemptuous huzzas." Yet he overstressed the difficulty of creating it. Only the absence of any "federal" centralization, as well as South Carolina's shocking willingness to bow to the Crown sooner than free blacks, barred the measure's realization. Still, the father invoked a noble family tradition that extended back to his own father, also named John:

> I knew the pride and the naughtiness of the hearts of some of our fellow citizens would seduce them to spurn . . . the mode you speak of for completing our Confoederal Regiments; that the avarice of others would impel them to revolt from the proposition for erecting black battalions. . . . Nothing wonderful in all this. . . . It is certainly a great task effectually to persuade rich men to part willingly with the very source of their wealth. . . . You have encountered rooted habits and prejudices, than which there is not in the history of man recited a more arduous engagement. If you succeed you will lay the cornerstone for accomplishing a prediction of your Grandfather and your name will be honorably written and transmitted to posterity; but even the attempt without perfect success will, I know, afford you unspeakable self-satisfaction.

The work will at a future day be efficaciously taken up, and then it will be remembered who began it in South Carolina.[145]

The attempt was not easy. On July 14, 1779, John Laurens wrote angrily to Hamilton of "the successless harangues" he delivered in the legislature against South Carolina's treachery: "Ternant will relate to you how many violent struggles I have had between duty and inclination—how much my heart was with you while I appeared to be most actively employed here— but it appears to me that I shd be inexcusable in the light of a Citizen if I did not continue my utmost efforts for carrying the plan of black levies into execution, while there remains the smallest hope of success."[146]

Patriot troops had departed from South Carolina for Virginia, and South Carolina now had, Laurens wrote, a force "reduced to nothing."[147] If the Crown invaded, this remnant could not guarantee the state's security. South Carolina's militiamen had enlisted for only nine months, and few served long enough to become battle hardened, even when not used to catch escaped slaves. The need for black regiments had become ever more glaring.

Laurens wanted to excoriate his colleagues. In a letter to Hamilton, he exclaimed: "Oh that I were a Demosthenes—the Athenians never deserved more bitter exprobation than my Countrymen."[148] Demosthenes, the great orator, heroically fought for democracy against Phillip of Macedon and committed suicide rather than be captured by Antipater, the minion of Alexander "the Great."[149] In the Whig neoclassical tradition, Laurens saw himself as part of a grand heritage in which leaders speak out and some-times sacrifice themselves standing up for a democratic republic against the seductions of empire. Laurens valued principle above mere existence. He made "a final effort" in the assembly.[150]

For Hamilton, Laurens's proposal represented the interests of the com-mon good on both pragmatic and principled grounds, but he doubted its prospects: "I think your black scheme would be the best resource the situ-ation of your country would admit—I wish its success—but my hopes are very feeble. Prejudice and private interest will be antagonists far too pow-erful for public spirit and public good."[151] From this letter and the later *Federalist Papers*, we can see how easily Hamilton could abandon his con-victions on bondage. Still, in 1799, he fought for gradual emancipation in New York. Like Henry Laurens's and Washington's, Hamilton's affection for John Laurens brought out the best in him.[152]

In the nineteenth century, one of John Laurens's relatives, Martha Laurens Roper, owned the table on which delegates to the Continental Congress had signed the Declaration of Independence. To proclaim South Carolina's secession in the Civil War, the Confederacy requested its use. "[I will] burn it to ashes first," Martha Roper replied, her sense of honor fierce.[153] Central in South Carolina history, the Laurens family, across generations, fought for emancipation. As of the 2000 election, South Carolina still flew the Confederate flag. The state's "official" history effaces the history of the Laurens family, as has American history. However, they played a significant role in simultaneously advancing both of the two American revolutions.[154]

> *It is justifiable that Negroes should have their freedom, and*
> *none amongst us be held as slaves, as freedom and liberty is the*
> *grand controversy that we are contending for.*
> —Lieutenant Thomas Kench, "To the Honorable Council in Boston,"
> *April 3, 1778*

he second revolution could have sustained the first. The emancipation of America's black slave population in the name of the liberty for which the American Revolution was fought could have transformed a self-contradictory claim for universal natural rights restricted to whites into a genuine aspiration for equal freedom. In addition, from a practical point of view, the exclusion of blacks crippled the Patriot cause. In 1775 the colonies' population totaled two and a half million; of roughly half a million blacks, all but fifty thousand were in bondage. Many free Americans, perhaps one-third, became Loyalists, but a much higher percentage of blacks did.

Compared with the South, a smaller proportion of slaves and Tories lived in New England, where citizens were often more deeply committed to freedom. New England provided a disproportionately large number of troops to the American Revolution. The central role of free or newly freed black soldiers in Rhode Island, Connecticut, Massachusetts, and Pennsylvania served as a symbol of emancipation to more reactionary states. In their efforts to supply troops to the Continental army, the states soon exhausted the pool of available whites, and to fill enlistment quotas, several legislatures in the North focused on and occasionally manumitted blacks. Moreover, opting out of the Revolution, many white "citizens" presented blacks in their stead.[1] Thus, many Patriot soldiers were slaves or new ex-slaves.

As a consequence, in some northern states even before the Continental Congress passed the Laurens proposal to free and recruit blacks to the Patriot cause, the role played by free or newly freed black soldiers both paved the way for acceptance of the proposal and served as a symbol of emancipation to more reactionary states. While the enlightened opinions of elites and the pragmatic exigencies of the Revolutionary War motivated decision makers to accept freedom for America's black slaves, the ardor for liberty and the performance of black troops already enlisted in the Patriot cause contributed significantly to the mutual progress of the two revolutions.

Initially, Connecticut, Massachusetts, and Virginia barred slave enlistment with the Continental army. As in the South, elites there feared insurrections by armed blacks. But slave owners throughout the colonies could free individuals and offer them to the military in the master's place.[2] For instance, in what was a typical case, Elkanah Watson of Plymouth, Rhode Island, sent "Dolphin Negro" for "thirty days' service." Jonathan Giddings of New Fairfield, Connecticut, hired a black substitute throughout the war. In North Carolina, William Kitchen, a recaptured deserter, proffered Nate Griffin in his stead.[3] In turn, these blacks hoped that the Patriots would eventually grant freedom to those who fought. Yet these practices also make the ratio of enslaved to free blacks among Patriot troops hard to estimate. Ironically, these masters' very lack of patriotism for the new country led to freedom for many individuals.

Until defeat and lack of money to pay troops added their stimuli, however, Dunmore's example did not lead George Washington to emancipate slaves in exchange for recruitment. Still, a substantial number of the already free, as well as these substitutes for their owners, joined the Continental army in Rhode Island, Connecticut, and Massachusetts.[4] As a Hessian officer put it, "One sees no regiment in which there are not negroes in abundance, and among them are able-bodied, sturdy fellows."[5] Between October 22 and November 20, 1777, Colonel Christopher Greene led four hundred soldiers, mainly free blacks, in defending Fort Mercer on the Delaware River. According to historian Phillip Foner, "The black Continentals . . . successfully held off waves of attacks by superior numbers of Hessians and British regulars. Faced by overwhelming odds, Colonel Greene . . . abandoned the fort and withdrew with the surviving black soldiers in good order. He had been commended by Congress and his assignment to head the Rhode Island black battalion was a logical aftermath."[6]

In June 1778, two months after the battle of Monmouth, New Jersey, Alexander Scammell, an adjutant general, drafted a roster or "return" of blacks under Washington's command (see table 1). The list does not include those already recruited in Rhode Island; these were but a fraction of the black soldiers enlisted by the Patriots. In contrast to the Crown, however, this return reveals an aggressive American response to military necessity. These blacks were predominantly soldiers. "They were enrolled

TABLE 1. Return of Negroes in the Army, August 24, 1778

Brigades on command	Present	Sick	Absent	Total
North Carolina	42	10	6	58
Woodford	36	3	1	40
Muhlenburg	64	26	8	98
Smallwood	20	3	1	24
2d Maryland	43	15	2	60
Wayne	2			2
2d Pennsylvania	33	1	1	35
Clinton	33	2	4	39
Parsons	117	12	19	148
Huntington	56	2	4	62
Nixon	26		1	27
Patterson	64	13	12	89
Late Learned	34	4	8	46
Poor	16	7	4	27
Total	586	98	71	755

Source: Reprinted from George H. Moore, *Historical Notes on the Employment of Negroes in the American Army of the Revolution* (1862), 17.

in fourteen different regiments and represented several States," Scammell wrote. "Five hundred and eighty-six were in active service, out of a total muster of seven hundred and forty-two."[7] The list reveals substantial recruitment by Maryland, North Carolina, Pennsylvania, and even New Jersey, a bastion of slave-owning in the North.[8]

Nineteenth-century abolitionists and some modern historians maintain that blacks opted for whichever side would give them freedom.[9] Opposing bondage in the new United States, these abolitionists would have elicited no sympathy from mainstream American politicians by recognizing that initially blacks fought mainly for the Crown. However, these historians rightly argued that the same person could go back and forth between sides and that blacks from the same family sometimes fought for different sides. According to William Nell, a black abolitionist writing in the mid-nineteenth century:

Seymour Burr was a slave in Connecticut. . . . Though treated with much favor by his master, his heart yearned for liberty, and he seized an occasion to induce several of his fellow slaves to escape in a boat, intending to join the British, that they might become freemen; but being pursued by their owners, armed with the instruments of death, they were compelled to surrender. [Burr's owner] asked what inducement he could have for leaving him.

Burr replied that he wanted his liberty. His owner finally proposed, that if he would give him the bounty money, he might join the American army, and at the end of the war be his own man. Burr, willing to make any sacrifice for his liberty, consented, and served faithfully during the campaign, attached to the Seventh Regiment.[10]

In 1784, Nell also reports, the Loyalist Claims Commission in London heard the tragic story of Benjamin Whitecuff, a twenty-year-old New Yorker. Whitecuff's father, a Patriot sergeant, tried to recruit Benjamin and his elder brother. Out of conviction and perhaps a rebellion common among younger brothers, Benjamin sided with the Crown. He became a spy. Patriots captured and hanged Whitecuff from a tree. Before he strangled, however, imperial troops miraculously rescued him. According to the account, "His Father took the American side. . . . He would have persuaded him to go too but he refused. His older Brother went with [the Father]. . . . He was employed for 2 years as a Spy by Sir Henry Clinton and Sir William Ayscough. . . . He says he was hung up by the Rebels at Cranbury in the Jerseys for three minutes but was saved by a Detachment of the 5th light Company. . . . He has heard his Father was killed at Chestnut Hill. His Brother was killed at German Town."[11]

But lists compiled by today's historians often dramatically understate the number of blacks on the American side. They tend to be based only on the clearest indication that the names were of blacks, for instance, African, ancient Greek and Roman, and geographical first names or occasionally the surnames "Freedom" or "Negro." On most lists, however, these names make up but a fraction of the blacks enlisted by the Continental army.[12]

RHODE ISLAND

Among the earliest and most distinguished group of black recruits to the Patriot cause was the First Rhode Island Regiment. Scholars have often neglected the First Rhode Island, but even when they invoke it, they obscure the wider role of free black and Native American soldiers from that state.

In 1777 the Crown reconquered Newport, the capital of Rhode Island. Encamped at Valley Forge, the two Rhode Island Patriot battalions had few soldiers. On January 2, 1778, General James Mitchell Varnum wrote to Washington: "The two Battalions from the State of Rhode Island being Small, & there being a Necessity of the State's furnishing an additional Number to make up their Proportion in the continental Army; the Field Officers have represented to me the Propriety of making one temporary Battalion from the two, so that one entire Corps of Officers may repair to Rhode Island, in order to receive & prepare the Recruits for the Field. It is imagined that a Battalion of Negroes can be easily raised there."[13]

Writing for Colonel Christopher Greene, Lieutenant Colonel Jeremiah Olney, and Samuel Ward Jr., Varnum urged Washington to "give the officers employed in this business all the assistance in your power."[14] Washington forwarded Varnum's letter to Rhode Island governor Nicholas Cooke. In February, Cooke submitted the proposal to the state legislature.

The subsequent Rhode Island Resolution for Negro Recruitment of 1778 combined the two revolutions for American freedom. It declared: "That every slave so inlisting shall, upon his passing muster before Col. Christopher Greene, be immediately discharged from the service of his master or mistress, and be absolutely FREE, as though he had never been incumber'd with any kind of servitude or slavery."[15]

Debating the proposal in the legislature, a proslavery delegate suggested that the state could not consistently recruit "a band of slaves" to defend American liberties. In a revolution for the natural rights of man, the inconsistency lay in the bondage this delegate commended. As another delegate imagined, this act would subject Americans to ridicule by the British similar to the one "we so liberally bestowed upon them on account of Dunmore's regiment of blacks."[16] Yet opponents could suggest no alternate source of recruits.

The resolution recalled that the Roman Republic freed slaves to defeat Hannibal, stating that "history affords us frequent Precedents of the wisest, the freest, and bravest nations having liberated their Slaves and enlisted them to fight in Defence of their country."[17] In Rhode Island, imperial forces had conquered "the Capital . . . and a great part of this State," and the legislature declared that "every able-bodied *Negro*, mulatto, or *Indian* man slave . . . may inlist into either of the said battalions."[18] It mandated that "every slave so inlisting shall be entitled to and receive all the bounties, wages, and encouragements allowed by the Continental Congress." Rhode Island recruited Narragansett Indians mainly into the First Regiment.[19]

To recruit soldiers, the state offered to purchase slaves "at the rate of £120 for the most valuable." The resolution created a committee of five members of the Rhode Island General Assembly to oversee black enlistment: Thomas Rumreil of Newport; Joseph Humphrey of Warren; Judge Thomas Tillinghast of East Greenwich; Christopher Lippitt, former colonel of the Second Rhode Island Regiment; and Samuel Babcock of South Kingstown. Babcock had signed a slave-owners' petition against the resolution.[20] Even these committee members embodied the conflict over emancipation.

The resolution also called for reimbursement of the Rhode Island legislature by the Continental Congress for the purchase of slaves to free in order to fight on the Patriot side.[21] But Congress had not promised to recompense owners. Governor Cooke had written to Washington that whites would not enlist for what the Continental army could pay. The Patriot cause in and of itself did not inspire enough whites. Emancipation would move blacks more deeply. Enrolling blacks was thus feasible; it was, Cooke insisted, "impossible to recruit our battalions in any other way."[22] William Greene, the next governor, argued in the legislature that the demoralization of soldiers arising from "not having been paid their wages for several months past" was serious. [23] In contrast, he argued, freedom was a profound form of "pay" for blacks, though until long after the war it was their only wage.

On passage of the resolution, Cooke wrote to Washington, "Liberty is given to every effective slave to enter the service during the war; and upon passing muster, he is absolutely free, and entitled to all the wages, bounties and encouragements, given by Congress to any soldier enlisting into their service." Cooke added, "The number of slaves in this State is not great but it is generally thought that three hundred and upward will be enlisted."[24]

On February 19, 1778, a large crowd of blacks gathered in South Kingstown. According to Captain Elijah Lewis, some whites, notably Hazard Potter, attempted to frighten recruits.[25] Cuff Greene, a former slave of James Greene,[26] and Dick Champlin and Jack Champlin, who had belonged to Stephen Champlin, enlisted in the Continental army. In Narragansett or South County, which had the largest ratio of blacks to whites, approximately one in three joined. But owners campaigned to discourage blacks from enlisting. As Governor Cooke wrote to Nathanael Greene on April 19, 1778, "Your observation upon South Kingston in respect to the Negro Rigment is very Just; they are not pleased with it at all and grumble a good deal."[27]

Yet on the general treasurer's account, from February 25 to October 14, 1778, sixty-seven blacks joined: twenty in April, seventeen in May, thirteen in June, thirteen in July, one in August, two in September, and one in October.[28] Along with slave-owner "grumbling," the general assembly found its new defense of freedom frightening. On June 10, it decreed the great resolution "expensive and impractical" and sought to halt black recruitment.[29] But the combination of black zeal for freedom and Patriot military necessity rendered the later decree ineffective. According to muster rolls, enlistment in the black and Narragansett battalion continued until the close of the war.[30]

According to an initial return for the First Rhode Island Regiment, July 6, 1778, the four companies had 19 commissioned officers and 144 noncommissioned officers and privates.[31] On July 16, Nathanael Greene wrote to Washington that the regiment was "about 130 strong."[32] An additional company soon brought the total to 226 officers and enlisted men.[33] Historian Lorenzo Greene estimates that between 225 and 250 blacks—mostly slaves—signed up.[34] Given casualties, desertions, and discharges, as well as incomplete muster rolls, treasurer's lists, payrolls, and casualty lists, that figure is probably low.

Aside from the First Regiment, other free or newly freed black recruits served in Rhode Island. In December 1778, Captain Ebenezer Flagg's company had twenty-nine black privates and, in the ranks of those whose duties would later become icons in depictions of the American Revolution, one black fifer and one black drummer. In November 1778, Captain David Dexter's company had thirty-two blacks, and in April 1779, it had thirty-one. On December 31, 1779, the Second Company had thirty black privates and one black fifer.[35] In addition, skilled black workers included two tailors, one carpenter, seven coopers, three wagoners, three teamsters, and one blacksmith. Fifty-four black laborers amounted to roughly 10 percent of all minority recruits. Another 5 percent fought at sea. Twenty-three served as sailors, three as "captain's boys," three as waiters, two as "ships carpenters," two as cooks, and one as surgeon's mate.

More often than others, Rhode Island recruits kept their owner's surname. Some blacks came from the largest slaveholding families: Brittain Saltonstall from Dudley Saltonstall; Cato Greene from Governor William Greene; Cato Vernon from William Vernon of Newport; Jack, York, July, Newport, and Sharper Champlin from the slave merchants Hazard and Stephen Champlin of Newport and South Kingston; Mingo Robinson from Sylvester Robinson; and Jacob and Peter Hazard from Robert Hazard, one of the biggest landowners in New England. Curiously, no black on the list "belonged" to John Brown, the wealthy Providence revolutionary and slave trader after whom Brown University is named.

In 1855 William Nell recounted how freedom for blacks moved some owners who were patriotic about liberty. In *Colored Patriots of the American Revolution*, Nell reported, "When his master told him [the man's name is, unfortunately, not mentioned] that they were on the point of starting for the army, to fight for liberty, he shrewdly suggested, that it would be a great satisfaction to know that he was indeed going to fight for *his* liberty. Struck with the reasonableness and justice of this suggestion, Gen. S. [John Sullivan] at once gave him his freedom."[36]

To Patriots, the black First Rhode Island Regiment served as a standard of dedication. In the Battle of Rhode Island between August 5 and 31, 1778, the regiment defended the Continentals' right flank. According to Samuel Greene Arnold's *History of Rhode Island*, "Posted behind a thicket in the valley, [Sullivan's brigade] three times drove back the Hessians who charged repeatedly down the hill to dislodge them." The Hessian colonel promptly asked for a transfer "because he dared not lead his men into battle, lest his men shoot him for having caused so much loss."[37] In that encounter, the British suffered 247 dead or wounded, the Americans 167. Eleven were members of the First Rhode Island Regiment.[38] The regiment then fought in the South, including at the Battle of Yorktown. Its example contrasts strikingly with the slave-hunting Patriot militias of South Carolina and Georgia.

The average term of service in the regiment was three years. Many served for five.[39] The British killed 116 soldiers—18 percent of the regiment: one in five of them died in the Patriot cause. Thus, if we factor in shorter terms due to death, the average service among surviving soldiers probably nears four years. Coming from warrior cultures, Native Americans also served longer terms. In contrast, white militiamen engaged for, at most, twelve months. As Yorktown would reveal, blacks provided the core of American fighters.

In the Battle of Rhode Island, the redcoats took seventeen black prisoners.[40] The regiment's officers reported seven blacks as wounded.[41] In general, blacks suffered heavier casualties. At the battle of Fort Oswego on Lake Ontario in 1783, for instance, many lost fingers and limbs from frostbite. Like whites, blacks and Native Americans often deserted: eighty-two (nearly 13 percent) fled from the regiment during the war.[42] In the *Rhode Island Gazette*, the army advertised for twenty-seven of these men.[43] Revealing the Patriot's desperation for recruits, six were allowed to rejoin the regiment. Four were retaken. Five deserted twice.

Officers whipped black soldiers more frequently than they did whites. Colonels Greene and Olney ordered this punishment for leaving camp, abandoning one's post, or stealing. For instance, on June 15, 1779, for absence from camp, officers lashed Peter Hazard twenty times. On July 14, 1779, Prince Bucklin and Solomon Wanton arbitrarily received fifty lashes for the same offense. In contrast, on November 2, 1779, officers gave Fortune Watson only fifteen. Over five years, whippings brutalized 2 percent of the regiment. These examples terrorized others.

Yet these officers also staunchly defended black soldiers. On February 28, 1778, when the city of Providence arrested Prince Randal for a minor offense, Colonel Jeremiah Olney bailed him out. In 1858 abolitionist William Lloyd Garrison's *Liberator* reported a letter from a Captain Perkins to Brigadier General Nathanael Greene displayed at the commemoration of Crispus Attucks's death that year in Boston. Perkins told of the arrest of a Lieutenant Whitmarsh for abusing a black soldier at "Newport Rhode Island."[44]

Motivated by freedom and continually engaged in battle, the First Rhode Island Regiment developed its own spirit of militancy. It would become the most fearsome unit on the American side and inspire others throughout the war. In 1781 the regiment camped at Points Bridge in Croton, New York. On May 4, the redcoats staged a surprise attack, killing the commander, Christopher Greene, and a number of black soldiers, who defended him to the death.[45] Led by Lieutenant Colonel Olney, these Rhode Island soldiers would go on to fight at Red Bank, Yorktown, and Fort Oswego.[46]

No writing by any member of the First Rhode Island Regiment survives. Following the Revolution, however, Elleanor Eldridge, daughter or niece to three of these men—her mother was a Narragansett—learned to read and write and told her story. In contrast to the pretensions of biographers of the "great," she articulates the dignity of ordinary lives. On behalf of a younger brother and sister, Eldridge claimed land promised to her father for his revolutionary service. But she did not get it. Thus, the U.S. government betrayed both father and daughter. [47]

Still, Eldridge celebrates freedom. Her account sometimes seems grandiloquent to our ears, but is pointedly accurate: "At the commencement of the American Revolution, Robin Eldridge [her father], with his two brothers [Dick and George] presented themselves as candidates for liberty. They were promised their freedom with the additional premium of 200 acres in the Mohawk country, apiece."[48] Slave traders had abducted her grandfather (an African ruler), grandmother, and their children. Owners renamed them. In this case, kidnapping effaced the memory of original names, even in the next generation.

Eldridge is concerned, however, with the transfiguring aspect of freedom: "Oh, LIBERTY! What power dwells in the softest whisper of thy syllables, acting like magic upon the human soul! He who first woke thy slumbering echoes, was a magician more potent than ever dwelt in the halls of genii; for he had learned a spell that should rouse a principle of the soul, to whose voice, throughout the whole wide earth, every human spirit should respond." Freedom's "fires," she writes, moved her relatives to fight longer, in more difficult circumstances, and with greater enthusiasm than others, for instance, at the battle of Fort Oswego: "These poor slaves toiled on in their arduous duties; and while they literally left footprints of blood, upon the rough flint, and the crusted snow; they carried a fire within their bosoms which no sufferings could extinguish."[49]

Eldridge's words capture the exhilaration of liberty: "These slaves fought as bravely, and served as faithfully, under the banner of Freedom . . . as if the collar had never bowed down their free heads, nor the chain oppressed their strong limbs. . . . Did they not already see the morning star of FREEDOM, glimmering in the East? . . . Were they not soon to start up from the rank of goods and chattels into MEN?"[50]

In 1783 Rhode Island released Elleanor Eldridge's emancipated relatives from military service. But the Eldridges lacked resources to claim the promised land: "At the close of the war they were pronounced FREE; but their services were paid in the old Continental money, the depreciation, and final ruin of which, left them no wealth but the one priceless gem, LIBERTY. . . . Having no funds, they could not go to take possession of their lands on the Mohawk. And to this day, their children have never been able to recover them."[51] In effect, they weren't paid at all.

On behalf of her siblings, Elleanor Eldridge would pursue Robin Eldridge's claims. She spoke for her silent father, uncles, and thousands of others. Aside from her autobiography, these Eldridges have faded from history. Even Louis Wilson's list of members of the First Rhode Island Regiment does not include names that sound English. This omission again suggests how extensively such lists underestimate the number of black Patriots. Historians guess that five thousand blacks enlisted in the Continental army. Though others may, in the future, emulate Wilson's meticulous work, no way exists at this time to get an exact picture. The actual number was probably substantially higher.

The fate of black Patriot soldiers is a gauge of the uneven progress of American freedom. Lifting the independence movement from the bottom of the social order to victory at Yorktown, these men were a measure. On June 13, 1783, at Saratoga, New York, Rhode Island disbanded the regiment. Like other American soldiers, its members may not have been paid, but they had won their freedom. In a farewell address, Lieutenant Colonel Olney praised their "unexampled fortitude and patience through all the dangers and toils of a long and severe war." He lamented that "such faithful service has heretofore been so illy rewarded, and painful indeed is it to me to see the officers and men retire from the field without receiving any pay, or even their accounts settled and the balances ascertained."[52] These soldiers' dedication profoundly moved Olney. In 1784 Rhode Island would pass a gradual emancipation law that would free newborn boys and girls only at twenty-one and eighteen, respectively.[53] But the federal and state governments offered no payment to the soldiers. In 1789 black soldiers again petitioned the Treasury for lost wages, but to no avail.[54]

In 1791 Olney urged Arthur Fenner, secretary of the Rhode Island Abolition Society, to take up the case of Jack Burrough, one of the first "free black men" in the regiment.[55] New Orleans authorities had imprisoned him. Olney hoped the society would consider "his unhappy condition . . . and prosecute such Just and Efficacious measures as will prove the happy Consequence of his Speedy release and Return to the State in whose service he was engaged in the late War and thereby obtained his Freedom." Olney offered "cheerfully" to contribute expenses toward "delivering the Unfortunate." In addition, he reported that authorities had reenslaved Jack Champlin, another of the first recruits, at the island of Hesperides near Spain.[56]

On April 2, 1794, to Oliver Walcott, comptroller of the U.S. Treasury, Olney urged payment for seven members of the regiment: Job Burton, Jabez Remington, Abraham Devons, Wally Allen, Cato Bannister, James Northrup, and Peter Harris.[57] Because the last three had died, Olney requested income for their relatives. He also mentioned a March 13 letter, which has not survived, supporting five others.[58]

By the 1820s, Rhode Island finally honored these heroes of the Revolution, providing pensions and land to 23 percent of the blacks who were members of the First Regiment. Many had died, but the benefits also went to relatives: sixty-six received land, fifty-nine received pensions, and twenty-four received both land and a pension.

In Connecticut, Massachusetts, and Pennsylvania, similar fitful synergies between the struggle against British oppression and the struggle against the oppression of slavery played out in the years surrounding the American Revolution. As a result, in an epochal achievement, through legislation or judicial decisions, the northern states would gradually and, again, fitfully, unite the two revolutions.

In Connecticut many citizens took the idea of democracy seriously. Joining the army in 1775, Thomas Hooker of Farmington freed his slave: "I will not fight for liberty and leave a slave at home." In 1778 a Connecticut woman emancipated another "because I believe that all Mankind ought to be free."[59]

In 1776, on the grounds that bondage was "injurious to the poor and inconvenient," the Connecticut General Assembly banned the slave trade.[60] In May 1777, it formed a committee "to take into consideration the state and condition of the negro and mulatto slaves in this State, and what may be done for their emancipation." Written by Matthew Griswold of Lyme, the committee's report called for recruiting newly freed blacks to the Continental army. For determining "value" to be paid to former owners, it mandated estimates by town selectmen. The state would pay an owner the recruitment bounty ordinarily given the soldier and half the soldier's salary up to "value." Furthermore, if freed blacks could not subsist in their new circumstances, owners would owe them no support.[61] Though the lower house passed the bill, the upper house rejected it.

This proposal preceded Rhode Island's creation of a black regiment. Just as Washington's urging prompted the creation of the First Rhode Island Regiment, according to J. Hammond Trumbull, the mid-nineteenth-century Connecticut recorder of records, Washington's permission to enlist blacks "was regarded as a rule of action, both by the selectmen in making up, and by the State Government in accepting, the quota of the towns."[62] In May 1777, the assembly allowed that any two men "who should procure an able-bodied soldier . . . [for] either of the Continental battalions" could avoid military service.[63] As in Massachusetts, a lack of conscription for owners paid for black freedom: two owners were exempted for each black recruited.

This practice resulted in the case of Prince Dupleix, among others. From 1777 to 1780, Dupleix fought for Connecticut. Discharging him on June 1, the state paid him eleven pounds, two shillings, and three farthings. In Farmington, on September 18, Dupleix signed over his wages for the entire war—forty-four pounds, eight shillings, and three farthings—to one Jonathan Barnes.[64] Like most slaves, Dupleix could not write. A justice of the peace named Heart signed the certificate transferring the money in Dupleix's name.[65] From these records, we may infer that Barnes had been Dupleix's owner, that Prince had kept a different owner's name, that Dupleix had gone to war as a substitute for Barnes, and that Barnes had granted Dupleix his freedom for doing so. Alternately, Barnes might have paid Dupleix's owner and gotten Dupleix to substitute for him or for both Barnes and the owner. Dupleix then reimbursed Barnes in exchange for liberty.

Only Rhode Island enlisted more black soldiers than Connecticut. To celebrate their emancipation, Connecticut recruits often changed their names from those they had received in slavery. For instance, in the Second Company of the Connecticut Fourth Regiment, forty-eight blacks included ten—more than 20 percent—who did so: Jeffrey Liberty, Pomp Liberty, Sharp Liberty, Cuff Liberty, Dick Freedom, Ned Freedom, Cuff Freedom, Peter Freedom, Jube Freedom, and Prinnis Freedom. Among the 389 possibly black Connecticut soldiers identified by historian David White, twenty-four emancipatory names appear: Cash Affrica and Buel Africa, seventeen named Freedom or Freeman, and five named Liberty.[66] These contrast with a very large group, 139, indicated only by first name and the surname "Negro."[67] The choice of "Freedom" or "Africa" reveals black aspirations. The prevalence of "Negro" attests to the recruiters' slave-owning mentality.

Unlike what happened in Rhode Island, Connecticut's liberation of blacks in exchange for service was not universal, and not all blacks who fought for Connecticut were emancipated. The situation of Brister Baker, a New Haven soldier in the Second Regiment, is a case in point. Baker's discharge certificate, signed by George Washington, awarded him "the Badge of Merit for six years faithful service," from 1777 to 1783.[68] But Baker's owner liberated him only in 1784, saying that Baker "has been a good soldier . . . and capable of Business Equal to most white men in Way of Husbandry, and being . . . but about 38 years old . . . it is reasonable that he should be set free as he has been fighting for the Liberties of the Country."[69] Because, on average, blacks lived to around forty, Baker may not have enjoyed a long experience as a free man.

Perhaps because a public act emancipated those who served, no Rhode Island blacks took the name "Freedom." They had a deeper sense that they were free. Manumitted only haphazardly, perhaps Connecticut blacks adopted the name "Liberty" to inspire others and push Connecticut whites toward decency.[70]

Declaring themselves "friends to America, but slaves," eight blacks from Lyme—Great Prince, Little Prince, Luke, Caesar, Prue, and her three children—petitioned the general assembly for freedom. Ironically inverting the then-ordinary relationships between whites and blacks, they suggested that their "master," Colonel William Brown, fled "from his native country to his master, King George; where he now lives like a poor slave."

They prayed that "our good mistress, the free state of Connecticut, engaged in a war with tyranny, will not sell good honest Whigs and friends of the freedom and independence of America." This plea should have awakened the assembly. Appealing to whites, however, the blacks took too seriously the metaphorical enslavement of Patriots: "because the Whigs ought to be *free* and the *Tories* should be sold."[71] On the contrary, one might say, Tories should be vanquished, but no one should be enslaved.

Benjamin Harrison, a future president, leased out William Brown's confiscated estate. The lessee, Harrison suggested, could pay the rent and free the blacks.[72] Once again, the lower house assented to the petition, but the upper house "negatived" it. Exemplifying Connecticut's tepid fealty to freedom, a conference committee deadlocked.

Among Washington's aides, David Humphreys of Connecticut, like John Laurens and Alexander Hamilton, urged emancipation in exchange for fighting and sought to abolish slavery. According to Frank Landon Humphreys, David Humphreys's relative and biographer, "There were about one hundred [black troops] scattered throughout the fifty or more companies in the Connecticut Line. When the . . . consolidation took place . . . on January 1, 1781, the Connecticut negro soldiers appear to have been brought together into one company in Colonel Butler's regiment and put under the nominal command of Col. Humphreys. It is a tradition that he was one of the first men in the country to recognize the possibilities of the Negro as a soldier, and by his own influence and that of his faithful body-servant, Jethro Martin, among people of his own race, created much enthusiasm for the cause of freedom among the Negroes of Connecticut."[73]

Servants often fought heroically for the Crown. On the American side, Jethro Martin, Humphreys's servant, and William Lee, George Washington's, fought alongside them. On both sides, the status of servant was not sharply distinct from soldier. But imperial servants were free.[74]

The Second Company of Connecticut's Fourth Regiment had black privates and white officers.[75] As White found, "Close to three hundred black soldiers can be unmistakably identified as serving either in Connecticut's regiments of the Continental Army or with the State militia. Names on Connecticut's military rolls suggest that more than one hundred others were also black. These three to four hundred soldiers made up less than two percent of Connecticut's Revolutionary troops. While this is a small percentage, it should be noted that blacks made up only three percent of Connecticut's population and that almost all of the black enlistees served in the Continental Army which saw more duty than the State militia."[76]

White's cautious estimate discounts even one hundred whom he lists by name and who were probably black. As in guesses about blacks in Rhode Island, White's number understates—perhaps quite dramatically—the number of blacks who served in the Continental army from Connecticut. In that state, legislative debates and the widely known role of black soldiers encouraged a general recognition of freedom. In 1784, the same year that Rhode Island freed its slaves, the Connecticut legislature, too, affirmed gradual emancipation.

MASSACHUSETTS

Like Rhode Island and Connecticut, Massachusetts had difficulty recruiting white soldiers. In 1777, to fill its quota of fifteen regiments, the Massachusetts legislature reversed Washington's ban on black enlistment and recruited everyone but Quakers. In 1778 it included enlistment of "Negroes." On April 3, 1778, Thomas Kench, an artillery captain, proposed to the state representatives to recruit a black regiment in return for immediate freedom. Kench offered to lead the troops himself: "A re-enforcement can quickly be raised of two or three hundred men. Will your honors grant the liberty, and give me the command of the party? And what I refer to is negroes."[77]

Massachusetts already has "divers of them in our service,' Kench noted, "mixed with white men." With keen insight into the military impact of slaves' hunger for freedom, he suggested that it would be "proper to raise a body by themselves," to recruit an all-black regiment, for "their ambition would entirely be to outdo the white men in every measure that the fortune of war calls a soldier to endure." Subduing the invader, they would win "a peaceful inheritance" for themselves and their former masters.[78]

Mirroring British companies, Kench envisioned white commissioned officers and an orderly sergeant. Yet he also suggested "three sergeants black, four corporals black, two drums and fifes black, and eight-four rank and file."[79] Though Kench asked for one company, he left open the possibility of more. "And I doubt not," he concluded too easily, "that no gentleman that is a friend to his country will disapprove of this plan, or be against his negroes enlisting into the service to maintain the cause of freedom, and suppress the worse than savage enemies of our land."[80]

On April 7, however, Kench wrote of a "disturbance with Col. Seares, Mr. Spear, and a number of other gentlemen, concerning the freedom of negroes, in Congress Street." Even in Massachusetts, with its comparative zeal for liberty, the cause of freedom for blacks often lost. In contrast, with a telling sense of America at its best, "as freedom and liberty is the grand controversy that we are contending for," Kench argued to the

Massachusetts House of Representatives, Patriots should emancipate blacks. But he now knew the legislators better: "I will not enlarge, for fear I should give offense."[81]

The legislature rejected Kench's proposal. Still, it appointed two committees, one from each house, to study the recent Rhode Island measure to recruit a black regiment. And ultimately, Massachusetts formed two black companies, one under Major Samuel Lawrence and the other, "the Bucks of Massachusetts," commanded by Colonel George Middleton. The latter was the only Patriot unit led by a black man.

Few traces survive of this Massachusetts company. The Bucks were the last black company formed on the American side, and they fought at Yorktown in 1781. Atypically, no record of numbers of men or their service in particular battles exists. But in 1783, Governor John Hancock would present the company with an elegant white-and-blue silk flag embroidered with a rearing deer, a pine tree growing out of the earth, and thirteen stars. It had initials on it—J GW H—from Hancock and George Washington.[82]

Though abolitionists would celebrate black revolutionary efforts, a tidal wave of racism flooded over many stories. For instance, reprintings of John Trumbull's engraving of the Battle of Bunker Hill "white out" black soldiers.[83] Apparently, although the Bucks fought for the Continental army, they did not do so as regular troops. They may have fought as guerillas. Alternately, the Bucks may have served as a local militia to defend Boston. At age fourteen, however, James Forten encountered black companies marching through Philadelphia to join Washington and confront "Lord Cornwallis, [who] was overrunning the South, when thick gloom clouded the prospect." According to William Nell, Forten recalled that "I saw . . . when the regiments from Rhode Island, Connecticut, and Massachusetts marched through Philadelphia, that one or two companies of Colored men were attached to each."[84] His glimpse suggests the striking role of blacks, though not the larger estimates—25 percent of the Continental forces at Yorktown—of Baron Ludwig von Closen, an aide to Rochambeau, and Georg Daniel Flohr, a private in Rochambeau's forces, who observed the troops more closely. Very likely, the Bucks were one of these units.[85]

Except for the account of Nell, no official records connect Colonel Middleton to the Bucks. Yet the family of abolitionist Lydia Maria Child lived across the street from Middleton, and she referred to him as "Colonel" and "commander of the Bucks." Like many white Christian opponents of bondage, Child had a patronizing bent.[86] In an odd remark, she wrote that Middleton "was not a very good specimen of the colored man. . . . His morals were questioned." Middleton married three times, which perhaps provides part of the reason for her comment. She added, "He was passionate, intemperate and profane." Child, however, might have dwelt on another of her observations: "He was greatly respected by his own people, and his house was thronged with company."[87]

Each year, she recalled, racists attacked black celebrations of the congressional ban on the slave traffic: "Our negroes,[88] for many years, were allowed peaceably to celebrate the abolition of the slave trade; but it became a frolic for the white boys to deride them on this day, and finally, they determined to drive them, on these occasions, from the [Boston] Common. The colored people became greatly incensed by this mockery of their festival, and this infringement of their liberty, and a rumor reached us, on one of these anniversaries, that they were determined to resist the whites, and were going armed, with this intention."[89]

As a veteran of the Revolution, Middleton brooked no intimidation by racist thugs. When a melee broke out, Middleton appeared with a gun and rallied the blacks:

About three o'clock in the afternoon . . . terrified children and women ran down Belknap Street, pursued by white boys, who enjoyed their fright. The sounds of battle approached; clubs and brickbats were flying in all directions. Col. Middleton opened his door, armed with a loaded musket, and, in a loud voice, shrieked death to the first white who should approach. Hundreds of human beings, white and black, were pouring down the street, the blacks making but a feeble resistance, the odds in number and spirit being against them. Col. Middleton's voice could be heard over every other, urging his party to turn and resist to the last. His appearance was terrific, his musket was leveled, ready to sacrifice the first white man that came within its range.[90]

Middleton disrupted the terrorizing of blacks. Following his resistance, Captain David Lewis intervened with the racists, while Child's father interceded with Middleton. Child's account shows that Middleton was accustomed to leading in battle.

As it did a century and a half later, when the color barrier in the U.S. armed forces finally was dismantled after World War II, the participation of black troops and black leaders such as Middleton on the Patriot side in the American Revolution helped advance the revolution that led to the abolition of slavery in the North. In 1780 the state legislature added a Bill of Rights to the Massachusetts Constitution. Ruling on a series of cases brought by slaves, the courts outlawed bondage. However, that did not mean that free blacks and whites enjoyed equal rights, and the role being played by black recruits in the revolt against Great Britain supplied those who would further the revolt against inequality with arguments for equal treatment under the law.

For example, Paul and John Cuffe were free citizens of Massachusetts, yet they could not vote. Income restrictions on suffrage denied the vote to free blacks and poor whites alike.[91] In response, in a precursor of Thoreau's civil disobedience, the Cuffes refused to pay their taxes. On February 10, 1780, in a petition to the legislature, they invoked the Boston Tea Party, indicting the first revolution from the standpoint of the second by the core moral standard of its proclamation "No taxation without representation": they were disenfranchised and not represented, but "contrary to the invariable custom and practice of the Country, we have been, and now are, taxed both in our Polls and that small pittance of estate which, through much Hard Labor and industry, we have got together to sustain ourselves and families." The Cuffes also noted that "by reason of Long Bondage and hard Slavery, we have been deprived of enjoying the profits of our Labor or the advantage of inheriting estates from our Parents, as our Neighbors the white people do, having some of us not long enjoyed our own Freedom."[92]

On May 10, 1780, petitioning a Dartmouth town meeting, the Cuffes condemned the inconsistency of denying the vote to free blacks "with the liberty we are contending for." Their petition asked to expunge a clause that required for suffrage "an annual income of three pounds or an estate of the value of sixty pounds." The Cuffes' measure linked the interests of whites and blacks, long visible in ethnically diverse revolutionary crowds. I found no record, however, that the Dartmouth council responded to the petition.[93]

On February 18, 1781, the Cuffes had praised the numerous black Patriots of Massachusetts: "We think that we may be clear from Being Called tories though some few of our Colour hath Redcoats & some wickedly however we think that there is more of our Colour gone into the Wars according to the number of them into the Republican [word unclear] troops."[94] This petition shows why at least five thousand blacks fought to extend the liberties spelled out in the Declaration of Independence. Yet the General Court ignored it. In 1783, however, finally responding to the Cuffes, the Massachusetts legislature voted to unite taxation to suffrage for all citizens.[95] Politically and philosophically, in northern states such as Massachusetts, the second revolution's abolitionists, both black and white, understood liberty and democratic representation more profoundly than the Patriots of the first.

The situation in Pennsylvania was more complicated. Given the powerful impact of Quakers on other Protestants and the role of urban artisans, Pennsylvania had a strong abolitionist movement. It also had a strong proslavery interest, and many slaves in Pennsylvania had fled to the Crown to gain freedom. In 1780 Pennsylvania was to become the first major colony to emancipate blacks. (Vermont, though not part of the thirteen original colonies, freed blacks in its 1777 constitution.[96]) Also, Pennsylvania enlisted fewer blacks in the war than Rhode Island, Connecticut, or Massachusetts. Only gradually did Pennsylvania's antiracists proclaim abolition as a goal, and this gradualism interfered with the mutual progress of the two revolutions.

In April 1775 at the Rising Sun Tavern in Philadelphia, ten citizens founded the Society for the Relief of Free Negroes Unlawfully Held in Bondage. Initially, Quaker artisans and shopkeepers, led by Thomas Harrison, a tailor, made up the society's membership. Unfortunately, they took a retrograde legal position, challenging only wrongful or illegal enslavement of individuals.[97] Referring to individuals held unlawfully as slaves, even this group's name indicates liberty's precariousness in America.

The society proceeded only on a case-by-case basis. For example, when slave traders seized Dinah Nevell, a free black and Indian woman, and her three children and sold her to a Virginian, Benjamin Bannerman, Harrison and Israel Pemberton, a merchant, sued on her behalf. A Pennsylvania court ruled for Bannerman. Harrison then convinced Samuel Moore, a Philadelphia brewer, to purchase Nevell and two of her children. Moore transferred ownership to Harrison, who manumitted them. I found no information about the fate of the third child.[98]

The first emancipations in Pennsylvania were acts by individual owners. Between 1767 and 1774, thirty-eight owners freed forty-four blacks (one in fifteen of those in slavery in the colony).[99] During the Revolution, fifty-six owners emancipated another one hundred—15 percent of the slaves in Pennsylvania. Practical motivations joined spiritual insights into equality and humility. Many artisans and merchants concluded that wage labor protected them against economic downturns. While they could fire the workers, they would have to provide for slaves, however miserably.

And as in the South, the Loyalist cause seemed to offer greater prospects for the success of the second revolution than did the Patriot standard. In 1777 British commander William Howe's victory at Philadelphia spurred black escapes. Historians Gary Nash and Jean Soderlund found that "scores of slaves from the region fled their masters when the British occupied the city in September 1777, and still more when the British evacuation began in 1778. Probably at least one hundred were crowded onto the ships . . . with the British army. Eighteen months later, a Philadelphia newspaper reminded readers that 'by the invasion of this state . . . [a] great part of the slaves hereabout, were enticed away by the British army.'"[100] However, this dynamic would spur Patriot efforts to unify the two revolutions in Pennsylvania. A concatenation of causes—Christian doctrine, public discussion of natural rights, fear of insurrection, imperial recruitment, and the unprofitability of slavery—all shook the legitimacy of bondage.[101]

In August 1778, when George Bryan, an abolitionist, became acting president of the Pennsylvania Executive Council, competition with the British for the recruitment of black slaves to the Patriot cause exerted a powerful influence on Pennsylvania law. As Bryan wrote, "No period seems more happy for the attempt [at abolition] than the present, as the number of [slaves] . . . ever few in Pennsylvania has been much reduced by the practices & plunder of our late invaders."[102] But gradualism remained characteristic of Pennsylvania's response to the contradiction posed by slavery in a revolution undertaken in the name of freedom. In November the council endorsed gradual emancipation. Freeing black children at age twenty-one would provide for "the general abolition of Servitude for life . . . in an easy mode."[103]

Yet the Pennsylvania house did not respond to Bryan.[104] Three months later, however, the council proclaimed that bondage disgraced a nation ostensibly fighting for liberty. Its draft emancipation law required children to work for their mothers' masters as indentured servants and freed girls at eighteen and boys at twenty-one. Affirming the rule of law, the measure mandated the use of the same courts for free blacks and whites. It barred subjection of black redcoats captured by the Patriots to beating or hanging and banned the further importation of slaves.

Still, this document limited the testimony of slaves to cases involving other slaves. Furthermore, it barred interracial marriage.[105] For violations, this measure fined blacks one hundred pounds or sentenced them to servitude for seven years. Another reactionary clause bound blacks to service "if they refused to support themselves."[106] But the legislature would not pass the measure.

Responding to an abolitionist groundswell among citizens, however, a legislative committee that included Bryan revised the bill. A new preamble likened American despotism toward blacks to British tyranny. Abolition would provide "substantial proof," in Bryan's new preamble, of

Pennsylvania's gratitude for escaping the Crown. This bill dropped the ban on intermarriage and the threat of renewed servitude for blacks who could not support themselves.[107] Still, even the new bill delayed emancipation until blacks reached age twenty-eight.

Lively public deliberations marked the long Pennsylvania campaign against bondage. For instance, when Chester County's representatives resisted, Bryan published a series of "Letters to a Minister." Invoking Quakers to shame Presbyterians, he noted, "Quakers, who we think have but clouded views of the gospel, have nearly cleared their society of this opprobrium of America." Would Presbyterians be "so void of charity and justice, as to . . . labour for the continuance of it?" By maintaining a class of internal enemies, Bryan argued, bondage conflicted with democracy. He stressed the military threat of English recruitment and emancipation. Only American abolition could remove the cause. Moreover, the labor of free workers would outproduce that of bondsmen. In a burgeoning workforce, Bryan suggested, emancipation would accompany a new emigration from Europe. Competing with states dependent on servitude, Pennsylvania would benefit from reliance on free workers.[108]

In November 1779, by a vote of thirty-eight to eight, the house adopted the bill. But Philadelphia slave owners soon moved to restore bondage. In 1781, in the *Freedmen's Journal*, Cato would avow that "I am a poor negro who with my wife and children have had the good fortune to get my freedom. I am told the assembly are going to pass a law to send us all back to our masters. . . . This would be the cruellest act. . . . To make a law to hang us all would be merciful."[109] Even Pennsylvania's emancipation enabled slave owners to exploit bondspersons and their children for nearly their whole lifetime. For the first two generations, blacks such as Cato found promises of "gradual" emancipation hollow.

In the South, on the Patriot side, John Laurens had struggled, with limited success, to recruit and free black fighters to fight for the colonies' independence. In the North, emancipation and independence more often could serve as common ends, although even there, proponents of the first revolution resisted the second. As we will see next, however, in the South, where proponents of independence often feared the consequences of emancipation, it was the opposition between the two revolutions, not their possible consonances, that drove the recruitment of blacks—recruitment on the side of those fighting to prevent the independence of the colonies.

chapter 5 ¶ Black Fighters for Freedom
British Recruitment and the Two Revolutions

But the instant that the King's Troops are put in motion in those Colonies, these poor Slaves would be ready to rise upon their Rebel Masters, and be a great means for compelling them to seek refuge in the interior Provinces.
—Lieutenant Colonel Moses Kirkland of the South Carolina Royal Militia to His Majesty's Commissioners, October 21, 1778

ritish recruitment of blacks was massive, and, particularly in the South, blacks aided the British more than the Patriots. On March 16, 1777, Lord William Howe briefly repudiated black recruitment, including his own Company of Negroes, declaring "The Commander in Chief being desirous that the Provincial Forces should be put on the most Respectable Footing, and according to his first Intention be composed of His Majesty's Loyal American Subjects, has directed that all Negroes, Mullatoes, and other Improper Persons who have been admitted into these Corps be immediately discharged."[1] Yet nothing could silence the reverberations from Dunmore's 1775 proclamation. In August 1777, Howe emancipated blacks who joined his Chesapeake armada to attack Philadelphia;[2] a surviving return—a military roster list—records 518 recruits.[3] And in 1779 and 1780, in Georgia and South Carolina, blacks thronged to the Crown. Surviving rosters and stories underline black participation in the American Revolution on the British side. Freed slaves would fight prominently in the siege of Savannah and the battle of Charlestown. By relying on blacks, the British pressed the Patriots to do the same.

Because Tory slave owners in the South feared a Patriot victory, they could not prevent the commandeering of blacks to royal forces or overly lament their flight to the defense of their former owners' other interests. In any case, Tory slave owners had cast their lot with the imperial side and could not suddenly become Patriots because of the loss of some slaves. However, the attitudes of those on the British side who employed the blacks who fought for freedom were sometimes as racist as those of the slave owners from whom the black soldiers and their families had escaped. Even with the British, freedom for blacks, especially former slaves of Tories, was uncertain. Nevertheless, as surviving stories of blacks reveal, a fairy-tale heroism characterizes escapees from Patriot plantations—especially the exploits of a black recruit from Colt's Neck, New Jersey, who would become known as the tactically brilliant Colonel Tye.

PRAGMATISM, NOT PRINCIPLE

The motives that led many British military leaders to advocate the emancipation of black slaves and their recruitment to the British cause tended to be pragmatic in the extreme. They were not themselves abolitionists, but they did not let their racist attitudes interfere with what seemed like a winning military strategy. In a letter to His Majesty's Commissioners, Lieutenant Colonel Moses Kirkland, a sawmill owner in South Carolina, explained his rationale for enlisting blacks to defeat their "Rebel Masters": "It is well known that the principal resources for carrying on the Rebellion are drawn from the labour of an incredible multitude of Negroes in the Southern Colonies, who are daily driven by their hard task-masters in the manufacture of Rice, Indigo, Tobacco, Hemp, Wheat and Indian Corn, and also in raising stock of all kinds. These are the [unreadable word] that support the credit of the Paper-Currency, and enable the Congress to draw supplies from every part of this Continent as well as from Europe and the West Indies." [4]

Kirkland wanted to deprive the Americans of resources and secure them cheaply for the British. As his memorandum argued, "That prodigious quantity of Hemp, Tar, Pitch and Turpentine, which support the Navy of the Congress, might then be converted to the cause of His Majesty, and those Colonies abroad. . . . The Army might in great measure be supplied with Provisions without the expense of transporting them across the Atlantic." [5]

In addition, Kirkland suggested that an attack by imperial troops would cause blacks "to rise upon their Rebel Masters" and at the least force them to flee their estates. Yet given his attitude regarding blacks as a source of labor, not as humans endowed with natural rights, it is not surprising that his letter nowhere mentions arming former slaves. While the Crown would organize black redcoats and even irregular black units in South Carolina, its failure to rely mainly on armed blacks would undercut a powerful advantage.

Instead, the Crown extensively relied on blacks in other, quasi-military roles. As foreigners, the redcoats would have foundered without local information, and in exchange for freedom, the British set up many companies of "Black Pioneers," composed of guides and spies. For instance, the

1778 capture of Savannah, which initiated the imperial reconquest of the South, was aided by Quamino Dolly, an "aged Negro" who appeared at the tent of Lieutenant Colonel Archibald Campbell, British commander in Georgia. Dolly offered to show the British forces a "private way" through the swamps behind the American lines.[6] And German captain Johann Hinrichs wrote in his journal that "negroes" had reported an enemy patrol in South Carolina that captured imperial soldiers at "William Ashby's house." They also guided redcoats to "South River."[7] In addition, blacks did most of the heavy work for the Crown. They lugged artillery and constructed and repaired forts. Blacks cooked, worked as servants or mistresses to imperial officers, found horses, foraged, and did many other jobs.

Just as the will to free blacks to serve in their respective causes waxed and waned on both sides with the needs of the war, the roles played by blacks swiftly shifted as well. On the British side, Boston King had originally entered "the service of the commanding officer" of Nelson's Ferry, South Carolina. But servants often served as messengers. The Americans had 1,600 soldiers nearby, the British 250. "We expected to be made prisoners every day," King wrote in his autobiography. But 1,200 royal soldiers camped only thirty miles away. "Promising great rewards," King recalled later, the commander sent him with a letter to obtain help. In his story, the perils stand out. That King bore such risks attests to how much he valued British freedom:

> I refused going on horse-back, and set off on foot about 3 o'clock in the afternoon; I expected every moment to fall in with the enemy, whom I well knew would shew me no mercy. I went on without interruption, till I got within six miles of my journey's end, and then was alarmed with a great noise a little before me. But I stepped out of the Road. And fell flat upon my face till they were gone by. I then arose . . . and again pursued my journey till I came to Mums-corner tavern. I knocked at the door, but they blew out the candle. I knocked again, and intreated the master to open the door. At last he came with a frightful countenance, and said, "I thought it was the Americans; for they were here about an hour ago, and I thought they were returned again." I asked, "How many were there?" He answered, "About one hundred."

King was near the lines of the British he was seeking. He asked the man "to saddle his horse for me, which he did, and went with me himself."[8]

Among white Loyalists and redcoats, the necessities of war thus sometimes broke through the general climate of racism toward blacks. Still, a

Colonel Small rewarded Boston's courage mainly with words: "When we had gone about two miles, we were stopped by the picket-guard. . . . As soon as he knew that I had brought an express from Nelson's-ferry, he received me with great kindness, and expressed his approbation of my courage and conduct in this dangerous business. Next morning, Colonel Small gave me three shillings, and many fine promises which were all that I ever received for this service from him. However he sent 600 men to relieve the troops at Nelson's-ferry."[9]

In terms of pragmatic military strategy from the British point of view, one of the ways in which the emancipation and recruitment of black slaves could serve the British cause was simply by diverting the resources of the enemy into trying to suppress the revolt and escape of slaves throughout the South. In South Carolina and Georgia, colonial militias fought the Crown only occasionally. Instead, these states assigned their regular troops to quell black insurrections or impede black flight to the British. In 1777 American general Robert Howe suggested that the state assembly deploy seven thousand to eight thousand soldiers to check the "numerous black domestics who would undoubtedly flock in multitudes to the Banners of the enemy whenever an opportunity arrived."[10] In 1778, fearing "the vast number of Negroes we have, perhaps of themselves sufficient to subdue us," the Georgia Assembly assigned one-third of each county's forces to local patrol. In 1779, faced with royal campaigns in the South, the legislature allowed South Carolina to be conquered rather than mobilize slaves to fight. On January 9, 1779, Lieutenant Colonel Campbell wrote that southern blacks "do ten thousand times more Mischief [to the cause of independence] than the whole army put together."[11]

As the British attempted to reconquer the South, Patriots especially punished black Loyalists. In 1779 a rare South Carolina list "of persons . . . taken in arms against the united states" included a "negro fellow of Mr. Odum's." This unnamed prisoner jauntily "broke custody[,] insulted the centry & carried off his hat & gun." The Americans recaptured him. Revealing the emptiness of Patriot slogans about freedom, they "tried [him] as the law directs in such cases," in accordance with the 1740 Negro Act.[12]

Conversely, the British were delighted to recruit former slaves from prominent Patriots. Thomas Jefferson was among those who lost slaves to the prospect of freedom offered by the British: Jefferson's farm book recorded at least thirty blacks from Monticello who "joined [the] enemy" or "fled to the enemy & died" or "caught smallpox from [the] enemy and died."[13] After the Revolution, Jefferson wrote a surprising letter to Dr. William Gordon. In an owner's rather than a citizen's lament, he denounced

Cornwallis for ravaging his estate in 1781 and "carrying off" the thirty. Jefferson could not acknowledge that black hatred of him ran high or that the Crown had brought freedom for many blacks that he had celebrated only for whites. According to Jefferson, Cornwallis showed special venom for the property of the author of the Declaration of Independence: "Lord Cornwallis destroyed all my growing crops of corn and tobacco; he burned all my barns, containing the same articles of the last year; he used, as was to be expected, all my stock of cattle, sheep, and hogs, for the sustenance of his army, and carried off all the horses capable of service; and he burned all the fences on the plantation, so as to leave it an absolute waste. He carried off also about thirty slaves. . . . Had this been to give them freedom, he would have done right."[14] Ironically, his last remark reflects English conduct accurately. The Crown did right to free blacks. Jefferson could not, however, praise this emancipatory element in an empire seeking to crush the independence of the comparatively privileged.[15] Writing to Gordon, Jefferson also guessed at the number of blacks who escaped in Virginia—thirty thousand to Cornwallis in 1781 alone. Yet this figure would make the overall numbers escaping in Virginia throughout the war, including those who fled to Dunmore, Howe, and Arnold, even higher.

Tory slaveholding and royal participation in the slave trade could deter British enlistment, and because so much Loyalist wealth stemmed from bondage, John Adams hoped, in vain, that the Crown would shun freeing and recruiting blacks. Of Archibald Bullock and John Houston, two Georgia delegates to the Continental Congress, Adams wrote in his diary: "These gentlemen gave a melancholy account of the State of Georgia and South Carolina. . . . The negroes have a wonderful art of communicating intelligence among themselves; it will run several hundreds of miles in a week or fortnight. They say their only security is this: that all the king's friends, and tools of government, have large plantations, and property in negroes."[16]

But military necessity often overrode private advantage. Pragmatism and principle had combined to foster black recruitment and emancipation on the Patriot side in the North in the wake of Britain's Dunmore Proclamation in the South. Military necessity could, in turn, serve as a rationale for more extensive black recruitment and emancipation by the British in the South, despite the interests of Tory slave owners to the contrary.

One result was British commander Henry Clinton's 1779 proclamation: "Whereas the Enemy have adopted a practice of enrolling Negroes among their troops, I do hereby give notice that all Negroes taken in war or upon any military Duty shall be purchased for the Public Service. . . . I do most strictly forbid any person to call or claim right over any Negro the property of a Rebel who may take refuge with any part of this army. And I do promise to any Negro who shall desert the Rebel Standard full security to follow within these Lines any occupation which he may think proper." From July 3 through September 25, 1779, each issue of *Rivington's Royal Gazette* ran the proclamation.[17] Recapturing Charlestown in 1780, Clinton renewed the promise. His proclamation brought large numbers of blacks—women and children, as well as men—to the imperial side.

Subsequently coining the slogan "Freedom and a Farm," Clinton proposed postwar resettlement of freed blacks on lands forfeited by Patriots. When ex-slaves swore allegiance to the Crown, they hoped to receive the same benefits as other Loyalists: land, provisions, and the rights of an Englishman.[18] As the pseudonymous Patriot writer Antibiastes observed in 1779, "Our non-emancipated soldiers are almost irresistibly tempted to desert to our foes, who never fail to employ them against us."[19] Following the Rhode Island example, Antibiastes's implication was to emancipate them and others.

Under Clinton's proclamation, freed blacks, including those previously deemed unfit for military service, could take up any occupation, and many became soldiers. Clinton's proclamation inspired the formation of the Black Carolina Corps in South Carolina and—despite Clinton's attempt to discourage it—the arming of blacks throughout the South.

BRITISH RECRUITMENT

Only a few returns for British troops survive in the William L. Clements Library at the University of Michigan and in the Public Records Office in London. They list unexpected numbers of black soldiers, and they also illuminate the magnitude of black enlistment and where the soldiers were assigned. Inferences from these spotty records to the composition of imperial forces cannot be exact. Nonetheless, these returns amplify eyewitness accounts and buttress the huge numbers reported in the literature.

For example, several rosters exist for "Capt Stuarts [name spelled as both "Stuart" and "Stewart"] Black Pioneers" in Philadelphia and Charlestown. Continually replenished from the thousands of escapees who followed British forces, the size of "Stewart's Pioneers" varied considerably over time. On July 23 and 29, 1778, the company numbered 60: 47 men, 9 women, and 4 children.[20] By October 7, 1778, "Stewart's Company of Black Pioneers" had swelled to 96.[21] On March 24, 1779, "Stuart's Black Company" had declined to 69,[22] but on August 22 to 29, it grew again to

103[23] and on September 26 to 107.[24] An influx of black recruits in the British forces retreating from Virginia may account for this increase in numbers. An order of June 18, 1779, assigned the "negroes" to "Capt. Stewart" and the Black Pioneers.[25]

Another return mentions three companies of "Stewart's." The numbers vary only for "casualties" and the dead.[26] The many identical figures probably indicate some haste or laziness on the list maker's part. In addition, each company included seven servants. Thus, the three white officers per company each had at least two servants. If such a ratio existed in imperial forces generally, then one might surmise that some of the blacks listed with the troops in the returns below were servants. But the Crown regularly identified "servants" separately. Thus, blacks recorded with companies most likely enlisted as soldiers.[27]

The first company of Pioneers totaled 95 or 105, counting the dead,[28] the second totaled 95 (or 123), and the third totaled 95 (or 115). Anywhere from one-ninth to roughly one-third of the companies had perished, probably many in fighting. According to these records, women worked, for instance, as servants or cooks. Thus, the three companies numbered 285 active workers and soldiers, along with 45 children. Including the dead, the total number of blacks in these companies was 343.

These troops served mainly in the South. But according to this return, while in New York, they received "60 great coats" and "60 sailor jackets." The Crown offered blacks worse supplies than whites. Even the return notes, "They being ten men left at New York which got no cloathing."[29]

The blacks who enlisted in the British cause shared the defeats that eventually gave victory to the Patriots. Retreating to New York in 1779, British major general Edward Matthews, who had fought in Virginia from the beginning of the Revolution, took a large contingent of escaped blacks with him on the *Margery* and other ships. A "Return of Persons Who Came Off from Virginia with General Matthews in the Fleet the 24th May" includes 518 blacks: 256 men, 135 women, and 127 children.[30] That record of recruitment, broken down by ship—possibly for Matthews's whole expedition, possibly for only a part of it—demonstrates, once again, the vast movement of blacks to join the fighting.[31] That half were women and children again shows how families fled bondage together. In contrast, only 46 white men, 27 women, and 17 children joined Matthews.[32] Judging by the return, of the Virginian Loyalists who adhered to the British troops, 11 black men came for each white. For women, the ratio was 5 to 1, for children 8 to 1. The presence of so many black nonsoldiers, combined with the thousands who followed imperial regiments and were not yet soldiers, created a major problem for the Crown: so many mouths to feed. But black escape had provided at least as significant a source of civilian or "irregular" recruits to the redcoats as white enlistment.

As in some units in the North, for example in Massachusetts, the British forces employed not only segregated, all-black companies but also "mixed" units. Compared with the information available on the Black Pioneers, however, reports on mixed units are more difficult to assess. One is a return for soldiers and others fed at New York between November 14 and 21, 1779, who would soon fight in the South. The return does not differentiate blacks from whites by regiment.[33] Only the entry for "Stuart's Black Company" indicates 101 blacks.[34] The report as a whole, which registers 22,401 male troops, also includes 3,347 women and 3,163 children.[35] Redcoats from England, as well as Hessian and Danish mercenaries, did not bring wives and children. Neither did the white Tories recruited to fight. Mistresses accompanied some officers, but some of these were black.

Some of this information was described in the field by the Danish officer Johann van Ewald and others and enumerated in returns for "Stuart's Black Company" and the *Book of Negroes*, an archive largely of freed Whig slaves who had become black Loyalists and requested permission to leave the United States to resettle in Nova Scotia. The figures for women and children mostly indicate families of blacks who served in the Royal Army. Because the number of woman and children—6,510 in this return[36]—was roughly equal to that of black men in other returns, one might even imagine that as many as 6,500 of the 22,401 male troops could have been black. If so, blacks would have constituted 25 percent of the British force. That estimate parallels the German officer von Closen's estimate of blacks on the American side at Yorktown. Even a smaller number, say one-eighth of the imperial troops, would still have been a substantial number.[37]

The return lists women and children by unit. Following Clinton's proclamation in 1779 promising blacks emancipation whether they became soldiers or not, the Crown employed women to cook and wash clothes. The men whom they "victualled," however, were soldiers in the imperial army. The roster does not include the separate mass of several thousand escapees who were not yet assigned. The two sets of blacks composed a very substantial part of imperial forces. Still, the goals of British military victory and escape by black families often conflicted.

On June 22, 1779, officers in Emmerich's Chasseurs denounced German captain Andreas Emmerich "for employing Soldiers, Negroes & Refugees to robb and Plunder the inhabitants of West Chester Country and dividing the property with them."[38] These officers again drew the racist demarcation between "Negroes" and "soldiers." Plainly, though, there were black chasseurs. As part of the company, the New York return lists as chasseurs 179 men, 18 women, and 29 children. Once again, if we assume that the number of black men is roughly equal to the total of women and children—47—nearly one-third of Emmerich's Chasseurs were black. Presumably, Emmerich pursued similar policies when his chasseurs moved south.

A company listed as De Lancey's Brigade appeared in September in Daniel Wier's report as "Battalion of De Lancey's Brigade": 262 men, 39 women, and 75 children.[39] A breakdown of a roster for "De Lancey's Second Battalion" in Savannah for the next month, October 1779, includes 18 black men—roughly 7 percent—and 228 white.[40] This ratio suggests that some of the women and children may have been white. But it is unclear why white redcoats needed to bring them or why the Crown—increasing its need for supplies—would have encouraged it. Very likely, the earlier report does not underline a substantial black presence.

An "Abstract of the Number of Men, Women, and Children, Negroes, and Prisoners Victualled at Savannah from 11th to 20th October, 1779," signed by Peter Paumier, deputy British commissary in Georgia, records only 235 Negroes, compared with 4,477 whites in the regular troops, which is roughly 5 percent. But this figure is probably low.[41] First, it is unusual that this list does not indicate women and children, though they are mentioned in its title. At Savannah, the Crown may, again in what would have been unusual, not have "victualled" them. But more likely, denying them food would have caused great discontent, possibly rebellion, among the troops. Paumier probably failed to record the details correctly.

Also, depending on occupations, the ratios of blacks to whites diverged sharply. For instance, 27 blacks participated in the Royal Artillery at Savannah, compared with 109 whites: 19 percent of the total. In the First and Second Troop Light Dragoons, 5 blacks in each unit—16 percent—served, compared with 25 and 27 whites, respectively. In the Second Battalion of South Carolina Royalists, 12 blacks fought, compared with 109 whites— 10 percent; in the Georgia Loyalists, there were 10 blacks, compared with 104 whites—9 percent (the figures for these last two units contrast markedly with Patriot troops from South Carolina and Georgia, which had few black soldiers).[42] In General De Lancey's Second Battalion, 18 blacks served, compared with 228 whites—7 percent. A nonfighting unit, however, the Engineers Department, was more than half black: 41 blacks and 39 whites.[43]

Eight other companies listed only one or two blacks. These individuals—a total of twelve—may have served officers, though the records do not indicate this status. But like Boston King, even servants worked as messengers or fought. For instance, in 1782 the *Charlestown Royal Gazette* praised an unnamed "negro man, a servant to Capt. Alex. Campbell," who was killed in a skirmish with American cavalry "after making a most gallant defense."[44] Such instances suggest that many more blacks engaged in combat for the empire than it formally listed as soldiers.

The Crown also employed blacks in separate, perhaps mainly non-fighting companies and at sea. The same roster listed "Negroes employed in Redoubts—14," "Volunteer Negroes—58" and "Black Pioneers—218," "His Majesty's Ship *Rose*—15," "Seamen—15" and "Brigade Major Skelly—2"—for a total of 620 blacks,[45] compared with 5,112 whites, just over 8 percent.[46]

That list also does not include two black companies created contemporaneously. As French and Patriot troops besieged Savannah during September and October, Lieutenant Colonel Campbell recruited 218 blacks to arms. These troops nearly double the 235 on this list.

In addition, the large number of "Black Pioneers" commanded by Scottish captain Angus Campbell refers to a different unit than "Capt Stuarts Black Pioneers."[47] The unit was irregular, neither paid nor clothed as redcoats. Instead, it depended for subsistence on the civil government, military contingency accounts, or the seizure of resources from both Whig and Loyalist estates.[48]

Thus, at Savannah, roughly 10 percent of total imperial forces were black. Even on this list, blacks made up 5 percent of the soldiers, though as we have seen, they made up around 10 percent in many units and 20 to 25 percent in a few. But given the thousands of unorganized blacks trailing the redcoats, these numbers could rapidly increase. With the recruiting of two fighting units by Archibald Campbell, black soldiers became 10 percent (and blacks in all occupations 14 percent) of the total.

We lack other lists with this depth of detail. Nonetheless, distributions roughly similar to this one, and, again, reasonable inferences from the New York list, suggest that in "mixed" units, substantial proportions of blacks worked and soldiered with the Crown throughout the war.

An "Abstract of Men Victualled at Gibb's Landing, Camp Charlestown Neck" in South Carolina from April 7 to 9, 1780, however, lists a smaller percentage of black soldiers among Loyalist troops. Only about 5 percent served in the Infantry British Legion—11 blacks, 200 whites—and 5 percent in the infantry commanded by Major Graham—12 blacks, 231 whites. The British concentrated blacks in the Savannah Pioneers, which now had 186 black men, 96 women, and 74 children, for a total of 356, as well as 20 white men. This report indicated that women and children accompanied the Pioneers, but no other troops, which was unusual. For the whole force at Camp Charlestown Neck, 209 black men constituted 3 percent of the troops, which included 7,281 white men.[49] Like the Georgia list, however, this one is incomplete. Separate units of black troops and workers also played a substantial role in the imperial victory at Charlestown in 1780.

Another return, this one of skilled workers for the royal "Quarter Master General's Department," South Carolina, June 1, 1780, first lists whites by name. Then, casually and anonymously, the return indicates boatmen— the actual term, "Batteauxmen," is an oddly corrupted French—"Seventy two Negroes" and "Labourers Sixty Nine Ditto." The total of 141 blacks out of 310 (169 of these were whites) is 45 percent.[50] A hasty perusal of this list would indicate few blacks, but, in fact, they are almost half the total.

Similarly, a "Muster Roll of the Civil Branch of Ordnance" in Charlestown on June 30, 1780, identifies fifty skilled workers. The roll notes "negroes"—in little parentheses—"13." That is 26 percent of the total list. All nine carpenters were black—John Duncan, Peter Young, Cato Burding, John Jones, Simon Slain, Samuel Sterling, Isaac Moore, Francis Carter, and Friday. "Wheelers" included "Negro Isaac Williams"; collarmakers were "Negroes" Hector Edwards and Pompey Pool. The British often did not list blacks by name or even ascertain the full name. Whoever wrote the roll dismissively lists one "Wheelturner" as "Negro Bunge."[51] This muster roll indicates with what varied skills blacks worked for the Crown. One has to stare at it for a while to see how much of it was black. On other rosters, the reporting officer might simply not have listed blacks separately or by name.

In a British troop muster in Rhode Island on July 1, 1779, the Civil Branch of Ordnance totaled thirty-one. Several names that are probably names of blacks appear, but are not so indicated: Prince Jackson and then three first names—Danl, John, and Richard, next to Peleg Carr.[52] Blacks may have composed one-seventh of the company. By the time it reached South Carolina in the following year, the Civil Branch of Ordnance had grown, numbering fifty, as had its black membership, thirteen (26 percent).

A "Return of Negroes" for one Royal Artillery Department in Charlestown on April 28, 1780, identifies 154, which includes, in an incomplete listing, 7 carpenters, 2 collar makers, 1 blacksmith, and 92 laborers. Thirty—one-fifth—had smallpox. In addition, twenty-two were "sick and lame." Petter Traille, its author, characterizes the blacks' current assignment as "transporting Stores in the Schooners."[53] This return indicates routine imperial diversion of blacks with specialized military functions to menial labor. But as with servants, black artillerists often fought.

For a six-month period in 1781, several "General List[s] of Negroes Employed in the Royal Artillery Department" under General George Wray, from Charlestown, survive. A roster for April includes fifty-six blacks; for May, sixty-eight; for June, seventy-four; for October, ninety; for November, ninety-one; and for December, ninety-two.[54] The Wray lists identify the participants, including a number who retain African first names: Quaco Miles, Quash Wood, Quash Wilkinson, Mingo McPherson, and Mingo Tropia. As we have seen, those who knew each other often escaped together and would have joined military units at the same time. On the December list of ninety-two, for instance, twenty-eight, or roughly 30 percent, shared surnames, those of a former "owner." Some may have been brothers or cousins.[55]

Officials did not keep exact count. The Wray list for November is one fewer—ninety-one—than December's. Several lone members on December 1, however, share common surnames with others on the earlier report. Thus, December lists only Paul Wearon; November reports Joe, Will, and Adam Wearon as well. November reports Monday, July, and Jack Miles; December includes only Jack. Whether the lists are inaccurate from month to month or whether five were killed or deserted and six recruited between November and December is unclear.[56] But we can infer more information about some of these. Joe Postell, an artilleryman, probably escaped from John Postell, a former American governor of South Carolina. Quash Wilkinson escaped from Eliza Wilkinson.

In his *History of the Campaigns in 1780 and 1781 in the Southern Provinces*, Colonel Banastre Tarleton recalled: "Upon the approach of any detachment of the King's troops, all negroes, men, women and children, thought themselves absolved from all respect to their American masters, and entirely released from servitude. . . . They quitted the plantations and followed the army."[57] Patriots named Tarleton, a cavalry commander who took no prisoners, "Bloody Ban."

Among the Patriots, many South Carolina slave owners fled the Crown, leaving blacks to run the plantations. Those owners who remained spoke of a "petit marronage," the escape of small groups of slaves to form independent communities or join the British. Clinton's proclamation escalated such flights.

For instance, in 1780 John Ball, a Cooper River owner, kept a "list of the Negroes that is gone from Kensington [plantation] to the British Army."[58]

On learning of nearby imperial encampments, overseers tried to terrorize blacks to prevent them from leaving with their families. But in the upheaval of war, sporadic slave-owner violence could not quell escapes. In Ball's record, "Tanner Charles" left on May 11 and then "came home & went away again." Owner Samuel Mathis of Camden, South Carolina, recorded that one Sunday in 1781, Esther, his slave, visited the royal forces nearby. On Monday, when she returned, Mathis "threatened her and set her to work." Two days later, she "had taken her child and cloaths" and departed.[59] Historian Sylvia Frey speculates that the imperial army siphoned off the leaders of a potential black rebellion.[60] But ironically, massive defection to the Crown in exchange for freedom, together with competitive Patriot recruitment of blacks, became that very rebellion.

In addition to the blacks who served both in irregular bands and as redcoats, the thousands of blacks who trailed the British troops also organized themselves behind the lines for independent combat against slave owners. Sometimes they took arms from the field of battle; sometimes sympathetic royal officers supplied them. Thus, returns of regular forces, either because they are partial, as in the case of Savannah above, or because they omit the thousands of unorganized followers, dramatically understate black participation.

EMANCIPATION AND BIGOTRY

As on the Patriot side, racist attitudes often stood between black fighters for freedom and the equality for which they hoped to fight. Danish captain Ewald provides an example of this casual bigotry. Ewald had recruited twelve black horsemen. As he wrote in his diary, "Because I lacked some cavalry and the little at Portsmouth could not be spared, twelve Negroes were mounted and armed. I trained them as well as possible and they gave me thoroughly good service, for I sought to win them by good treatment to which they were not accustomed."[61] Ewald recognized black fighting ability and the powerful individual response to decent treatment. Yet even with increasing royal losses, he could not imagine that recruiting blacks mainly to fight might revive the British cause. He mostly saw them as manual laborers—slaves in all but name.

Ewald did condemn imperial hubris toward the Patriots: "On every occasion during this war, one can observe the thoughtlessness, negligence, and contempt of the English toward their foe."[62] After retaking Savannah, the British commander had repaired only a few redoubts. With a bold attack, the Americans and their French allies under Comte d'Estaing might easily, in Ewald's estimation, have conquered the city. In June 1779, d'Estaing's fleet appeared suddenly in Savannah harbor. To prepare Savannah's defenses, Ewald wrote, "Three hundred Negroes had to work head-over-heels at once under [Captain] Moncrief [of the Engineers]."[63] Luck alone, according to Ewald, had saved the Crown.

At Charlestown on March 3, 1780, Ewald "requested thirty Negroes provided with axes and shovels to repair the works [of the redoubts across the Stono River] and strengthen the abatis surrounding them."[64] On April 1, Ewald noted that given an absence of horses, "the sailors and Negroes were used to drag [heavy pieces, munitions, entrenching tools] to their places" from Linning's Creek over the Ashley River to Gibbes' Ferry.[65] Once again, Ewald made the standard racist distinction among troops. Blacks did the heavy work for the Crown.[66]

As Ewald noted, itinerant blacks did provide vital information to the liberating imperial army. After one battle, he hid in a garden: "[I] rummaged through the area on my hands and knees for an hour, I luckily found an old Negro. . . . He told me that the marshy Black's Creek, which fell into the Ashley River, lay in front of me a thousand paces away. While crawling around I had fallen more than once into the water and swamp over my knees, but how could I have guessed that this wet area was not passable?"[67]

Escaped blacks, Ewald wrote, camped near the troops in horrifying circumstances. In 1780 the worst smallpox epidemic in seventeen years ravaged South Carolina's Low Country. David Ramsay, a Patriot physician and historian of the Revolution, inaccurately describes escapees as slaves, though they had freed themselves: "The slaves . . . being crowded together were visited by camp fever . . . and the small-pox . . . broke out among them, and spread rapidly, from these two diseases and the impossibility of their being provided with proper accommodations and attendance in the British encampment, great numbers of them died and were left unburied in the woods."[68]

During a ten-month campaign, however, the Danish mercenary Ewald fixated on the appropriation by British officers of a large number of blacks as servants. He suggested luxury and languor by the British: "Lord Cornwallis . . . permitted each subaltern to keep two horses and one Negro, each captain, four horses and two Negroes, and so on, according to rank. But since this order was not strictly carried out, the greatest abuse arose from this arrangement. . . . Every officer had four to six horses and three or four Negroes, as well as one or two Negresses for cook and maid. Every soldier's woman was mounted and also had a Negro and Negress on horse-back for their servants. Each squad had one or two horses and Negroes, and every noncommissioned officer had two horses and one Negro."[69]

From surviving returns, especially for "victualling," Ewald's figures seem a vast exaggeration, even for Cornwallis's command, and certainly in other commands. At this point, Ewald's picaresque tale sweeps him away: "Yes, indeed, I can testify that every soldier had his Negro, who carried his provisions and bundles. . . . Behind the baggage followed well over four thousand Negroes of both sexes and all ages. Any place this horde approached was eaten clean, like an acre invaded by a swarm of locusts. Where all these people lived was a mystery to me. Fortunately the army seldom stayed in one place longer than a day or a night. . . . What made this strange baggage train so comical was the motley clothing of the black people, most of whom looked rather like monkeys."[70]

Ewald indicates how hungry and rebellious blacks seized food with their own hands. He thus underlines a conflict between the capacity of the invading British army to supply each person, particularly women, children, and men who had not yet been organized, and the needs of black escapees. Ewald then offers what was for him a surprising thought: "These people were given their freedom by the army because it was actually thought this would punish the rich, rebellious-minded inhabitants of Carolina and Virginia." He added: "They had plundered the wardrobes of their masters and mistresses, divided the loot, and clothed themselves piecemeal with it. For example, a completely naked Negro wore a pair of silk breeches, another a finely colored coat, a third a silk vest without sleeves, a fourth an elegant shirt, a fifth a fine churchman's hat, and a sixth a wig.—All the rest of the body was bare! The one Negress wore a silk shirt, another a lounging robe with a long train, the third a jacket, the fourth a silk-laced bodice, the fifth a silk corset, the seventh, eighth and ninth—all different styles of hats and coiffures."[71]

Most blacks could not have been on horseback. As Patriot Landon Carter of Virginia reported, escapees occasionally took the "master's" weapons.[72] But because they risked their lives to escape, most sought to draw no attention to themselves. They brought their families. They did not ride horses by day or deck themselves in the "master's" finery, a sure way to be identified as a rebel rather than as a "local" wandering on an owner's assignment. Ewald imagines "coiffures." Hiding in swamps and along the road, would black women who had once worked on the wife's hair take time out to style each other's? Owners in Virginia did force some blacks to work naked. Perhaps once they were with the Crown, some escapees mocked their former owners in the way Ewald describes. Still, this depiction is mainly Ewald's fantasy.

We have seen how Patriot recruitment of blacks in the wake of the Dunmore Proclamation, founded on claims of military necessity, allowed the British in turn to extend the recruitment and emancipation of blacks on their side, using the same pragmatic arguments. But the reverse occurred as well. Bigots on both sides derided the policy of emancipation. Just as some Patriots ridiculed Dunmore's proposal to free slaves to be soldiers, some Loyalists mocked the Laurens proposal to raise black Patriot regiments. For instance, on June 8, 1779, a Tory, William Smith, chief justice of New York, gloated to Frederick Howard, an English diplomat: "Their order to take 3,000 Negroes into their service gives great Disgust to the Southern colonies."[73] While Clinton's proclamation further undercut Tory resistance to emancipation on the pragmatic level, imperial emancipation during the American Revolution had a notoriously British patchwork quality.

Committed only to royal victory, rather than to abolition, Clinton distinguished blacks who fled from rebels from those who escaped Tories. He sometimes returned ex-slaves to Loyalist masters.[74] Furthermore, he instructed Cornwallis, his successor in South Carolina, "to make such arrangements as will discourage . . . [slaves of Tories] joining us."[75] Yet even slaves of Tories still escaped to the British forces. And Clinton instructed Major General Alexander Leslie, a British commander in Charleston, to assign the vast number of blacks who had answered his proclamation to any job except soldiering. Clinton's directive to Leslie echoes the imperial racism exemplified by the likes of Captain Ewald. As a contrast, the French Jacobins, responding to the Saint Domingue insurrection in one sweeping 1794 measure, would abolish slavery throughout the French colonies.

In the American South, the British were frightened by the independent actions of black crowds, which ranged from deserting or looting Tory estates to shooting white Loyalists who sold members away from their families. And the necessity of many mouths to feed was beyond the British capacity to supply. To the Board of Police of South Carolina, imperial Brigadier General James Patterson spoke of the "very great Inconveniences . . . found from Negroes leaving the service of their masters and coming to the British army." He hoped to protect from punishment blacks who were returned to their owners. Black "crowds" would disappear, he suggested obtusely, only "if the slave could be persuaded to return voluntarily to the service of his master."[76]

Most royal officers were engaged in the war against the Patriots, and the

Crown had little time to suppress rebellions on Loyalist plantations. But a few officers struck against black insurrections. Responding in July 1780 to the "ill-behaviour and insurrectious conduct of Mr. Isard's Negroes towards their Overseer," Colonel Nesbit Balfour ordered "a party of soldiers under a sergeant to be sent to Mr. Isard's plantation to inflict such punishment upon the principle offenders in the insurrection as may be adequate to their Crimes."[77] In January 1781, redcoats suppressed an insurrection on a James Island plantation and executed one of the leaders.

Lieutenant Colonel Archibald Campbell provides an example of the way in which racist attitudes prevented the British from benefiting from the energies and skills of the slaves they recruited and freed. In campaigns at Savannah and Charlestown, Campbell himself had recruited some two hundred black soldiers and five thousand black aides, victuallers, teamsters, valets, spies, and laborers.[78] He had issued a proclamation of freedom for blacks. He could have learned from the skill and heroism of Quamino Dolly, who guided him to victory at Savannah, or from his unnamed gallant servant who died fighting next to him in 1782. He could have relied on black soldiers. Yet Campbell grasped neither the strategic nor the moral opportunity before him.

In fact, Campbell only uses black escapees in a tactic to trap blacks who had fled from Tories or is annoyed by such escape for disrupting his plans for a surprise attack. For instance, on January 1, 1779, at Zubly's Ferry, near Savannah, Campbell recaptured the slaves of white Loyalists. To gull the escapees, he used his own black troops. He reported in his journal:

> Observing that the Negroes were scarcely 100 Yards from the other Side of the River, and that the Two Ferry Boats were hauled up close to the opposite shore, I fell upon the following Expedient to recover a part of them for their proper Owners.
>
> To a Confidential Mulatto . . . I gave a Musket, and sent him forward with a Number of Negroes to the Bank of the River to call out to the Rebels for God's Sake to send over the Boats and save his Master's Slaves from falling into the hands of the King's Troops. Captain Lieutenant Charles Campbell of the 71st Regiment with his Company of Light Infantry was ordered to pass through the Wood and get as near to the River as possible without shewing themselves to the Rebels on the Opposite Shore. The Mulatto had Orders to shew his Negroes on the bank of the River, and to make them all cry out in the most pitiful manner for Relief. He had likewise Orders to fire off his Musket the Moment the Ferry Boats reached our Side of the River, which Captain Campbell

was to notice as a Signal for his party to rush out of the Wood, seize the Boats, and push across the River in quest of the Slaves who lay there. This stratagem succeeded.[79]

The trick, however, only showed Campbell's blindness to the potentials of emancipation. He did not grasp, before his very eyes, the prospect for British victory relying on blacks. In addition, to betray escapees from Tory masters, the blacks on the British side would have had to have been very intimidated. The "Confidential Mulatoo"—"confidential" here means "trustworthy"—seems a coward. Had he asked the lieutenant colonel what he thought he was doing, perhaps some deeper thought about strategy involving blacks would have crossed Campbell's mind.

On January 30, 1779, Campbell struck at a Mr. Golphin, who had mobilized Creek Indians and backcountry whites against the Crown. Ninety of Golphin's slaves had "joined the troops under my command," Campbell wrote in his journal. As pawns, Campbell dangled these now-free men before Golphin's son, whom he had captured. Campbell sent a message with the son that "upbraided [Golphin] for his Perfidy. He was likewise informed that there was but one Method of receiving his Negroes, and saving himself and property from immediate Destruction; which was to send me his Brother in Law . . . accompanied with all the Information he could give me of the Enemy's Force and movements."[80]

Note that Campbell threatens blacks—Golphin's "property"—with destruction. Honor was not his strong point. On obtaining the intelligence, however, Campbell transferred the blacks to General Augustine Prevost to hold for Golphin "in Case he continue to act the same friendly part towards us, during the rest of the Campaign."[81] Campbell betrayed these blacks, who had freed themselves based on royal promises.[82]

Many British officers emancipated and relied on blacks to fight and work for freedom. In utilizing blacks for diverse purposes, however, others failed to understand the resource they had. A few used blacks as pawns or, even worse, as weapons against slave insurrections. Despite Dunmore's persistent efforts, some royal military leaders preferred defeat to mobilizing ex-slaves as soldiers. In this, they shared the prejudices of Patriot South Carolina.

But British defeats once again spurred efforts to recruit blacks to the British cause by freeing black slaves. As on the Patriot side, pragmatism motivated what principle often could not. In 1782, following Cornwallis's defeat at Yorktown, Dunmore would again try to awaken Clinton and George Germain, British secretary of state for America, to the potential of black irregulars. Dunmore discussed black recruitment with South Carolina Loyalist John Cruden, who was the commissioner of "sequestered"—that is, captured—estates, including Patriots' slaves, in the South. Dunmore forwarded two of his letters to Clinton and Germain.

As Cruden put it, "While there was a ray of hope left for believing that Lord Cornwallis had made his escape with a small part of his army, I was easy and happy, convinced that he would not have hesitated a moment in giving freedom to men of all complexions that would faithfully serve the King, and assist in crushing a most infernal rebellion."[83] But Cornwallis had not escaped. It now fell, Cruden thought, to Dunmore to extend freedom to all of America with a local force—"I mean the Provincial troops and black troops to be raised." Cruden's mobilization would free up redcoats and Hessians to attack the French.[84] As to the number of blacks to be recruited, Cruden envisioned "ten thousand," the largest figure so far proposed.[85] Dunmore and Cruden intended to transform the war.

Cruden's letters mocked potential objections: "'What! arm the slaves? We shudder at the very idea, so repugnant to humanity, so barbarous and shocking to human nature,' etc." A racist, he insisted that black soldiers were a last resort. Still, this resource could make the American continent a source of "power, strength and consequence to Great Britain again." Otherwise, the Crown would "tamely give it up to France, who will reap the fruits of American Independence."[86]

Alone among others, Cruden focused on recruiting troops from Loyalist masters. Though Dunmore forwarded his letters, he never had quite this emphasis. Perhaps Cruden risked driving Tory slave owners to the Patriots, but the military situation was increasingly dire, a point that could not have escaped these Loyalists, who were threatened with the loss of everything. In addition, a considerable number of Tory slaves already had left and soldiered with the Crown. It would have been easy to pass to the Crown under an assumed name, and redcoats did not look closely at escapees. Thus, Cruden would have regularized and expanded an already occurring practice. Finally, Cruden pledged recompense to slave owners. He wrote these startling words:

In the province of South Carolina, ten thousand Black troops may be raised, inured to fatigue and to the climate, without impoverishing the plantations so much that they might not be able to produce crops equal to the maintenance and support, not only of the women and children that are left on the estates, but also sufficient to feed, clothe and pay the Black Troops.

When these men are raised, there can be no doubt, that, with the force here, they will be able to drive the enemy from the Province and open a large door for our friends from North Carolina to join us, till such time as it may be policy and we may have a sufficient command of the sea, to enter Virginia.

When the country is again in our possession, with proper and effectual support, I will engage to maintain and clothe those Black Troops from the estates of the enemy; and I will also engage to pay the interest on the receipts granted to our friends, at the rate of eight per cent. And to convince the world that we never adopt any measure at the expense of individuals, let three or more gentlemen of the country—men of honor and probity—be appointed to value the negroes that belong to our friends, and at the rate they would have sold for in 1773, and Government to be accountable for the amount at the expiration of the war, paying interest at the customary rate, so long as the parties concerned maintained their allegiance.[87]

To the expected objection that the Crown would harm Loyalist slave owners and drive them to the Patriots, Cruden answered that merchants constituted the majority of the "friends of Britain" in the South. To preserve slavery, most slave owners had already declared for the Patriots. But royal recruitment of intrepid blacks in exchange for freedom, Cruden suggested, would provide an alternative to "cabals, tumult and even [slave] rebellion." It would prevent blacks escaping to join the British military on their own and enable Tory owners to keep other slaves in "good order." Fear of a black uprising encouraged by the British, he continued, would make "lukewarm" allies of the Crown "better friends."[88]

Yet Cruden's office circumscribed his vision. He did not see the main source of potential black enlistment as escapees from the Patriots. In motivating soldiers, Cruden had no grasp of the moral force of emancipation.

Enclosing Cruden's letters, Dunmore recommended to Clinton that "Your Excellency would adopt the measure on some such footing"—he was well aware of freedom as a motive for the slaves of Patriots—and volunteered "to hazard my reputation and person in the execution of it." He altered Cruden's proposal to suggest that while the ten thousand soldiers would have mainly white officers, the Crown should "fill up the vacancies of the non-commissioned officers now and then with black people, as their services should entitle them to it."[89] The more direct the appeal made to blacks and the more they could affirm their freedom in positions of leadership, the more vigorously and creatively they would fight.

Dunmore recommended giving each black "one guinea and a crown, with a promise of freedom to all that should serve during the continuance of the war."[90] Emphasizing the moral motivation of liberty, his proposal clashes with Cruden's. As Dunmore knew, Clinton shied away from recruiting blacks, let alone former slaves of Tories, to fight. For this reason, Dunmore also sent copies of the letters to Lord Germain. In 1775 Dunmore had called for the slaves and indentured servants to join him. Unlike Cruden, Dunmore did not care whether recruits came from Tory or Patriot estates. Relying on black soldiers—Dunmore referred to them as "the people of the country"—Dunmore believed that Germain could reconquer the South and sunder the new America: "If His Majesty and your Lordship should approve of this plan I am fully convinced that the people of the country, embodied and led forth by those in whom they could confide and that would pay due attention to their merits, would even now give such convincing proofs of their Spirit . . . as would give a favourable turn to affairs in the southern colonies at least. . . . This country must now be conquered by its own force or not at all, for after a seven years war with I know not how many thousand regular troops we now find ourselves confined to very narrow limits indeed."[91]

Black irregulars, Dunmore believed, offered hope for the imperial cause: "I would therefore beg leave to recommend to your Lordship that the Governor of one of the provinces should be authorized to raise and embody men of all descriptions to serve during the continuance of the Rebellion and to act under him perfectly independent of the Commander-in-Chief of the Regulars, and that all the appointments belonging to this Army should be entirely under the direction of that governor . . . [that] would have given a very different turn to affairs in this country."[92] Speaking cautiously to a superior, he did not ask Germain for permission to command, but rather to accompany whomever his lordship would appoint.

Clinton did not respond. On March 30, Dunmore wrote again to Germain about the persistent efforts of John Laurens and Nathanael Greene to raise an American black regiment in South Carolina. Dunmore saw the competitive threat and potential of Patriot and imperial recruitment. He used Laurens's proposals to arouse London to rely on black irregulars. Again invoking "these people"—those especially who escaped from Patriots—to Germain, he insisted: "Since writing to your Lordship on the 5th of February, there has been a motion made in the Rebel Assembly of this Province for raising a brigade of negroes, which was only negatived by a very few voices, and it's supposed will be re-assumed and carried on a future day; and we by neglecting to make a proper use of these people, who are much attached to us, shall have them, in a short time, employed against us."[93]

Besides this, he argued, most South Carolinian slave owners sought not to arm blacks but to spirit them away: "They are now carrying them up the country as fast as they can find them."[94] But Dunmore was now isolated in England, having fled from Virginia to New York in July 1776 and then to the metropolis, although he officially remained the royal governor until 1783. He was out of touch. Most South Carolina blacks had long deserted the plantations. By escaping and fighting for the Crown, southern blacks provided even stronger evidence than Dunmore supposed that if mobilized en masse as guerillas, they could revive the flagging imperial cause. Yet General Carleton, who replaced Clinton, discouraged further fighting. Between May and October 1782, Dunmore lobbied unsuccessfully for his plan.[95]

Other officers urged Dunmore's idea on Clinton. For instance, in March 1782, General Leslie wrote Clinton that white Loyalists would not fight. Faced with an American confiscation law to seize Loyalist property, Leslie argued, most would defect. And he spoke of "the necessity I shall in all probability be under of putting arms into the hands of negroes," because "it appears to me a measure that will soon become indispensably necessary shou'd the war continue to be carried on in this part of America."[96]

FREE BLACKS AND THE "BLACK DIASPORA"

From 1779 on, the imperial army in Charlestown had set up independent black bands and mobilized black redcoats. In New York and New Jersey, British commanders had also pursued this combined strategy mainly for free blacks formerly enslaved by Patriots. But slave-trading interests, racism, and fatigue triumphed in the imperial leadership. Still, the British had gone far in freeing and recruiting blacks. In the end, their decision not to expand the use of black troops was political: by 1782, London simply lacked the boldness to reinvigorate the war.

However, tales of unrest on particular plantations suggest the magnitude of the actual and potential resources that black troops could have represented to the Crown. The slaves of entire plantations often escaped together. On a South Carolina Patriot estate in 1779, for instance, "sixty-four negroes went away in one night." The next three years "were years of general . . . calamity in which all but the particular friends of the British thought themselves fortunate if they could raise provisions, and save their negroes from being carried off."[97] In correspondence, Thomas Pinckney, a South Carolina representative to the Continental Congress, complained that blacks were de facto "now perfectly free & live upon the best produce of the plantation." Managing the estate, Eliza Lucas Pinckney, his wife, found blacks "insolent and quite their own masters." In the spring of 1779, Thomas Pinckney returned from Congress to discover the plantation empty of slaves, except pregnant women and the old. In 1780 his wife estimated that the crop would be "very Small by the desertion of Negroes in planting and hoeing time."[98]

In March 1780, Prussian captain Johann Hinrichs wrote in his diary, he observed "thirteen Negroes fleeing from Young's plantation on Wadmalaw Island."[99] On March 2, Patriot governor John Rutledge ordered Colonel Benjamin Garden to hunt those who incited insurrection or escape: "I repeat . . . that I must have one-half of your regiment here, with the utmost expedition; that part of the Regiment which remains in the District are to do patrol duty for keeping the Negroes in order, and be employed in suppressing any insurrections of the disaffected and in apprehending . . . persons who . . . mak[e] it their business to propagate false news, spread groundless reports and sow discontent among people."[100] Such commands did little to stop black escape to the British side.

On March 29, 1780, John Lewis Gervais wrote to Henry Laurens that "thirty-four of Mr. Lowndes's Negroes have joined the enemy." Gervais warned, "This will be the fate of many."[101] When David George's master fled from the approaching British army, George wrote in his autobiography, his family "and fifty or more of my master's people . . . [walked] about twenty miles . . . where the King's forces were."[102]

The isolation of American blacks in a sea of whites had long curtailed revolt. Still, over the entire epoch of North American bondage, a steady stream of individuals, roughly two-thirds of them men between the ages of sixteen and thirty-five, slipped away.[103] According to historian Peter Kolchin, "Taking advantage of wartime chaos and the proximity of British troops, tens of thousands of slaves fled their homes, sometimes in large groups." As William Wells Brown, an escapee, abolitionist, and novelist, would state, "The slave is brought up to look upon every white as an enemy; twenty-one years in slavery had taught me that there were traitors even among colored people."[104]

As historian Ira Berlin argues, even those who remained on the plantations refused to do onerous tasks. Instead, they worked their own plots. Overseers who sought to force them to do other work discovered that the balance of power had swung dramatically. For example, in the summer of 1779 on a Maryland plantation, blacks "cut [overseer William Elson's] throat from Ear to Ear with an Axe."[105] At the redcoats' approach, blacks often took their Patriot "masters" prisoner.[106] In furthering the British cause, blacks acted on their own initiative.

And despite the equivocal reception of escaped slaves by the British forces, many black fighters for freedom fought valiantly on the British side for a king and country that, more so than the Patriot defenders of "life, liberty, and the pursuit of happiness," promised to value their fundamental human rights. In search of the actual enjoyment of those rights, both during and after the Revolutionary War, former slaves who supported the British would become part of what historian John Pulis names "the black diaspora."[107] We will explore the search for both freedom and equality on the part of black former slaves after the war in the final chapters that follow. Here, it is enough to note the heroism of those few whose tales are to be found in official records and the twists and turns of their fate.

For instance, after the war, Scipio Handley, a black soldier, petitioned the treasury commissioners in London for payment for his injuries. He had been a ship's captain and knew Thomas Jeremiah in Charlestown, South Carolina. He was thus a scary figure to the Patriots. Handley, a recorder of his petition wrote, had left his Patriot master to join Governor William Campbell of South Carolina in 1775. Patriots had arrested him and sentenced him to death.

Provided a file "by the hand of a Friend," he had escaped to the Barbados.[108] In 1780, to fight the Patriots' siege of Savannah, Handley returned on the *Eagle*. "As [Savannah] was very bare of troops all that was in it were Employd both White & Black, in order to Endeavour to keep the [Patriots] off as if they had succeeded in the attempt they would have had no mercy on many." Comparatively, whites could expect decent treatment, but Handley declared that "your Petitioner could Expect none, as they had often threatened his life if Ever he should be caught for quitting Charles Town in One Thousand Seven hundred & seventy five when they were contriving to put him to death."[109]

For six weeks, the imperial army employed Handley at the armory shop, "running grape shot and Carrying them out to the Redoubts and Batteries." At four o'clock on a Saturday morning in 1780, he "unluckily received a Musket Ball in his right leg, which proved to be a very dangerous wound, as the surgeons thought they would be obliged to Cut it off." After Handley underwent a "long & Tedious" recovery, the leg healed. Yet, he declared, "the pain of it, at times [is] so very great that he is Obliged to keep his Bed for two or three days and therefore rendered entirely unfit for service."[110] Scipio Handley was one of many free blacks who left South Carolina for London after the war. No record survives about whether the London committee granted Handley an award.

Surviving by doing needed jobs around British camps, two black ministers also left stories. Blacks served in a graduated number of ways: as unorganized followers of the troops, as support workers, as irregulars or "plunderers," and as redcoats. For instance, after David George escaped from his owner, he worked as a butcher in Savannah. He would eventually end up in Sierra Leone.

Under Clinton's 1779 proclamation, George was one of many who were freed by the Crown without enlisting. But emancipated blacks living in British-held territory needed protection and luck. In Savannah on December 11, 1779, George rented a "house Garden and field situate . . . near the little Ogeechie" from a white Loyalist, John Wright. "Any person Molesting or disturbing him in the possession of the premises," Wright threatened in an official notice, "will be prosecuted to the Utmost rigor of the Law."[111] From Edward Cooper, Savannah town adjutant, George received papers certifying his freedom and that of his wife, Phyllis, and their three children—Jesse, David, and Ginny. Cooper also gave George a pass to pursue his business. But George found no work. To move, he obtained yet another certificate to ensure safe passage from Alured Clarke, the British commander in Georgia.[112]

In 1780 he moved to Charlestown. What the emancipated could do with their freedom behind royal lines was often astonishing, and George decided to get his family out of the war-torn South. For two years, George's *Life* reports, he operated a "butcher's stall in a hut belonging to Lawyer Gibbons." His wife's brother, half Indian and half black, sent them a steer that George butchered. He sold the beef for "13 pounds and about 3 guineas besides, with which I designed to pay our passage, and set off for Charles Town." But before he could leave, imperial soldiers stole his money. "However as it was a good time for the sale of meat, I borrowed money from some of the Black people to buy hogs, and soon re-paid them and agreed for a passage to Charles town where Major P. the British commander, was very kind to me."[113]

White redcoats could be thieving and treacherous or helpful and generous. "Major P." advised George to go to Halifax and "gave the few Black people, and it may be as many as 500 White people, their passage for nothing."[114] These "few Black people" were part of 6,500 to 7,800 Tories who, during the early 1780s, journeyed to Canada separately from the 3,000 who left New York in 1783. On January 15, 1792, George moved again, embarking for Sierra Leone in West Africa, where he would play a leading role in the free colony that abolitionists established there. Filled with perils and setbacks, George's path to freedom typifies that of many blacks emigrating from the South.

In the 1770s, Virginian George Liele came to Burke County, Georgia, with his master, Henry Sharp. A Baptist deacon, Sharp baptized Liele and authorized him to preach to slaves at plantations along the Savannah River. At his master's church, Liele also gave sermons. Finally, Sharp granted him freedom to "follow any thing he thinks proper."[115] In Savannah and Charlestown, Liele would work as a teamster and sell provisions.[116]

Redcoats killed Henry Sharp, and Sharp's relatives tried to reenslave Liele, but he was in imperial territory; the British colonel Kirkland freed him.[117] In 1782 Liele joined the royal forces fighting at Savannah. He and Andrew Bryan, another former slave, later established a black Baptist church, and in 1783, Liele immigrated to Jamaica, where he served a two-year term as an indentured servant. Like many whites who had gone from Britain to North America, black servants, emigrating with the Crown, often agreed to be indentured for a specified period.[118] Once liberated, Liele founded the first black Baptist church on the island, the Windward Road Chapel.[119] He prospered, became a planter, and purchased the freedom of several others.[120]

COLONEL TYE

Among the black recruits to the British cause, however, the daring acts of "the famous negro Tye, justly much more to be feared and respected than any of his brethren of a fairer complexion," as the *New Jersey Gazette* put it, stand out in the few existing extensive accounts of the actions of black troops on either side in the Revolutionary War.[121] Tye, or Titus, as he was called by his slave master, had "belonged" to John Corlis, a Quaker farmer from Colt's Neck, New Jersey. An exception among Quakers, Corlis did not intend to free Titus, who was twenty-one in 1775, or three other slaves, aged twenty-five, fourteen, and twelve.[122] From living with the Friends, however, Titus had learned that slavery is unjust. Corlis and his mother, Zilpha, were the last two Quaker slave owners in Shrewsbury, which included Colt's Neck. In late 1775, the Shrewsbury Friends Meeting convened with Corlis. In what would prove an unintentionally ironic reflection about Tye, the Friends asserted, "They [blacks] have no learning and he [Corlis] is not inclined to give them any."[123]

On November 8, 1775, the day after Lord Dunmore issued his proclamation, Titus escaped from Corlis. Along with several other New Jerseyans, he joined the Royal Ethiopian Regiment. With Dunmore, Titus would go to New York and join the Black Brigade there. The brigade's membership came not only from survivors of Dunmore's Royal Ethiopian Regiment but also from New Jersey. These guerillas would terrify the Patriots. In 1776 "a Mechanic" from Middlesex County warned a Tory that "a deluded King and a corrupted and venal ministry have endeavored to raise up our own domestics to cut the throats of their masters."[124] Henry Melchior Muhlenberg, a Protestant minister, wailed: "The worst is to be feared from the irregular troops whom the so-called Tories have assembled from various nationalities—for example, a regiment of Catholics, a regiment of Negroes, who are fitted for and inclined towards barbarities, are lacking in human feeling and are familiar with every corner of the country."[125] In New Jersey, these guerillas opened up a second front.

Unlike regular battalions on either the imperial or Patriot side—with the exception of the shadowy Patriot "Bucks of Massachusetts"—blacks led these "mixed" forces. Fighting at Monmouth, New Jersey, Titus, a former slave, became Colonel Tye. Between 1778 and 1780, his guerilla band killed or arrested Patriot leaders and secured supplies for Loyalist New York. Flashing out in the night sky of war, his brilliance incarnated the second revolution: a black uprising against former masters. His actions inspired other multiracial bands, for instance, ones led by Stephen Blucke and George Fraction. Even under British authority, Tye generated acts of black independence and, sometimes, rebelliousness.

Monmouth County had a large population of mostly pro-British Anglicans and neutral Quakers. Patriots were isolated. In early 1778, Patriot colonel Asher Holmes reported, "Depredations have been committed by the Refugees (Either Black or White)" from Staten Island and Powles Hook.[126] During the 1778 Battle of Monmouth, Tye's forces captured Elisha Shephard, a captain in the Monmouth militia, and took him to Sugar House Prison in New York City.

On the other side, Patriot confiscation of their homes enraged Loyalists. Furthermore, the rebels often hung Tories. The Monmouth vigilante law of 1779 licensed such executions.[127] According to a report in the *Royal Gazette* of June 5, 1779, "A Loyal Refugee" incited retaliation for these hangings. Only a narrow strip of water separated Monmouth from Staten Island. Royal headquarters in New York badly needed supplies and commissioned Tye to gather food and strike back at the Americans.

Tye's initial military successes shaped a dramatic proposal by former New Jersey governor William Franklin.[128] Franklin sought to intimidate

"Rebels" and relied on forces who knew the country. Though his proposals do not mention blacks, Tye's was the most striking example of the sort of irregular force on which Franklin planned to rely.[129]

In May 1779, Franklin proposed to Major John André, the British spy, the creation of a Loyalist "Intelligence Board." Officially, such a board would subpoena and examine under oath anyone coming from enemy lines into Manhattan. It would copy papers captured by imperial troops, pay informants, and launch military expeditions. In practice, the board would enable Loyalists to act as guerilla fighters, independently of the Crown. It would form bodies of black-led irregular troops, notably the multiracial band commanded by Captain Tye, who could act with complete freedom. André supported the board. Clinton, however, feared such a plan would give Tory civilians too much authority.[130] He did not acknowledge the proposal.

In June, Franklin sent a revised version to William Tryon, commander of provincial forces in New York. The board's army, Franklin argued, would "distress the Enemy in any Quarter not expressly forbid by the Commander in Chief." It would avoid cruelty "unless by way of Retaliation"—an admission of the vengefulness that marked the Patriot and Tory rivalry. It would conduct guerilla operations, share in plunder, and control its own prisoners. In return, Clinton would receive intelligence and enlist locals dedicated to destroying the Patriots. Tryon submitted the new plan. Still fearing Loyalist independence, Clinton again rejected it.[131] Nonetheless, the imperial leadership widely discussed Franklin's proposal. New York authorities sponsored "Captain Tye" and organized the Black Pioneers, led by another black officer, Colonel Stephen Blucke.[132] (The Crown did not formally appoint Tye captain or colonel. In a sign of respect, however, imperial officers addressed him by these titles. New York authorities paid Tye for his efforts, sometimes as much as five gold guineas per raid.[133])

On July 15, 1779, Tye's guerillas, aided by the white Tory John Moody, launched a series of raids in New Jersey. According to one newspaper report, "About fifty Negroes and refugees landed at Shrewsbury and plundered the inhabitants of near 80 head of horned cattle, about 20 horses and a quantity of wearing apparel and household furniture. They also took off William Brindley and Elisha Cook."[134]

According to historian Graham Russell Hodges, Tye's raids against his former masters combined banditry, marronage—his forces lived as a small colony in the swamps and in Refugee Town, Sandy Hook, New Jersey—and formal commissions from the redcoats.[135] Tye took Monmouth

Patriot officers and soldiers prisoner and seized cattle, clothes, and silver plate. Like a mountain lion, Tye knew places of refuge. Patriots were able to kill only a few of his men.

In the spring of 1779, Tye again launched raids into New Jersey. Historian Margaret Washington estimates that he commanded eight hundred men. This figure seems high, though reports in contemporary New Jersey and Philadelphia papers are almost certainly low. No one saw the irregulars coming. Few Patriots formally reported the battles. Washington rightly judges that "he was probably more feared in that region than any other British loyalist, black or white." Many blacks joined him. Others, according to Washington, "certainly got a big charge out of the fact that here was this black man, who was leading these raids against the patriots, freeing slaves. And it gave them a sense of their own capacity."[136]

On March 30, 1780, a letter from Trenton in the Whig *Pennsylvania Evening Post* reported that "a party of Negroes and Refugees, from the Hook, landed at Shrewsbury in order to plunder."[137] Tye captured Captain Warner, Captain James Green, and Ensign John Morris. Warner purchased his freedom for "two half joes" (coins with the value of eighteen shillings each). Tye took the two remaining prisoners to Sugar House Prison. Tye's men also killed John Russell, a Patriot who had raided Staten Island. Labeling Tye's guerillas "ruffians" and "banditti," a letter in a Whig newspaper praised Russell for "making some resistance to their depredations." He killed one of Tye's fighters. Tye's men set fire to his house and, in a grim consequence of war, wounded Russell's grandchild.

Tye carefully distinguished among Monmouth Patriot leaders. He executed those who had hounded and hung Loyalists. These raids brought consternation to the Patriots and inspired black and white Tories. Three weeks later, near Newark, a different band of black and white refugees captured Patriot Matthias Halsted at his home. They took "bed, bedding, family wearing apparel and 7–8 head of creature [cattle]."[138]

In leading multiracial victories, Tye provided a second chance after the Dunmore Proclamation for the imperial army to rely on a second revolution to defeat independence, an opportunity that was even more militarily promising. The Crown could have emancipated blacks and, aided by black recruits, perhaps could have retained many colonies, particularly in the South. In New Jersey, led by William Franklin, Tories sponsored many irregular units such as Tye's. In addition, after 1779 in South Carolina, the Crown would rely on "Black Dragoons." Some of the thousands of not yet organized blacks who followed British troops may also have formed irregular companies.[139]

On November 27, 1780, the *New York Mercury* lamented that "a desire of obtaining freedom unhappily reigns throughout the generality of slaves at present."[140] Journeying from nearby states, blacks crossed the border between New Jersey and New York to freedom under British rule. One year earlier, William Livingston, New Jersey's Patriot governor, proposed gradual abolition, but the New Jersey legislature had not supported him. In correspondence, however, the governor kept silent about Tye's raids. Yet he sent to Congress a copy of a captured letter from the Earl of Dartmouth to Dunmore as proof that the royal governor of Virginia had recruited blacks.

Joseph Murray, a private in the Patriot Monmouth County militia, twice joined attacks on Refugee Town. He denounced two leading Loyalists.[141] On June 7, 1780, at Murray's house in Colt's Neck—Captain Tye's hometown—Tye and his men assassinated him. On June 9, Patriot general David Forman notified Governor Livingston of this raid—without mentioning Captain Tye, as if afraid of the name—and requested aid: "The Day before yesterday Joseph Murray was murdered by a party of those Refugees while he was at His Harrow in his Corn field—this we doubt not when taken in to account of our other Numerous distresses will induce your Excellency to exert your self in Establishing such a guard and will tend to restore in some measure the Security of this County."[142]

Forman, notorious as "Black David" for lynching Tories, did not know that on June 6, Governor Livingston had instructed the assembly to supply the Monmouth militia "with provisions as a matter requiring all possible dispatch, lest the Post be deserted, & a greater part of the Country be thereby exposed to the depredations of the Enemy."[143] Forman also wanted more troops.

On June 8, Forman had also notified Livingston that "a party of Negroes about 30 in Number did this afternoon Attack and Take Captain Barns Smock and a Small party that were Collected at his House for their Mutual Defense."[144] On June 21, the *Philadelphia Gazette and Weekly Advertiser* announced: "Ty with his party of about 20 blacks and whites, last Friday afternoon took and carried prisoners Capt. Barns Smock and Gilbert Vanmater; at the same time spiked up the iron four pounder at Capt. Smock's house."[145] Smock had used a four-pound cannon to warn neighbors of the raid and to summon others to fight. Tye captured twelve Patriots. Accounts of hostile troops in combat are rarely exact. Note the difference of one-third in the estimates between the *Gazette* and Forman reports.

In response, Livingston declared martial law. Like Henry Laurens, he favored abolition in the abstract. Yet instead of calling for Patriot emancipation and soldiering, he fought against blacks rebelling for freedom. The diversion of Tye's raids, along with planting season, which left slaves unguarded in the fields, favored escape. According to the *New Jersey Journal and Political Intelligencer*, "Twenty-nine Negroes of both sexes deserted from Bergen County in early June [1780]."[146]

On June 20, "a party of the enemy, consisting of Tye, with 30 blacks, 36 Queen's Rangers, and 30 refugee Tories" landed at Conascung, according to a letter from Monmouth County in the *Pennsylvania Evening Packet*. Tye's forces "got in between our scouts" undiscovered, "plundered [James Mott's] and several . . . neighbors houses of almost every thing in them, and carried off the following persons, viz. Mr. James Mott, sen., Jonathan Pearse, James Johnson, Joseph Dorset, William Blair, James Walling, jun., John Walling, sen., Phillip Walling, James Wall, Matthew Grigs." Having given the exact names of ten whites, the writer also mentions "several negroes." For the Patriots, "property" did not have names. The irregulars also took "a great deal of stock." An American raid, the letter announced, reenslaved "all the Negroes, one excepted"; it also recaptured "horses, horned cattle, and sheep." Apparently, though, it did not free the whites.[147]

Mott, captured in that raid by Tye, was a major in the Monmouth militia, and Captain James Johnson led soldiers from Hunterdon. Tye also arrested six privates serving under these officers. He thus captured or killed ten Patriot officers and conveyed eight additional prisoners to Sugar House Prison in New York.

In late August, Tye captured Hendrick and John Smock, brothers of Barnes Smock, whom he had previously detained. On September 1, he trapped Captain Josiah Huddy in a house. Hanging Loyalist Stephen Edwards from an oak tree near Monmouth Courthouse, Huddy had bragged that he "Greased the Rope well" and "pull[ed] the Rope hand over hand," along with "Black David" Forman.[148] With "two loaded guns," the *Pennsylvania Packet* reported, Huddy and "a girl," Lucretia Emmons, defended the house. Huddy ran from room to room, firing. Emmons reloaded. After a two-hour battle, Tye set the house on fire. His troops captured Huddy. In an account published on October 3, the *Packet* imagined an attack on the house by "72 men, comprised of New Levies, Refugees and Negroes." Huddy "wounded their brave Negro Tye (one of Lord Dunmore's crew)" and arranged a truce. "On their entering the House, when [Tye's forces] found that none but he defended it . . . it was with the greatest difficulty he was prevented from being murdered." In the Patriot account, violating the truce, Tye's raiders arrested Huddy. They then made, the *Packet* suggested, "a shameful and silent retreat, loaded with disgrace."[149] But Tye released Lucretia Emmons.

While Tye's troops were returning to Refugee Town, six Patriot militiamen intercepted them on the river. If the guerillas had numbered seventy-two as the *Packet* reported, they would have overwhelmed the Patriots. In the fighting, the prisoner jumped from the boat. Shouting "I am Huddy," he waded to the Patriot forces. Soon after the battle, Tye contracted lockjaw and died.

BLACK FREEDOM FIGHTERS AND GUERILLA WAR

Tye's actions were conspicuous, but far from unique. Along a broad New Jersey front, both free blacks and slaves had preceded Tye in flocking to the British standard, and others followed in his footsteps. For instance, in September 1776, when General Howe's redcoats conquered Long Island and New York City and established an outpost in New Barbadoes Neck, New Jersey, freeborn blacks, including John, Jacob, and Betty Richards, joined them as soldiers. Escapees Sam Albert, Peter Jackson, and Jacobus Westervelt of Bergen County worked for the Wagon Master General's Department or as woodcutters. In the Black Pioneers, "Jack" from Hackensack became a spy. The Crown employed Thomas Lydecker, his wife, and John and Kitty Ryerson, also from Hackensack.

In Closter, Tenafly, and Tappan, New Jersey, black soldiers fought in imperial raids. On November 23, 1776, they sacked Patriot homes, including that of the Reverend Dirck Romeyne in Schraalenburgh. On October 30, 1778, Patriot Richard Varick mourned the loss of his father's slaves: "In the beginning of the war, my father had two middle-aged Negroes and wenches—he has lost the wench. . . . One Negro died and the last wench and one Negro left with the enemy to my mother's distress."[150] In early 1779, Loyalist soldiers from British blockhouses, including blacks, raided homes in Bergen and Essex Counties. The blockhouses provided refuge for escapees.

On March 28, 1779, Ward's Blacks, commanded by Thomas Ward, raided Closter. On April 11, they attacked English Neighborhood; on April 12, Little Ferry; and on May 11, Closter again. Ward's Blacks were one of two companies in the Loyalist Refugee Volunteers. The other, led by Abraham Cuyler, also enlisted many blacks, including women, to cut wood for New York City. Stephen Blucke, freeborn, headed a new company of Black Pioneers that fought in Morris County, New Jersey.

Black escapees crossed to New York from ferry landings at Fort Lee,

Bull's Ferry, and Fort Delancey at New Barbadoes Neck, New Jersey. At Weehawken, blacks rolled logs down the natural gorge, strapped them together, and floated across the Hudson to freedom in British-occupied New York.

From Bull's Ferry, imperial troops forayed into Tappan and Schraalenburgh.[151] In 1780, commanding one thousand Patriots, Anthony Wayne attacked the landing. It was defended by 112 troops, including 20 blacks, led by Captain Ward.[152] Ward's troops inflicted sixty casualties. In embarrassment, Wayne retreated. Loyalist New York celebrated Ward and his men.[153]

In this context, Tye's actions set an example of what multiracial guerillas could accomplish. Many Patriots admired Tye's daring. After he died, a New Jersey paper extolled Tye as "a brave and courageous man whose generous actions placed him above his white counterparts."[154] Tye had avenged crimes perpetrated by Continental troops. His selective targeting of Patriots did not inflame his opponents, who in death praised him.

In 1780 Colonel Blucke replaced Tye as commander of irregular raids in the New Jersey area. Following Tye's example, many other blacks felt empowered to launch such battles.[155] In New York, Captain George Fraction, who had escaped from a slave owner in James River, Virginia, became the new leader of the Black Brigade. According to the *New Jersey Gazette*, in June 1782, at Forked River, a party of "about 40 whites and 40 blacks" set fire to Samuel Brown's salt works. It proceeded to Barnegat, "burning the salt-works along the shore."[156]

Black soldiers acted independently against slave auctions. In July 1782, according to Reverend Dirck Romeyn of Schraalenburgh, a Patriot captain Hessius from Totowa Falls, accompanied by a Mr. Van Houten, journeyed to New York "to enquire about some runaway Negroes and 'tis said sold a wench of his." Selling others flaunted bondage, enraging freed blacks. Hessius "was beset upon and murdered by about 12 or 15 of Ward's Blacks not far from Bergen."[157] Historian Graham Russell Hodges draws an analogy between such incidents of Afro-American self-defense or vengeance and black riots against slave owners—which were plainly struggles for freedom—in the 1790s and early 1800s.[158] "In consequence of this affair," Romeyn conjectured to fellow Patriot Richard Varick, "it is said that the Refugee Negroes are all disarmed and that they will be transported and sold."[159] They were not.

According to the October 28, 1783, *Pennsylvania Packet*, the Black Brigade continued to operate independently in alliance with white artisans and sailors: "Capt. Stewart's vessel with the colours of the United States of America flying, was boarded by the Canaille [French word for "rabble"], who, in a riotous manner, tore down and carried [them] through the streets in triumph, attended by a Chosen group of blacks, seamen and loyalist leather-aprons."[160] The continuing unity of black and white sailors and artisans threatened the Patriot elite.

In a war within the war, Patriots murdered Tories, and Tories, led by Franklin and Tye, retaliated. A cycle of unnecessary death and terror marked the Patriot and Tory clash. It helped create an atmosphere in which many Tories had to flee. Patriot brutality often started the cycle. Patriots were at least as barbarous to whites as were the Loyalists. Toward black soldiers, however, they were uniquely murderous.

After the British defeat at Yorktown, New Jersey Tories, led by William Franklin, correctly feared that the Crown might abandon them. To prolong the war, they retaliated against Josiah Huddy, the Patriot who wounded Colonel Tye. In the spring of 1782, the Royal Armed Boat Company, commanded by Captain Nathan Hubbell, included several blacks. On March 23, joined by forty "Associated Loyalists," among them black soldiers, Hubbell attacked a blockhouse at Toms River. Both sides lost several dead and wounded. The Crown imprisoned the American garrison, including Huddy.

In a March 30 skirmish, the Patriots had captured six Associated Loyalists, including "Negro Moses." According to the prisoners, the Patriots murdered Phillip White, a white Tory. The Patriots played up White's dangerousness. In a letter to the *New Jersey Gazette*, one wrote:

> On Saturday, the 30th of March last, [White] was surprised by a party of our people, and after he had laid down his arms, in token of surrendering himself a prisoner, he again took up his musket and killed a son of Col. Hendrickton; he was however taken by our light horse, and, on his way from Colts-Neck to Freehold, where they were conducting him, he again attempted to make his escape from the guard, who called on him several times to surrender, but he continued running, although often crossed and re-crossed by the light horse, and declined to stop, and finally, when leaping into a bog, impassable by the horse, he received a stroke in the head with a sword which killed him instantly.[161]

Samuel Taylor, a Loyalist farmer, reported White's death to William Franklin and urged retaliation against Huddy. Franklin concurred and assigned Captain Richard Lippincott, another Associated Loyalist, to assassinate him. Rebels had stolen Lippincott's property and had "executed in the cold blood" many of his neighbors.[162]

On April 8, the Crown assigned Lippincott to exchange Huddy for Captain Peter Tilton. Instead, Lippincott ordered a black soldier, perhaps in revenge for Tye, to hang Huddy and pinned a note to the dead man's chest: "We, the Refugees, have with grief long beheld the cruel murders of our brethren, and finding nothing but such measures daily carrying into execution, we, therefore, determine not to suffer without taking vengeance for the numerous cruelties, and having made use of Captain Huddy as the first object to present to your view, and further determine to hang man for man, as long as a refugee is left existing. UP GOES HUDDY FOR PHILIP WHITE."[163]

This execution stirred a furor among Patriots that lasted through the peace negotiations.[164] In the *New Jersey Gazette* for April 15, 1782, a letter from an anonymous Patriot insisted: "This murder was attended with so much deliberate injustice and wanton cruelty, that the circumstances ought to be . . . made publick . . . as a shocking instance of the blackness of that guilt of which human nature is capable."[165]

On April 20, with icy politeness, General Clinton informed William Franklin, the leader of the Associated Loyalists:

Murder ha[s] been lately committed in Monmouth by the Refugees from New York on the Body of Captain Huddy; and . . . Brigadier General Forman, who commands in that District, [h]as gone to General Washington to complain of the Outrage.

As the Report is further ascertained by an authenticated Copy of a Label found on the said Huddy's Breast; and I understand that the deceased was a Prisoner in the Custody of the Commissary to the Board of Associated Loyalists, I . . . request you will signify to them that they will be pleased to cause an immediate Enquiry to be made into this Matter, and report to me as soon as possible.[166]

On April 26, in a worried afterthought that the board might continue killing prisoners, Clinton ordered it to cease retaliations: "It is my positive command that the [board] shall not in future remove or hange any Prisoner of War in the Custody of the Commissary without having first obtained my Approbation and Orders, and that they will be pleased to make me an immediate Report of the Names and Numbers of the Prisoners of War at present in their Power and where confined."[167]

In an extension of the guerilla war led by Tye and Blucke, black redcoats sometimes fought their own war against Tory slave owners. On July 7, 1782, nine black Refugee Volunteers took two Tories prisoner at Bergen Neck. They set one free. The other, Cornelius Niffee, had just sold the wife of Henry Scobey, one of the soldiers, in New York. To sell human beings away from their families was a great crime of bondage. Forming a firing squad, the soldiers executed Niffee.

In a subsequent court-martial, no one would confess to firing the fatal shot. Some refused, they said, to fire. One or two shot into the air.[168] Major Thomas Ward stressed the independence with which these soldiers had acted. The recorder speaks of him in the third person:

> Q: Was any Report made to him [Ward] by Sisco, who they termed Colonel or any of the Prisoners, of Cornelius Niffee being put to death?
> A: He never heard a word concerning it from any of them.
> Q: Did he give Orders to any of the Prisoners to apprehend Niffee, or put him to death?
> A: No; he knew nothing of the matter 'till a fortnight after such a thing had happened.
> Q: Were any of the Negroes, who they term Officers and Serjeants, appointed by him or any other Officer under his Command?
> A: No; the Officers were appointed among themselves, and them they obeyed as implicitly as if [Ward] had appointed them.[169]

That the blacks selected their officers testifies to their independence of the British hierarchy. Under Ward's formal command, they organized themselves and, in this case, defending justice, defied imperial authority.

The hearing sentenced four prisoners—Daniel Maffis, Thomas Cadmus, Caesar Totten, and William van Riper—to death. Ironically, it acquitted Scobey and four others. But the Crown executed no one. Instead, it transferred these soldiers elsewhere in the British Empire.[170]

The other black and multiracial guerillas that Tye's exploits inspired provided a potentially lethal weapon to the British, which, however, Clinton and other leaders—imperial hierarchs—could neither control nor fully trust. Such guerillas encouraged a spirit of independence and, as witnessed by the execution of Cornelius Niffee, even occasional rebelliousness against racist acts by Tories.

chapter 6 ¶ Black Fighters in the Two Revolutions

Would it not be as well to liberate and make soldiers at once of the blacks themselves, as to make them instruments for enlisting white soldiers? It would certainly be more consonant to the principles of liberty, which ought never to be lost sight of in a contest for liberty.
—*James Madison to Joseph Jones, November 28, 1780*

Until the British surrendered, Patriot and imperial rivalry to bring blacks into the war steadily eroded bondage. Driven more by pragmatic considerations than by principled objections to slavery, the revolution for the human rights of America's slaves proceeded in parallel with the revolution for American independence. However, both proceeded haltingly, and the second revolution encountered much resistance and several setbacks on both the Patriot and British sides. On both sides of the American Revolution, emancipated black slaves fought for their freedom, but the story of black fighters' contribution to the Revolution is the story of one victory achieved and of another victory deferred. On both sides of the conflict, however, visions of victory motivated black fighters in the two revolutions.

On the British side, Murphy Steele, who had once been a slave in North Carolina, had a vision of royal victory that relied on black soldiers and on Dunmore's strategy of emancipation. Steele prophetically elaborated a widespread insight that promised to revive British fortunes in the South.

In 1778 Steele had escaped to the British and had become a sergeant in the Black Pioneers. A return of Captain George Martin's company lists Steele as formerly a slave of Stephen Daniel. As a guide, his expertise included the vicinity of "Lookouts Folly," where he had lived, and territory ranging from "Rock fish to [the] South."[1] In Philadelphia, however, the Crown demeaningly required the company "to attend the Scavengers, assist in Cleaning the Streets and Removing all Newsiances being thrown into the Streets."[2] This experience shaped Steele's contrasting vision of blacks as fighters.

On August 16, 1781, Murphy Steele reported a series of visions to a British officer, who duly transmitted them to General Clinton: "About a fortnight ago at Noon, when he was in the Barracks of the Company in Water Street, he heard a Voice like a Man's (but he saw no body) which called him by his Name, and desired him to go and tell The Commander in Chief, Sir Henry Clinton, to send Word to Genl. Washington That he must Surrender himself and his Troops to the King's Army, and that if he did not the wrath of God would fall upon him."[3] This "Voice" offered shrewd political advice, requiring that Clinton "raise all the Blacks in America to fight against" Washington. If Clinton had followed it, the Crown would have won the war or at least would have forced the Americans to match its policies on the emancipation of slaves. "The Voice also said that King George must be acquainted with the above."[4]

But Steele did not initially accept this prophecy. The "Voice" had to reiterate its message. The speaker had come to Steele "three days ago in Queen Street and insisted that he should tell it to Sir Henry Clinton, upon which he answered that he was afraid to do it, as he did not see the Person that spoke." The "Voice" explained its origin: "That he must tell it, that he was not to see him, for that he was the Lord, and that he must acquaint Sir Henry Clinton that it was the Lord that spoke this; and to tell Sir Henry, also that he and Lord Cornwallis was to put an end to this Rebellion, for that the Lord would be on their Side."[5] Steele's is one of the few surviving black voices that resonate with "enormous power . . . from this period. Given imperial racism and the illiteracy in which slave owners kept most blacks, a vision came to him. But he also thought strategically. The voice helped to make Steele's startling words heard."[6] Clinton allowed blacks to serve the Crown in different ways, including soldiering. But he would not hear the sage advice of Murphy Steele.

Luckily for George Washington, Clinton, not Dunmore, commanded the imperial troops. Neither British leader was a competent general. Dunmore, however, understood the strategic potential of black emancipation and an "irregular" army. In contrast, as we have seen, Clinton did not, and he certainly did not attend to wisdom emanating from below, particularly from a black soldier. On December 27, 1781, Major General Alexander Leslie would report the Tories' despair to Clinton: "The people are daily quitting the town and the great part of our militia are with the enemy, after getting all they could from us. In short the whole of the country is against us but some helpless militia with a number of officers, women, children, Negroes, etc."[7]

Inadvertently, in this report Leslie suggests that blacks were the reliable rank and file. Yet he viewed them as hangers-on, an afterthought to women and children, listed ritualistically in British hierarchical order. Leslie did not recognize that, if asked, blacks who had escaped bondage with their families would fight fiercely as redcoats and guerrillas. He projected on them his own and Clinton's frailties. A year later, however, Leslie would advocate arming negroes. By then, however, Clinton and the administration in London had given up on the war.

Although imperial generals, notably Clinton and Cornwallis, recruited blacks, they were hierarchs and had no principled conception of human freedom. In contrast, as we have seen, revolutionary Americans such as John Laurens and others like him were more imaginative and principled. Yet as the example of Murphy Steele shows, blacks on the English side sometimes went even further than black Patriots in their allegiance and commitment to victory.

BRITISH DRAGOONS AND IRREGULARS

On the British side, the emergence of black and multiracial irregulars opened a second front for the Crown. Using surprise tactics, these troops struck at Patriot slave owners in their homes and crystallized their terror of slave insurrection. Patriot masters characterized black raids on plantations as "plundering." In 1779 Eliza Wilkinson described the "plundering of everything . . . worth taking" from her South Carolina plantation by irregulars, including "several armed Negroes who threatened and abused us greatly."[8] On December 30, 1779, from Charlestown, Patriot general Benjamin Lincoln informed Colonel Francis Marion: "The matter respecting winding off the cattle on the River, destroying the rice on Wright's Neck, the negroes' plundering, etc., I have shewn to the Governor."[9] In the South, nothing grew without slave labor. Those who plundered blacks of their lives accused black soldiers of "plundering."

In addition, black battalions defended Savannah when, in October 1779, a substantial Franco-American army, including blacks from Saint Domingue, besieged the city. On October 16, a British observer noted, "Our armed Negroes [were] skirmishing with the Rebels the whole afternoon." Two days later, "the armed Negroes brought in two Rebel Dragoons and eight Horses, and killed two Rebels who were in a foraging party."[10] On November 18, the *Royal Georgia Gazette* reported: "Saturday, the 16th [of October] in the afternoon, there was a good deal of skirmishing on Mr. McGillivray's plantation between some Negroes and a party of rebels, and the latter were several times driven from the buildings on the plantation into the woods. Want of ammunition, however, obliged the blacks to retreat in the evening with the loss of one killed and three or four wounded, the enemy's loss is not known."[11] In April 1780, the American John Louis Gervais wrote to Henry Laurens that "Col Pickens had been down with a party within 5 miles of Savannah, [and] . . . killed about 60 Negroes in arms."[12]

Late in the war in South Carolina, the Crown also relied on black irregulars. In 1782 William Matthews, a Patriot slave owner, lay sick. After a visit by "Negroe Dragoons," he described his fears in a letter to fellow Patriot farmer Gideon White. Beneath his slave-owner's braggadocio, his account reveals the decency of the blacks: "On the night of the 17th Janr. a Party of armed Negroes . . . surrounded the House & endeavoured to get me out by stratagem—failing in their first attempt they threaten'd to break in by force—but I was not to be intimidated or cajoled into their Power—after having demanded and obtained some refreshment they departed—swearing . . . that had I not been an Invalid they would have fired the House and cut me in Pieces."[13] Their decency contrasted with Patriot barbarism toward slaves and particularly toward black Loyalists.

Matthews continued to fear for his life. To White he wrote that "their Pilot went from this neighborhood where he has large connexions & as the surrounding Plantations are People[d] with large gangs of unruly Negroes . . . [whose masters are] absent from them I cannot think myself safe a single night."[14] To Matthews, this familiar "pilot" had no name. But like Captain Tye in New Jersey, these dragoons represented a sophisticated black army and an attractive royal presence.

Imperial troops robbed South Carolina Patriot Eliza Wilkinson's mansion on June 2, 1782. Hers is one of the few women's voices in the surviving manuscripts; she especially feared black Loyalists. To a modern sensibility, accustomed to rape and murder by soldiers on all sides, including by Americans, her indignation seems exaggerated. In this case, the British are represented as comical, petty thieves. Still, the violations were intense. The whites were menacing, "inhuman monsters"; the accompanying black Loyalists were, just by their presence, worse. In her letter book she wrote:

They were up to the house—entered with drawn swords and pistols in their hands . . . crying out: "Where're these women rebels?" (pretty language to ladies from the *once famed Britons!*) . . . The moment they espied us, off went our caps, (I always heard say none but women pulled caps!) And for what, think you? why, only to get a paltry stone and wax pin, which kept them on our heads; at the same time uttering the most abusive language imaginable and making as if they'd hew us to pieces with their swords. But it's not in my power to describe the scene: it was terrible to the last degree; and what augmented it, they had several armed Negroes with them, who threatened and abused us greatly.[15]

Here was the intimidating effect on Patriots—insurrection's incarnation of black troops.

To save her possessions, Wilkinson remonstrated with the redcoats: "I ventured to speak to the inhuman monster who had my clothes. I represented to him the times were such we could not replace what they'd taken from us, and begged him to spare me only a suit or two; but I got nothing but a hearty curse for my pains; nay, so far was his callous heart from relenting, that, casting his eyes towards my shoes, 'I want them buckles,' said he, and immediately knelt at my feet to take them out, which while he was busy about, a brother villain, whose enormous mouth extended from ear to ear, bawled . . . 'Shares there, I say; shares.'"[16]

Wilkinson was a Patriot sympathizer. Caught at her home on Yonge's Island, South Carolina, she argued with the British. Once, she and her household escaped to her sister's home in Wadmalaw. Another time, on a three-mile march to her father's plantation, she had compassion for a free Loyalist soldier whom one of her slaves bloodied. Yet she showed no inkling that bondage was wrong, that the Revolution was fought against freedom for blacks as much as for freedom for whites.[17]

Americans especially feared black guerilla war. On February 20, 1781, Patriot general Thomas Sumpter of the South Carolina militia worried about black troops, irregular and regular, who stripped the plantations, and to General Francis Marion he wrote, "I wish . . . that you may suppress every species of plundering, as the greatest evils to the publick, as well as individuals, are experienced thereby. You cannot be too particular. The enemy oblige the Negroes to make frequent sallies. This circumstance alone is sufficient to rouse and fix the resentment and detestation of every American who possesses common feelings."[18] Contrary to Sumpter's assertion about the British forcing them, however, blacks had their own motivations for "frequent sallies." Furthermore, many Americans had democratic "feelings." Sumpter records only the emotions of slave owners.

Officers such as Marion acted barbarously toward blacks. Marion defeated Tory major Micajah Ganey and five hundred soldiers at the battle of Bowling Green. The second article of their treaty, concluded on June 17, 1781, required that Ganey "deliver up all Negroes, horses, cattle, and property that have been taken from this or any other State."[19] On September 2, Governor Rutledge wrote to Marion from his Ackermans plantation in

South Carolina: "Severe examples must be made of all Negroes who carry any provisions of any kind, aid, or assist, or carry any intelligence to or for the enemy; agreeably to the laws of this State, all such Negroes shall suffer death."[20]

Marion feared that British general Leslie would soon embark from Charlestown and take many blacks to freedom with him. On March 10, 1782, Marion ordered Colonel Peter Horry, a plantation owner near Wiyanh Bay, to seize all who did not have written permission to travel: "Every Negro in custody of whatever person that has not a pass from Governor Matthews, Gen. Greene, or myself must be stopped, and kept in close confinement until further orders."[21] On October 6, under the Negro Act of 1740, John Matthews, the new governor, ordered Marion to apply draconian measures: "As they were taken in arms, [blacks] must be tried by the Negro law; and if found guilty, executed, unless there are any whose cases are so far favorable as to induce the court to recommend them to mercy, and the executive authority interpose and pardon them."[22]

Many slaves of Tories escaped with the British, and the fabled Marion sought to terrorize the escapees. On November 27, 1782, Jonathan McKinnon, British deputy quartermaster general, reported the head of a black known only as Harry planted on a stake along the roadside. He had been owned by a Mr. Galliard, a Charlestown Tory and, as McKinnon underlined, had remained enslaved.

However, according to McKinnon, Lord Rawdon, the commander of Camden, and Lieutenant Colonel Nisbet Balfour had employed Harry as a spy, "in which capacity He was very serviceable." Even the ugly racist Balfour made use of black recruits. Technically, the Quartermaster Department had enrolled Harry as a guide. On a mission to Monk's Corner, Marion's troops had taken him prisoner. Later, when General Charles Gould and his royal troops passed Greenland's swamp, they saw with horror that the Patriots had beheaded Harry.[23] This beheading was another act in the depraved Patriot campaign for bondage.

As the war continued, the Crown increasingly commissioned Black Dragoons. In contrast to blacks on the Patriot side, it paid these irregulars. A 1782 abstract lists four black officers by name, again pointing to a transformation in imperial strategy to expand the responsibilities of black soldiers: "Captain March, Lieutenant Mingo, Adjutant Garrick, and Quarter Master Robins." As shown in table 2, Paymaster Robert Andrews commanded Colonel Robert Gray to pay Captain March the following sums for thirty soldiers for July 1 through September 30, 1782.[24]

TABLE 2. Payment to Black Dragoons, July 1–September 30, 1782

	Pounds	Shillings	Pence
1 Captain at 2/4	10	14	8
1 Lieutenant at 1/2	5	7	4
1 Adjutant at 1/2	5	7	4
1 Quarter Master at 1/2 5	7	4	
3 Sergeants at 8d	9	4	0
23 Rank & File at 6d	88	18	8

Two accounts remain of someone who may have been Captain March. In a battle with Black Dragoons on April 22, 1782, the Patriots killed and hacked to pieces "a brave soldier named March"—perhaps the captain cited here—and "two or three" companions.[25] Alternately, in a postwar petition, a March Kingston asked the London Loyalist Claims Commission for relief for crippling injuries. He had fought as a guide under Lord Cornwallis, Kingston reported, "in which Service your Memorialist was wounded in the Knee which is now broke out again and Rendered him Quite Incapable of Any Service and is fearful of being a Criple for Life." In the British army, blacks took enormous risks. Kingston had also lost "His Horse and Acutriments" to the Patriots.[26]

Irregular war mainly spurred imperial efforts and intimidated Patriots. But on January 17, 1782, as we have seen, Black Dragoons led by John Jackson raided the mansion of a Tory, William Matthews.[27] The Crown could have punished Jackson for raiding a friend and supporter, but it would not give up black leaders or soldiers. In the Book of Negroes of 1783, John Jackson and his wife, Hannah, both listed as thirty years old and members of the New York Black Brigade, would leave on HMS L'Abondance.[28]

To join Governor Dunmore in Virginia in 1776, Jackson had fled slave owner Peter Curtinas of Morristown, New Jersey; his wife had escaped from Aaron Gilbert. After returning with Dunmore to New York, Jackson may have served with Captain Tye in New Jersey. Perhaps to enhance guerilla warfare in the South, the New York leadership sent him to South Carolina.[29] After the strike against Matthews, however, Jackson was ordered to return, and he immigrated to Canada.[30]

Independently organized Black Dragoons sometimes operated with white troops and sometimes on their own.[31] On August 11, 1782, Charles Cotesworth Pinckney, president of the South Carolina Senate, wrote in a letter to Arthur Middleton, signator of the Declaration of Independence, that "the black Dragoons . . . are daily committing the most horrible depredations and murder."[32] In 1782 Major General Leslie formed an irregular black unit to cover the imperial retreat. Serving with the Second Pennsylvania Regiment in the South, Patriot lieutenant John Bell Tilden wrote in his journal of a clash "with one of ye British negro Captains and his Troop."[33] His phrasing testifies to a broad emergence of irregular imperial forces under black leadership.

On August 29, from Uxbridge, Governor John Matthews warned General Marion about the militia's slackness and about unimpeded raids by black irregulars: "I cannot help thinking it reflects no great credit on our cavalry in this part, to lie still in their quarters and suffer about a dozen or twenty Negroes to come out almost every night in the week and carry off cattle, horses, and anything else they want." Matthews, however, hoped that Marion could prevent blacks from supplying the Crown: "I must entreat you, sir, to form some plan which will be most effectual to stop such a shameful commerce; it is no less villainous than true that the Charlestown markets are now daily supplied with the greatest plenty of everything they want."[34] In this peculiar moral logic, traffic in blacks and slave ownership were not shameful. The act of blacks reappropriating what they had produced and selling it in Charlestown was shameful.

In late August, Marion's irregulars deflected an attack made by several hundred British troops and "some Colored Dragoons."[35] On December 9, 1782, within a week of the British departure from Charlestown, Judge Thomas Bee, "at the request of several inhabitants of the Goose Creek neighborhood," wrote to Governor Benjamin Matthews that "the black dragoons . . . have been out four times within the last ten days plundering & robbing between the Quarter house and this place—last night they came as high as Mrs. Godins, where they continued from 11 o'clock till 4 this morning & carried off everything they could, except what was in the house which they did not enter—all her cattle, sheep, hogs, horses, & half the provisions she had was moved away." Again, the black troops' lack of murderousness contrasts with the barbarism—Harry's head on a stake—of South Carolina Patriots. The decency of black soldiers also contrasts with the insurrection in Saint Domingue. North American blacks acted as a comparatively disciplined army of freedom. "[Mrs. Godins] thinks they number at least one hundred all Blacks. . . . At going off they said they would return this evening or tomorrow night & pay a visit to Mr. Parker and Mr. Smith, which they may possibly do."[36]

Guerilla resistance in support of the British had become a leading feature of the war. It reflected the independent initiative of blacks, many thousands of whom escaped and joined the Crown or followed its troops. These included mostly former slaves of Patriots but some slaves of Tories as well. As Murphy Steele's vision expressed, many blacks had a sustained vision of fighting the Patriots. Thus, until 1787, the "Soldiers of the King of England," as some roughly three hundred black Loyalist irregulars called themselves, honoring the lost cause of Cornwallis and London, fought for freedom in Georgia and South Carolina. Led by Captains Cudjoe and Lewis, they constructed a maroon colony of twenty-one houses. They planted rice fields near the Savannah River and raided nearby plantations.

In 1787 the Georgia militia attacked, killing six. It captured, tried, and beheaded Captain Lewis. But these soldiers retreated deeper into the South Carolina swamps and fought on.[37] These courageous men were the last breath, within the war itself, of the second revolution.[38]

BLACK PATRIOT TROOPS IN THE
REVOLUTION: SOUTH CAROLINA

On the Patriot side, while blacks fought for the independence of the colonies from British rule, their contributions to the first revolution did not always advance the second. Indeed, in the South it was a struggle for men of principle, such as John Laurens, who had been sent home by the Continental Congress in 1779 to raise a force of freed black troops, to try to accomplish that task, coupled with attempts by Patriot general Nathanael Greene to second his efforts. As on the British side, racism and prejudice often trumped both pragmatism and principle. In South Carolina and Georgia, many elite Patriot slave owners remained blind even to the principles of the first revolution, let alone to the pragmatic reasons for freeing and recruiting black slaves to advance their cause.

On January 18, 1781, at the Battle of Cowpens, in South Carolina, General Daniel Morgan led an American victory in which, Morgan reported to Nathanael Greene the next day, the "young slave William Bell" shot a British officer who menaced Colonel William Washington, George Washington's cousin. An 1845 painting by William Ranney depicts Bell on horseback with a gun and the British officer with a sword raised over Washington.[39] This is the sole indication that some blacks, though still enslaved, fought for Patriot South Carolina during the Revolutionary War.[40]

Instead, the story of black participation on the Patriot side in the American Revolution in South Carolina is in some measure the story of the trials faced by John Laurens and General Nathanael Greene to secure that participation despite the efforts of Patriot slave owners to prevent it. In South

Carolina after 1779, when the Crown had conquered Charlestown, the task of the Continental army was to prevent further British successes and retake the capital. Writing to Governor John Rutledge on December 9, 1781, General Greene insisted that blacks "would make good Soldiers" and that confronted with black as well as white troops, the British would hesitate before "making further attempts upon this country." Such troops would secure South Carolina "if the Enemy mean to act vigorously upon an offensive plan, or furnish a force to dispossess them of Charlestown, should it be defensive."[41] In addition, South Carolina's weak finances made black recruitment necessary and viable. Freedom would substitute for wages.

In the same letter, Greene described blacks—many times the number of whites in several counties—as South Carolina's natural strength. With a frankness typifying the military attitude of the Continental army toward South Carolina, he added that had the legislature initially recruited blacks, it could have blocked imperial reconquest of Charlestown. Instead, in devoting its militia to slave catching, South Carolina's leaders betrayed even the fight for independence.

Like Laurens, however, Greene imagined only a limited impact on the remaining slaves of emancipating some in exchange for soldiering: "And I am persuaded, that the incorporation of a part of the negroes, would rather tend to secure the fidelity of the others, than excite discontent, mutiny and desertion among them."[42] But as South Carolina slave owner Aedanus Burke angrily insisted in the legislature, Greene would probably not have regretted the abolition of bondage. South Carolina was no Rhode Island. In any case, most blacks had already escaped to the Crown and emancipation. For the Patriots, the economic dependence of their aristocratic supporters on bondage trumped all other considerations.

From the legislature, Greene requested two regiments for the Continental army and two for the South Carolina militias. All soldiers "should have their freedom and be cloathed . . . without which, they will be unfit for the duty expected from them."[43] In addition, he requested "a corps of Pioneers, and a corps of Artificers, each to consist of about Eighty men." Here, he bowed to South Carolina's reactionary intransigence: these corps would remain in bondage.[44]

Governor Rutledge stalled. The council could not give an opinion, he wrote on December 18, because "three members . . . left for Martin's Tavern, where the election for the Assembly was to be held 'Yesterday and today.'"[45] On December 23, Rutledge reported that the council had referred the issue to the assembly, which would not convene for several weeks.[46]

As an officer in the field, John Laurens supported Greene's proposal for a "black levy" and on December 28 warned Greene of British reinforcements headed to Charlestown: "It appears to me that the Governor & Council should not lose a moment in carry[ing] the black levy plan into execution but I know that unless they are goaded upon the subject, their deliberations and delays will lose the opportunity which offers."[47]

A month later, Laurens denounced the council's decision to Washington: "The Governor & Council of this State, notwithstanding the hopes that had been given me, declined complying with Gen Greenes recommendation to reinforce this department with black Levies—alleging that the business wd come with more propriety before the Legislature which was shortly to be convened." He would make "a last effort," Laurens promised, "for the execution of a plan which appears to me so essential to the deliverance and happiness of this state."[48]

In 1779 John Rutledge had supported the Laurens proposal to the Continental Congress to free and arm three to five thousand blacks. But on January 18, 1782, the governor's speech to the South Carolina Assembly focused on the ostensible horrors committed by Loyalist blacks and Native Americans. Still Rutledge offered a backhanded, slave-owner's tribute to freedom: "Thus, the lives, liberties and properties of the people were dependant solely on the pleasure of British officers, who deprived them of either or all, on the most frivolous pretences. Indians, slaves, and a desperate banditti of the most profligate characters, were caressed and employed by the enemy to execute their infamous purposes." To racism, he appended the patriarchal fear that blacks and Indians would violate women and murder children: "Nor were their violences restrained by the charms of influence of beauty and innocence; even the fair sex, whom it is the duty of all . . . to protect, they and their tender offspring were victims to the inveterate malice of an unrelenting foe."[49]

On January 25, 1781, Rutledge sent an owner's lament to General Dan Morgan, praying that Morgan's troops might move Rutledge's slaves and ensure a crop: "I am in great hopes that the late affair with Master Tarleton will afford an opportunity of bringing away all my Negroes from Ninety-Six to Salisbury.[50] If an attempt can be made to remove 'em, with a probability of Success, I wish it may as soon as possible. . . . Tho' I have no doubt of recovering and holding So. Carolina [his sole public-spirited clause in the letter], yet as I have lost the two last years crops entirely . . . I w'd wish to send my Negroes, if I can, to some place where I may perhaps make a little by them." In a brief flash of conscience, Rutledge apologized for his corruption: "You will excuse my giving you any trouble about a private concern when you have so much about the publick Trusts (fortunately for me) committed to your charge."[51]

On January 21, 1782, General Greene appealed again to Rutledge's patriotism. With blacks, he noted, the redcoats had easily conquered Charlestown; with blacks, the Patriots could drive them out. Yet Greene recognized the net of bigotry spread against him: "If my zeal urges me to impress a measure which is opposed by common prejudices I hope it will be imputed to it's [sic] true motive, a desire to secure this unfortunate country from a repetition of the calamity under which it has groaned these two years past."[52] Imagine the regret that would ensue, Greene suggested, if peace were signed under the common international principle of uti possidetis, by which combatants retain the territories held at the conclusion of hostilities. Britain would rule Charlestown, Savannah, and the Deep South.

"The remedy [recruitment of blacks] may be disagreeable but who among you could they have foreseen what has happened would not have adopted this measure disagreeable as it is to have prevented so great an evil?" By both "reason and information," Georgia and South Carolina appeared to be targets of "the last efforts of British power." Would not the northern states see themselves as justified, Greene counseled, in giving away South Carolinian territory captured by the Crown "after you have refused to avail yourselves of these means?"[53]

Greene reminded Rutledge that the British were already "arming a considerable body of negroes." Perhaps exaggerating the number, he wrote, "I am well informed that they determine to compleat them to the number of 3,000 for the defence of Charles Town." In an April 15 note, however, Greene estimated to Marion that the English actually had "about 700" blacks under arms. But he also invoked a 1781 declaration in Parliament by John Montagu, first lord of the admiralty, that "the Ministry would avail themselves of every thing that God and Nature had put in their power to crush this rebellion."[54]

Greene subtly used the example of imperial recruitment and the constricting influence of Tory slave owners to suggest that the failure of the Patriot South Carolinian defense arose from a like influence of Whig slave masters:

Had not private avarice got the better of national policy in the british Army you would at this moment have been fast fettered with your own chains. Perhaps it was fortunate for you that the country fell so easy before the british army immediately after the reduction of Charles Town. A greater resistance of the period might have drawn their attention to this great resource that you had neglected to avail yourselves of which if you had adopted before the reduction of Charlestown . . . by removing the hopes from the ministry of Great Britain and increasing the difficulty of conquest of the Southern States might have given peace long since to all America.[55]

His words "this great resource" recall those of John Laurens. On January 24, 1782, to Washington, Greene sketched the desperate situation of his troops: "Our men are almost naked for want of overalls and shirts, and the greater part of the Army barefoot. We have no rum nor the prospect of any."[56] Intoxication would have perhaps dulled the horror. To South Carolina governor Matthews, Greene also bemoaned the lack of liquor.[57] "Had the enemy got knowledge and availed themselves of our situation," he informed Washington, "they might have ruined us."[58] He recommended that South Carolina "raise some black Regiments" because "to fill up their Regiments with whites is impracticable and to get reinforcements from the Northwards precarious, and at best difficult, from the prejudices respecting the climate." Though some South Carolinians supported his proposal, he told Washington that "the far greater part of the people were opposed to it."[59] As Laurens remarked, however, twice the number of assembly delegates now affirmed this proposal compared with those who had voted for the Continental Congress's 1779 resolution.[60]

On February 2, Greene wrote to Governor John Martin of Georgia: "From a persuasion that the State of South Carolina could not fill their Continental battalions, as well as from many other political reasons, I recommended to the State to raise a body of Negroes. I recommend the same measure to you. . . . One common evil threatens you both. This State has not acted upon it yet, but it is much to be feared, that private interest and imaginary evils will frighten the Legislature out of a measure that cannot fail if adopted to fix their liberties upon a secure and certain footing."[61]

As a source of political "vigor," Greene now bitterly recommended to Washington greater subordination of the states to the will of Congress:

When any State can be made to feel an inconvenience from disobeying a requisition of Congress, then, and not till then can we hope our measures will have vigor; and a combination of our force take place. We may write 'til we are blind; and the local policy of the States in perfect security will counteract our wishes. From this very same source I apprehend it impossible to establish matters of finance upon such a footing as to answer the public demands. If such of the States as refused or neglected to comply with the congressional requisitions were deprived of the liberty of trade either foreign or domestic out of their own State, it might serve to fix a little Obligation to effect compliance.[62]

By 1782 John Laurens was a representative in the South Carolina legislature, as well as a soldier. As Aedanus Burke noted, "Laurens tried yesterday to carry in the house his favorite scheme of raising 2500 blacks. Only himself, Ramsay, Mr. Ferguson & about 13 others joined in it."[63] Eleven days later, Laurens made a second attempt. Though "strongly urg'd in the Assembly and warmly debated," the legislature defeated the motion.[64] On February 7, 1782, Patriot general Lewis Morris complained from South Carolina to Major Jacob Morris, his son, that "the prejudices against the measure are so prevailing that no consideration could induce them to accept it."[65]

While the British mobilized Black Dragoons, the Patriot army stole slaves from undefended Loyalist plantations and perhaps redistributed them among officers and recruits. For instance, in 1781 American light troops—those who operated, like guerillas, outside the regular lines of battle—raided Loyalist Josiah Smith's Peedee plantation. In addition to rice and hogs, they "took away four of the estates' Negroes."[66] One owner, John Hopton, "heard [that his slaves] were distributed by the American General Sumpter in bounties for raising soldiers."[67]

The Patriots sometimes sacked deserted Loyalist plantations—deserted except for slaves. On James Island, John Peebles, a British officer, wrote in his diary in 1780 that the war reduced "poor Negroes to a starving condition in many places hereabout."[68] Hunger drove many to seek refuge with the Royal Army.

Governor Matthews feared the continuing redcoat mobilization of black troops. On the day that the legislature last rejected Patriot black recruitment, Matthews informed the representatives that the Crown had dispatched black forces to South Carolina. He invited General Greene to apply for non-arms-bearing black recruits.[69] Greene replied that he could use about 440: "140 wagoners, 150 pioneers, 120 artificers, and 20 or 30 servants."[70] In a typically racist observation, Matthews informed Greene that recruitment of blacks would free up "valuable soldiers." He commended Greene's request to the legislature: "If the propositions therein made of furnishing the army with a number of Negroes for the different services he has mentioned should meet your approbation, it will enable Gen. Greene to throw into the ranks a considerable number of valuable soldiers." The representatives approved this proposal.[71]

In response to Laurens's letters about the legislature's opposition to black recruitment, Washington argued that private interest, not the public good, "influences the generality of mankind."[72] As a slave owner, Washington had vacillated about Laurens's proposal to the Continental Congress, but finally had supported it. While Washington acted in the public interest during the Revolution, however, many Southerners did not.[73] Nevertheless, "with all the tenacity of a man making a last effort," Laurens wrote to Washington, he would throw himself into the task.[74]

On August 26, 1782, John Laurens spent a long night partying near the Combahee River. The next morning, he rode out with his troops. In a meaningless skirmish, he was ambushed and killed.[75] Among his family and friends, Laurens's death unleashed a torrent of sorrow. His influence is visible in the continuing unfolding of the abolitionist movement. In addition, Laurens was a charming, charismatic figure. His death contributed to the later personal and political weakening of his friends' support for abolition. Still, Hamilton continued to oppose slavery in New York.

About ending slavery, Henry Laurens tried to keep faith. Writing to William Henry Drayton on February 23, 1783, he advanced a republican insight that the security of a state depends on the equal property holding and vigorous work of citizens. No republic, Laurens contended, can survive the parasitism of the slave-owning few: "Should the future importation [of blacks] be prohibited or greatly restricted, the land already granted will be parceled out to poor white adventurers at easy rents or moderate purchases. There will not be such a glare of precarious riches as we have formerly seen in the possession of individuals; but the riches of the State will be greater and more permanent."[76]

Republican theorists had long emphasized the importance of smallholding farmer-soldiers and an army of citizens rather than a standing force. But equal citizen-soldiers would be the opposite of South Carolina's slave-owning elite, which had rejected John Laurens's proposal. Perhaps through timidity, Henry Laurens did not press this republican ideal.

He hoped, however, that the antislavery Moravians would send missions to South Carolina. As Laurens wrote to Drayton, "Such persons as you allude to, I have no doubt will make a happy exchange, mechanics will find full employment and good wages. Husbandmen may obtain land upon much better terms than they have been accustomed to. But I dare not speak positively of encouragements from the State." He added presciently, "I won't say "tis over our head the old House totters'; but 'tis certainly true that want of wisdom in that House may soon throw us again into a flame and retard the building of our own."[77] On February 15, 1783, he asked Drayton simply, "Have you reflected upon the great point of the abolition of slavery?"[78]

Nevertheless, Laurens, a latecomer to the peace negotiations ending the war, added Article VII, demanding the "return of slaves and other American property" that the British had taken. The other negotiators had forgotten this issue. John Laurens had fought to end slavery. Here, Henry Laurens betrayed his son.[79]

In England, however, Laurens befriended Richard Price, a leading abolitionist. To members of the South Carolina legislature, he circulated Price's 1784 *Observations upon the Importance of the American Revolution.* Some decried the book's denunciation of slavery. In a January 31, 1785, letter to the speaker of the assembly, Laurens replied, "I have not had time to read a single page of the Doctor's book, but if it contains attacks against the slave trade & slavery I am of opinion with yourself & Mr. Izard, the doctrine will not in the present day be pleasing to the generality of the inhabitants of this State; yet the time may come, the time was, when we solemnly engaged against further importations under a pretence of working by graduate steps a total abolition. We were then indeed in a religious mood & had appealed to God."[80] Here, he kept faith with his son.

Alexander Hamilton's friendship and alliance of principle with John Laurens affected him enormously. On August 15, 1782, on his election to Congress, Hamilton wrote to Laurens enthusiastically, "It is said your father is exchanged for Cornwallis, and gone to Paris to meet the other commissioners." On "our terms . . . peace made, my dear friend, a new scene opens." Henry Laurens's Article VII for the British to return the free to bondage would, however, disfigure "their terms." But that travesty would make Hamilton's next thought even more poignant: in "secur[ing] our Union on solid Foundations—a herculean task—and to effect which, mountains of prejudice must be levelled," he hoped John Laurens would join him. "Quit your sword, my friend; put on the toga. Come to Congress. We know each other's sentiments; our views are the same. We have fought side by side to make America free; let us hand in hand struggle to make her happy."[81]

On October 12, 1782, writing to Nathanael Greene, Hamilton memorialized his "dear and estimable friend": "His career of virtue is at an end. How strangely are human affairs conducted, that so many excellent qualities could not insure a more happy fate! The world will feel the loss of a man who has left few like him behind, and America of a citizen whose heart realized that patriotism of which others only talk. I shall feel the loss of a friend I truly and most tenderly loved, and one of a very small number."[82] Unlike Henry Laurens, Hamilton found apt words about John's death. His stress on John Laurens's democratic patriotism, his allegiance to a republic, recapitulated, in a modern evolution, the spirit of the Rousseauian *citoyen de Geneve*, that is, the theory of egalitarian—abolitionist—citizenship.

Yet the course of Hamilton's subsequent career resembled that of Henry Laurens at the Paris peace conference. In the *Federalist Papers*, Hamilton brilliantly designed institutions for commercial, antidemocratic purposes and, with President Adams, defended the Alien and Sedition Acts. Increasing embitterment about democracy emerged in Hamilton even as he became famous for commercial proposals such as the National Bank. In 1800 he campaigned against the unprincipled Aaron Burr. His death in a duel with Burr four years later revived, flickeringly, the honor he had shared with John Laurens. Laurens's charisma brought out the best in Hamilton. If they could have gone on together, Hamilton's later career would possibly not have been so dismally antirepublican.

On November 6, 1782, John Adams—poles apart from John Laurens politically—wrote to Henry Laurens that the new country had lost "its most promising character."[83] In a 1784 letter to Dr. William Gordon, George Washington praised Laurens, his former aide: "No man possessed more of the *amor patria*. In a word, he had not a fault that I ever could discover, unless intrepidity bordering on rashness could come under that denomination; and to this he was excited by the purest motives."[84] Without Laurens's influence, Washington, too, would become less principled over time.

BLACK PATRIOT TROOPS IN THE REVOLUTION: VIRGINIA

In Virginia, where thousands of blacks escaped to the Crown, the role played by blacks on the Patriot side in the first revolution was greater than in South Carolina. Given the resistance that Laurens and Greene encountered, however, almost any role at all would have been greater. In Virginia, Patriots recruited free blacks and still-enslaved substitutes for whites, but pitting the first revolution against the second, they also aggravated bondage—"enticing" white recruits with slaves as a motive for "independence" among whites. Powerful forces pressed for Patriot emancipation in Virginia—the logic of the revolution, the threat of English competition for troops, gradual emancipation in Pennsylvania, and the

Laurens resolution. Still, Virginia Patriots did not act. It was there, however, that free blacks on both sides played a role in the decisive battle of the Revolution.

In 1775 some one thousand free black men of military age lived in the state, and at least 179, including 25 slaves, fought for the Patriots.[85] Thus, the rate of enlistment of free blacks on the Patriot side, 15 percent, was high.[86] And Patriot Virginia's records understate the number of black soldiers. Official lists identify only thirty-three. By correlating pension requests, tax books, marriage registers, and "registers of free Negroes and mulattoes" with recruitment lists, however, historian Luther Jackson uncovered a larger number, 154.[87] Half a century after the Revolution, Virginia became solvent enough to provide veterans with pensions and land grants. Blacks had to petition, and in the process, they became identifiable. Blacks who had already died (most blacks lived then to about forty) do not appear on these lists. As Jackson argues, "The exact number of Virginia Negroes who fought in the Revolution may never be determined."[88]

Recruitment of free blacks thus created opportunities for the unfree. If a white "Patriot" sent a black substitute, he avoided going to war, but blacks who substituted for whites in the Revolution often later sued for freedom. Thus, in the Patriot navy, David Baker took the place of his "owner," Lawrence Baker. Later, Lawrence forced David again into bondage. In 1781 David Baker petitioned the legislature for freedom. Even in Virginia, slaves could appeal for redress. No record survives, however, of the legislature's decision. Other veterans were freed. Serving in the navy, William Boush and Jack Knight "belonged" to the Commonwealth of Virginia. In 1789 the legislature emancipated them.

Sometimes whites hired free blacks to substitute for them. For instance, John Key of Lunenberg took Christopher Carlton's place. In the First Virginia Regiment, Key served under General Nathanael Greene in the battles of Ninety-Six and Eutaw Springs. In the latter, he was severely wounded.

The Patriot forces had no need for blacks as guides. Nonetheless, slaves, notably James Armistead Lafayette and Saul Matthews, became invaluable Patriot spies. At Portsmouth, James Armistead, who would take Lafayette's name as an emblem of freedom, gathered information for the marquis about Cornwallis's movements. Camped seventy-five miles from Richmond and Williamsburg, the Americans and French needed to know whether Cornwallis would go north to New York, join royal forces in South Carolina, or retreat to Yorktown. Armistead told them of his retreat. In 1786 the legislature freed him.[89] Similarly, Saul Matthews entered the

British camp at Portsmouth. Lafayette, Greene, and Baron von Steuben praised his work. In 1792 the legislature granted his liberty.

At sea, record keeping was even more casual than on land. Blacks often appear in the Patriot rosters only with first names. "Toby," for example, escaped and enlisted under the name "William Ferguson." Slave owners traced him, however. Whether he continued to serve in the navy is unclear.

Patriot Virginia employed bondsmen as pilot-boat captains. For instance, Caesar Tarrant engaged Dunmore's flotilla near Hampton. As commander of the *Patriot*, Tarrant captured the *Fanny*, a brig loaded with supplies for imperial forces in Boston. In 1789 the Virginia General Assembly purchased Commander Tarrant from his "mistress" and manumitted him.[90] Slave traders had kidnapped Captain Starlins from Africa as a child. At James River, Starlins fought Dunmore. Before the war ended, however, he died, still a slave.

Preferring military service to bondage, many blacks served long terms in the Patriot armies. For instance, Shadrack Battles of Albemarle County joined the Tenth Virginia Regiment for three years, fighting at Brandywine, Monmouth, Germantown, Stony Point, and Savannah. (Perhaps he took his surname from his many experiences in combat.) An observer at Stony Point remarked that Battles served as "the right hand man of Clough Shelton, and in all the daring acts of that most intrepid officer."[91] This praise paints the black hero as but a satellite to a white officer. Actually, often with greater valor than whites, blacks fought for emancipation—their own and others.

Enlisting in 1776, Sylvester Beverly, a free black from Franklin County, fought at Monmouth, Stony Point, Paulus Hook, White Marsh, Guilford Courthouse, and Yorktown. After the Patriots defeated Cornwallis, Beverly guarded British prisoners.

William Flora of Portsmouth served in Captain Grimes's company at the battle of Great Bridge. When an imperial detachment attacked, other sentries fled. Flora alone kept firing. In typical racist perspective, a soldier reported that even though Flora was a "man of color," white officers and soldiers held him in high esteem. He fought for eight years in the Revolution and again in the War of 1812.[92]

At least seventy-five men, roughly 42 percent of black Patriot soldiers in Virginia, became seamen. On land, white Patriots feared that blacks might turn arms on their masters. Black sailors frightened white colonists less. At most, blacks could throw officers overboard. But the navy offered other opportunities; some blacks used service at sea to escape bondage.

Abel Spriggs was one of "a group of sailors who deserted the ship *Dragon*." In 1777 Francis Arbado, a "West Indian," departed from the navy without leave.[93]

On the Patriot brig *Northampton*, James Thomas of Norfolk served three years as a boatswain. James Barron Jr., a commandant in the Virginia navy, testified that Thomas fought bravely: "He was a fellow of daring and though a man of color was respected by all the officers who served with him." In this climate of contempt, blacks proved themselves only by extraordinary effort. As another example, James Nickens served in the Patriot navy for three years and fought under General Nathanael Greene in South Carolina. Yet at the battle of Eutaw Springs, a white officer stationed him with the baggage at the rear.[94]

When blacks who substituted for whites in the Revolution sued for freedom, sometimes their owners murdered them. On December 11, 1824, Margaret Brandum wrote to Colonels John and Charles Tucker. She was heir, she said, to "old Ned Brandum who was in the old Revolutionary war in the service of old Mr. Roaney as a substitute." In her account, three of Roaney's servants had enlisted. After the Revolution, Robin, Ned's brother, petitioned the legislature for emancipation. "In consequence of suing for his freedom," she reported, Roaney slew him. Virginia did not prosecute the malefactor.[95]

In addition, Margaret Brandum wrote for two other women, identified only as Dolly and Fanny, who hoped for pensions for soldiers in their family. For forty-one years, Margaret Brandum had been "somewhat afraid," she noted, and did not look to "white persons to protect me." She would, however, "trust to your two gentlemen's honour to see me right." She urged them to verify her claims. "In case you recover any thing for me," she suggested, "you'll keep the same as your property until you are satisfied." She also invited them to inquire about her "character," which had "never been blemished by no persons in my Neighborhood."[96]

Probing official records, however, historian Luther Jackson found only a Thomas Brandum, alternately "Brandon." During the Revolution, Brandum purchased 130 acres in Mecklenburg and would live there for fifty-six years. In 1780 Brandum joined the Continental army. He served in the battle of Camden under General Gates and at Yorktown. He married Margaret who, as his widow, drew a pension. The official story appears inaccurate in major respects. Thomas Brandum was probably the third substitute for owner Roaney, along with Ned Brandum, whom Margaret Brandum announces herself "heir to," and Robin Brandum. Possibly through the intervention of the Colonels Tucker, Margaret Brandum's request for aid was answered; only the note that Virginia provided a pension to the widow survives. The records that Jackson reviewed do not mention Ned and Robin Brandum. Thus, three blacks served, but officials recorded only one. They also depict Thomas Brandum's military service differently while mistakenly supposing that he was married to Margaret. Once again, Margaret Brandum's letter suggests a serious underestimate and misinterpretation of black participation on the Patriot side.

As the critical battles of the American Revolution approached, Patriots in southern states besides Virginia tried to recruit blacks. On June 5, 1781, John Cadwalader, a representative in the Maryland legislature, wrote to Washington, "We have resolved to raise, immediately, seven hundred and fifty negroes, to be incorporated with other troops; and a bill is now almost completed."[97] Presumably, these blacks were to be freed.

The possibility of emancipating blacks also struck James Madison. Writing to Virginia legislator Joseph Jones on November 28, 1780, Madison, who had long feared black revolt as the Revolution's "Achilles heel," insisted to Jones that of these recruits "no imaginable danger could be feared from themselves." Madison would cordon off blacks "with white officers and a majority of white soldiers." In addition, he hoped to sever any relationship between the newly freed and the enslaved, "experience having shewn that a freedman immediately loses all attachment and sympathy with his former fellow-slaves."[98] That claim was false, however. Free blacks sided with the Americans in the hope of liberating enslaved blacks, including in Virginia. Theirs, not Madison's, was the patriotism of liberty.

However, on December 8, 1781, Jones wrote that the legislature had introduced several new proposals for a "negro bounty," giving slaves to whites for enlisting. He agreed that "the freedom of these people is a great and desirable object," yet he reported that the majority in the legislature had accepted the owners' rationalizations to repel Madison's proposal: "The negro scheme is laid aside . . . because it was generally considered as unjust, sacrificing the property of a part of the community to the exoneration of the rest. It was reprobated also as inhuman and cruel."[99] Only a man who could not face his own despotism—the common torture, rape, murder, exploitation, degradation, and the breaking up of families involved in slavery—could write of freedom that it is "inhuman and cruel."

On the other hand, Jones argued, if provoked, the Crown would out-recruit the Americans, and bondage would collapse: "How far your idea of raising black regiments, giving them freedom would be politic, in this and the negro States, deserves well to be considered, so long as the States mean to continue any part of that people in their present subjection; as it must be doubtful whether the measure would not ultimately tend to increase the army of the enemy as much or more than our own. For if they once see us disposed to arm the blacks for the field they will follow the example and not disdain to fight us in our own way."[100]

Yet, starting with Dunmore, the Crown had long recruited blacks in Virginia. Furthermore, blacks had reason to escape and become fighting Tories. Jones underestimated these facts, but he rightly stressed that to the extent southern Patriots armed blacks, the British would, very likely, respond in kind. Military competition could thus result in gradual emancipation. If this competition enlisted the most able blacks, Jones added, plantations would collapse. The war effort "would draw off immediately such a number of the best labourers for the culture of the earth as to ruin individuals, distress the States, and perhaps the Continent, when all that can be raised by their assistance is but barely sufficient to keep us jogging along with the great expense of the war." But Jones lived in a fantasy world. Imperial emancipation had already diminished production. In 1781 and after, thousands more would escape. Yet Jones averred that, he, too, favored gradual emancipation—in some indefinite future.[101]

YORKTOWN

The culminating battle of the American Revolution was the siege of Yorktown, ending with Cornwallis's surrender on October 19, 1781. Here, the role played by freed blacks in the first revolution on both sides can be seen in juxtaposition, along with the obstacles and incentives that both deferred the second and promoted its parallel development with the first.

Cornwallis's 1781 orderly books in Virginia record over one thousand black laborers and soldiers, but do not include a much larger number of unorganized blacks who followed the troops. The books also reveal imperial callousness. For instance, a September 15 entry reports: "Great abuses have been committed in victualling the Negroes, the Dep Qr Mr Genrl [Deputy Quarter Master General] has directions to receive the returns of the deficient departments and to appoint a person to attend to the issuing of provisions." Blacks also suffered from smallpox. A brigade order for the Fortieth, Seventy-Sixth, and Eightieth Regiments, including "Negroes," indicated a requirement "to have them inoculated."[102]

In a strategic error, Cornwallis diverted many blacks from soldiering. Entries assign the latter as servants to officers and allot them to the Black Pioneers under a "Captain Brown" (as we have seen, guides and servants also fought). For instance, a June 5 entry purportedly regulates blacks in the Artillery, Wagon Master General Department, and other companies: "Lord Cornwallis desires the Commanding officers of corps to Examine strictly the number of Negroes that are with these respective corps. See that no more are kept than those allowed by the regulation and they will order all the ablebodied Negroes which they find above their number allowed to officers to be taken up and sent to Capt. Brown with the Pioneers."[103]

These orders seek a hilarious, numerical precision, unintentionally satirizing Cornwallis's aristocratic pretensions. They also lump "Negroes" together with livestock:

> Lord Cornwallis regulations Respecting the No of Negroes and
>   horses—
> Field Officer of Infantry 5 Horses and 2 negroes
> Captains 3 Horses 1 negro
> Subalterns and staff 2 Horses and 1 negro—
> Qr Msr, Sergt, Sergt Major 1 Horse and 1 Negro.[104]

The racism of imperial officers often matched that of Patriot plantation owners. Several entries actually rank servants below horses, listing "Ball horses and servants,"[105] though one lists "Negroes and horses."[106] The army treated freed servants as belonging to their corps: "The number or names of Corps to be marked in a conspicuous manner on the Jacket of each negro. No woman or Negro to possess a Horse nor any Negroe to be suffered to ride and march except such as belong to publick departments."[107] The orders, however, also assigned many blacks to "publick departments," the Black Pioneers, and battle.

On the Patriot side, as the army prepared for Yorktown, Baron Ludwig von Closen described in his diary the black soldiers on review in Westchester, New York:

> I had a chance to see the American army, man for man. It was really painful to see these brave men, almost naked, with only some trousers and little linen jackets, most of them without stockings, but would you believe it? very cheerful and healthy in appearance. A quarter of them were Negroes, merry, confident and sturdy. On the 9th [of July near Dobbs Ferry], all the American army presented arms; General Washington invited our headquarters staff to come to see it. . . . Three-quarters of the Rhode Island regiment consists of Negroes, and that regiment is

the most neatly dressed, the best under arms, and the most precise in its maneuvers.[108]

Based on firsthand observation, Closen's report that a quarter of all American soldiers to fight at Yorktown were black—of six thousand, roughly fifteen hundred—is very likely accurate. The experience of bondage toughened these men as survivors and, with a more profound vision of freedom than most of their white comrades, as warriors. As Closen's comment shows, even revolutionaries such as John Laurens underestimated how rapidly and with what determination blacks would become soldiers.

At Yorktown, the First Rhode Island Regiment marched off to take two strategic British redoubts. Success would come, the Americans imagined, only with surprise. So that no shot would alert the redcoats, the soldiers fixed bayonets. As they departed, Washington watched with trepidation. Captain Stephen Olney recalled Washington's speech to his troops: "to act the part of firm and brave soldiers." His memoir recalls, "I thought then that his Excellency's knees rather shook, but I have since doubted whether it was not mine." Black soldiers, Olney continued, "marched in silence . . . many no doubt thinking that less than one quarter of a mile would finish the journey of life with them."[109] The British were alerted to the Patriot attack. Shots rang out. In this moment, the Patriots merged the two revolutions.[110] Blacks and Native Americans carried the day for the American cause.

After the battle, Georg Daniel Flohr, a private with the Royal Deux-Ponts, saw "all over the place and wherever you looked, corpses . . . lying about that had not been buried; the larger part of these were *Mohren*"—Moors.[111] A great number fell on the American and French side.[112] Many blacks also fought and died for the Crown. By not primarily organizing blacks to fight, the British had squandered the advantage that their larger pool of black soldiers, workers, and unorganized supporters might have provided. Yet they had forced the Patriots to rely on blacks. Both British and American historians have obscured this role of black Americans in the pivotal battle of the Revolution. In effect, they have mistakenly "whitened" the battlefield.

Defeat at Yorktown came suddenly. Cornwallis had made few preparations for its possibility and had no provisions for the thousands of blacks following his troops. Cornwallis drove these people into no-man's-land to die of disease and starvation, to be recaptured by Americans, or, rarely, to escape to freedom.[113] In his diary, Ewald, the Danish mercenary, reported, "I would just as soon forget to record a cruel happening. On the same day of the enemy assault, we drove back to the enemy all of our black friends, whom we had taken along to despoil the countryside. We had used them to good advantage and set them free, and now, with fear and trembling, they had to face the reward of their cruel masters."[114] The Crown had made use of these followers and freed them. It had an obligation to them. But Ewald's phrase probably does not refer to those already enlisted in the British army, for Cornwallis depended on these forces in the fighting and did not intend to lose. That he drove unorganized blacks between the lines, however, was an act, as a commander, of treachery to his supporters and troops.[115]

In addition, the Patriot triumph at Yorktown probably meant recapture and redistribution of blacks. Black soldiers were courageous and honorable and, on the American side, delivered the victory. But in this paradoxical and dizzying moment of American freedom, "Patriots" have left no formal record of their zeal for recovered bondage. The first revolution was still diminished by its opposition to the second.

Ewald recalled his own ignoble participation for the Crown: "Last night I had to make a sneak patrol, during which I came across a great number of these unfortunates. In their hunger, these unhappy people would have soon devoured what I had; and since they lay between two fires, they had to be driven on by force. This harsh act had to be carried out, however, because of the scarcity of provisions; but we should have thought more about their deliverance at this time."[116]

Ewald mourned killing "all the artillery and baggage horses for there was no forage." The British dragged the horses into the York River. In his diary, Ewald told of a vision: "Several days after their death, these poor animals came back in heaps with the tide, nearly up to the sunken ships. It seemed as if they wanted to cry out against their murder after their death."[117] As an aristocrat, Ewald valued horses over blacks. But the spirits of the free blacks whom the British drove into no-man's-land also cry out.

I must confess that the mere supposition that the King's Minister
would deliberately stipulate in a treaty an engagement to be guilty
of a monstrous breach of the public faith towards people of any
complection seems to denote a less friendly disposition than I would
wish [and] think, less friendly than we might expect.
— *Sir Guy Carleton to Lord North, June 6, 1783*

Although the American Revolution did not officially end until the Peace of Paris was finally signed on September 3, 1783, two years earlier, when British prime minister Lord North was informed of Cornwallis's defeat at Yorktown, he is reputed to have said, "Oh God, it's all over."[1] It was, but the second revolution was not. Instead, at no time more sharply than in victory was the first revolution pitted against the second.

In victory, the worst attitudes of those elites who espoused the American cause paradoxically came to the fore. Conversely, however, in defeat, the British often exerted themselves to honor and protect those freed slaves who faced a possibly disastrous future in a newly "free" United States of America, where they would bear the double stigma of escaped black slaves and defeated Tories. But Article VII of the Treaty of Paris required the Crown to return emancipated blacks: "And his Britannic Majesty shall, with all convenient speed and without causing any Destruction or carrying away any Negroes or other Property of the American Inhabitants withdraw all his Armies, Garrisons, and Fleets from the said United States."[2] This article simultaneously betrayed the American cause of seeking liberty for all and the solemn oaths of the British to free the blacks who had supported them.

Many of the British officers who served in America were men of honor. At royal headquarters in New York on April 15, 1783, the commander, Guy Carleton, officially ordered: "All Masters of Vessels are particularly cautioned, at their Peril, not to commit any breach of the above article," which already was known to be part of the peace treaty.[3] Yet as a matter of honor, Carleton himself countermanded it.

On May 3, Carleton met George Washington. "Without animation & in a low tone," as one of Carleton's aides wrote of the meeting, the American leader broached the issue of "preservation of [American] property . . . especially the Negroes." Many had departed for Canada, Carleton replied. "Mr. Washington appeared to be startled," the aide recorded. "Already embarked says he." Washington "express[ed] his Surprize" at the violation of the treaty. As the aide related, "Sir Guy Carleton observed that no interpretation could be put upon the article inconsistent with prior [promises] binding the National Honor which must be kept with all colors." The Crown, Carleton added, must keep its "Faith to the Negroes who came into the British lines." He rebuked Washington for the suggestion that an imperial officer would consent to a "notorious breach of the public faith towards people of any complection."[4]

In fact, during the last years of the war, the British had honored their commitment to the freedom of their black recruits and supporters under pressures that could have led them to renege on them, and they did not abandon them now, in defeat. Whether British soldiers and Tories had acted out of principle or pragmatism in recruiting black slaves, in the final years of the war, many felt honor bound to attempt to defend them against the prejudices of some of their fellow soldiers and the claims of Tory slave owners. In defeat, many upheld their responsibilities to those who had embraced their cause, aiding black Tories, as well as whites, to escape from a land where they were despised.

EMANCIPATION AND EVACUATION

As Lieutenant Colonel Alexander Clarke had told Lord Cornwallis on July 10, 1780, "I cannot help remarking to Your Lordship, that however policy may interfere in favor of the Masters, an attention to Justice, and good faith, must plead strongly in behalf of the Negroes, many of whom, having certificates of service performed, come to me to protect them from the violence of some of the most notorious offenders that Carolina has produced." Clarke had received Loyalist complaints about slaves who had escaped and fought against the Patriots. He reported, "I have daily applications from the Masters of Negroes who left them under the sanction of Sir Henry Clinton's Proclamation, on that Subject. The arguments used by the Masters are, that they have conformed, and become good subjects. Those of the Negroes; the Proclamation, above mentioned, and most of them add, having served in the defense of Savannah, and on many other occasions, and the apprehensions they are under of being treated with cruelty in consequence of it, if they go back."[5] To Cornwallis, Clarke praised the service of the large number of blacks—some two hundred soldiers and five thousand other workers—who had been recruited by Clinton and

Campbell and who had helped defeat the American and French siege of Savannah in 1779.

On June 27, 1782, Alexander Leslie, now a lieutenant general who commanded royal southern troops after Cornwallis's surrender at Yorktown, wrote to Carleton, the new imperial commander in chief, contemplating a British retreat. Leslie distinguished those emancipated for service from many bondsmen "sequestered" from "Rebel" estates and worried about the latter's fate: "If this town is to be evacuated, what will be done with the sequestered negroes now under charge of Mr. Cruden, and employed in the different departments. . . . There are many Negroes who have been very useful both at the siege of Savannah, and here; some of them have been Guides, and from their Loyalty been promised their freedom."[6]

On October 18, Leslie insisted more sharply "on the impossibility of delivering up, under any stipulation a certain description of Negroes, who having claimed our protection have borne arms in our service or otherwise rendered themselves more peculiarly obnoxious to the resentment of their former masters, and the severity of the Rebel Laws, and You was pleased to express Your approbation to that effect."[7]

While the former slaves that the British had recruited and freed had contributed to the imperial war effort, they had also posed a series of problems for the British as the war continued and as the Patriot victory loomed. On the one hand, British recruitment and emancipation of slaves appropriated what Loyalist slave owners regarded as their property. The British army in the South sometimes commandeered blacks from Tory estates, as well as from those of Patriots, to strengthen their forces, and although these acts did not produce any large defection of white Loyalists, sometimes former owners tried to reclaim slaves. On the other hand, the recruitment and emancipation of slaves made the British responsible for the fate of freed blacks who had rallied to a losing cause.

The issue of Tory slaves had vexed imperial leaders throughout the war. On November 6, 1778, Alexander Innes, secretary to South Carolina's royal governor, wrote a letter for Daniel Manson, who had lost his plantation near Charlestown and who thus came "with the wreck of a very good fortune from his attachment to the Government." On the ship *Rose*, underlining that officers had no desire for Tories to ferret out former slaves, Captain Reid had "Severely Persecuted" Manson, Innis reports. Yet "this Poor Man has found one of his Negroes in the Black Company. The fellow loves his master and would wish to go to him." Racist literature makes much of the supposed "love" of slaves for masters. Unsurprisingly, actual examples of slaves loving their masters were rare.[8] Manson gave Innis's letter to Major William Crosbie, General Howe's aide-de-camp. But Howe did not take the master's or an officer's hearsay for gospel. To Innes, he responded cautiously: "If the Negro wishes it, I have no objection."[9]

Loyalist owners also clamored for recompense for their slaves who had fled to or been taken by the British. They clashed with officers who wanted to retain servants as well as those who recognized the contributions of black soldiers. On August 8, 1782, Rawlins Lowndes, a Charlestown plantation owner, apologized for writing to Carleton, the imperial commander in the South, yet could not forebear suggesting how widespread the recruitment of slaves of Tories was: "The continual deprivation of my property is not warranted by any principle of war or policy. What I particularly allude to is the prevalent practice of carrying off negroes from this province, scarcely a vessel sails but some of the inhabitants lose this kind of property. Many of my own are now at New York and other places. Captain Durnford of the Engineers has lately carried with him a valuable house servant woman, wife to a man in my employ." Though the woman now served Durnford, her status was ambiguous; perhaps she had become, de facto, free.[10]

Lowndes continued: "Hearing that Georgia was to be evacuated, I waited on Colonel Moncrief to request his interposition for the recovery of the negro woman, but Captain Durnford did not permit her to come on shore and after lying a day or two off the bar the vessel proceeded to New York. I desire the interposition of your authority and the restoration of the woman to whom my family are much attached, who raised my children and had the care of their infancy."[11]

In 1782 Carleton asked General Leslie to return slaves to Tory "owners." On October 18, Leslie wrote to him about the difficulties of prying these servants loose, because blacks feared bondage, and British officers got work out of them. But whether, as Leslie suggested, these officers saw such blacks as their "property" is unclear. Many blacks pointed to certificates of service and, hence, emancipation, provided by Generals Prevost, Cornwallis, and others. Imperial officers frequently emancipated those who worked for or fought with them. Their attitudes probably varied case by case. Nonetheless, many blacks previously owned by white Tories were free.

In a bureaucratic argument to Clinton, Leslie also noted that the chain of command went through naval officers. He passed the buck and suggested that Admiral Robert Digby write to Captain Swiney about ordering the return of servants, but then added:

It is a most interesting business and I wish to do my best—but must fall very short of your expectations, for officers long in this country look on negroes as their property, and the slaves are exceeding unwilling to return to hard labor, and severe punishment from their former masters, and from the numbers that may expect to be brought off, including their wives and children, if to be paid for, will amount to a monstrous expense.

If your Excellency will please mention any number of blacks, or (if paid for) a certain sum of money to be paid (or receipts given) to a certain amount, this will be a guide for my conduct, for every department, and every officer wishes to include his slave into the number to be brought off. They pretend them Spys or Guides, and of course obnoxious, or under promises of freedom from Genl. Prevost, Ld. Cornwallis, Ld. Rawdon or some other officer of rank or free by Proclamation.[12]

Leslie underlined a "monstrous" potential cost, but the Claims Commission in London would make that decision. They specially rewarded white Loyalists, yet they hardly paid "full price" to those who had lost slaves and land in the United States.

Still, Leslie called for an assessment of potential losses to Tories: "If your Excellency intends them paid for, suppose receipts given of their names, occupations, ages, sex, owners, &c., &c., and this to be settled by some men at home well informed in the value of Slaves of all degrees."[13] As he did in New York, Carleton probably freed a considerable number of slaves in the South. Sadly, from a historian's point of view, neither Leslie nor others compiled a record of these emancipations.[14]

Conversely, occasional stories indicate the possibility of reenslavement by Loyalist officers. On September 16, 1782, Mary Butler, wife of Patriot leader Pierce Butler, wrote to Carleton that Cornwallis had assigned the entire slave corps of her husband's plantation to the Royal Engineers Department in Charlestown. She "is well informed that Major Moncrief . . . boasts of his determination to remove the whole of her negroes, about 200, to his own lands in East Florida," Butler insists, and bids "His Excellency . . . prevent this."[15] But the rumor on which she based her "well informed" judgment has no independent source. Carleton did not intervene.

During the war, large numbers could escape from their Patriot masters, travel for considerable periods unnoticed, and find a new home with the Crown, but the chances for accidental recapture were high. Surviving imperial "certificates" confirming the emancipation of individual blacks and allowing them to travel testify not just to the freedom gained by southern blacks under British rule but to the threat of reenslavement and the ways in which free blacks sometimes used their freedom, with the help of sympathetic Tories, to try to get away from that threat—often by escaping the war-torn colonies altogether in the evacuation of Tories and Tory sympathizers.

Blacks were freed in British America to fight as soldiers, regular and irregular, and to work with the Royal Artillery, Wagon Master General's Department, Black Pioneers, or otherwise as support personnel in the camps; yet anytime that free blacks traveled, they had to show passes or permits. White Tories sometimes tracked and attempted to reenslave escapees, and free passes and certificates provided at least some official protection against such a disaster. Furthermore, although black freedom with the British was real, betrayal by unscrupulous redcoats or Tories was possible. In a tug-of-war, officers tried to secure their freedom. And although most black redcoats were former slaves of Patriots, officers would have been unclear on the status of blacks who worked with them. Possession of certificates could clarify their freedom, and hence, as we have seen, officers would often issue them.

Like the "returns" in the military, these passes add to what we can know about free blacks in the areas controlled by the British in the wake of the Dunmore Proclamation and subsequent proclamations and recruitment efforts.[16] Among the things these passes show is the way in which free blacks, having seized the opportunity to escape from slavery in the midst of a war between the white colonies and the metropolis, further sought freedom and safety beyond the war zone with the help of British officials, finding a refuge from the dangers of both slavery and war in other colonies under metropolitan control or in Africa. With the help of their British supporters during the various evacuations of the colonies, freed black American slaves became cosmopolitan citizens of the British Empire and the world.

For example, on July 24, 1779, in Savannah, Commanders Augustine Prevost and Alured Clark hailed Michael Thomas, a former slave, as "a friend and Loyalist since the arrival of Col. Campbell into Georgia." They also noted the freedom of his wife and children. On October 12, 1782, Robert Ballingall, the commander of claims in Charlestown, gave Phyllis Thomas, Michael's wife, "permission to go to the Island of Jamaica or elsewhere at her option." This certificate may indicate that her husband and children were dead or that she was separated from them.[17]

On November 19, 1779, in Savannah, Colonel Metland employed Ned, "a Free Negro," his wife, and three children "in getting him Publick Horses for the Space of Eight Months." In his certificate, Metland warned others "not to trouble or Molest" them. On October 14, 1782, Robert Ballingall gave Ned and his family, Jimmie, Castle, Ned [Jr.], and Dublin, permission to immigrate to "York, Halifax, or elsewhere at their Option."[18]

As prospects for a British victory waned and, in retreat, as the British army evacuated Tories, the British acknowledged responsibility for the fate of blacks whom they had encouraged to join their cause. On March 13, 1782, before retreating to the North, Lieutenant Colonel James Moncrief asked General Clinton for instructions, noting, "The number of slaves who have attached themselves to the Engineer Department since my arrival . . . and who look up to me for protection has been for some time past a matter of serious concern." Here, by "slaves" he probably refers to already free blacks.[19] Moncrief praises "the advantage of their labor" and asks, "Upon what footing are they to be fixed before my departure?"[20]

Of course, Tory slave owners seeking refuge from the impending defeat hoped to take their human "property" with them. On June 27, writing to Carleton about the planned imperial exodus, General Leslie's mind turned to evacuation not only of free blacks but also of slaves of Loyalists: "The enemy have it from the Northward of our intend'd evacuation, the people in town don't much believe it: when it happens it will be severely felt by many. I've taken no steps towards it yet, knowing the jealousy of the people. I fancy every thing could be put on board in fourteen days; but I apprehend the want of a great deal of shipping, and I am confident many of the owners of negroes would wish them sent to Jamaica, and others to St. Augustine, or St. John's, Florida."[21]

IMMIGRATION TO THE SOUTH

In addition to fleeing to the North, some Tories, black and white, fled southward—to Florida and beyond.[22] Patrick Tonyn, the governor of British East Florida, estimated the number of settlers who had come from Georgia into Florida before the evacuation to be "about a thousand [whites] and three thousand blacks," but additional "refugees from Georgia are about fifteen hundred whites and a thousand negroes." His estimates do not differentiate the free and the still-enslaved. An aristocrat, Tonyn scorned ordinary white Georgians: "There are a few respectable families but they consist chiefly of backwoodsmen who are intolerably indolent; perhaps about four hundred may be found fit to bear arms, but their appearance is against them."[23] Of note in the governor's thoughts of the Georgians is that blacks were better suited to arms, compared with these whites. An August 29, 1782, return refers to a missing list of British Tories from Charlestown, "also the number of their Negroes."[24] More slaves than free blacks probably left from the South.[25]

To Lieutenant General Leslie on October 30, Lieutenant Colonel Archibald McArthur in St. Augustine wrote that the "Refugees and blacks" were still coming—no exact count was yet possible.[26] He noted the appointment, with paid assistants, of "Col. Ball & Cassells for Carolina & Cols. Tatnall & Douglas for Georgia" to distribute provisions "and prevent confusions & impositions." On January 29, 1783, McArthur enclosed a roster of the number, now lost, to Carleton in New York. He also noted a new "importation; no return of them being sent here, it will take some time to ascertain their numbers, as many of them are looking out for habitations; but by the best acct. I have been able to procure, there are more than fifteen hundred souls ['Refugees and Negroes"] arrived with the fleet."[27] On May 23, McArthur estimated to Carleton that "the number of souls [in the province] is about sixteen thousand, the proportion nearly three blacks to two white."[28] Among this very large group of blacks—more than ten thousand—he provides no estimate of how many were free. Many were still slaves.

But even Tory owners realized that as an arena for slave labor, the British Empire was shrinking. On July 31, 1782, Georgia loyalists had complained to Carleton about how "at least 4000 persons Whites and Blacks have removed from Georgia into this province [St. Augustine, Florida], that in case of the evacuation of this place, you may be able to judge the number of Transports necessary for their accommodation . . . in case of such removal, Jamaica or some other of our West Indian Islands is the only part of the British dominion where we can employ our Slaves to any advantage."[29]

It was indeed to the Caribbean, not just to the loyal British colonies in Canada, that many fleeing Tories looked for refuge. Tory slave owners headed this way in part because the islands offered the sort of climate in which their human "property" could again be put to use in agriculture, which was not the case in northern climes. But both free blacks and those who had supported and employed them, whether for practical or principled reasons, saw the islands as a place of refuge as well. However, with its own history of slavery, the Caribbean was not a place where free blacks could enjoy unfettered freedom.

On July 2, 1782, writing to Henry White, a Loyalist merchant in New York, Major General Edward Mayhew sought to recruit free black laborers from New York and South Carolina to construct barracks and guardhouses in Antigua. Although Mayhew was a racist—blacks were the British army's laborers of choice—freedom was also, somewhat elliptically, assumed: "What is particularly required is negroes and if any are to be procured at New York (without purchase[30]) to enter into H.M. service at 6d. a day and rations they are to be sent. You are authorised to grant John Cruden of Charlestown power to send 200 from there."[31] In August, differentiating between "men" (perhaps soldiers) and "Negroes" (perhaps laborers), Carleton responded that he had ordered Cruden, in charge of sequestered estates, "to supply horses and cavalry appointments for fifty men by the first safe convoy, and I have also desired him to endeavor to procure two hundred Negroes on the terms pointed out by you if possible and to send them at the same time with the horses."[32] That Carleton routinely drew such distinctions between "men" and "negroes" underlines the racism of even the best of the British.

On September 10, 1782, Carleton ordered Leslie to enlist two hundred negroes to be sent to Saint Lucia—one of the Windward Islands—who "will be paid per day & rations. Could you find such in Charlestown who are willing to enter that service, you will take proper steps."[33]

On August 21 and 22, 1783, the British ships *Nautilus* and *William* transported sixty-six free black Loyalists from New York to Abaco Island in the Bahamas.[34] On September 3, with a crew of 220, roughly half of them black, Andrew Devereux, a South Carolina Tory colonel, sailed from St. Augustine to wrest the Bahamas from Spain.[35]

In all, a minimum of 776 free blacks emigrated from the United States to the Caribbean, including 200 to Jamaica, 200 to Antigua, 200 to St. Lucia, and 176 to other parts of the Bahamas. Some may not have stayed; this number is but an indication. It does not include indentured servants, such as George Liele, or soldiers temporarily in London, such as Scipio Handley. Thus, the total who escaped to the Caribbean is probably two or three thousand and may be higher.[36] Carleton's order to Leslie resulted in the creation of the Black Carolina Corps, which became permanent imperial troops after the war. Tragically, in the 1780s, this force would suppress black revolts.[37]

On October 18, 1782, Leslie responded with questions about recompense to owners of blacks held by imperial officers, but announced in a letter to Carleton that the army "shall attend that all those that are paid for, or carryed off by permission, shall be sent to St. Lucia under a proper officer for the public service there."[38] On July 19, 1782, in perhaps the largest direct reference to Tory slaves, however, Leslie wrote to Carleton of "the request of Sir James Wright and the inhabitants [of Charlestown] to desire Capt. Swiney to supply shipping to transport about 2,000 of their negroes to Jamaica."[39]

Historian John Pulis estimates that 200 free black Loyalists immigrated to Jamaica and believes that 4,904 slaves of Tories were also shipped there.[40] Given the threat of slave revolts, the Crown forced free blacks to register at church vestries and to provide information about where they were emancipated.[41] Some may have avoided such listings, however. Still, free blacks needed to register to achieve important, if limited, recognition. Even so, imperial Jamaica denied them political participation, forbade inheritance of estates worth more than two thousand pounds, and barred them from government employment.

Black Loyalists joined a free black community of perhaps four thousand.[42] Roughly fifty free black people petitioned for recognition in each legislative assembly.[43] According to vestry records, nineteen men and nine women served as Black Pioneers in Jamaica. The Crown had recruited them for nine-year terms in Savannah and Charlestown. They belonged to the Nineteenth Regiment and were among twelve hundred who joined the Loyalist officers Campbell, Clarke, Coote, and Balcarres.[44]

The British Public Records Office has two scant numerical "returns of Loyalists" arriving in Jamaica that include 200 "blacks" out of 493 total immigrants and "130 blacks" out of 700.[45] Imperial records ordinarily indicate the status of slave. One wonders, again, whether more arriving blacks were free than Pulis estimates. James Walden, an aide-de-camp with the Loyal Irish Volunteers of New York, received a certificate of freedom in 1778 and came to Jamaica in 1780. Yet he is not recorded in vestry registers.[46]

Officers often freed those who worked for them. For instance, in Jamaica, Archibald Campbell emancipated three blacks: Mary Miles, Hector Lloyd, and Cuffee, as well as two Native Americans, Mary Bown and Sarah Willis. With certificates from Clinton, Tom, Dublin, and John Waters, Nancy and her daughter Mary, and Christobal (the last three with no surnames), arrived from Charlestown. In 1785 Governor Tonyn of East Florida issued certificates to Kate, Phoebe, and Windsor.[47]

In 1783 William Bull, former royal governor of South Carolina, received land in the Jamaica parish of St. Elizabeth. He brought two hundred slaves from Charlestown. But Bull also certified the emancipation of Solas and Amelia Duberdue, John and Frances Lampert, George (the minister) and Elizabeth Vinyard, Susan Towers, Rosetta Douglass, Susan Burrows, and Dublin Waldren.[48]

On December 6, 1782, Lieutenant Colonel Campbell in Jamaica sent a letter of introduction to Carleton for "Major William Lewis, who is appointed Commandant of a Provincial Battalion to raise from blacks and people of color of Jamaica, the Windward Islands and America [soldiers] for the defense of Jamaica." He "desires" Carleton to appoint a "public officer at New York to inspect these recruits."[49]

The largest number of émigrés to Jamaica came from Charlestown. Others, however, arrived from New York, Nova Scotia, and the Bahamas. Blacks faced many problems in their new homes. Emigration from the latter two places underlines myriad black journeyings for freedom in the black diaspora. With a certificate from Peter Dubois, magistrate of police, dated June 20, 1780, Frank Lope came from New York. Ishmael York, Oly Adams, William Kenty, and a woman named Silva had certificates from Edward Williams, New York major of brigade, issued in 1783. As in New York, however, imperial officials often recognized testimony of freedom without certificates. Authorities in Jamaica emancipated William Kitt, Henry York, Cesar Moncrieff, Prince George, and Augustus Ryall on the word of Moses Baker, their fellow ex-slave, New Yorker, and minister.[50]

But it was not so easy for free blacks to escape from slavery in the British Empire in the last decades of the eighteenth century—especially if they had fled from the Revolutionary War to the slaveholding colonies of the Caribbean islands. Reenslavement was always a threat, even from—or especially from—racists among the British.

For example, in 1782, to revive the royal cause, John Cruden had proposed black recruitment from Loyalist estates in exchange for freedom, but his idea was based on simply a tactical judgment. The institution of slavery did not trouble him. On March 25, 1783, in a property-holder's memorandum from Tortola in the British Virgin Islands, Cruden complained about officers selling blacks—but only because they were selling blacks whom they did not own: "Since my arrival on this Island, I have been informed that many Negroes the property of the inhabitants of the Southern Provinces, have been offered for Sale and by people who have no right to dispose of them." In particular, he sought "condign Punishment" from the chief magistrate for a Charlestown émigré who had brought "a number of Negroes and is offering them for Sale."[51]

Shifting to what at first seems a humane tone, he also urged a Major C. Nesbit, to whom he sent the memorandum, to bring the case before Commander Edward Matthews "to take such measures in all the Wyndward Islands, as will prevent unprincipled individuals from making a property of these poor Wretches." Cruden's compassion for the "poor Wretches" suggests that he might have wanted to free them, but he did not. His proposal to recruit blacks to fight for the British had focused on paying former owners with interest, involving them in making decisions about who would be recruited. As we have seen, Rawlins Lowndes had complained to Carleton about how many of his slaves had been sent to New York. Honoring his promise to Lowndes, Cruden merely insisted on restoration of "slaves" to their "proper owners."

In 1786 English Caribbean administrators would sell previously emancipated Loyalists to French plantation owners.[52] But the zeal of some officers to "market" some blacks did not stop many of the emancipated from settling in, or passing through, the Caribbean. On his way to London, for example, Benjamin Whitecuff, the free black soldier, would sojourn in Tortola.[53]

IMMIGRATION TO THE NORTH

The fate of freed blacks who had supported the British cause and who had escaped to the North before the end of the war could be equally fraught with danger. In a Manhattan soon to pass to the Patriots, Carleton organized hearings concerning the possible reenslavement of a small number of blacks. Breaking up families and returning women and children to slavery, these hearings often resulted in tragedy. Yet Carleton's maneuver allowed a vast majority to escape. The *Book of Negroes*, which compiles an exact record, reveals that 3,000 blacks, some 2,600 of whom were free, immigrated with the Crown by ship to Nova Scotia.[54]

Boston King, whom we have met before, was among them. His autobiography, composed at Kingswood School in England, offers stunning insight both about the realities of bondage and those that freed blacks who had supported the Crown faced during and after the war. Even a hard life among the British could not dull King's ardor for freedom. In exchange for liberty, the imperial army employed King as a hospital nurse, a servant to an officer, and a messenger behind enemy lines. King accompanied the army from Charlestown to New York. As defeat neared and supplies grew short, however, the British stopped feeding emancipated blacks. To eat, King and others had to obtain private employment.

King worked on a Loyalist pilot boat. An American whaler captured it, again enslaving him. Surprisingly, King praised the physical conditions of his renewed bondage: "The slaves about Baltimore, Philadelphia, and New York have as good victuals as many of the English; for they have meat once a day, and milk for breakfast and supper; and what is better than all, many of the masters send their slaves to school at night, that they may learn to read the scriptures. This is a privilege indeed." Partly because of this night-school experience, King became a minister.[55]

In allowing King and others to study the Bible, the masters hoped to produce obedience to a slave-holding "Caesar." However, King's Christianity empathized with the slaves who left Egypt: "Alas, all these enjoyments could not satisfy me without liberty! Sometimes I thought, if it was the will of God that I should be a slave, I was ready to resign myself to his will; but at other times I could not find the least desire to content myself in slavery." Separated from his wife and family in New York, he was "sorely distressed." Early one Sunday morning, as his American guards slept by the riverside or drank the night away, he slipped off.[56]

When hostilities ceased, Britain still held Manhattan, but Patriots surrounded it and were eager to enforce Article VII's provision for the reenslavement of blacks who had escaped to the Tories. Southern slave catchers, King would later fearfully recall, entered the city and seized blacks on New York streets: "A report prevailed [there] . . . that all the slaves, in number 2000, were to be delivered up to their masters, altho' some of them had been three or four years among the English. . . . Many of the slaves had very cruel masters, so that the thoughts of returning home with them embittered life to us. For some days, we lost our appetite for food, and sleep departed from our eyes."[57]

According to one British observer, Washington urged the return of the blacks to their former owners "with all the Grossness and Ferocity of a Captain of Banditti."[58] To his credit, General Carleton did what he could to protect those such as Boston King who had risked their lives to seek freedom under the British flag. To his superiors, Carleton insisted that Article VII applied only to slaves freed *after* the peace.[59] On June 6 to Lord North, he enclosed a copy of a slave-owner's resolution from "New Ark in New Jersey": "This meeting alleges a violation of the Treaty on our part in the case of Negroes who have come in under the faith of proclamations, an allegation which will probably in the same narrow spirit be adopted by others."[60]

London had betrayed King and thousands more. Not realizing Carleton's unique role in reversing the meaning of the treaty, King praised the British in general: "The English had compassion upon us in the day of our distress, and issued out a Proclamation, importing 'That all slaves should be free, who had taken refuge in the British lines, and claimed the sanction and privileges of the Proclamations respecting the security and protection of Negroes.' In consequence of this, each of us received a certificate from the commanding officer at New York, which dispelled our fears and filled us with joy and gratitude. Soon after, ships were fitted out, and furnished with every necessity for conveying us to Nova Scotia."[61] As a matter of honor, General Carleton got three thousand mainly free blacks out of New York, evacuating them to Halifax, Nova Scotia.

Too late, Lord North inquired angrily of Carleton what he had done with the black soldiers. On May 12, 1783, the general responded mildly that he had only recently "learned with concern, that the embarkation which has already taken place in that a large number of negroes had been carried away, appeared to your Excellency as a Measure totally different from the letter & spirit of the treaty." Reminding his superior that blacks had fought for the Crown, he argued: "The negroes in question I have already said, I found free when I arrived at New York. I had therefore no right, as I thought to prevent them going to any part of the world they thought proper."[62]

Carleton contended, implausibly, that even without his aid, as many blacks would have escaped. These lists of departing blacks, he avowed, allowed owners the possibility of recompense: "Had these negroes been denied permission to embark, they would in spite of every means to prevent it, have found various methods of quitting this place so that the former owners would no longer have been able to trace them, and, of course, would have lost, in every way, all chance of compensation."[63]

Several thousand additional blacks also escaped to Canada by other means, and Carleton's words pointed to an important reality: black resourcefulness in avoiding reenslavement. Yet with the enemy surrounding New York, fewer would have escaped without Carleton's help. Because of London's unprincipled policy and fierce American pressure, Carleton caused to be created, and thus left to us, what is known as the *Book of Negroes*: the logs of ships naming three thousand blacks.[64]

However, unleashed by Article VII, slave owners, like hounds, bayed after prey. Throughout the war, owners had hunted "lost" slaves. According to a royal official in Savannah, "Not a day has elapsed without some persons coming in from South Carolina, to enquire after Negroes."[65] Imperial defeat only intensified the masters' ferocity. John Beckley reported the testimony of "Dr. Thomas Walker," guardian of Thomas Jefferson, to the Virginia General Assembly. He stated that together with several other people from Norfolk and Princess Anne Counties, "in or about the month of April 1783, [Walker] went to New York with a View of recovering the Slaves which had been taken from them by British Troops during the War, that not being permitted to take Possession of those Slaves which they found in that City, the said Walke[r] made a personal application to General Carleton, and requested a delivery of the said Slaves in compliance with the 7th Article of the Treaty."[66]

Carleton "peremptorily" refused, Walker reported. Using bureaucratic obfuscation to check evil, the general insisted that "he was not authorized to [return blacks] without particular instructions from the British Government." Not all imperial officers favored resistance, however. An aide to Carleton showed Walker the "Register of Slaves," which, due to Carleton's evasiveness, Walker could not exploit.[67]

Maryland plantation owner John Stewart also averred, Beckley noted, that Carleton "invariably" rejected applications for the return of blacks. Though professing "no inclination to interfere with the power of making Treaties with foreign Nations," the Virginia Assembly nonetheless insisted that "the national Honor and Interest of the Citizens of this Commonwealth [require the representatives] . . . to withhold their Co-operation in the complete fulfillment of the said Treaty until the success of the aforesaid Remonstrance is known."[68] In practice, this meant Virginia would not approve American independence. That the Virginians refused to sign until they recovered their escaped slaves reveals, once more, their primary motivation: waging the first revolution mainly to prevent the second.

The logs in the Public Records Office in London report ten trials in Manhattan in which blacks had to argue for their freedom in order to join the evacuation to Canada.[69] That small number testifies to the brilliance of Carleton's stratagem. These trials provided cover for the escape of thousands. Typical of British adherence to the rule of law, blacks had a right to bring these cases; two even resulted in their favor.

The commission of American and English "inspectors" that Carleton had set up to oversee the immigration of former black slaves from the lost American colonies to Canada and to administer the compilation of the *Book of Negroes* referred four to Brigadier General Samuel Birch, the British commandant. Because the English soon left, these cases very likely resulted in the former slaves' emigration. Four verdicts forced blacks back into bondage. In all but one, Patriots had sued to reenslave women and children. A modern American finds these cases painful to read.

"A. Bartram, a Negro complains that his Daughter Nancy is detained by Henry Rogers of Queen Street," names one case. A certificate from Captain Nathan Hubbell recorded that Bartram and two daughters, Nancy and Flora, "came within the British Lines in July 1779." On June 2, 1783, the commissioners ordered Rogers to "set [the child] at Liberty."[70] Here, in the commission's most honorable decision, a black soldier saved his daughter. Attempting to follow law and to honor service, the court did not simply bow to the masters.

In another case, a Captain Hewetson claimed "a Negroe Woman named

Sally." In the West Indies, a court had convicted Sally as an accomplice in a robbery and had imprisoned her for four months. Taking her from jail, Hewetson declared her to be an indentured servant. The board ruled that the indenture was "founded on false principles." Surprisingly, even a defendant's criminal record did not prevent the commission from ruling in her favor.[71]

Though not always with such success, black women could sue for freedom in these courts. In a third case, Violet Taullert "complains of being detained by David Campbell as a Slave without sufficient Authority." Campbell had a bill of sale from one Thomas Gilchrist of Virginia. Campbell added a second, contradictory line of ownership: on his death, Gilchrist's brother, William, had left her to him. The commission could have noted this conflict. Instead, it ruled against her.[72]

On June 4, however, the commissioners asked Commandant Birch not to send them cases unless "the Property is embarked or about to be embarked." Their reference to "the Property" points up the racist tenor of the proceedings.[73]

The board also examined the "claim of Philip Lott to a Negroe Man named Thomas Francis now enlisted by Captain Thelwell in the Jamaica Rangers and about to be sent off on the *Fair American*." Lott had supposedly purchased Francis in New Jersey. Testifying to his service with the Crown, however, Francis had a certificate signed by Birch himself. This case troubled the commissioners. Given controversies, they asked Carleton for authority to make all witnesses swear an oath. Carleton concurred.[74] Here we can see the seriousness of the rule of law and a touching, if naïve, Anglo-Saxon faith in its probity. The transcript does not report a resolution. According to the *Book of Negroes*, however, Thomas Francis, identifying himself as formerly a slave of Isaac Vermilla, Phillip's Manor, New York, had escaped in 1777. Possessing a Birch certificate, in 1783 he embarked on the ship *Elizabeth* bound for Port Roseway.[75]

In another case, "Doctor Abraham . . . claims a Negroe man, Samuel Doron as his property." Four witnesses testified that they had seen Doron with Abraham. Doron replied that he "belonged" to the claimant's mother, Allida Teller. Perhaps as a Loyalist—the record does not specify—Doctor Abraham had crossed imperial lines and Doron had "assisted him." When they returned, however, Patriots suspected Doron's loyalty. In 1780, with the mother's permission, Doron went again "behind British lines." To a striking query from Lieutenant Colonel Smith, an American representative, Doron answered that he considered himself a "Subject of the King of Great Britain." The commissioners decided that they were "not authorized to determine the Question" and sent the case to General Birch.[76] Unusual here was that, among black émigrés, Doron had not fought for the British. In New York in 1780, however, he had supported their cause.[77]

The British law of slavery then current—that it was lawful to traffic human beings—governed these cases. Representatives of the Crown under Carleton sought to abrogate bondage for those who had answered the call of imperial proclamations. Yet in some cases, they upheld bondage. Another trial involved Samuel Doron's two children, Peter and Elizabeth, whom he had taken "behind British lines" and on board ship for Nova Scotia. On August 2, Gerrard G. Beekman, a New York merchant, produced a document signed by Pierre Van Cortlandt of Westchester. Van Cortlandt had given "the Wench"—unnamed in this official document—who had borne the children to "Cornelia," his daughter and Beekman's wife. In such cases, parents could not protect their children. The commission delivered Peter and Elizabeth to the slave owner, who was "permitted to take and dispose of them as he may think proper."[78] Though free, Doron may have decided not to emigrate. He is not listed as departing in the *Book of Negroes*.

In another case, "Thomas Smith" of Aquaquanunk, New Jersey, "claims a Negroe Woman named Betty." She was not addressed by her full name, Elizabeth Truant, until later in the testimony. Truant, too, produced a Birch certificate. As if referring to cattle, Smith stated that she had "been bred in his Family and lived with him." On April 20, 1782, Truant had escaped to New York. She acknowledged that she had been Smith's slave. Had she insisted that she was a subject of the king, her case might have remained "unresolved." Her "crime" was her honesty, coupled with a failure to volunteer information about which side she had supported in the war—the commissioners did not ask. They sent Truant back into bondage.[79] By the same logic, however, the commission would have had to return any black with a Birch certificate listed in the *Book of Negroes*, for each had left an American owner.

In another case, Jonathan Elbeck of Norfolk, Virginia, "claims a Negroe woman named Judith Jackson." In response, Jackson offered a Birch certificate, dated "5th June, 1783" in the name of Jenny Jackson. Under the protection of the proclamations, she testified, she had come behind the British lines. Without explanation, however, she acknowledged that her name was Judith. "On account of the War," Jackson testified, her "master," John McLean, had fled to England. She had joined General Leslie in Charlestown and come to New York. Elbeck produced a bill of sale from McLean, dated "16th July, 1782." Ironically, Elbeck "upon being asked declares himself to be a British subject." The Americans made no effort to help him. In both parties' testimony, the "master" was a Tory. The English were reluctant to override Jackson's service to the military and referred the case to General Birch. No record survives of how he settled it.[80]

Nonetheless, the *Book of Negroes* records a Judith Jackson embarking on the ship *Ann* for Port Roseway. This Jackson is identified as formerly a slave of John Bell of Cape Fear, North Carolina. She escaped and joined Sir Henry Clinton in 1776 (because Clinton's proclamation occurred in 1779, the date listed is premature). Because Jackson's details differ from those later brought out in her trial, this report may have preceded her being taken back for a hearing. Still, the ship's log indicates that she embarked.[81]

In another case, William Farrer "claims a Negroe Woman named Dinah Archey." A separate letter from Archey to Sir Guy Carleton, August 2, 1783, recorded by an aide, conveys her own words: "Has she says been free five years & Came in agreeable to his Excellency General Howe's Proclamation." She also had a Birch certificate, dated "2 May, 1783," which granted her "permission to pass from this Garrison to whatever Place She may think proper."[82]

Archey testified that she had been a slave to John Bains of Crane Island, Virginia, who had sold her to a William Fancey. She lived on Fancey's property "about three years." Fancey fled to England. Bains told her that he had never given Fancey a bill of sale and forced Archey back into bondage. She escaped to "the Expedition up the Chesapeake under Sir George Collier and General Mathews," one of the 518 black Loyalist recruits from Virginia in 1777, and came with the troops to New York. On being asked, Archey declared herself a British subject. Because she possessed a Birch certificate of service with the military and declared her loyalty to the Crown and because there was no bill of sale, the commissioners might have ruled in her favor. Instead, they referred this case, too, to General Birch.[83]

Still the *Book of Negroes* records that Dinah Archer, forty-two, who had "lost an eye"—again, the brutality of bondage is hidden in the choice of words—was formerly enslaved to John Bayne, Norfolk County, Virginia. She left him "5 years ago" and now was to depart on the ship *Grand Duchess of Russia* bound for Port Roseway. The name Archey is close to Archer; both are from Norfolk, and both came to the British troops five years before. This entry, too, suggests that the case was resolved by her leaving with the British.[84]

In an August 7, 1783, case, Gabriel Legget of Westchester, New York, "claimed a Negroe Wench named Mercy and her three children." Legget related that he lived behind British lines until October 2, 1779, holding Mercy and her children, when a Major Bearmore "turned [him] out of the Possession of his farm" and Bearmore's family took over. Yet in a contradictory account, Legget also stated that Mercy had served Patriot colonel Stephen Delaney and his wife in Long Island. After Delaney fled Westchester with his troops, Mercy took her children to New York and claimed the benefit of the British proclamations. Meanwhile, Legget put himself under British general Howe's protection. As a witness to Mercy's servitude, Gabriel summoned Ebenezer Legget, apparently by name a relative. Ignoring the relationship, the commissioners treated Ebenezer as a disinterested observer.

Mercy had worked at the Brooklyn Ferry. On June 26, 1783, at the recommendation of Doctor Peter Huggeford, she obtained a Birch certificate. She also produced a note from British aide-de-camp George Beckwith, dated October 6, 1779, announcing that Wilhelm Knyphausen, British commander of New York City in 1779 and 1780, "is pleased from the bad character of Gabriel Legget to order him to quit Morrissania tomorrow with his Family and Effects and Major Bearmore . . . to take Possession of his late House and Property." Conflicts in the testimony—was she a former slave of the Patriot Delaney's and legitimately emancipated under the British proclamations, or did she belong to Gabriel Legget?—might have prompted the commission to forward the case to General Birch, but the commission seemed prejudiced against "the Wench." With no contrary evidence except that of the accuser's relative, they ignored the testimony of Legget's bad character. Unmercifully, the commission delivered Mercy and her children back into slavery.[85]

Still, the *Book of Negroes* records several blacks whose cases were referred to General Birch as on board the departing ships for Canada. Sending a case unresolved to General Birch may, in fact, have settled them in the former slaves' favor.[86]

Carleton's ruse voided most Patriot claims for the return to bondage of freed blacks. Only a handful of owners from New York, New Jersey, and Virginia had a chance to bring cases. The *Book of Negroes* and the appointment of a joint committee to oversee the trials appear consistent with the letter of the treaty. As Carleton had written to Lord North, "Every Negroes' name is registered, the master he formerly belonged to, with such other circumstances as serve to denote his value that it may be adjusted by compensation, *if* that was really the intention and meaning of the treaty."[87]

On May 12, 1783, Carleton had stressed to Lord North the absence of pragmatism in the treaty as well as the absence of principle involved in breaking "the public faith towards people of any complection": "restoration, where inseparable from a breach of the public faith, is, as all the world I think must allow, utterly impracticable." As Carleton put it simply, "The Slaves which have absconded from their Masters will never be restored to them."[88]

Reversing the obvious meaning of Article VII, North responded in August 1783: "The removal of the Negroes whom you found in possession of their freedom upon your arrival at New York . . . is certainly an Act of Justice, due to Them from Us." He now concurred with Carleton's principled view: "Nor do I see that the removal of those Negroes who had been made free before the execution of the preliminaries of peace can be deemed an infraction of the Treaty." With an eye to the potential compensation of former American slave owners, North praised Carleton's stratagem: "It was, however, a very proper precaution to have a correct list of the said Negroes taken and their respective values ascertained."[89] Imperial "justice" was not abolitionist. But the Book of Negroes in fact estimates no prices for former slaves. Carleton meant the list to soothe Lord North. Patriots and Tories alike clamored for the return of their former slaves. Carleton's cunning interpretation of the treaty marks the height of English honor during the war—the triumph of justice over policy.[90]

As an American revolutionary suddenly and ironically inflamed with legalism, and perhaps unconsciously with shame, James Madison denounced Carleton's "shameful evasion . . . a palpably scandalous misconstruction of the Treaty."[91] Not content with merely winning independence, the Continental Congress threatened to use British prisoners of war as a bargaining tool. Undermining the great American victory, Congress mimicked the Virginia Assembly. In 1779, in its best moment, Congress had endorsed the Laurens proposal, which might have prefigured gradual abolition throughout the new nation. In 1783, with hubris, Congress acted as but a megaphone for slave owners. Even retention of bondage within the territorial United States was insufficient. Zealous representatives wanted the émigré former slaves returned. Ultimately, however, the American government returned British prisoners of war and confirmed the peace.

THE BOOK OF NEGROES AS A ROLL OF HONOR

As the defeated empire left America, thousands of other blacks departed from Charlestown and Savannah on British ships or private vessels chartered to take the overflow north to Canada. Researchers have not unearthed comparable records for them.[92] In New York, fortunately, controversy generated unusual record keeping. On November 24, 1783, Carleton sent a list, a "Return of Loyalists Leaving New York," to Lord North. This list was far less detailed than the subsequent *Book of Negroes*. It enumerated 1,423 blacks, distinguishing men, women, children over ten years of age, and those under ten. Carleton reported the immigration of "black companies" numbering 222 persons to River St. John, Canada.[93] Another 430 immigrated to Port Roseway and Shelburne.[94]

And the *Book of Negroes* provides an enormously significant numerical sample of the population of former slaves and free blacks who immigrated to Canada from the newly independent colonies under the aegis of the imperial troops whose cause they had espoused—a symbol of a vast movement. Of the 2,555 listed as free or slave in the National Archives version of the *Book*, Loyalists "owned" 365 (14 percent).[95] In the more complete Public Records Office version of 3,000, this figure increases to 407 slaves. The group mentioned in Carleton's previous return was probably included in this larger number.[96] After fighting, disease, and betrayal, that nearly twenty-six hundred free men, women, and children, drawn from all the colonies, emigrated with the Crown from New York in 1783 highlights the scope of black escape and resistance during the Revolution.

However, a major reason that this story has remained buried for two and a quarter centuries on both sides of the Atlantic is that the records are fragmentary and scattered. Only by making inferences to the best explanation from several cases—Dunmore's Royal Ethiopian Regiment, Captain Tye's raids, the American First Rhode Island Regiment, the scale of immigration to Nova Scotia, and the like—does the centrality of slave revolt and of black soldiering, both for the Crown and the United States, emerge.[97]

Still, the *Book of Negroes* offers a way to trace the electrifying impact, across colonies, of the Dunmore Proclamation, recording those among the British who implemented it and similar proclamations and the journeys to freedom that the former slaves listed in it undertook. The names it lists thus form a kind of honor roll of the liberators and the liberated.

The entries in the *Book* are laconic. "Upon the landing of British troops on New York island" in 1775, Henry Spincell "fled" B. Benson. "At the evacuation of Boston," Pompey Fleet "left" Thomas Fleet. "At the evacuation of Philadelphia," Sukey Coleman "left" Mr. Teaboult. August Griggs and Caesar Hassell escaped, respectively, at the 1779 "siege of Savannah" and the 1780 fall of "Charlestown." David Devonshire went from John Hamilton of South Carolina to "Augustine" in British East Florida and subsequently embarked for New York.[98]

The inspectors often failed to note rudimentary information about black Loyalists' service. They asked only about who had owned the blacks, when they had left their "masters," whether they possessed certificates of freedom, and the like. Nonetheless, a typical page lists thirty-one, all but one from Virginia,[99] with a "General Birch's certificate," along with seven born "within British lines" and one with a certificate that she had "purchased her freedom."[100]

The *Book* provides a horizontal column for each name, listing categories such as age, where each person was from, who the former owner was, and, sometimes, comments about whom they had fought under. Indicated in the *Book* by the initials "GBC," "GBCertificate" or "Certificate of General [Samuel] Birch" at the conclusion of the column, most blacks had received papers indicating their imperial service. Yet few Birch certificates survive. One that does shows the importance of British proclamations of black freedom: "Cato Hamanday [his mark] a Negro, resorted to the British lines in consequence of the Proclamations of Sir William Howe, and Sir Henry Clinton."[101] With the same wording about resorting to English lines in response to proclamations, on April 19, 1783, Edward Williams, major of brigade, signed John Williams's and his wife's certificates.[102] At the least, such certificates listed the commander for whom the soldier had fought. They also freed the bearer "to go to Nova Scotia or wherever else (s/)he may think proper."[103] Seven hundred and fifty-nine émigrés— 30 percent—out of 2,555[104] possessed a Birch certificate. In addition, another 173—7 percent—held a "GMC": the certificate of General Thomas Musgrave. To honor General Birch, black refugees named their community near Shelburne Birchtown. The precision of these few remaining certificates—military documents—contrasts with the vagueness of many entries in the book.

Cato Winslow escaped in New York to fight for Dunmore in mid-1775 (several months before the actual proclamation); at the same time, his future wife, Rose, and her son, Toby, fled from Boston to Dunmore.[105] From Charlestown, Thomas Holmes, twenty-two years old, responded to the Dunmore Proclamation, as did Mary Thompson, aged fifty-four, from Newark.[106]

If their certificates had survived, one could specify the numbers of these blacks who fought with each commander. Nonetheless, the *Book* highlights the role of General Sir William Howe in furthering black efforts to gain freedom. In the *Book*, thirty-three report escaping to Howe's forces, the largest number to any general.[107] As "Certified by William Walker, magistrate," Charles Williams, formerly enslaved in Virginia, answered "Howe's Proclamation." So did Henry (no last name),[108] Lydia Williams,

Kate Stout, and Alvin (no last name).[109] Perhaps the four British inspectors (Captains Armstrong, Gilfillan, and Cook and Major of Brigade Phillips) simply knew blacks had fought. Given their lack of interest and the disappearance of most Birch certificates, one may fairly infer that a much larger number responded to Howe's proclamation.

By asserting proudly with whom they fought, the blacks upheld the Crown's tattered honor against the disinterest of the inspectors, beyond indicating a Birch or Musgrave certificate. The *Book* notes other British liberators unmentioned by historians, including Edward Matthews,[110] commander in the Chesapeake, to whom Will Pitt of Virginia escaped; General James Patterson in New York, with whom former slaves Joseph Talbot and Nancy Talbot enlisted; General Alured Clark, "with his troops" at Savannah, to whom escapee Sam Willie came; and the American traitor, Benedict Arnold, whom Geo[111] Geddons (age twenty-two), Nancy Chaimett (likewise), and Samson Johnson (age sixteen) joined in Virginia in 1781. Some declared that they had fought with Dunmore in Virginia, more with Howe—with whom perhaps the majority, leaving between 1777 and 1779, had enlisted—and others with Benedict Arnold and Cornwallis.[112] Another page includes some seventeen with "General Birch's Certificate" drawn from all over the country.[113]

When one soldier broke the monotony of the lists by naming whose proclamation he had rallied to or in which battles he had fought, ten or twelve others did likewise. For instance, John Jones (aged forty),[114] formerly enslaved to Richard Jones, Williamsburg, Virginia, "left him with Lord Dunmore in 1776." Lucretia Jones (twenty-seven), freeborn, "left Philadelphia with British troops." Then came William Wells (thirty), once bondsman to Captain John Wells, Mulberry Island, Virginia, "left him with Lord Dunmore, 1775," as did his wife, Mary Wells (thirty-five).[115]

Previously in chains to "John Van Wyck, N. Castle Province of N York," William Francis (thirty) "left him with General Clinton in 1779."[116] "Born free in Virginia," Robert James (twenty-six) "served the British fleet in the Chesapeake [commanded by Howe] in 1777." Rebecca Williams (twenty-five), formerly a slave in Maryland, "joined Lord Howe's fleet in 1777." Sarah Gordon (twenty), once in bondage to George Ancram [nearly illegible] at Charlestown, "left him with Lord William Campbell in 1775." In the *Book*, the largest number, sixty-seven (3 percent of the 2,555), tell of scouting and sometimes fighting as Black Pioneers.

Given the date and place of escape, one might infer in which regiment each person enlisted. For instance, Lucy Lydacre (twenty-four), bound to William Lydacre in New Jersey, "left him in the year 1776 by Proclamation."

This phrase refers to the Dunmore Proclamation. In 1777 a similar comment identifies Howe; in 1779 it refers to Clinton. Thus, Billy Williams (twenty-three) and Rose Jackson (twenty-two) of Charlestown responded to "[Clinton's] Proclamation." As occasions for leaving, blacks often refer to the battles of Savannah (1779) and Charlestown (1780).[117]

In addition, the literature depicts most royal governors as differing with Dunmore's strategic boldness. [118] Yet as recorded in the *Book*, they, too, signed certificates enabling freed blacks to embark to Canada.

Many other imperial and Tory officials issued emancipatory documents—for instance, one Colonel Borelick, to John Annis; Mr. Hicks, "late Mayor of New York," to Patty Vankyle and her daughter; "Mr. David Matthews, Mayor" [town unspecified], to "Chas Rogers"; "Danl Randall, Phila[delphia]," to Mary Bright and her children; "Att. Hugh Millis," to Lucy [no last name] and her infant; "Certified to be free by M. Walton, Magistrate of Police" [city unspecified], to Cathy Christopher and her daughter, Saturn. The *Book* lists Francis Herbert, aged sixty-five, "certified to be free says she came from West Indies," without a certifier. Casually, to five others on one page, an inspector records: "Certified by [blank]."[119]

Some Tory owners manumitted blacks in their wills. Others gave slaves their liberty earlier—for example, Sarah,[120] "free at the Certificate of her last owner Thos Brown of London." As an indication that the imperial army generally stood for freedom, blacks' testimony was believed and served to emancipate some, as in the case of Violet Moore and her daughter, Dorothy: Moore "says [William Geddon of New York] left her free."[121]

Newly emancipated blacks experienced a world of danger. White Tories hunted escapees. Opportunist redcoats sometimes seized the free as well. But the vast number of black supporters following the British army probably limited such treachery. Officers could recruit among the many who were emancipated and hungry. In addition, many redcoats treated blacks respectfully.

The *Book* also reveals that a very substantial group of free blacks chose to fight with the British. Some blacks even "purchase[d] themselves" and enlisted with the Crown. Thus, "by a Bill of Sale produced," Esther Roberts bought her own and her daughter Diana's freedom. Roberts fought for the British. Similarly, Nancy Mumford's father purchased her liberty from "Mr. Mumford, Rhode Island." She, too, rallied to the Crown.[122]

A total of 307 men and women, 12 percent of those listed in the *Book of Negroes*, were born free or emancipated in the thirteen colonies.[123] If we add to these Americans 72 free blacks from Jamaica,[124] Barbados, Antigua,

Bermuda, Grenada, and St. Croix, the sum—379 free[125]—is 15 percent of those listed in the National Archives as having served the British cause. Five of these soldiers, John Twine, Black London, Anthony Smithers, James Franklin, and Stephen Blucke, despised "what they Call Free in this Country."[126] Many free blacks fought for the Patriots, but to many, British emancipation appeared noble compared to a revolution, ostensibly for freedom, fought only for slave owners.

The *Book* includes blacks of all ages, one a remarkable ninety-three. On the last page of the Public Records Office version, the inspectors provide a precise numerical breakdown. Of 3,000 listed, 1,336 were men (45 percent),[127] 914 (30 percent) were women, and 750 (25 percent) were children. The difference between men and women—nearly half again as many men as women—is significant. Blacks were intent on keeping their families together. The number of children—one-quarter—and of women together exceeds the number of men.[128]

Young people, who were hardier, often escaped. Between ages sixteen and thirty, 1,305 (51 percent) joined the British,[129] and 23 percent were aged thirty-one to ninety-three.[130] At least 450 families—more than 300 with children—emigrated.[131]

The emigration rates are dramatically higher and then slightly higher for infants in their first two years, compared with older children.[132] These figures suggest that blacks experienced a new sense of freedom and hope, registered in Boston King's glittering remark about reaching British lines: "I began to feel the happiness of liberty, of which I knew nothing before."[133] Emancipated, they made babies. One hundred and eighty-five infants, 7 percent of the total number of émigrés, were born within British lines. Families brought nearly four-fifths of the children from the plantations.

Notably, lone women often came with children. Tam Barclay, a forty-two-year-old mother, brought six: Rachel, sixteen, Elizabeth, twelve, George, nine, Israel, six, Tishy, three, and Jane, six months. Mary Stratton (twenty-four) came with Rose (four), Johnny (two), and Peggy (an infant).[134] The *Book* describes some mothers bearing babies in their arms, but does not list them separately. Thus, the Public Records Office list of three thousand understates the number who left. In the nineteenth century, bondsman John Washington described the horror of the American slave market that had shattered his family—his owner sold his mother and siblings to a far-away plantation—and that had consigned him as a child to care for a white woman.[135] Thus, to hold their families together, blacks went to great lengths. As the hearing of Samuel Doron, divided from his two children, shows, the Crown, too, sometimes broke up families. Nonetheless, that families escaped to the Crown and had babies in the camps testifies, in this respect, to the comparative humanity of the English.

Although a number of blacks listed in the *Book* had African names and facial markings, most had been born in America. African male names included Juba, Mimbo, Mango, Mingo, Quash, Quaco, Quomo, and Vig; female names included Cutto, Tenah, Mima, and Cudja.[136] Reflecting once again the English inspectors' laziness, only a return of two companies of Black Pioneers documents Quash's military service.[137]

The *Book* also testifies to the retrograde character of the empire. White Loyalists claimed ownership of about 16 percent of the blacks listed. The *Book* records, for example, individuals as "Captain Phillips' property clearly" or registered with a colonial "Office of Police." A complex pattern of freedom and enslavement appears: at the fall of Charlestown, John Mauze (twenty-three) escaped "with Colonel Thompson" and emigrated as a free man. But three entries above, a Colonel Gruden, a Tory owner, "gave" Henry Gruden (thirteen) to Thompson, who transported the child as a slave. Only fourteen people list themselves as "taken prisoner." For instance, James Collin (forty-three) was captured by General Arnold at Pittsburgh, Virginia, in 1780 and Zach Leich (twenty-six) by "the St. Albans man of war" in 1778. How the status of prisoner affected their future is unclear. Yet no imperial representative "claimed" them. Even for the free, a category demeaningly lists "Names of the Persons in whose Possession They Are."[138]

The Book of Negroes thus also reveals the complex practice of British repressiveness even toward those whom it freed. Officers still referred to blacks in the language of slave owners, and the *Book* reeks of the slave market. The most common word in the inspectors' abbreviated lexicon is the adjective "stout," as in "stout wench" or "stout fellow." Sometimes they append "old," as for Phyllis Hutchins (forty-four) or, for Jack Hand (fifty), "almost past his laboring." For those maimed by torture, they mention, as in the case of Isaac James, a "blind left eye." Occasionally, they add adverbs or adjectives, as for Dinah Ellis (twenty-five), "very little wench"; Sarah Cross (thirty), "stout squat wench"; Jane Parks (fifteen), "feeble wench"; and Cathleen Drayton (four), slave of William Henry Drayton of South Carolina, "ordinary wench."

Of such children as Peter Martin (twelve), inspectors burble "fine boy." Writing of others in a sexist vein, they describe both Ann Hazard and Rebecca Williams as a "likely wench" and Minnie (no last name) as a "remarkable fine wench." Whether from the point of view of productivity or desire, an inspector writes of Nancy Hill, a woman with a child, as "well made." He describes William Wells as a "stout fine fellow," and to show creativity, William Francis becomes a "fine stout fellow."

In the slave-owner sensibility of the time, inspectors, with subtle attention, designate by "race" 434 persons. They categorize them in thirteen subdivisions: 2 "half indians," 11 "half mulattoes," 3 "3/4 whites," 175 "blacks," "1 black Mulatto," 1 "Black & Indian," 1 "Mustee" [another name for black and Indian], 2 "Guinea born," 223 "Mulattoes," 2 "Mulatto and Indian," 7 "Negroid," 5 "Quadroon," and 1 "Yellow." Two hundred and forty of those listed by race—better than half—had a white parent. Thus, the variety of categories suggests how many children owners fathered through rape.

The slavocracy distinguished minor differences in color and status in extraordinary ways. When I embarked on this project, I did not know, for example what "mustee" or "quadroon" meant. Like the Nazi categories for putative racial differences, the vocabulary of the slave owners is, fortunately, almost lost.

In listing American "owners," the *Book* was not unique among British documents. A manifest of Black Pioneers commanded by Captain George Martin has a similar category of entry for freed soldiers: "to whom they belonged." Thus, "Bob Quince" and "Friday" are listed with former owner "Richard Quince" and "Quash" and "Morris" with "Parker Quince." Not all such records tracked former slave owners, however. For instance, a list of Black Pioneers commanded by Lieutenant Colonel Allen Stewart contains only the names of members.[139] Still, representatives of an empire that stood for emancipation during the Revolution often act without self-awareness, as if they were rating and swapping horses.

The *Book* would even serve as an instrument for continuing slave-owners' zeal. Perusing it in 1786, the Rhode Island legislature reported to Congress the names and information about thirty-eight blacks who had escaped with the Crown. It called on owners in other states to do likewise.[140] On the Rhode Island list, five of the thirty-eight blacks, around 12 percent, had classical, place, or African names, once again revealing the understatement of most of today's lists of the blacks who fought on either side, which single out only such names.

DELIVERANCE AND THE PERILS OF FREEDOM

The *Book of Negroes* is laconic about the perils of freedom, but a petition from London reveals the special suffering of black Loyalists in such a casually racist environment. After the war, Shadrack Furman requested compensation for his modest property, lost to the Patriots, from William Pitt, chancellor of the Exchequer. A free man, Furman, who lived in Acamack County, Virginia, entertained British troops in his home and, in his letter to Pitt, noted that he had "suppli[ied] them with provisions when they came into Virginia." On January 1, 1781, the Patriots "burnt and destroyed or commandeered the property of many Loyalists and the whole effects of your Petitioner."[141]

The Patriots had battered Furman: "After dangerously wounding him in diverse parts the Marks of which Petr can still shew, then Stripped, tied up and gave him 500 lashes and then left him almost dead in the Field by reason of which your Petitioner lost his Eye Sight and the use of one of his Legs by a stroke of the axe they gave him." Head wounds so impaired Furman's health "that he is sometimes bereft of reason."[142]

When he healed sufficiently, he fled on a privateer, commanded by one Captain Robeson of Cape Cod, to Portsmouth, Virginia, and enlisted with Captain Frazier's Department of Pioneers. He worked until illness "rendered it necessary to send him to Head Quarters under the Care of the General Doctor, and he was accordingly sent by order of Genl. Leslie who promised him that if he was not cured, he should be maintained out of the Royal Bounty." In Virginia, Furman was among the black Loyalists who caught black Patriot spies. As a certificate of Sergeant John McDonald of the Seventy-Sixth Regiment indicates, Furman identified "Cabb Tigel and one Rose two notorious Rebels whom he had known to come as spies to Portsmouth under the Disguise of Friendship."[143]

After the war, Furman immigrated with the Crown to Nova Scotia. When the commission sent by Pitt met at Shelburne in Canada, Furman needed treatment by Doctor Huggeford and could not attend.[144] "Discharged Incurable," he journeyed to London. The commission, however, would not grant his petition for relief. Without "friends, Credit or Money," he and his wife relied on the "Charity of the Public." As a last plea, Furman petitioned Pitt. No record survives of his decision.[145]

In defeat, the empire was thus both decent and evil. In Savannah, David Ramsey, a Patriot, observed that "in order to get off with the retreating navy, [blacks] would sometimes fasten themselves to the sides of the boats. To prevent this dangerous practice, the fingers of some of them were chopped off and soldiers were posted with cutlasses and bayonets to oblige them to keep at proper distances."[146] Perhaps Ramsay, who opposed the Crown, exaggerated, but escape was necessary to blacks, and to depart desperately with the British was a lesser evil than awaiting Patriot vengeance. To this racist Whig, empathizing with imperial officers who maimed the escapees, the danger here was not to the blacks, but to British authority. Recalling Cornwallis's driving blacks who followed his army between the lines at Yorktown, the story underlines English dishonor.

Nonetheless, the vast multitude who escaped to the Crown dwarfed those enslaved by white Loyalists.[147] Drawn in groups of three, five, ten, or twenty—after fighting, plagues, starvation, recapture, and death—as a conservative estimate, some twelve to fifteen thousand free blacks emigrated with the Crown. This figure again demonstrates the social magnitude of black resistance.

Recall Dunmore's estimate that two thousand might have joined the Royal Ethiopian Regiment in 1775, but perhaps seventeen hundred died on shore. Recall the six to eight who arrived each day at Gwinn's Island, with its epidemics and mass graves. Recall the diseases that ravaged black recruits throughout the British camps. Recall the several thousand black escapees who accompanied each large formation of redcoats and the unorganized blacks that Cornwallis drove between the lines at Yorktown. Recall that most corpses at Yorktown were black, as well as the steady attrition of black soldiers captured or killed in other battles. Recall the black guerillas of New Jersey and South Carolina, some of whom, like Captain Tye, were killed or wounded in the field. Recall that many escapees faded into the American population or fought on as "Soldiers of the King of England." The number of escapees is, as Gary Nash once put it, "gigantic," even if some numbers which previously circulated in the literature, say, sixty thousand and certainly a hundred thousand, are probably too large.[148]

After the Revolution, blacks went to Nova Scotia, Jamaica, East Florida, England, and Germany.[149] For instance, at least four hundred free black Loyalists immigrated to London.[150] Perhaps two to three thousand free blacks left for Jamaica, St. Lucia, Antigua, and the Bahamas. With its corps of Afro-American drummers, a mercenary unit under Baron von Riedesel returned to Germany.[151] Of blacks on ships from New York to Canada, 40 percent went to Port Roseway (1,065 of 2,679), 20 percent (533) to Annapolis, Annapolis St. John, and Annapolis Royal, 19 percent (496) to St. John's and St. John's River, and 10 percent (274) to Port Mattoon.[152]

In defeat, the Crown took some thirteen thousand black refugees, six thousand from Charlestown and four thousand from Savannah, most still slaves, but many free, and three thousand, mainly free, from New York.[153] Perhaps another ten thousand had sailed or escaped on foot from New York earlier. Once again, two to three times as many free blacks—between 9,100 and 10,400 total—settled in Canada, as the *Book of Negroes* records.

In 1786 the empire ceded East Florida to Spain. In London, on May 2, William Brown wrote a "Return of Persons who Emigrated to Different Parts of the British Dominions" from East Florida, which included 3,390 whites and 6,540 blacks. Blacks are neither listed by name nor identified as emancipated or slave, though many had become free.

The return includes the following blacks:

35 to Europe
155 to Nova Scotia
714 to Jamaica and the Spanish Main
444 to Dominica
2214 to the Bahamas
217 to other foreign lands
200 remain with the Spaniards.

A little better than a third, 2,561 blacks returned to, or perhaps were forced to return to, as the document describes it, the "States of America." The return offers no breakdown, however, of their status.[154] Though the realization of freedom for many, emigration also meant an uncertain future, far from what one had known. Perhaps some returnees sought to escape vengeance or reenslavement by former owners and to vanish into the new America.

chapter 8 ¶ Postwar Black Emigrations
The Search for Freedom and Self-Government

*The poor people I have brought with me from America begin to feel the
sweets of a free government, and I am convinced they would follow the
government of France should they be disturbed in their endeavours to
maintain their newly acquired freedom.*
—*John Clarkson, writing to the Marquis de Lafayette, July 2, 1792*

he story of the freed former slaves and free blacks
who fled the new United States after the British defeat is the story of a continued search for freedom
and of ongoing struggles to continue and to expand
the second revolution in the wake of the first. From
Canada to the Caribbean and from the New World to Africa, freed slaves
sought to fulfill the promise of their original efforts to achieve liberty and
equality. Unhappily, what they often encountered instead was misery, exploitation, and racist violence.

Nevertheless, after the American Revolution, among émigrés from the
newly independent former colonies, the second revolution, the revolution
for black freedom, took on a new dimension. It became part of an international revolution devoted to incipient stirrings of democracy around the
world as well as to freedom from slavery. In Canada, for example, Thomas
Peters, an ex-slave and a giant figure, strove relentlessly to win democracy
and subsistence for himself and others there.

Peters would eventually lead some twelve hundred free blacks to emigrate from Nova Scotia to Sierra Leone. There, in the face of repeated setbacks, Peters and other radical democrats, such as Isaac Anderson, forged
a novel democratic regime. In Canada, Sierra Leone, Jamaica, and elsewhere in the British Empire, the ideas of the American Revolution, combined with imperial emancipation and the promptings of Christianity,
spread the aspirations of former slaves not only to be free but also to govern themselves.

IMMIGRATION TO NOVA SCOTIA
After the Revolution, many blacks found freedom and even
the American idea of natural rights by immigrating to Canada with the

Crown. How many did so has been in question. Some historians cite four thousand free blacks as the number who escaped to Nova Scotia. This total includes the three thousand listed in the *Book of Negroes*. By such an estimate, however, three blacks would have come on the ships from New York with Sir Guy Carleton for every one who immigrated separately. Nonetheless, in the *Book of Negroes*, only some twenty-six hundred were free.[1] Had they examined the logs of ships listed in the *Book*, these scholars should have estimated that a total of thirty-six hundred free blacks arrived in Nova Scotia.

Still, a simple way exists to figure out how many free blacks escaped to Canada through New York earlier or subsequently on ships from the South. One can compare the musters of black settlers at Annapolis and Birchtown in Nova Scotia with the *Book of Negroes*. For Annapolis in 1784, 78 heads of household came separately from Carleton's fleet. In contrast, only 29 emigrated with it, a ratio of roughly 2⅔ to 1. Including entire families, 163 persons escaped to Annapolis by means other than Carleton's ships. Fifty-two are recorded also in the *Book of Negroes*. That is a ratio of more than 3 to 1 of blacks who arrived in Canada by other routes.[2]

In the same year, the *Muster Book of Free Blacks* at Birchtown recorded 464 heads of family who immigrated to Canada independently of Carleton and 253 heads of family who sailed with Carleton from New York. This muster does not list individual family members. However, its ratio of roughly 9 to 5 (those who came separately divided by those who came with Carleton) among heads of household would probably grow toward 3 to 1, comparable to the Annapolis list, if family members were included.[3] The British colonial government directed blacks into these main communities and some others in Nova Scotia. The roughly similar proportions for large settlements in Annapolis and Birchtown are very likely typical of other towns in Nova Scotia as well. No evidence suggests that some larger concentration of immigrants from the 1783 ships, compared with those who came by other means, was segregated elsewhere in the region.[4] Thus, an additional two and two-thirds to three times as many blacks as left from New York in 1783 escaped to Canada, making a total of between 9,100 and 10,400 free blacks. Unlike the standard guess, this range is supported by the foregoing evidence from Annapolis and Birchtown.[5]

Furthermore, some twelve hundred blacks would soon emigrate from Canada to Sierra Leone. If the standard guess of four thousand émigrés to Canada were right, that would mean that better than one in four went on that great adventure. But because agitation to immigrate to West Africa varied from town to town and in some places met violent opposition from white landowners who profited off cheap black labor and sought to bar further exodus, that ratio seems high. In contrast, my figures yield an estimate of one in eight to one in nine, which seems more plausible.

Nova Scotia was not a promising place of refuge for anyone after the Revolution. It was the northernmost European outpost in North America, and in the late eighteenth century, its economy had crashed as London's grants to settlers declined and immigrants fled to the Ohio Basin. Yet, after the Revolution, the Crown brought or encouraged some thirty thousand refugees, white and black, from the United States. Note that whites outnumbered blacks substantially (two to one, if blacks numbered roughly ten thousand). In the Nova Scotia communities of Shelburne and Digby, Lieutenant Governor John Parr's proclamation offered a quarter of an acre in the towns, along with a larger plot outside. But Parr did not make sure that suitable rural land was available. Often, the available land was not arable.[6]

Faced with sudden defeat, the Crown had no plan to resettle the emancipated. Lieutenant Colonel Robert Morse, an engineer, improvised. He wrote to H. E. Fox, the commander in Halifax: "As a number of Negroes are at Port Roseway . . . for whom lands are not yet located nor other provisions made, that such as may chuse voluntarily to engage in the Service of the Government shall be enlisted for one year upon the same pay and Terms with the Black Pioneer Company and be employed and paid in the Engineer Department to the number of 100 at Halifax and 40 at Roseway."[7]

Royal policy promised one thousand acres to former Loyalist officers, seven hundred to captains, five hundred to subalterns, two hundred to noncommissioned officers, one hundred to other soldiers and civilian heads of families, plus fifty for each family member. But Parr assigned tinier and fewer plots to blacks. Furthermore, bureaucratic corruption in land distribution undermined even these plans. Judge Alexander Howe reported "an unjudicious and unjust Mode of assigning [blacks] their Lands."[8] Only a few blacks who settled among whites at Preston, near Halifax, received equal grants.[9] To earn provisions offered gratis to whites, blacks had to perform public labor.

In Shelburne, even some whites waited up to three years for land; they received grants of varying sizes, from 5 to 350 acres, with an average of 74. Yet at Birchtown, out of 649 black men, only 184—28 percent—received land. Nearly three in four did not. Furthermore, even the fortunate had to wait five years—that is, two years longer than the worst-treated whites—to obtain grants averaging thirty-four acres, less than half the average for whites.[10]

Mirroring government segregation, blacks kept their distance from whites. Under Colonel Stephen Blucke's leadership, they founded Birchtown—the lone black city in North America—on Port Roseway harbor in 1783.[11] As John Wesley, founder of Methodism, put it, "The little town they have built is, I suppose, the only town of Negroes which has been built in America—nay, perhaps in any part of the world, except only in Africa. I doubt not but some of them can read. When, therefore, we send a preacher or two to Nova Scotia, we will send some books to be distributed among them; and they will never want books while I live."[12] Baptists created literate ministers; Wesley nurtured religious learning among the many.

Blucke's company of Black Pioneers built barracks, storehouses, and wharves for the imperial army. A Pioneers' return from September 1783 to July 24, 1784, lists ten heads of family along with eighteen women and children. On August 28 and 30, 1783, surveyor Benjamin Marston allocated land to Blucke and his "black gentry." Singled out for privileged treatment, Blucke received a two-hundred-acre grant, comparable to those of white noncommissioned officers, near Port Roseway. In turn, Blucke mobilized "80 souls" to do compulsory public labor on roads from Birchtown to Round Bay and Blucke's own land.[13] In Birchtown, Blucke was both the civil authority and a schoolteacher.[14] The authorities rewarded him; Blucke delivered, both for them and for his own community.

On March 14, 1789, William Booth, a British officer, wrote in his diary: "Birch Town is the Black's settlement under the care and charge of a Colonel Blucke, a Mulatto man, of surprising address, being perfectly polite, and I believe, he has had superior education. If he has not been so fortunate, he has certainly made good use of his time. He don't appear to exceed eight and twenty. His wife is a Negro woman as is his Mother—They are people from Barbadoes."[15]

In his diary for October 1788, General William Dyott praised the "poor but really spirited" settlers and caught their sense of freedom. Yet he punctured Blucke's ambitions: "This poor man, like many others in Shelburne Settlements—set off on the great scale, with his expectations much too far exalted, not having sufficiently examined and reflected, whether the land they were seated upon, or the water . . . would be profitable enough to tempt an increase of Companions—He began by Building a spacious house, and laying out an excellent garden—a garden he has well attended to . . . but the Building he has been obliged to stop the progress of, having only, as far as I could see, completed his Kitchen with a small room."[16] Blucke's incomplete house symbolizes the weaknesses of imperial resettlement of blacks in Nova Scotia.[17]

British authorities also indicted Blucke for assaulting one George Johnston, whom he "did beat, wound and ill-treat so that his life was greatly despaired of."[18] But the British could not toss Blucke aside and did not jail him. In 1792, when others immigrated to Sierra Leone, Blucke and his Black Pioneers petitioned the Crown for "so much as may enable us to purchase a Cow and two Sheep." With understandable resentment, they contrasted this "humble" cost with "the vast expense of transporting so many of our fellow subjects to Africa."[19] No record survives of whether the authorities granted this request.

Life was hard for the freed blacks who settled in Nova Scotia. They faced both economic hardships and the racist attitudes of their fellow white settlers. While enslaved or fighting for the redcoats, many blacks had become artisans, but in Nova Scotia, many became farmers.[20] Soon, however, the settlers learned that the soil was too shallow for crops and the growing season too short. On March 8, 1786, comparing the residents' complaints to those of Jesus, William Jessop, a traveling white Methodist minister, responded to their misery: "I preached this day at Birchtown. I tarried all night with the black people, but the house being leaky, I found it disagreeable, but why should I complain? It was better lodging than my dear Master had which offers from his own words. 'The foxes have holes, the birds of the air have nests, but the son of man hath nowhere to lay his head.'"[21] Of course, Jessop could leave. Nonetheless, spiritual whites often reached out to "the least of these."

In 1787 the Crown cancelled rations to immigrants. As Boston King, who had journeyed with Carleton in 1783, reported in his autobiography: "A dreadful famine . . . not only prevailed at Burchtown, but likewise at Chebucto, Annapolis, Digby, and other places. Many of the poor people were compelled to sell their best gowns for five pounds of flour. . . . When they had parted with all their clothes, even to their blankets, several of them fell down dead in the streat [sic], thro' hunger. Some killed and eat their dogs and cats; and poverty and distress prevailed on every side; so that to my great grief I was obliged to leave Burchtown, because I could get no employment."[22]

"The wretched circumstances," King wrote, forced many to indenture themselves "to . . . merchants, some for two or three years; and others for five or six years."[23] On May 1, 1786, John Harris bound himself "to be put to any plantation or farm work" to William Stone until July 14. In exchange, Stone would "find [Harris] provisions."[24] At fourteen years and seven months old, Herman Horton indentured himself for six years, four months to one George Deinstadt to learn "the Art, Trade, and Mystery of a

Cordwainer" (shoemaker). Herman pledged to keep his master's "secrets" and not to "fornicate or play dice." Deinstadt would provide "papers, pens and other necessities" for school "one quarter of a year every year."[25]

Still, indentures were precarious for ex-slaves; they could lead to reenslavement. On April 22, 1794, James Cox, a black farmer, reported to a Shelburne court that a child "my family bound to John Stewart" had been sold in Liverpool and transported to the West Indies. A "Hand Jury" requested the judge to ask English justices to arrest Stewart. This example of callous reenslavement, the foreman of the jury noted, would cause "much injury to the community in preventing the negroes from binding out their children in the future."[26] But the jury's action did nothing to rescue the child.

Even inside Birchtown, blacks had little security. For instance, Mary Postell had served William Postell, a Patriot sergeant, in County Bam, South Carolina. He had taken Mary to Charlestown, where she escaped and worked on the British fortifications. At the evacuation, Mary went to St. Augustine, Florida, and—emigrating directly from the South—to Shelburne. There, she indentured herself and her three children to a Mr. A. Gray; he sold the children and a nephew to one William Maughan for a hundred bushels of potatoes. In Canada, however, Mary at least had the right and sufficient means to sue for their freedom. Furthermore, two witnesses from Birchtown testified that she had indeed escaped from a rebel and had worked with the Crown.

The black citizens of Birchtown, however, often faced virulent racism. To punish blacks for testifying on Mary Postell's behalf, white Loyalists burned the homes of several black residents and murdered a child. Gray had no record of ownership and claimed that he had lost his original bill of sale from a man in Florida. Despite all this counterevidence, the court ruled for Gray. The precariousness of black freedom in Canada was such that in desperation and risking recapture, some blacks even fled back to the northern United States.[27]

Life was not easy for white Loyalist settlers in Nova Scotia, either, and they missed their former privileged life in the United States. King described their self-destructive pride: "The circumstances of the white inhabitants were likewise very distressing, owing to their great imprudence in building large houses, and striving to excel one another in this piece of vanity. When their money was almost expended, they began to build small fishing vessels; but alas, it was too late to repair their error. . . . The place was reduced in a short time to a heap of ruins, and its inhabitants . . . compelled to flee to other parts of the continent for sustenance."[28]

Once again, whites often received no land in Nova Scotia. White and black Loyalists could together have protested imperial policies, and to prevent their joining forces, the Crown adopted a policy of divide and rule, pitting whites against blacks, who waited longer and received little or no land. The regime's treatment of blacks as lesser citizens was meant to redirect white anger at their own grievances from the elite onto those worse off.

Yet blacks and whites sometimes acted in concert. Loyalists had sometimes imbibed the spirit of New England towns; they would not just obey commands. Authorities had to offer reasons. In his journal, surveyor Benjamin Marston disparaged this immigrant democracy: "The cursed republican, town-meeting spirit has been the ruin of us already, and unless checked by some stricter form of government will overset the prospect which now presents itself of retrieving our affairs. Mankind are often slaves, and oftentimes they have too much liberty."[29]

Still, many white Tories were making a transition from urban jobs, before emigration, to the hard life of a farmer in rocky and frigid Nova Scotia.[30] They could not adjust. As Marston proclaimed in his journal, "They are upon the whole a collection of characters very unfit for the business they have undertaken. Barbers, Taylors, Shoemakers and all kinds of mechanics, bred and used to live in great towns, they are inured to habits very unfit for undertakings which require hardiness, resolution, industry and patience."[31] Black Loyalists, however, had escaped bondage. Despite all the difficulties of the farming life in inhospitable Nova Scotia, freedom was, for blacks, a genuine improvement.

Speaking as a would-be aristocrat, Marston insisted: "Real authority can never be supported without some degree of real superiority." He derided "lower class whites": "People turning very indolent, some parties not at work till 11 o'clock. Many of the people who came in this fleet are of the lower class of great towns. . . . They begin to be clamorous, and to have a thousand groundless rumours circulating among them to the prejudice of those to whom they ought to submit."[32]

Although in a May 24, 1783, entry, Marston denounced "republican principles," he sympathized with some refugees: "Thursday last the people drew for their town lots. By indulging their cursed republican principles they committed an irregularity which cost them another day's work. Yesterday I was ashore all day apportioning people to their lots—'tis a task trying to humanity, for while those engaged in settling them are justly exasperated at the insolence . . . of one sort of people, they can't help they must feel for the distress of the sensible feeling part who have come from easy situations to encounter all the hardships of a new plantation and who wish to submit cheerfully to the dispensations of Providence."[33]

On July 26, Marston reported, "Great riot today. The disbanded soldiers have risen against the Free negroes to drive them out of Town, because they labour cheaper than the soldiers."[34] Blacks, for Marston, were not also "disbanded soldiers," but merely "free." Yet black Loyalists had served in the military more often and for longer terms than whites and, by and large, fought harder and suffered more.[35] They "labored cheaper" because the Crown compelled them. White Loyalists "pulled down about 20 of their houses," burned others, and looted.[36] Given Marston's insistence on many whites' laziness in putting up their own houses against the coming winter, his understated reaction to the destruction of newly created, bare shelters for blacks stands out for bigotry.

Officially, Governor Parr blamed the riots on the delay in white soldiers' obtaining land.[37] He even expressed some sympathy with blacks: "As the Negroes are now in this country, the principles of Humanity dictate . . . to give them a chance to Live, and not to distress them."[38] But the colonial administration did not protect blacks; rather, the authorities reinforced the divisions that led to these atrocities.

To survive in Canada, blacks shifted to nonfarm activities or from one skilled line of work to another. Thus, Boston King, a carpenter, became a seaman. After a voyage to Halifax, he wrote, "We were paid off, each man receiving 15 pounds for his wages; and my master gave me two barrels of fish, agreeable to his promise.[39] When I returned home, I was enabled to clothe my wife and myself; and my Winter's store consisted of one barrel of flour, three bushels of corn, nine gallons of treacle, 20 bushels of potatoes which my wife had set in my absence, and the two barrels of fish; so that this was the best Winter I ever saw in Burchtown."[40]

Over the next four years, the imperial government also forced many survivors to become sharecroppers for whites. Battening off cheap black labor, Shelburne grew, as historian R. D. Eno puts it, into "the largest and most prosperous community in the province, with an estimated population of eight thousand in 1785."[41]

In May and June 1785, landless blacks seized vacant lots and commons. The authorities chose not to dispossess them. A governor's inquiry into "the Disorders and unhappy Dissentions at Digby" discharged Robert Tempany as a justice of the peace for participation in black resistance.[42]

Still, a countertendency existed among many whites, spurred by an egalitarian Christianity. In his autobiography, the minister David George reported that he received "a bag of seed potatoes from a white Baptist family named Taylor." That bag produced thirty-five bushels of potatoes, which sustained George and his dependents for a winter.[43] In contrast, for the oppressors of free blacks, Christianity had evolved into what sociologist Max Weber would later name a "theodicy of good fortune," ornamenting their position as the gift of the Lord.[44]

Whites who sided with blacks risked attack. In 1786 Freeborn Garrettson, a white Loyalist who had freed his slaves, preached in Shelburne. Racists pitched stones and rotten eggs at him. Persecution by the ignorant and privileged, however, is, for a believer, the image of Christ. Garrettson encouraged Boston King to preach in Birchtown and Shelburne. In 1791 the Methodist William Black appointed King minister to thirty-four parishioners in Preston, a black town near Halifax. Sometimes whites came to his services.[45] Nonetheless, the egalitarian Protestantism of some could not undo the racism of many whites and the imperial administration.

THOMAS PETERS, GRANVILLE SHARP, AND THE VISION OF "NATURAL EQUITY"

For black Loyalists, however, the Christian honoring of souls and the idea of natural rights fused in a vision of freedom and dignity. Such insights motivated the career of Thomas Peters.

In Halifax, Fredericton, and London, blacks demanded the rights of British subjects: to vote, to serve on juries, and, if accused or arrested, to be tried in a court of law. Peters, the leader of the movement, had been a Yoruba prince in what is now Nigeria. When he was twenty-two, slave hunters had imprisoned him aboard the ship *Henri Quatre* and had sold him in Louisiana. The owner named him Thomas Peters and took him to Wilmington, North Carolina. Three times, Peters attempted to escape. Each time, the "owner" whipped and branded him. Finally, in 1776, Peters freed himself. Heeding Dunmore's and Clinton's proclamations, he became a sergeant in the Black Pioneers. Twice, Patriots wounded him. On October 26, 1783, in New York, Lieutenant Colonel Allen Stewart attested that Peters "has served . . . in every respect becoming the Character of a good and faithful subject of Great Britain and has gained the good wishes of his officers and comrades."[46]

Peters, his wife, Sally, a twelve-year-old daughter, Clairy, and a son born in 1781 immigrated with the Crown to Nova Scotia in 1783.[47] Near Digby, he and his followers founded Brindley Town. Peters worked as a millwright.[48]

A fiery seeker of freedom, he would become spokesperson for Nova Scotian and Sierra Leonean blacks in their efforts to transform a nominal freedom into genuine equality and self-government.

In August 1784, Peters and Murphy Steele, who had also served in the Black Pioneers, petitioned Governor Parr for land, but received none.[49] In 1790, representing Annapolis blacks, Peters journeyed to New Brunswick—a distant region in Nova Scotia—to request land from its governor, Thomas Carleton. Peters's words to Carleton were forceful: "That your Petitioner and Numbers of other Blacks are unprovided with Lands, he humbly implores in the name of the whole that something May be done for them as he and many others are now Suffering. Their present Situation is Such that they are incapable of paying the poor tax."[50] Carleton proclaimed that black Loyalists would receive the same treatment as whites. Peters asked about open land near Fredericton. The Crown, the governor told him, had reserved those tracts for whites.

In St. Johns, Peters and other blacks applied for three blocks of land. The English, however, allocated them sparse plots far from the town; only five families went. One hundred stayed in St. Johns as laborers or subsisted on tiny lots.[51] After seven years, Peters had still received no land.

But Peters had become a sophisticated political organizer. From 202 black families in Brindley Town and New Brunswick, he collected powers of attorney, which he later used to petition Foreign Minister Grenville. The signatories praised the Reverend Joshua Weeks's charitable collections for them. Cagily, they also pledged to obey "the Episcopal Church of England" and to be "Peaceable and Obedient to the Ruling Powers." Yet going around Weeks and Governor Parr, they nominated a black representative. Parr would hardly have found this "obedient." The blacks averred that "it wou'd be to Our Advantage if our Affairs were to be transacted by One Person Nominated and Appointed to Act for and in behalf of the whole of us; in all matters both Civil and Religious . . . and do hereby Promise and engage to abide by, hold for firm and Effectual, and ratify all and whatsoever the said Thomas Peters shall for us and in our behalf do."[52]

Historians report that Peters was illiterate. But along with his eloquence, Peters seems to have acquired some learning—he could either recruit sophisticated help or write himself. In a surviving copy of the petition, fifteen black soldiers—illiterate former slaves—indicated their consent with an "X."[53] At this time, no white worked with Peters. Peters himself probably wrote it.[54]

In an epic pilgrimage in 1790, this former soldier journeyed to London.[55] Many British and Portuguese ships on the Atlantic trafficked in slaves and could have recaptured him. In England, he met many free, but unemployed blacks, including American Loyalists.[56] He also encountered Ottobah Cugoano, a former West Indian bondsman, who had written *Thoughts and Sentiments on the Evil and Wicked Traffic of Slavery*. On December 26, 1790, Henry Clinton introduced him to Secretary of State Grenville: "I wish to present to you a memorial of certain poor blacks who are deserving the Protection of Govt. & who seem to be the only Loyalists that have been neglected.... Perhaps you will suffer the poor Black who is the bearer of this to tell his own melancholy Tale. He is deputed by others in similar situations; I remember this man a very active Serjt. In a very usefull Corps."[57] A prince kidnapped into bondage, Peters became a celebrity among abolitionists. A 1790 portrait shows Peters, tall and regal, shaking hands with an imperial official.[58]

In London, through the Committee for the Relief of the Black Poor or through Cugoano, Peters met abolitionist leaders Granville Sharp, William Wilberforce, and Thomas Clarkson. Through them, and especially in association with Sharp, he became connected with the scheme of British abolitionists to resettle former American slaves in Africa.

As a minor government official, Granville Sharp had been inspired by the American Revolution's declaration of freedom but was horrified by its continuing embrace of bondage. This contradiction—and imperial mockery of a revolution against "slavery" that defended slavery—inspired him and other abolitionists to act to oppose slavery wherever Britain ruled in the world. Historian Christopher Brown rightly underlines this connection: "As the American crisis turned toward war, Granville Sharp's fight against the keeping of slaves in England widened into a broader campaign against the practice of slavery and the traffic in slaves throughout the British Empire." At the American Revolution's outset, he disseminated petitions by American blacks for freedom, among both the public at large and the elite. His actions probably stimulated imperial thinking about emancipating and recruiting blacks. In turn, the loss of the thirteen colonies provoked reflection, led by Sharp, about the connected harms of empire, the slave trade, and bondage. His opposition to these practices was not merely pragmatic and instrumental; he traced them to their illiberal conceptual root.[59]

Sharp's 1774 *Declaration of the People's Natural Right to a Share in the Legislature* developed a coherent theory of representation and freedom or "natural equity" throughout the empire—or, rather, throughout a postcolonial, democratic world that he believed should and would succeed it. In the book he emphasized the links between freedom, self-determination, and abolition. Thus, on the basis of the same principles, he supported the abolition of slavery and the right of the American colonies to be independent of Great Britain. For instance, he asserted that because the British Parliament could not represent Americans, American representatives would have to free white indentured servants, blacks, and Native Americans. As Brown notes, Sharp agreed with the Quaker abolitionist Anthony Benezet that "defending the rights of slaves 'should be a means of warning the Americans of the natural independence of their several assemblies with respect to the British Parliament.' The apparent complement between African and colonial rights satisfied Sharp's belief that all liberties stood on the single foundation of 'natural Equity.' When he framed the rights of colonists as inviolable as the rights of slaves, he drew himself into defending American resistance."[60]

After the British defeat, his thoughts became broadly influential in the emerging abolitionist movement.[61] In particular, he was one of the central figures in the project to establish an African colony of freed blacks and in the Sierra Leone Company formed to realize that project.

Although Sierra Leone became a British colony in 1808, it was originally founded as an independent colony by the Sierra Leone Company in 1792. The Sierra Leone Company was the successor of the St. George's Bay Company, itself founded in 1787 by the Committee for the Relief of the Black Poor, created in London the previous year to provide a home in Africa for London's black underclass, including freed Loyalist ex-slaves. The initial effort failed, done in by disease and by raids by local natives and slave traders, but under the aegis of Granville Sharp and other leading British abolitionists, including William Wilberforce and Thomas Clarkson, in 1792 the Sierra Leone Company sent eleven hundred black settlers from Halifax, Nova Scotia, mostly Tory ex-slaves who had fled with the British after the American Revolution, to a new colony based in the new settlement of Freetown.

For Africa, Sharp had imagined a democratic colony for free black settlers that he named the Province of Freedom. According to his 1786 "Short Sketch of Temporary Regulations" for the St. George's Bay Company colony that he projected, it would resemble an old "English system of mutual Frankpledge or free-suretyship given by all the householders." This was a system of equality based on an oath of responsibility. Sharp divided households into dozens, or tithings, each of which would elect a "tithingman." Every hundred households would choose a "hundreder." Sharp proposed suffrage for all males over sixteen for a common council or parliament (suffrage could not, of course, be universal without women). This new African regime would be more democratic than those of the United States or England. Every homeowner would serve in the militia.[62]

Sharp's "Sketch" saw labor as the medium of exchange, proposing a paper currency tied to the value of a day's work.[63] In contrast to the twelve-hour day customary in England, Sharp mandated that work begin after prayers at 6:00 a.m. and cease at 4:00 p.m., with a two-hour siesta. With a six-hour Saturday, blacks would work a forty-six-hour week rather than a seventy-two-hour week. They would convene their own assemblies and courts, elect their own leaders, and control the militia. Sharp declared that the settlers "would become the freest and the happiest people on earth; because the poor are effectually provided for, and their rights secured, the meanest cottager being allowed a due share of the land, besides a property and interest in the Settlement."[64]

The Sierra Leone Company continued to promote this vision of a free, democratic black colony in Africa. At the same time, Thomas Peters arrived in London representing a group of free British blacks suffering from their search for freedom on the British side in the Revolutionary War. The Sierra Leone Company's directors decided to promote Peters's cause and to help black Loyalists in Nova Scotia to immigrate to and establish a new colony in Sierra Leone. Perhaps with Sharp's help, Peters refined two petitions to Secretary of State Grenville.[65] The first invoked the bare, inaccessible lands offered to some new inhabitants at St. Johns, Canada, and stressed that more than a hundred black Loyalists had obtained no rural land: "The said Persons with their Wives and Children amounting together in the whole to the Number of 102 People . . . at Annapolis Royal have not yet obtained their Allotments of Land except one single Acre each for a Town sol."[66] The families petitioned to be settled decently.

News of a free black colony in Sierra Leone had reached Nova Scotia. Many black Loyalists there no longer had confidence that Canada would provide a setting for liberty. Peters's first petition reported: "Some Part of the said Black People are earnestly desirous of obtaining their due Allotment of Land and remaining in America but others are ready and willing to go wherever the Wisdom of Government may think proper to provide for them as free subjects of the British Empire."[67]

In a second petition, Peters denounced a "public and avowed Toleration of Slavery . . . as if the happy Influence of his Majesty's free Government was incapable of being extended so far as America." In Nova Scotia, whites had stripped black Loyalists of political rights. Peters condemned "such a degrading and Unjust Prejudice against People of Colour in general that even those that are acknowledged to be free Inhabitants and Settlers . . . are refused the common Rights and Privileges of the other Inhabitants, not being permitted to vote at any election or serve on juries." Blacks could not recover wages wrongly denied them. They had no legal recourse against violence.[68]

On December 18, 1790, Peters submitted these two petitions to Grenville. The one concerning land moved Grenville to action. In 1791 Parliament funded a second free black colony in Sierra Leone.[69] The second petition highlights the severity of racism in Canada; Grenville ignored it.

Endorsing Peters's first petition, however, Secretary of State Henry Dundas ordered the governors of Nova Scotia and New Brunswick to allocate the best available lands to blacks. They ignored him. Dundas also encouraged the new settlement in Sierra Leone. This second colony was initially composed of two hundred whites, with a smaller number of free blacks,[70] but English abolitionists helped four hundred blacks journey from London and supported émigrés from Nova Scotia.

Peters returned to Canada accompanied by Lieutenant John Clarkson, Thomas Clarkson's brother. Representing the Sierra Leone Company, Clarkson promised twenty acres of land to each man, ten to his wife, and five to each child.[71] Afflicted by misery, landlessness, racism, and violence, many free blacks in Canada signed up. Yet this exodus from Nova Scotia met fierce opposition from whites, who fought to keep cheap black labor. In addition, Governor Parr realized that a large emigration would prove he had failed to provide adequately for settlers. He, too, opposed the exodus.

On August 2, 1791, Clarkson and Lawrence Hartshorne, a Quaker from Halifax, circulated a Sierra Leone Company advertisement for a "Free Settlement on the Coast of Africa." Applicants would have to obtain a "Testimonial of their Character (more particularly as to Honesty, Sobriety and Industry)" signed by either Clarkson or Hartshorne. In return, they promised, black settlers there would receive equal treatment with whites:

> That every Free Black shall have a Grant of not less than Twenty Acres of Land for himself, Ten for his wife, and five for every child, upon such terms . . . as shall hereafter be settled by the Company.
>
> That for all stores, provisions, or supplies from the Company's warehouse, the company shall receive an equitable compensation, according to fixed rules, extending to blacks and whites indeterminately.
>
> That the civil, military, personal and commercial rights and duties of Blacks and Whites shall be the same and secured in the same manner.[72]

To recruit émigrés, Peters traveled several hundred miles from Birchtown to New Brunswick. Local officials opposed him. At St. John, 220 blacks signed up. Crossing the Bay of Fundy to Annapolis, Peters recruited ninety others. At Digby, a white man knocked him down. No arrest or prosecution occurred. Other whites forged indentures that named nonassenting blacks and refused to pay back wages or settle debts with those who sought to leave.[73] "The white people . . . were very unwilling that we should go," wrote an Annapolis black minister, "though they had been very cruel to us, and treated many of us as though we had been slaves."[74]

At Digby, whites attempted to bar four blacks, including George Corankapone, from leaving. Nonetheless, they escaped. Covering 340 miles in fourteen days, they made their way through dense forest and snow around the Bay of Fundy and joined Peters in Halifax. As historian Gary Nash puts it, "The return to Africa soon took on overtones of the Old Testament delivery of the Israelites from bondage in Israel."[75]

Starting on October 12, 1791, Clarkson traveled by horseback to the black towns of Preston, Birchtown, and Shelburne. He recruited Boston King and many others. In opting to immigrate to West Africa, Clarkson said, blacks looked to the future: "The greatest part of the people . . . had not done it with the idea of improving their own condition, but for the sake of the children whom they wish to see established upon a better foundation."[76]

On a rainy night in Birchtown on October 26, some 350 blacks came to the chapel of Moses Wilkinson, a blind and lame Wesleyan preacher, to hear Clarkson's proposals. In his diary Clarkson wrote, "It struck me forcibly that perhaps the future welfare and happiness, nay the very lives of the individuals then before me might depend . . . upon the words which I should deliver. . . . At length I rose up and explained circumstantially the object, progress, and result of the Embassy of Thomas Peters to England."[77] Wilkinson's congregation often applauded Clarkson's speech. In the next three days, the whole group—514 men, women, and children—added their names to the list of prospective emigrants.[78] Many who decided to go were connected through specific churches and communities.

IMMIGRATION TO SIERRA LEONE

Clarkson recognized the horrors of the "Middle Passage," which had murdered so many blacks. Aiming to prevent repetition, he and Peters inspected the ships.[79] On January 15, 1792, a flotilla of fifteen ships sailed from Canada with 1,193 settlers.[80]

A Nova Scotian muster lists 155 heads of households, consisting of 562 emigrants: 151 men, 157 women, 4 of whom led households, and 254 children.[81] This list is nearly half of the 1,193 émigrés to Sierra Leone in 1792. Several individuals had stood out in some way in the struggle for freedom in America. For instance, David George, the preacher, with his wife and six children, was first on this list. Despite George Washington's desperation to recover slaves, Henry Washington had escaped him and now immigrated to Africa.[82] "Chs Wilkinson" escaped Eliza Wilkinson, whose letters had expressed dread of black soldiers. John Quaker's surname honored that emancipatory group.

In the *Book of Negroes*, blacks bound for Canada had listed the place in the United States in which they had been born or to which they had been sold. The list of those leaving Canada, however, indicates that rejection of North America ran high. Nearly one-third of the men on the Nova Scotia list—49 (32 percent), including the oldest, Richard Herbert at eighty and the youngest, Chas Jenkins at twenty-two—reported their birthplace as "Africa."[83] Three of five sixty-year-olds made a similar declaration. Isaac Anderson, who would become a leader of black democracy in Sierra Leone, reported being born in Angola.

In addition, three had African names: Mungo Leslie, Cudgoe Leslie, and Cudgoe Francis. But as the name "Norfolk Virginia" from "Africa" suggests in one entry, the Nova Scotia compilers were not notably more careful than the inspectors of the *Book of Negroes*. Many blacks who emigrated from New York had either come from Africa or identified with parents who had. Departing for Canada, however, they had not revealed that identification. Fused with egalitarian Christianity and republicanism, a longing for an African home now sustained these immigrants to Sierra Leone.

Many signatories reported their current or former military ranks: 148 soldiers, 2 captains, 1 corporal, 1 sailor, and 2 pioneers. Their service in the British military included terms in Canada as well as in the Loyalist forces in the United States. As captains in Canada, "Thos Hog" of Carolina and "Robt Nicholson" of Virginia achieved higher rank than other black officers in the imperial army except Tye, Blucke, and Fraction in New York. The manifest lists John Godfrey, twenty-five years old, of Virginia as a "wounded cripple." Blacks bore hardships in Canada and fierce conditions of passage to Sierra Leone. But inverting the coerced voyage into bondage, these blacks crossed the seas for freedom.

In addition, four free men came from the Caribbean: Thos Godfrey and Henry Walker from Bermuda, John Wearing from Antigua, and Charles Wright from Barbados. They had left a political regime of bondage, and in the American Revolution they had thrown in their lot with the Crown. They had joined freed blacks in immigrations to Nova Scotia and now to Sierra Leone, pursuing a continuously reenvisioned future in a free regime.

As in the New York *Book of Negroes*, these pilgrims came overwhelmingly from Virginia and South Carolina. Those who reported that they came from "Africa" had probably sojourned during their slavery mainly in those two states. Fifty-three out of 155 (34 percent)[84] named Virginia as their "place of origin"; this number nearly equals the 36 percent who emigrated from Virginia in the voyage to Nova Scotia. If we add a substantial proportion of those who stated their origin as Africa, however, then the percentage from Virginia soars to as much as one-half the immigration to Sierra Leone. Four Virginian ministers—David George, Richard Ball, the blind Moses Wilkinson, and another blind preacher, Cato Perkins—as well as family connections may have helped to recruit black Virginians. The presence of four ministers among Virginians, and Boston King among South Carolinians, underlines the force of an egalitarian, republican Christianity among the voyagers.

Thirty-six out of 155 (23 percent) came from Charlestown,[85] slightly higher than the 20 percent in the *Book of Negroes*. If we add in those designating "Africa" who had probably sojourned in South Carolina, however, this figure grows to between 30 and 35 percent. Compared with those in the *Book of Negroes*, only a handful came from other sites: four from New Jersey, three from Pennsylvania, and one each from North Carolina, Boston, Massachusetts, and Maryland.

This special concentration from two states again suggests a network of connections in the emigration. Blacks who came from other states were not swept up in it. Once again, that the émigrés were concentrated in terms of origin and social and religious connection suggests that many others remained. Thus, underpinning its acts of daring and hope, the emigration has a distinctive political sociology. That sociology accentuates the evidence that a much larger number of blacks went to Nova Scotia with the British than previously thought. Roughly 88 percent of those outside these networks—for instance, those linked through alternative connections to Stephen Blucke—remained behind.

In contrast to "married" and "ditto" to indicate wives, the list contains nine single women. The four it reports as heads of household are Lucy Banbury, Abby Roger (with five children), Mary Brown (with one child), and Dinah Jones (with two children). Reverting to patriarchy, the compiler lists Luke Dixon from Virginia as "young" and accompanied by a "mother" who brought eight other children. This unnamed woman symbolizes the heroic tradition of single black women emigrating with their children from America for freedom. Three other mothers came with their sons, Jos Bruill, John Townsend, and Chs Wilkinson, and their wives. Effey Black, sister of Jos Waring, emigrated from "Carolina."[86]

Emigrants from Canada to Sierra Leone had diverse skills. Better than half of the heads of households, eighty-five, were farmers. Two reported themselves "baker/farmer" and "carpenter/farmer." The return lists eighteen carpenters; ten sawyers; four sailors (as a nonmilitary occupation); three coopers, caulkers, and blacksmiths; and one shoemaker, baker, barber, weaver, and "taylor." The return records only eleven "labourers." In exchange for passage, it catalogues the items or land each returned to the Crown.

Illustrating John Clarkson's remark that blacks hoped to build a future for their families, 45 percent of the emigrants, nearly double the rate in the *Book of Negroes*, were children. With only three exceptions—Richard Richerson, Peter Francis, and Richard Herbert, who was eighty—all émigrés brought families. Families needed more food to survive. In hardscrabble Nova Scotia, they would have been especially restive.

The return is not precise about ages. Only those of heads of households are listed. As in the *Book of Negroes*, inspectors rounded off numbers. Thus, they reported that thirty-five—23 percent—were forty years old. An additional twenty-four—16 percent—were between forty and fifty, and sixteen—10 percent—were fifty. So nearly half—49 percent—were between forty and fifty.[87] Having aged nearly ten years in Nova Scotia, most adults, 134 out of 155, or 86 percent, were between thirty-two and fifty.[88] Twenty-five between the ages of fifty and sixty emigrated, though the inspectors recorded only four precise ages in this group.

These records include only half the voyagers. One not listed, by way of example, but nevertheless mentioned in the shipboard diary of John Clarkson, was "an old woman of 104 years of age who had requested me to take her, that she might lay her bones in her native country."[89]

Liberty, democracy, and Africa were the goals of this profound revolutionary force. That half the émigrés to Sierra Leone came from Birchtown underlined the imperial betrayal of certificates of freedom. Extending the first escape to Dunmore, the battles of the Revolution, and the second escape to Nova Scotia, the black pilgrimage for liberty continued. Inspired by Granville Sharp's vision, these freedom fighters had definite ideas about how to run their affairs.

The political experiment in Sierra Leone is one of the great attempts by poor people to organize a decent, nonhierarchical regime. However, they undertook it not so much with the assistance of their white abolitionist patrons as in spite of their attitudes and the corrupt practices that they fostered. In the mid-1780s, the Committee for the Relief of the Black Poor, composed of British merchants, lawyers, and politicians, saw indigent blacks as a nuisance, not as examples of humans wronged by the institution of slavery. They attempted to send four hundred to the Bahamas. Its members thus plotted to return London blacks, though free, to the uncertainty of islands that practiced slavery. The Royal Treasury Department overruled the committee. Nonetheless, the politics of the British abolitionists were far less democratic than those of former black soldiers who had fought for the Crown.

Between four hundred and one thousand black Loyalists had come to London.[90] Each Saturday, blacks gathered at Paddington or Mile End to receive the committee's subsistence allowance of sixpence a day. Alone in the empire, the London authorities assigned no plots of land to émigrés. They intended England as but a temporary refuge for blacks, not a destination. In 1787, when the Committee for the Relief of the Black Poor offered to transport London's free blacks to Freetown, Sierra Leone, the blacks refused. Freetown was near the slave-trading center of Bance, and they feared reenslavement.

According to the committee minutes, "[Jonas] Hanway reported that . . . he found them reluctant . . . [to go] to the Grain Coast of Africa unless they had some Instrument insuring their Liberty."[91] Hanway had "harangued" them about the noble intentions of the Treasury, the committee, and himself, "an old man." To deceive them, he averred, he would have to be depraved. He contrasted Africa's fertility to barren Nova Scotia. He had, he thought, convinced them. The following Monday, Hanway appointed eight as "Headmen" or corporals.[92]

Meetings with Granville Sharp, whom blacks trusted for his vision and honesty, invigorated the project,[93] but the committee used cudgels, as well as carrots, to encourage the London blacks to depart. The committee threatened to deny subsistence to those who refused to do so. On a pretext of vagrancy, the City of London jailed twelve blacks—eleven men, including Paul Clarke, a headman, and one woman. According to committee minutes, blacks petitioned, "threaten[ing] not to go if [Clarke] did not accompany them." Other corporals, however, "said they knew nothing of [the petition] and totally disavowed the same." It "was entirely out of their Power to stop the effect of the laws," the committee announced, but sent a letter to "Sherrif Le Mesurier to intercede in behalf of those Persons to get them released."[94]

Ottobah Cugoano, the minutes reveal, was "the Ninth Man, said to be a person of weight among the Blacks." In an anticolonial insight, Cugoano named an aspect of the project that had already caused problems and that would cause more: imperial arrogance in settling freed blacks in Sierra Leone without consulting the local inhabitants. A rare black voice surviving from this period, Cugoano's words capture the betrayals by white abolitionists and the fear generated in blacks by projects that ultimately, and despite great harms, helped them. In 1787, in *Thoughts and Sentiments on the Evil of Slavery*, Cugoano wrote, "Had a treaty of agreement been first made with the inhabitants of Africa . . . then might the Africans, and others here, have embarked with a good prospect of enjoying happiness and prosperity themselves, and have gone with a hope of being able to render their service, in return, of some advantage to their friends and benefactors of Great-Britain. But this was not done."[95]

The British held London emigrants aboard in the port in winter, the ships unheated. Some died of the cold. As Cugoano emphasized, the four hundred blacks had every reason to fear. because "they were to be hurried away at all events, come of them what would; and yet, after all, to be delayed in the ships . . . until many of them have perished with cold, and other disorders, and several of the most intelligent among them are dead, and others that, in all probability, would have been most useful for them, hindered from going, by means of some disagreeable jealousy of those who were appointed as governors, the great prospect of doing good seems all to be blown away."[96]

If the Sierra Leone Company had not restricted ships to the freezing harbor, Cugoano suggested, many London blacks would gladly have joined this abolitionist expedition. He put their fear colorfully: "A burnt child dreads the fire, some of these unfortunate sons and daughters of Africa have been severally unlawfully dragged away from their native abodes, under various pretences, by the invidious treachery of others, and have been brought into the hands of barbarous robbers and pirates, and, like sheep to market have been sold into slavery." Invoking a biblical parable, he doubted that authorities from Britain, the great slave trader and owner of a colony from which blacks continued to be kidnapped—"the bitter water"—could sponsor a "Free Town": "Many of them [took] heed to that sacred enquiry, Doth a fountain send forth at the same place sweet water and bitter? They were afraid that their doom would be to drink of the bitter water. For can it be readily conceived that government would establish a free colony for them nearly on the spot, while it supports its forts and garrisons, to ensnare, merchandize, and to carry others into captivity and slavery?"[97]

However, like the prospects for blacks living in Nova Scotia, the prospects for blacks remaining in London were bleak, and the incentives to emigrate were accordingly great. Racial discrimination was the norm. The verdicts delivered by the London Loyalist Claims Commission in the cases of free American ex-slaves who petitioned for recompense for their meager lost properties underline the commissioners' racism. There were few witnesses in these cases. The commission often denied black claims, even for back pay for military service. Yet without scrutiny, the commission granted much larger claims of white Loyalists.

Whenever a black brought a case, the commission listed him as "a Negro." John Baptist—the name probably indicates his religion—described himself in a petition as "freeborn" in Gloucester County, New Jersey. When the rebellion broke out, he lived with his sister. His father was white and "kept company with" and was "master" of his mother. More moral than Thomas Jefferson, who did not provide for his children by Sally Hemings, his father left Baptist property valued at ten pounds per year, a house, and three acres of land. Baptist estimated the value of the furniture, three horses, a cow, and twelve chickens at two hundred pounds. When General Howe captured Philadelphia in 1777, Baptist joined the imperial army.[98]

In exile in London, this six-year veteran had little evidence for his American property. The commissioners disparaged him: "In our opinion this case & the Cases of many of these Black Men is an absolute Imposition as he & many others pretend to have had exactly the same Quantity of Land which is both written & valued & certified by John Williams and Thos. Watkins, who have an Interest in representing a Falsity to us as many of these Blacks lodge with them." On the contrary, that these men took in former soldiers seems commendable. Blacks often had small properties. Again, with little evidence, white Tories received a sympathetic hearing. The commission ruled John Baptist "not entitled to receive the Bounty of Government."[99]

In 1775 John Brantford, freeborn, lived in the backcountry of South Carolina. He had a house and some cattle, worth by his estimate 150 pounds. In 1779 the imperial army took Savannah. As his petition noted, Brantford "came afterwards to Charlestown" and joined the redcoats. Ignoring some of his witnesses, the commissioners concluded, "In Consideration of Colo. Fanning's interfering so far in his favor as to write his Memorial, we must suppose that he knew him & we think that Circumstance alone sufficient to report the Sum of £5 to him."[100] The Crown thus awarded Brantford a thirtieth of the amount he claimed.

Born free in Charlestown, Samuel Burke joined the British army under royal governor William Browne of the Bahamas. Patriot commodore Isek Hopkins took Burke prisoner and transferred him to Hartford, Connecticut. Exchanged for Patriots, he went to New York, married a free Dutch mulatto woman, and acquired a little house and garden. After a year, a Sergeant Orchard confiscated his property to quarter soldiers. Mrs. Burke received a certificate from Governor Browne indicating the value of the house.[101] Burke then enlisted in the army, doing diverse support activities. When Burke petitioned in London, the commission noted that Colonel Fanning spoke "strongly of this man's Zeal & Loyalty." Burke also had a "very strong Certificate" from Governor Browne. The Commission awarded him twenty pounds.[102]

Thomas Johnson,[103] a free black, had worked as chief servant on John Izard's estate in Cedar Grove, near Charlestown. Petitioning the commission, Johnson said Izard gave him "Ten Acres of Land upon which he had Corn, Four horses, pigs and Fowls, and a Chest of good Cloathes + Linen, of the value of at Least Sixty Pnds Sterling." Given Izard's generosity and the common rape of black women in plantation households, one might wonder whether Izard was Johnson's father. In October 1780, the Royal Army pressed Thomas into His Majesty's service. He served as a guide with the British Legion commanded by Banastre Tarleton. According to his petition, Johnson "Conducted the Detachment which surprised Colonel Washington at Monk's Corner."[104]

After Yorktown, Johnson reported, the American general Robert Howe inquired about him "on account of his activity, and would have been Hanged, if he had not been privately sent on board the *Bonetta* sloop to New York, by Lord Cornwallis' direction where he joined the Legion again." With the legion's disbanding, Johnson "went on board the *Rhinoceros* commanded by Capt. Duncan, with which he came to England at the Peace." Izard died in 1781, leaving Johnson "an Annuity of Fifty Pounds Sterling which he has never received." He could not "hazard his Life as to go to Charles Town and the Executor of Mr. Izard's Will refuses to pay it on any other Terms." Johnson, his wife, and child "subsisted Poorly upon what little he had saved in the service. In London he has no Employment."

From the commission, Johnson "implore[d]" twenty pounds."[105] No disposition of the case is recorded.

THE REALITY: SIERRA LEONE AND THE
STRUGGLE FOR "NATURAL EQUITY"

Driven to seek freedom by emigrating once again after the American Revolution, free British ex-slaves thus arrived in Africa. Burning with fever, Thomas Peters led his people ashore in Sierra Leone, singing, "The day of jubilee is come; return ye ransomed sinners home."[106] In what blacks saw as a promised land, they repeatedly sang this hymn. Despite massive, ongoing casualties, this vision sustained them. And in the conditions they encountered in Sierra Leone, they needed a source of sustaining strength

On arrival in 1792, Peters, asserting his leadership, wrote to Prime Minister Dundas:

> We . . . desire to return our Sincere Thanks to your Lordship, and to our gracious Sovereign, for the Faviours [sic] we have received in our removal from Nova Scotia to Sierra Leone.
>
> We are intirely Satisfied, with the Place and Climate. . . . The treatment we received on our Passage was very good; but our Provisions was ordinary; we was allowed Salt Fish four Days in a Week and one half of that was Spoilt, the Turnips also was no use to us, for the greater part of them was Spoilt. . . .
>
> We also inform your Lordship, that the Natives are very agreeable with us, and we have a Gratefull Sense of His Majesty's goodness in removing us.[107]

John Clarkson was less pleased. Only God, Clarkson avowed, could save the settlers from "putrid fevers" stemming from lack of shelter, overcrowding, rains, and malnutrition. "Few of the Settlers have yet got huts erected." Anna Falconbridge, one of the cohort of whites whom the Sierra Leone Company sent to set up the colony, reported in her *Narrative*: "They are mostly encamped under tents made with sails from the different ships, and are very badly off for fresh provisions; indeed such is the case with us all, and what's worse, we have but half allowance of very indifferent salt provision, and . . . worm eaten bread." In the two-month journey from Nova Scotia, sixty blacks had died, followed within a few weeks after arrival by forty others. By the end of the rainy season in 1792, another one hundred perished. In all, nearly 20 percent of the Loyalists died during the passage to or settling in Africa.[108] They sang of a new day, but even for resilient former slaves, the realities of Freetown were hard to bear.

The Sierra Leone Company may have been founded by abolitionists, but it intended Freetown to be ruled by white autocrats. Like later imperial racists, the company's directors embraced a mission to "civilize" Africa. The company's "Orders and Regulations" stated, "Both with a view to [the settlers'] own happiness and [the] Company['s] great object of extending civilization in Africa . . . they should neither be left without instructions from [England], nor without a government consisting of Europeans."[109] Only Granville Sharp argued for a black democracy. Instead, the company appointed a council of white immigrants.

Settlers expected to be given farmland immediately. Instead, they had to clear forests. Supplies were short. On March 27, 1792, Councilor James Watt wrote Clarkson, "Dissatisfaction became very troublesome." On April 7, the company slashed rations by half. "With hunger," warned Watt, "comes mutiny."[110]

And then there was the issue of quitrents. The directors of the Sierra Leone Company had received some money from the Crown to support the blacks, but they had to raise the rest, and they sought to do so in part by means of a proposed tax on settler's land, an imposition historically related to the fees charged by feudal lords in lieu of the services their vassals were supposed to provide.[111] It was not exactly reenslavement, but it was an institution deeply rooted in the European traditions of lordship and bondage.

Although the prospectus for the company noted that settlers were expected to pay a small annual quitrent for all land granted, no mention of quitrents had been made during the efforts to recruit blacks to immigrate to the settlement. Instead, their flyer used the slippery phrase "upon such terms . . . as shall hereafter be settled by the Company" to open the way for exploitation.[112] When instituted, the company's quitrent would exceed by many times quitrents imposed on imperial land grants elsewhere in Asia and America.

Of course, first the settlers would actually have to be allotted land to work and be taxed, and such was the mismanagement of the settlement by the company that even the surveying and allocation of what little arable land there was proceeded fitfully, if at all. But once the settlers arrived and were told that a quitrent was to be imposed, the issue—and the deceitfulness of the directors of the Sierra Leone Company—rankled. It was, after all, taxation without representation. To win their freedom, they had fought against those who had objected to such impositions. Now they experienced the imperial yoke themselves.

The "obnoxious arrogance of their rulers" drove blacks to resist.[113] In Halifax, Clarkson had appointed three black superintendents, including Thomas Peters. From encounters in London, Peters knew of Sharp's democratic ideas. At Methodist gatherings in Nova Scotia and in London, he had invoked the promises of democracy. Yet historians often present the conflict between Peters and Clarkson as black versus white and the subsequent revolt of blacks in Sierra Leone as a precursor of black nationalism.[114] In this misguided perspective, David George, the black Baptist minister who opposed Peters, somehow becomes "white." Peters stood for the democracy promised by Sharp.[115] Because Clarkson was a tyrant, Peters opposed him.

As described earlier in this chapter, the black immigrants, following Sharp's vision, elected different levels of political representatives, "tithingmen," who represented each dozen settlers, and "hundreders." Other Sierra Leoneans and the English would ridicule these blacks, who had been stolen from Africa, lived in American bondage, and briefly sojourned in Canada, as "Nova Scotians."[116] But the Nova Scotians heroically implemented a radical democracy.

Many tithingmen and hundreders also preached. The Nova Scotians brought a sense of individual Protestant relationship to God that sustained democratic arrangements.[117] "While the white inhabitants are roaring with strong drink at one end [of Free Town]," Governor T. Perronet Thompson of Sierra Leone would report in 1808, "the Nova Scotians are roaring out hymns at the other."[118] They voiced a jubilee of democratic politics.

As with most colonialism and neocolonialism, "white," referring in the Sierra Leone case to abolitionists, meant dictatorial, exploitative, and racist. Among the directors of the Sierra Leone Company, Sharp and perhaps Thomas Clarkson sought democracy. The others[119] aimed to make money and to whiten or, in their phrase, to "civilize" Africa.[120] It was only as a secondary goal that they sought to end the slave trade.

In addition to the black male settlers, nearly one hundred white artisans, soldiers, colonists, and wives of blacks lived in the colony.[121] Looking down on these whites as well as blacks, the white councilors were arrogant.[122] As Falconbridge comments in her *Narrative*, "Perhaps the Directors imagine they were particularly circumspect in their choice of representatives, if so, they are grossly deceived, for never were characters worse adapted to manage any purpose of magnitude than some whom they have nominated." The blacks, she warned, "have not their promised lands; and so little do they relish the obnoxious arrogance of their rulers, that I really believe, was it not for the influence of Mr. Clarkson, they would be apt to drive some of them into the sea."[123]

In his memoirs, Sharp indicated that he feared a dictatorship by the white councilors over blacks. He noted, "I am very sure that such restraints cannot accord with ideas of perfect liberty and justice."[124] Blacks, however, had already organized from below on Sharp's democratic model. Enslaved in the United States and then abused in Nova Scotia and England, black Loyalists encountered mistreatment, starvation, broken promises, tyranny, economic exploitation, and the guns of white "patrons" in Sierra Leone. In the view of the company's antiradical ideology, they were troublemakers.[125]

Most black immigrants could not write, yet both their actions and petitions speak eloquently. In contrast, the company was an enemy, in practice, of the liberty its representatives espoused in speech. That whites left a written record does not mean that their perspective is true, coherent, or honorable. Given the moral inversion of much of the literature, the term "black" needs to be transvalued, as Nietzsche might put it, as "democratic." As we will see, what was going on in Sierra Leone, in the resistance mounted by Thomas Peters and other black settlers, was the local manifestation of an international movement for the realization of democracy, equality, and self-determination.

In early 1792, 132 Sierra Leone settlers signed a petition for Peters to present the grievances of the black settlers to John Clarkson. An April 7 meeting elected Peters "Speaker-General." On April 8, two men originally from Preston, Nova Scotia, warned Clarkson of a coming uprising to make Peters governor. Recovering from fever, Clarkson had stayed aboard ship. For that evening, he called an emergency meeting. He had now forgotten on whose behalf he had gone to Canada; he threatened Peters as a "traitor." If Peters could not clear himself of "sedition," he said, Clarkson would hang him.[126]

Even later, in retirement in London, he stuck to this bizarre threat: "It was always better at the beginning of a new government to hang three or four who might be the cause of future misery to the place."[127] Many blacks knew that Clarkson was actually on their side about the issue of quitrents, but they were probably aghast at his behavior.[128] To revolt against Clarkson would remove a partial friend and divide the settlers. Despite this support, Clarkson denounced black democracy and, with murder in mind, defended what would later be called the "white man's burden."

Two inconsistent accounts survive of the emergency meeting. According to the first, it occurred on April 8. Clarkson pledged that he would quickly make land available. He challenged the people to choose between himself and Peters. In this account, Peters did not speak, and no one moved to Peters's side.[129] According to the second version, the meeting occurred seven weeks later, on May 30. There, Peters asked, "Who is for me, who is for Mr. Clarkson? Let those who are for me come here, the others there." In this account, the settlers did not come to his side either.[130] For the moment, the democratic revolt subsided, and although tensions remained and sometimes flared, Clarkson managed to contain it for the remainder of his tenure as governor.

In Clarkson's account, blacks said they wanted Peters only to aid the governor. Thus, they allowed Clarkson to back off. In a moment of honesty, Clarkson acknowledged that he was "very glad to close the business with this explanation, for had matters appeared stronger against Peters, I should not have known what to have done with him."[131] By murdering Peters, Clarkson would have risked driving the settlers to rebel. Later, when Clarkson studied the list of 132 names, he found the name of David George—who opposed Peters—on it. So the settlers' claim that they had only wanted Peters to support Clarkson appears to be true.

In Clarkson's account, Peters's followers threatened the two informers. Once again, Clarkson and some subsequent historians have superimposed a putative black-versus-white split on the rivalry between Methodists led by Peters and the Baptists led by George. They too easily perfume the abolitionists' autocracy. Rather, convictions about individual responsibility and each individual's relationship to God, as well as escaping slavery, fighting heroically, and claiming the rights of Englishmen in Canada, had empowered these blacks to participate in a novel, democratic politics.

At all-night prayer meetings, Peters criticized the white councilors. Clarkson attended. Privately, he raged against Peters as a man "of great penetration and cunning," a "rascal who had been working in the dark from the time he landed to get himself at the Head of the People, and if I had not acted by them as I did by taking care of their sick and indeed the whole of my Conduct . . . this Wretch would have driven all the Whites out of the Place and ruin'd himself and all his brothers."[132] In fact, Clarkson was himself the abusive and paternal "Head." Note his assumption that the well-being of black Loyalists depended on a few whites, or even Clarkson alone.

On May 1, Laury White, a black, accused Peters of stealing from John Salter, a dead man. But White himself was an interested party; he claimed Salter's estate. Perhaps influenced by Clarkson and his allies, the jurors did not accept Peters's defense that the money was owed to him. Peters testified that some ten years earlier, he had helped Salter, a fellow Black Pioneer, to purchase the freedom of his wife.[133]

Historians often credit Clarkson's story about the theft, for which we have only Clarkson's testimony.[134] Here again the words of an insecure tyrant silence a democrat who was perhaps illiterate and did not record his version. Tensions already existed among the black immigrants about how to deal with an elitist authority. Worse, Clarkson regarded Peters as a mortal enemy. Very likely, he and the council would have stirred up differences among blacks and used the outcome against Peters. In white records, Peters's silence speaks eloquently.

Thus, while the democratic revolt subsided for the time being, fundamental tensions remained between the settlers and the Sierra Leone Company. In a May 10, 1792, letter to Clarkson, Duke Gordons, a black immigrant, requested a "spot of land." He dreaded the deadly "Rainey Season" to come.[135] The company's surveyor would not work, however. Like Nova Scotian officials, Clarkson could make almost no land available. Even those who obtained a plot had no equipment to cultivate it.

On May 16, the "black captains"—the leaders from Nova Scotia—confronted Clarkson. They demanded land and cancellation of debts at the company store. As Clarkson grudgingly acknowledged, they "were not quite without reason." Subsequently, in less heated circumstances, he would affirm their claims. They also demanded democratic representation. That these leaders supported Peters shocked Clarkson. They addressed him, he said, with "inappropriate expressions." Patronizingly, Clarkson dismissed their "strange notions . . . as to their civil rights."[136] But these democrats had fought for the British and thought—rightly— that they had rights.[137]

On June 15, Peters and others petitioned Clarkson to allow the election of twelve blacks as peace officers. This petition accorded with some of the Sierra Leone Company's principles. Following Enlightenment ideas, the company's charter barred capital punishment. That Clarkson thought of hanging Peters, however, reveals how little the company's principles affected what governors might do in practice. In deciding each lesser sentence, the petitioners asked for twelve blacks to serve as a jury. Clarkson responded that all officials would have to meet his approval. His opposition even to nominal representation shocked blacks.

As the tensions grew, Clarkson became even more autocratic. On the council, each member had an equal vote. Clarkson complained to the Sierra Leone Company that his orders "were either slovenly and partially executed, or countermanded by other officers." He requested special powers. On May 22, the directors gave Clarkson authority to override the white council "to act according to his sole direction in all [pressing matters] and emergencies."[138]

On June 25, Henry Beverhout, a black captain, urged inclusion of blacks in the government, restoration of credit at the company store, a speedy allocation of land, and abolition of the governor's veto power in the council. He reminded Clarkson of his promises in Canada. He also remarked how extreme Clarkson's demands were:

> 1st. Sir, the people of our Company consent to the Wages that your Honour proposes, that is to work at 2s [shillings] per day as long as we draw our provisions. 2ndly. We are all willing to be governed by the Laws of England in full, but we do not consent to give it to your honor without having any of our Color in it. . . .
>
> 3rdly. there is none of us would wish for you to leave us here & go away, but your honor will be pleased to remember, what your honor told ye people in America at Shelburn that is whoever came to Sierra Leone they should be free, & have laws & when there was any Trial, there should be Jury of both White & Black, and all should be equal so we take it that we have a right to chuse men that we think proper to act for us in a reasonable manner.
>
> . . . 7thly. We would wish for peace if possible . . . but to give all out of our hands we cannot.[139]

On the night of June 25, Thomas Peters died. Indicating his influence, for several months settlers reported visitations of Peters's ghost. The movement for democracy temporarily receded.

As much as Captain Tye in New Jersey, Thomas Peters fought for freedom for himself and others. Through his journeys to Canada, London, and Sierra Leone, he became a hero of democracy. In comparison with Peters, both Clarksons, who were important elitist leaders of the English emancipation movement, seem small. Among modern historians, only Gary Nash has done Peters justice:

> Peters lived for fifty-four years. During thirty-two of them he struggled incessantly for personal survival and for some larger degree of freedom beyond physical existence. He crossed the Atlantic four times. He

lived in French Louisiana, North Carolina, New York, Nova Scotia, New Brunswick, Bermuda, London, and Sierra Leone. He worked as a field hand, millwright, ship hand, casual laborer, and soldier. He struggled against slavemasters, government officials, hostile white neighbors, and, at the end of his life, even some of the abolitionists backing the Sierra Leone colony. He waged a three-decade struggle for the most basic political rights, for social equity and for human dignity. His crusade was individual at first, as the circumstances in which he found himself as a slave in Louisiana and North Carolina dictated. But when the American Revolution broke out, Peters merged his individual efforts with those of thousands of other American slaves who fled their masters to join the British. They made the American Revolution the first large-scale rebellion of slaves in North America. Out of the thousands of individual acts of defiance grew a legend of black strength, black struggle, black vision for the future. Once free of legal slavery, Peters and hundreds like him waged a collective struggle against a different kind of slavery, one that while not written in law still circumscribed the lives of blacks in Canada. Their task was nothing less than the salvation of an oppressed people. Though he never learned to write his name, Thomas Peters articulated his struggle against exploitation through actions that are as clear as the most unambiguous documents left by educated persons.[140]

Thomas Peters was Sierra Leone's most decisive and most democratic leader.

DEMOCRATIC REVOLT

Following Peters's death, like the swell of the sea, most black immigrants in Sierra Leone moved to democratic dissent. The French Revolution in 1789 and the revolution in Saint Domingue in 1791 had terrified the colony's governor and company officials. Racism, greed, and fear motivated their provocations. In 1793 the company replaced the autocratic, but abolitionist Clarkson with John Dawes. A total of thirty-one hundreders, tithingmen, and ministers petitioned London with "the most earnest solicitation for Mr. Clarkson to be sent out again." An anonymous letter alluded to the guillotining of Louis XVI as Dawes's likely destiny.[141]

The aura of the slave trade in Bance hovered over the free blacks in Freetown. Falconbridge spoke of nearby "predatory wars." She guessed that "upwards of two thousand slaves have been shipped . . . to the West Indies from this river, within these last twelve months." King Tom, leader of the local African people, the Temne, who had originally ceded the Sierra Leone Company the territory it occupied, had raided the colony and had sold captives into bondage. Despite the custom "to compromise disputes amicably," his successor, King Jemmy, had also driven off settlers, and he burned the new town in 1789. The threat of reenslavement thus hung over the free blacks of Sierra Leone, and such uncertainties created an environment in which the company's racist or careless policies caused terror. Blacks received no promised "spots" of land. Falconbridge witnessed "the universal discontent which has prevailed among the Settlers."[142]

In 1793 thirty-one "Nova Scotians" funded Isaac Anderson and Cato Perkins—the blind minister—to travel to London.[143] A free carpenter from Charlestown, Anderson could read and write. He had fought with the Crown and had immigrated to Birchtown. Following Methodist minister Luke Jordan, Anderson had then immigrated to Sierra Leone and become a farmer. Governor Dawes attempted to evict him as a "squatter."[144] Anderson resisted.

In their 1793 letter to the directors of the Sierra Leone Company, Anderson and Perkins still imagined that the company supported the democratic project that Granville Sharp had envisioned and that Thomas Peters had tried to make a reality. The company had appointed a halfway decent governor, Clarkson, but the conduct of later governors and other officials had shocked the settlers. "They[145] are grieved beyond expression to be forced to complain of hardships and oppressions loaded on them by the managers of the Company, which they are persuaded the Directors are ignorant of." No promise made by the company's agents in Nova Scotia had proved true, and they complained that "it has been insinuated to the [settlers] that Mr. Clarkson had not authority for making any." Anderson and Perkins again declared their equality with whites: "Notwithstanding they labor under the misfortune of wanting education, their feelings are equally *acute* with those of *white men*, and they have as great an anxiety to lay a foundation for their children's freedom and happiness, as any human being can possess."[146]

Anderson and Perkins's letter noted that "Clarkson informed them . . . the Company had been mistaken in the quantity of land they supposed themselves possessed of, and in consequence only one fifth part of what was originally promised them could be at present performed." Furthermore, the lands were "mountainous, barren and rocky," and "it will be impossible ever to obtain a living from them." And on Clarkson's departure, James Cocks, the surveyor, who would not do much work before this time, stopped working altogether. As Falconbridge sardonically remarked, "The surveyor being a *Councillor* and *Captain* of our *veteran host*, is of too much consequence to attend to the servile duty of surveying, notwithstanding he is paid for it."[147]

Blacks could get supplies only from the company store, which jacked up prices and diluted the rum. According to Anderson and Perkins, "Mr. Clarkson had promised in Nova Scotia . . . they should be supplied with every necessary of life from the Company's stores, at a moderate advance of ten per cent on the prime cost," and "while Mr. Clarkson remained in the Colony they paid no more; but since then they have been charged upwards of 100 per cent. That they would not grumble even at that, if the worst of goods were not sold, and paltry advantages taken of them, particularly in the article of rum."[148]

Zachary Macaulay, the next governor, said, in what was a bizarre claim, that Alexander Falconbridge, the white engineer, had shown black immigrants charges for rum that did not include freight and insurance.[149] But Dawes had just jacked up the price. Anna Falconbridge suggested that Governor Dawes had acted from Protestant motives: "a fear the consumers would neglect to dilute the spirit sufficiently." But she recognized the impact: "Had such a trick been played at a Slave Factory [at Bance], how would it be construed?"[150]

Dawes, Anderson and Perkins wrote, "seems to wish to rule us just as bad as if we were all Slaves which we cannot bear." They explained: "You will pardon us gentlemen, for speaking so plain, however, we do not think your conduct has proceeded from any inclination to wrong us, but from the influence and misrepresentations of evil minded men, whose baseness will some day or other be discovered to you." Yet Henry Thornton, the head of the company, dismissed their letter of complaints as "frivolous and ill grounded."[151]

Anderson and Perkins sought Clarkson out: "The Directors never would give us Mr. Clarkson's address. . . . However, in the midst of our distress, accidentally hearing he lived at Wisbeach, we wrote him without hesitation, enclosed a copy of our Petition, requested he would interpose his influence with the Director, and in vindication of his character, endeavour to get justice done for us."[152]

In an open letter to the company and to Anderson and Perkins, Clarkson stressed that he had promised land free of quitrents: "The promises I made them were from the Directors of the Sierra Leone Company, and . . . they have as great a right to the performances of them as they have to dispose of their own property."[153] Stalling, Thornton insisted that Anderson and Perkins put what they had been promised in writing. In that document, dated November 1793, Anderson and Perkins focused on voiding the prospect of quitrents: "That those land grants should be given directly on our arrival in Africa, free of any expence or charge whatever." In addition, they insisted on fairness: "We should be provided with all tools wanted for cultivations, and likewise, the comforts and necessaries of life, from the Company's stores, at a reasonable rate, such as about ten percent, advance upon the prime cost." They avowed themselves free Britons: "We should be protected by the laws of Great Britain, and justice should be indiscriminately shewn Whites and Blacks."[154]

Anderson and Perkins came to London as moderates, and they left as radicals: "We did not come upon a childish errand, but to represent the grievances and sufferings of a thousand souls. We expected to have had some attention paid to our complaints, but the manner you have treated us, has been just the same as if we were *Slaves*, come to tell our masters, of the cruelties and severe behaviour of an *Overseer*."[155]

Relations between the company's autocratic governor and council and the settlers and their democratically elected representatives deteriorated, eventually leading to a democratic rebellion. In a 1794 incident, a crowd of Sierra Leone settlers working at Bance "insulted Captain Grierson of the slave ship *Thomas*," according to the captain's complaint. On June 13, Robert Keeling, the chief porter of the wharf, urged blacks to attack. Scipio Channel, the complaint alleged, "attempted to knock out said Capt. Grierson's brains with a hammer." Governor Macaulay sided with the slave-trading captain, and the council fired Keeling and Channel, but neither Grierson nor the governor offered any reason for the black hostility.[156]

On June 14, representing the hundreders and tithingmen, Joseph Leonard, a teacher, and Myles Dixon, a farmer, issued a "Warm remonstrance" to the council for their reaction to the Captain Grierson affair. If they were not treated honorably, they said, they and other blacks would resign their official posts. Macaulay tyrannically asserted that no settler "has a right to censure the Governor and Council." On June 20, Channel, Samuel Goodwin, Simon Johnson, Lewis Kirby, Matthew Sinclair, and Joseph Tybee, all free black farmers, "demanded an explanation," Macaulay reported, and insulted him "and even threatened my life." Hundreders and tithingmen prevented George Corankapone, the black marshal, from serving a warrant for their arrest. According to Anderson and Perkins, Governor Macaulay had overreacted. They concluded, "We are sorry to think that we left America to come here and be used in that manner."[157]

Macaulay had three leaders of the demonstration arrested. He summoned company employees to his home and told David George to mobilize his followers. Demanding the release of the prisoners, the democrats attacked George's supporters, wrecked the company's office, and destroyed Macaulay's journal.[158]

On July 1, 1797, the threatened quitrent was finally due. Baptists, led by George, paid. A far larger group, the Methodists, did not pay. Addressing the council on August 17, Isaac Streeter, a tithingman, and George Carroll, a farmer, named the company's abuse: "We are to inform you that we have left Lands to come here in expectation to receive Lands in the same condition as we received them in Nova Scotia, but . . . the Company says the Land is theirs. Sir, if we had been told that, we never would come here. . . . If the Lands is not ours without paying a Shilling pr Acre, the Lands will never be ours, no not at all."[159]

On August 21, Macaulay reported to the directors, "The People had flocked in from the Country. Meetings & Cabals were holdg in every Street. Every individual had in his countenance the marks of an anxious mind."[160] On August 22, Macaulay held a meeting to answer the democrats. The governor maintained that the company had told potential émigrés from Canada of the quitrents. After he left, Isaac Anderson read passages from Anna Falconbridge's *Narrative* to emphasize that Clarkson had never spoken of quitrents. Of Macaulay's supporters, Thomas Cooper, a black born in England, alone rose to speak. The crowd shouted him down.

Macaulay feared the overthrow of his government. He posted guards around the powder magazine and ordered whites and fifty "reliable Nova Scotians" to defend his Thornton Hill residence. He threatened to hang anyone who burned a government supporter's house. Macaulay noted in his private journal that he would lynch two or three of the "ringleaders."[161] His forces and the democrats split the population. In the end, the governor could not collect the quitrent.

In 1798 settlers presented a resolution to Macaulay for a self-governing legislature according to which the tithingmen and hundreders would divide themselves into two houses to make decisions. A joint committee would meet with the governor and council. Ironically, the American Revolution's ideas—particularly no taxation without representation—now inspired the Nova Scotians. They proposed a road tax of six days' work per year, equivalent to and in place of the quitrent. They invoked "precedents . . . from the Colonial Carolinas, Virginia, New York, and Nova Scotia."[162] Once free, blacks learned from North American and English ideas of liberty and modified both in a democratic direction.

Finally, in late summer 1799, 150 settlers declared independence from the Sierra Leone Company. The hundreders and half the tithingmen joined the revolt, electing militant spokespeople, notably Isaac Anderson. On September 3, at preacher Cato Perkins's meetinghouse, these democrats created a code of laws "just before God and Man," stripping power from the company's council and firing the governor. Signed by Anderson, James Robinson, and Anzel Zizer, three hundreders, and Nathaniel Wansey, chairperson of the tithingmen, their statement concluded: "All that came from Nova Scotia shall be under this law or quit this place." On September 7, the tithingmen declared that the settlers were the sole "Propriatives of the Colenney." Only hundreders and tithingmen could grant "forenners" the right to make laws or vote.[163] In 1800, in the first democratic uprising in Africa, most settlers rebelled.[164]

REPRESSION

The African tribes had not opposed the second settlement of Sierra Leone, in Freetown.[165] Still, the company could pit Temne chiefs such as King Jemmy and David George's followers against the rebelling democrats.[166] In July 1799, the British Parliament granted a "charter" to the company that abolished tithingmen and hundreders. Parliament also mobilized Jamaican maroons.[167] In August 1800, 550 blacks sailed for Sierra Leone as soldiers. Following the Roman logic of *divide et impera*,[168] the Crown used moderation toward one group of escaped blacks to suppress the stirrings of democracy in another. Initially, the forces of revolution and reaction in Freetown were evenly matched. In October, however, maroons swung the war against the democrats.[169]

In an outburst of antiradical ideology, William Wilberforce derided the claims of the democrats. Blacks were "thorough Jacobins as if they had been trained & educated in Paris. Nothg. but the greatest firmness of wisdom & temper in our governors could for 9 years have prevented their ruining the colony & rendering themselves miserable."[170]

Ironically, the Earl of Abingdon, an advocate of slavery in the House of Lords, rebuked Wilberforce for an abolitionism that mirrored French radicalism: "For in the very definition of the terms themselves . . . what does the abolition of the slave trade mean more or less in effect, than liberty and equality? What more or less than the rights of man? And what is liberty and equality, and what the rights of man, but the foolish fundamental principles of this new philosophy?"[171]

With its Jamaican troops, the company suppressed the revolt in 1800 and took thirty prisoners, executing Isaac Anderson and one other. The victors banished seven to Gorée Island, in Senegal, and twenty-five to Bulom Shore. Among the latter were British Freedom and Henry Washington, a former slave at Mount Vernon. Some rebels escaped and joined with the Temne in 1801 and 1802 to attack Freetown. The company also crushed this insurrection.[172]

The Nova Scotians continued the fight for freedom. Eli Ackim was a black officer. Responding to the Militia Act of 1811, which proscribed blacks from becoming officers, Ackim declared: "We was British subjects eighteen or twenty years before we came here, and after our arrival here we all took the Oath of Allegiance to our King and Country, we therefore refused to comply." In 1817 Ackim spoke again for equality: "We are in our own Country and as British Subjects we ought to have as much preveliges and profits as any white people."[173] In 1820 black petitioners led by Jonathan Thorpe condemned a white surgeon's bigotry: "The distinction of colour, the ungenerous doctrine of any man being . . . superior to another, can never exist in this settlement." They warned, "No one shall dare to curtail us of our privileges, as British subjects with impunity."[174] John Kizell was a follower of David George. In 1826 he petitioned for equal treatment to the British commissioners for the west coast of Africa: "It was promised by the Hon. John Clarkson that the Nova Scotians and the whites should be as one, but instead of this they have set a parcel of white and mallater boys over us as magistrates."[175]

Against great odds, blacks had fought for equality in North America and for democracy in Sierra Leone. Woven into the experience of Freetown and the struggles of many others in the coming century and beyond, however, the ideas of freedom and the rights of individuals lived on in an international movement for democracy and equality that swept former colonies in the Americas and elsewhere around the world.

chapter 9 ¶ Democratic Internationalism and the Seeds of Freedom

To those in our Country who do not yet see the necessity of abolishing the Commerce & Slavery of the unhappy Africans the efforts making in France may be held up so as to countenance & support our measures & we trust there is reason to expect that the conduct of several of the States in discouraging the practice of Slavery & abolishing the Slave trade will not be without influence in the Councils of France.
— Benjamin Franklin to the Amis des noirs, December 8, 1788

he American Revolution came to a happy end with the successful attainment of American independence, but the second revolution, the revolution for the emancipation of America's slaves, did not. The obstacles that it had faced during the first revolution and that it continued to face, from racism to entrenched economic interests, did not melt away with the signing of the Peace of Paris, and, as we have seen, the struggle for freedom, equality, and democracy continued without much mitigation on both sides of the conflict after the peace treaty was concluded. Not only did the new U.S. Constitution enshrine slavery in the nation's founding document, ultimately dividing the nation and deferring the realization of freedom and equal rights for all there, but even the blacks freed by the British in the contest for the colonies were still forced to struggle for freedom and self-government in Canada and Africa.

In 1808, when the Crown took over the Sierra Leone colony from the Sierra Leone Company, the new royal governor, Thomas Perronet Thompson, decried the "Nova Scotians" as "every thing that is vile in the American & all that is contemptible in the European. The most absurd enthusiasm is their religion & wild notions of liberty are their politics."[1] In an odious, imperial gesture, Thompson changed the name Freetown to Georgetown, imposing the concept of hereditary sovereignty in place of that of freedom. He denounced "Negro Sans Culottes" as embracing "half comprehended notions of American independence" and being "runaway slaves . . . full of every species of ignorant enthusiasm and republican frenzy."[2]

Ironically, despite his sneering rhetoric, Thompson was right. In the broader scheme of things, the struggle for freedom by blacks who fought for the British and who then sought equality and democratic self-government in Nova Scotia and Sierra Leone was indeed part of an international democratic movement that linked the energies of artisans, sailors, free blacks, and slaves seeking freedom with those of Enlightenment philosophers, Protestant divines, and people of honor in all walks of life in between.

With its principles rooted in Enlightenment philosophy and Protestant religion on the part of the white slaveholding nations and in the basic, universal desire to be free on the part of American slaves, the second revolution continued on an international scale. Following American independence, emancipation spread gradually through the North and was defeated in the South, but in England, France, and throughout the Americas, fighters for the abolition of chattel slavery and the recognition of the equal rights of freed slaves and their descendants persevered. Democratic internationalist movements sprang up, engaging in mutual support for abolition and the defense of emancipated slaves.[3]

Just as slavery itself was an international phenomenon, practiced by the great European empires of the sixteenth, seventeenth, and eighteenth centuries, so was opposition to it, especially in the glow of the Enlightenment's enthusiasm for universal moral principles and the awakenings of conscience that swept the Protestant world in the eighteenth century. The values espoused by these movements and the various schools, parties, and sects to which they gave birth knew no boundaries.

INTERNATIONAL ABOLITION SOCIETIES

Such was the case with the Quakers internationally and, in the United States, in the newly free state of Pennsylvania, where the first American abolition society was founded.[4] In the mid-1770s, the Pennsylvania Society fought for the emancipation only of wrongfully enslaved individuals. After the Revolution, however, a revived society adopted the broader cause of abolition in its ungainly name: the Pennsylvania Society for Promoting the Abolition of Slavery and for the Relief of Free Negroes Unlawfully Held in Bondage and for Improving the Condition of the African Race. It became better known simply as the Pennsylvania Abolition Society. The founding of similar societies in France and in England—the Amis des noirs (Friends of Blacks), headed by the Marquis de Condorcet and Jacques Brissot de Warville, and the Society for Effecting the Abolition of the Slave Trade, led by Granville Sharp, gave the movement a basis in the three transatlantic countries in which the struggle for equality and democracy was most conspicuously waged.

The adoption of the U.S. Constitution, enshrining bondage, spurred the society to greater efforts. In a June 2, 1787, "Memorial," Jonathan Penrose, vice president of the Pennsylvania Abolition Society, especially condemned the hypocrisy of the Constitution's extension of the traffic in slaves until 1808: "It is with deep distress [that the society is] forced to observe that the peace was scarcely concluded before the African Trade was revived, and American vessels employed in transporting the Inhabitants of Africa to cultivate as Slaves the Soil of America before it had drank in all the blood which had been shed in her struggle for Liberty."[5]

Against America's monarchical enemies, Penrose recognized the need for solidarity with the citizens of all countries against the injustices of slavery.[6] Because of the new nation's continued embrace of slavery, the American Revolution, that seeming beacon of freedom, had earned disfavor among democrats abroad—those who might work to block foreign interventions against the United States. "To the revival of this trade," Penrose explained, "the Society ascribes part of the obloquy with which Foreign Nations have branded our Infant States; In vain will be their pretentions to a love of liberty or a regard for National Character, while they share in the profits of a Commerce that can only be conducted upon Rivers of Human tears and blood."[7]

In 1787 the society selected Benjamin Franklin as its president. Outcompeting his Tory abolitionist son, William, who had worked with Captain Tye and who had fled America in 1782, the father became, at the end of his life, a fierce opponent of slavery. At the Constitutional Convention that same year, Franklin acidly distinguished property from southern[8] slave owning: "Sheep will never make any insurrection."[9]

Franklin's experience as ambassador to Paris stimulated mutual aid. For instance, Richard Price, author of *Observations on the Importance of American Liberty* (1785), informed Franklin about the founding of the London society and hoped that Franklin could influence deliberations concerning the American Constitution. On September 26, 1787, Price insisted: "This spirit [of liberty] originated in America. In consequence of the situation created by the American war and the dissemination of writings explaining the nature and end of civil government, the minds of men are becoming more enlightened; and the silly despots of the world are likely to be forced to respect human rights, and to take care not to govern too much, lest they should not govern at all."[10]

To the Amis des noirs on December 8, 1788, Franklin reported a Philadelphia meeting honoring Warville, the Amis's secretary, the previous April. Franklin praised the inspiring interconnection of a democratic internationalist movement: "We observe with sincere pleasure your overtures for establishing a relation of Brotherhood & mutual Correspondence between your Society & ours, which we also desire with equal earnestness, both on account of the respect we felt towards your Institutions & because we are convinced it will have a very favorable effect as well in Europe as America in promoting the interesting objects for which we have associated."[11]

In 1788 the Pennsylvania Society drafted two letters to the "Marquis of Fayette."[12] Praising Lafayette's abolitionist activity, the authors of the first letter reminded him of "the miseries of those unhappy people who are doomed to taste of the bitter cup of perpetual Servitude" and then praised the Enlightenment: "The present age has been distinguished by a remarkable Revolution. . . . Mankind began to consider themselves as Members of one family. The groans of our distressed & injured brethren from the shores of Africa have at length reached the Ears of the Citizens of the United States." Both letters speak of a common movement to abolish the "iniquitous" trade in North America and Britain. "National prejudices & jealousies," they fear, hinder this movement. In a premonition of Jacobin abolition of slavery throughout the French colonies in 1794, however, the second letter suggests that "nothing effectual will be done in this business until France comes in on it."[13] In 1789, in the spirit of the society's internationalism, citizen Thomas Bailly proposed for membership the "Marquis of Fayette."[14]

On February 3, 1789, writing to the Philadelphia Abolition Society on behalf of the Amis des noirs, Condorcet identified the paradox of the American Revolution: the reduction of the seemingly magnificent freedom for some, as the sophist Thrasymachus put it in Book 1 of Plato's *Republic*, to the mere "advantage of the stronger," to "might makes right": "At the same instant where America succeeded in breaking its chains, the generous friends of liberty feel that it will abase its cause if it authorizes by law the servitude of blacks. A free man who has slaves, or who approves that his fellow citizens have them, avows himself guilty of an injustice, or is forced to erect as a principle that liberty is nothing other than an advantage seized by force, & not a right given by nature."[15]

Condorcet condemned slavery as "*contraire a la raison & au droit naturel*," contrary to reason and natural right.[16] Like John Laurens, the French society relied on Rousseau's words in *Du contrat social* and *Discours sur les origines de l'inegalite*. Many ordinary people doubt the efficacy of actions by individuals, not imagining that great words can sometimes conjure movements that do not yet exist. Yet in the writings of the Amis des noirs we can see with startling vividness the impact of Rousseau's words in naming a great evil and triggering a movement from below to challenge it. However much this movement differed from Rousseau's vision of small, non-slave-owning republics, international abolitionists ultimately achieved the great object of emancipation.

Except for its impact on John Laurens, however, Rousseau's philosophy less directly shaped the movement in the United States and England than in France. In 1789, representing the London Abolition Society, Granville Sharp also addressed "a free and enlightened Nation on a subject in which its Justice, Humanity and Wisdom are involved." He named bondage "that detestable commerce."[17] Similarly, in a November 9, 1789, "Address to the Public" in Philadelphia, Benjamin Franklin invoked "the daily progress of that luminous and benign spirit of liberty, which is diffusing itself throughout the world."[18] This antislavery movement characterized the Enlightenment generally—and dialectically drew strength from and reinforced it—even though its most exact, profound, and striking arguments were French.

In 1789, to aid the French society "in their efforts to effect [slavery's] abolition which ha[ve] been more Spirited than could have been expected," one W. Dulvoyer reported, the London society had sent Thomas Clarkson, the evangelical abolitionist leader, to Paris.[19] Forged by its new revolution, the French National Assembly appointed a committee to focus on bondage. In this fundamental respect, the French Revolution's vigor contrasts with the fits and starts of inegalitarian America. In the latter, to suppress the rebelling democrats, the British Empire initially freed blacks. In France, a parallel would have required the aristocrats to strike down bondage while the sans-culottes, Girondins, and Jacobins upheld it.

Spreading antiradical rumors, British slave merchants used the specter of the French Revolution to fight abolition. As Dulvoyer wrote to his colleagues in 1789, "The most absurd Reports were industriously propagated to discredit them; among many others equally ridiculous, it was said that the London committee had found 10,000 stand of arms to encourage the Slaves of St. Domingo to assert their natural rights." To launch the fiercest social rebellion of the eighteenth century, which created Haiti, Saint Domingue's blacks needed no arms from abroad. As the British abolitionists' envoy to France, Clarkson defied the "Blusterers." In Dulvoyer's words, "T.C. was Several times openly threatened with assassination; and he told the persons that if such was their fixed purpose, he would give them the opportunity, as he was satisfied that their affecting it would instantly seal the destruction of the wicked Traffic + practice which they meant to support."[20]

SLAVERY AND RACIAL DISCRIMINATION
AFTER THE AMERICAN REVOLUTION

The new United States, however, lagged behind France and England in the second revolution not just in recognizing the institution of slavery in its founding document but also in sanctioning attitudes and practices that preserved it. After the American Revolution, even free blacks could not walk the streets of the new nation without fear of abduction. In 1788 the Pennsylvania Abolition Society praised that state's representatives for their "gradual, final abolition of Negro Slavery." Only this step, it suggested, could incarnate the principle of democratic government that "all men are born equally Free." But marauders, the society warned, threatened liberty: "The soil of Pennsylvania has been frequently polluted by the footsteps of kidnappers, who . . . have violated the sanctity of domestic repose with brutal violence making captive free people, descendants of Africans, and conveying them to remote places into hopeless bondage." Convictions for this "high offence," the society urged, should bring a fine "of no more than 100 dollars & 12 months imprisonment."[21]

Though incomplete,[22] the Pennsylvania Abolition Society's documents illustrate the twists and turns in the quest for freedom of free blacks in America, with individuals barely warding off slavery, having his or her "free papers" seized, or being returned to slavery. Local branches of the society worked protractedly to defend the liberty of free individuals in danger of being wrongfully reenslaved. For instance, on May 5, 1790, Richard Waln, a lawyer, member of the Pennsylvania Abolition Society, and congressman, wrote with hope to his son about Betty, a New Jersey black woman freed on the death of her master, John Horsfield.[23] As her owner, Horsfield had previously indentured Betty and another slave, Nelly, each then about fifteen years old, for a term of fifteen years. During that time, Betty had five children and one grandchild. But Betty was now free, and, by implication, her children were free as well. Yet the executor of Horsfield's will sold the children. On May 7, Elias Bond, a fellow member of the Philadelphia Abolition Society, wrote to Waln, expressing optimism that they "will all be freed next Supreme Court as the Chief Justice was gone to Trenton" to meet.[24]

The society solicited a writ of habeas corpus that opened the doors of the New Jersey court to Silas, one of Betty's sons. In September 1792, Chief

Justice James Kinsey freed Silas. His owner's lawyers had maintained that Betty had continued a slave and, hence, so had her "Issue." By using the word "issue," appropriate to a horse or a pig, instead of "infant," they distanced themselves from Silas's humanity. Budinott J. Pattison of New Jersey and Fisher Sergeant of Philadelphia, the lawyers for Silas, countered that "no Child of a Servant could be Born in Slavery & that nothing was Slavery that was short of *All the Days of their Life*."[25] In other words, when Betty had borne the children, she had been indentured for a term, and her liberation freed the children as well.

On October 26, 1792, Waln reported that the Supreme Court had granted a writ of habeas corpus to Betty's other children. Yet without enforcing it, the court adjourned. Writing to his son, Waln said he hoped that when the court reconvened, "a Judgment will go in their favor." "The Masters," he noted, still "threaten to carry the Case to the Court of Errors and Appeals."[26]

In the Pennsylvania Abolition Society minutes for December 19, 1792, Thomas Harrison noted that the Supreme Court had finally freed Betty's children. Furthermore, the court discouraged "the Claimants from removing their Case to the Court of Errors and Appeals."[27] After two years, the society had won major judicial victories. Still, the ordeal of Betty's children illuminates the precariousness of black freedom in the new United States.

The society also took the case of one Robert, captured during the Revolution in Virginia by the French. Reporting that he was free, Robert probably fought with Dunmore. Yet American authorities sold him to a Godfrey Wainwood. The outcome of this case is unrecorded. Similarly, Jonathan Stoddard held Ann Massey in bondage. In his will, Job Carr of Philadelphia had freed Massey years before. Massey had borne two sons. Subsequently, however, she had fallen ill. The will appointed overseers in Philadelphia to make sure that she could support herself. Thus, former slaves had, at most, a circumscribed freedom. The overseers contacted the Carr family, who "took possession" of Massey and her sons and "sold her as a slave for twenty dollars."[28] The society sued to free her.

Even Patriot soldiering did not protect blacks. The society took up the cause of Emmanuel Carpenter, a free man confined for ten months in the "New Gaol" of New York City. Carpenter had served fifteen months on an American gunboat on the Delaware River. The British captured him, brought him to New York, and freed him in 1783. Carpenter then apprenticed as a cooper and worked for William Hamilton in Philadelphia and

New York. Without cause, he told the society, Hamilton had had him "apprehended as a Run away Slave in December last."[29] The society filed a writ, but once again, no record exists of a verdict.

Despite the support given to free blacks, many in the international democratic movement did not grasp how powerful the will of blacks was to make themselves free, and frequently they patronized blacks. Expressions of liveliness, including parties or eccentricities, especially nettled Quakers. Thus, to be free politically in Pennsylvania did not mean to be free in social conduct. On September 28, 1788, Phebe Pemberton and one D. Bacon recorded the minutes of an antisexist "men & women Friends of Philadelphia."[30] Although ostensibly concerned with "the welfare of the Black people," members at the meeting urged blacks "to circumspect conduct." In visiting sixty-five families, the Quakers urged "moral and religious improvement" to those who had obtained "their just right of freedom." They sought to remake blacks in the Quakers' image.[31]

Yet blacks welcomed Quaker aid. White visitors to the former slaves, Bacon and Pemberton recorded, "were received by them with much respect and expressions of gratitude for the exercise of care and concern for their good." To defeat continuing slave-owner allegations, some members of the meeting reported that most blacks lived "comfortably and decently in their dwellings, which to us is a proof of their industry and capacity to support themselves with Reputation."[32]

Benjamin Franklin's "Address to the Public" on November 9, 1789, proposed to train and employ free blacks. Yet Franklin misguidedly reduced the "unhappy man" in slavery to a "mere machine." A free spirit himself, Franklin would not likely have been as straight-laced about the conduct of blacks in their personal lives as the Quakers were. The latter intervened to supervise supposedly wayward activities, such as drinking, and urged that blacks stifle joy.[33] Yet even Franklin's address aimed to control the free. Perhaps Franklin was suspicious of black insurrection because most ex-slaves, including those led by his son William, had fought on the British side:

> The unhappy man, who has long been treated as a brute animal, too frequently sinks beneath the common standard of the human species. The galling chains that bind his body do also fetter his intellectual faculties, and impair the social affections of his heart. Accustomed to move like a mere machine, by the will of a master, reflection is suspended; he has not the power of choice; and reason and conscience have but little influence over his conduct, because he is chiefly governed by the passion of fear. He is poor and friendless; perhaps worn out by extreme

labor, age and disease. Under such circumstances, freedom may often prove a misfortune for himself and prejudicial to society.[34]

In what the modern French social theorist Michel Foucault would call a disciplinary design, Franklin proposed four committees. First, "A Committee of Inspection" would "superintend the morals, general conduct and ordinary situation of the free Negroes, and afford them advice and instruction, protection from wrongs, and other friendly offices." In other words, white abolitionists would not trust freedom to blacks. To be free, blacks would have to be tutored. Thomas Harrison, the original leader of the Pennsylvania Abolition Society, served on this committee.

Second, Franklin envisioned a "Committee of Guardians," which would apprentice blacks for a "moderate" period to "learn some trade or other business of subsistence." Surprisingly, this committee would try to acquire "the right of guardianship over the persons so bound." Such a policy might make sense where orphans were involved. In other cases, however, the guardians' assumption of authority over black children emulated the attitudes of slave owners.

Third, Franklin proposed a "Committee of Education" to "provide that pupils may receive such learning as is necessary for their future situation in life." But this learning included conversion to strict Quaker practices. James Pemberton, vice president of the society, would participate in this group.[35] Fourth, a "Committee of Employ" would find jobs for children and adults and deter "poverty, idleness and many vicious habits."[36] The society subsequently set up all four committees.

On January 20, 1790, Warville wrote Franklin that the French Amis had caused his "plan" for the four committees to be "published in all the Newspapers." Like the Philadelphians and the soon-to-be-formed Sierra Leone Company in London, the Amis were benevolent toward, but patronized former slaves. Warville and the Abbé Gregoire sent a statement to the Philadelphia society on the condition of blacks in North America and the French colonies. The "planters and their Abettors," a standard term for the proslavery movement, Warville averred, had tried to stamp out their cause. Given the explosion of the French Revolution a year earlier, however, "the National Assembly has too much of the Spirit of liberty and philanthropy to listen to their calumnies."[37]

On August 30, James Pemberton, who became the president of the Philadelphia Abolition Society after Franklin's death, told the Amis that he hoped to see from France "a decisive step in Europe toward the abolition of slave trade." In 1791 this international movement would spur a

resolution in London's House of Commons against the traffic. The insurrection of slaves in Saint Domingue that same year and the visit of three
ambassadors—a black, Jean-Baptiste Belley-Mars; a mulatto, Jean-Baptiste
Mills; and a white, Louis-Pierre Dufay—to the French Assembly would
contribute to the abolition of bondage in all French colonies in 1794.[38]

Thanking the Amis for their support of Franklin's plan, Pemberton
invoked Franklin's phrase about black misery—"the unhappy man"—
and celebrated the propagation of universal liberty: "Our application to
Congress in behalf of these unhappy Men did not meet with that Success
which their most Zealous friends expected; yet we have great reason to be
satisfied with the measure, as it has evidently served to disseminate our
principles by exciting a Commotion on the subject which has produced a
more general disquisition, and of consequence a more general assent to
those truths."[39]

In London on February 20, 1790, Sharp congratulated the Pennsylva-
nians: "The formation of so many other Societies affords the pleasing Pre-
sumption that the Benefit of your Labours have not been confined to your
own State and that the Day is not very Distant when your extensive Empire
will be thoroughly purged of the Evils which our common Endeavours
have been employed to remove." Sharp, too, approved Franklin's "Plan."
He hailed the increase in "the Number of our Friends in France . . . and
many of them being in eminent positions." He dryly acknowledged the
slave-owners' menace: "The more zealous of [humanity's] advocates have
been threatened with personal violence: a species of Argument offered
with peculiar propriety by Slave Dealers and their Abettors."[40]

In 1791 an abolition society in Plymouth, England, indicted the slave
trade with drawings of "a number of human creatures, packed, side by
side, almost like herrings in a barrel."[41] In 1791 the House of Commons debated, but rejected a resolution to abolish the slave trade. Sharp, however,
saw this rejection strategically, that is, as a delay but not a defeat: "We cannot persuade ourselves that the Prosperity of the West-India Islands depends on the misery of Africa; or that the luxuries of Rum and Sugar can
only be obtained by tearing asunder those ties of affection which unite
our species and exalt our nature. . . . Tenets like these will not, we believe,
long maintain their influence in a free country and an enlightened age."[42]

ABOLITION SOCIETIES IN EIGHTEENTH-CENTURY AMERICA

Despite the attitudes and practices of even the most enlightened of the American Founding Fathers, freedom and notably the call for
emancipation received a great impetus from the American Revolution. As

a sturdy tree trunk from which branches spring, the Pennsylvania Abolition Society inspired societies in Connecticut, Rhode Island, New York, New Jersey, Maryland, Virginia, and Pennsylvania beyond the Allegheny. On May 24, 1789, the Rhode Island convention deliberated ratification of the Constitution and sent the Philadelphia Abolition Society an amendment to bar the slave trade: "As a traffic tending to establish or continue into Slavery of any of the human Species is disgraceful to the cause of liberty and humanity—that Congress shall as soon as may be promote such laws and regulations as may effectually prevent the importation of Slaves of every description into the United States."[43]

The Connecticut Abolition Society elliptically described itself: "For the Promotion of Freedom, and for the relief of Persons Unlawfully holden in Bondage." Yet their constitution at last named the goal of emancipation: "And being desirous to co-operate in a systematick way with the several Societies which have been, or that may be hereafter formed in the United States, or elsewhere, for the purpose of pursuing the abolition of slavery."[44]

On March 29, 1790, to Representative John Page, St. George Tucker, a proponent of gradual emancipation, reported an advertisement in the *Virginia Gazette* by a Mr. A. Davis for a Virginia Abolition Society. Congressional funding of such societies in the "several states," Tucker suggested, could help "extirpate an Evil so abhorrent to the principles of our government as to the rights of humanity." "You have perhaps been injured in the Eyes and Opinions of your Constituents," Tucker warned Page, by a rumor that the latter had urged on Congress immediate abolition of slavery. If accurate, Page would have been too principled about abolition for Tucker's tastes. Page, Tucker advised, might want to correct the rumor.[45]

In the North, abolitionists were bolder. For instance, the Washington Society of Pennsylvania addressed itself to Samuel Johnson's telling criticism of the American Revolution—that those who sought political freedom for themselves kept others in bondage: "As a nation, America has asserted her rights, with a fortitude which never can be forgotten; and while she fought for her own liberty, it became her to cherish that of all. Many of the States in the Union have evinced to the World their Willingness to do that justice to *others*, which they asserted, and appealed to Heaven, was *their* right. The laws in favour of that distressed and injured race of beings, whose unhappy lot has been Slavery (a Term which ought never to have been heard of in America, & which we wish blotted out, as soon as policy can effect it) every man is peculiarly bound to support."[46] By achieving a second revolution, the abolition societies aimed to complete the American Revolution.[47]

Emancipation's cause also attracted the support of many individuals. For instance, writing on August 2, 1788, from Richmond, Edmund Randolph, an aide-de-camp to George Washington, swore allegiance to the cosmopolitan Franklin's ideals: "I write, merely as a private man: and in that character I am free to declare that whensover an opportunity shall present itself, which shall warrant me, as a *citizen*, to emancipate the slaves possessed by me, I shall certainly indulge my feeling as a man, impressed with a sense of the rights of this unfortunate people and regardless of the loss of property. For such an opportunity, my best endeavours shall not be wanting."[48]

From Hartford, Connecticut, on December 4, 1789, lexicographer Noah Webster sympathized with the Pennsylvania Abolition Society's educational plan. "Money I have not to give," he wrote, but offered the "fruits of several years labor," an early dictionary. "I have requested Mr. Thomas Dalton to make sale of a considerable number of my 'Dissertations on the English Language' in a way most likely to [unclear word] my views & the interests of the Society, and directed one half the net proceeds to be delivered to the order of the Society."[49] On February 19, 1790, John Adams reported that he had distributed to U.S. senators the society's "addresses and plans," for instance, for Franklin's four committees, sent to him by James Pemberton.[50]

The international emancipation movement thus extended the first revolution's principle of freedom to blacks. One could not coherently support the one and oppose the other. Like the turbulent ocean, campaigns to emancipate the slaves came in waves that struck fiercely in the efforts of the abolitionist societies and rose to the huge storm of the French and Saint Dominguen revolutions. Sometimes, the movement lapped in one place, as in the long campaign against bondage in England. It would then be energized anew by Gabriel's and Sancho's revolts in Virginia in 1800 and 1802 and by blacks fighting for Britain in 1812 and, as after the Revolutionary War though on a smaller scale, escaping in hundreds to Canada.[51] Through the turbulence of slave insurrections and international campaigns, this movement would shape the nineteenth century, causing the abolition of slavery in the British colonies in 1834 and the American Civil War.

DEMOCRATIC INTERNATIONALISM AND ABOLITION

Although the second revolution began in America in parallel with the first, the seeds of freedom that it sowed grew among the most oppressed around the world. Anatole France, one of the great twentieth-century French novelists, ironically maintained that political equality—the freedoms of conscience, association, speech, and suffrage—give the beggar and the rich man an equal right to sleep under a bridge.[52] Political equality combined with arms, however, inspired the poor to demand adequate social resources. Ordinary people fused the second revolution of social equality or "red republicanism" to the first revolution's political equality or "plain republicanism."[53] In the *Communist Manifesto*, Marx and Engels would later make this natural evolution of a democratic revolution the centerpiece of their strategy for Germany in 1848.[54] A democratic revolution, they suggested, "would be but the prelude to an immediately following proletarian revolution."[55] In Europe, twin revolutions linked demands for freedom and abolition of large-scale private property in the means of production, a dialectic of democracy and communism.

In independence movements in the Americas, however, where bondage, reinforced by racism, had imposed staggering social and political inequalities, abolition overshadowed other forms of redistribution as the main social issue. Emancipation redistributes to slaves property in their own persons. Equality meant liberation of each individual. In the Americas, the two revolutions thus joined independence and emancipation. In Saint Domingue, the latter dynamic triggered the most profound social revolution of the eighteenth century. In 1804 blacks made civic liberty universal and renamed the former French colony Haiti.

North Americans had launched the first revolution for a public freedom restricted to (some) whites. Though initiating suffrage and representation for citizens, it did not include poor whites and women. Because of blacks escaping from the Patriots, the British Empire could initially pit emancipation against independence. As in the later American Civil War, the South became independent to prevent slaves from escaping and to preserve the institution of bondage. The conflict between these two revolutions nearly eclipsed the American independence movement. But then Patriots sought to match British manumission, creating, for instance, the First Rhode Island Regiment, and freed blacks would ultimately provide nearly a quarter of Patriot troops and the key fighters on both sides at Yorktown.

In American ports, black and white sailors and artisans had dominated revolutionary crowds, including the Boston Tea Party of 1773. In 1787 the threat of dispossession triggered an uprising of former soldiers, now farmers, led by Captain Daniel Shays. That insurrection defended the power of democratic state legislatures to cancel debts. Another second revolution, that of the poor, but free, came into existence with sympathies for abolition.[56] In a "Dissent to the Massachusetts Convention" in the April 9,

1788, *Hampshire Gazette*, three farmers from western Massachusetts, Malachi Maynard, Samuel Field, and, writing under a pseudonym, "Consider Arms," offered a criticism of the American Constitution: "Where is the man, who under the influence of sober dispassionate reasoning, and not void of natural affection, can lay his hand upon his heart and say, I am willing my sons and my daughters should be torn from me and doomed to perpetual slavery? We presume that man is not to be found amongst us: And yet we think the consequence is fairly drawn, that this is what every man ought to be able to say, who voted for this constitution."[57] From fighting in the Revolution itself and their own experiences of oppression—experiences separate from those of artisans and sailors—these men had seen that freedom must be equal and universal. Revealing the unity of emancipation and independence, these farmers underline a separate and continuing cause of abolition.

The American Revolution had many features, including political institutions for popular influence, formally equal liberties, and judicial independence that others might wisely have adopted. If the American Revolution had liberated slaves not only in the North but also in the South, its model might have inspired social revolution and better political design elsewhere. In the battles of Savannah and Charlestown, for example, future Haitian leaders such as Henri Christophe had apprenticed with the French and the Patriots. Thus, the American Revolution spread the seeds of freedom. Nevertheless, the paradox of imperial emancipation and the failure of rebels from below to force gradual emancipation in the American South crippled the first revolution's international impact.

In contrast, the French Revolution profoundly stirred blacks. For instance, Toussaint L'Ouverture read Abbé Raynal's *Histoire des deux indes* (*History of Two Indias*), which foresaw a black liberator in Saint Domingue. In 1794 three Saint Domingue delegates influenced the Jacobins' outlawing of slavery throughout the French colonies. In 1800 the Haitian Revolution inspired Gabriel's revolt in Virginia—a democratic feedback of international politics. But the sprouting of the seeds of freedom in Haiti shocked Thomas Jefferson. He had once admired the Shays's Rebellion and had spoken of the need to water the tree of liberty every twenty years "with the blood of patriots and tyrants." Now he feared the insurrection in Saint Domingue against the French slave owners and encouraged reaction, an antidemocratic feedback of global politics.

Had it not thwarted the second revolution in the aftermath of the first, the United States could have supplied a concrete example of its professed belief in equality to the movement for democratic internationalism. Instead, that role fell to Haiti.[58] Not only did Haiti inspire Gabriel's revolt in the United States, but also the new Haitian republic lent support to Simon Bolivar, the revolutionary leader in Venezuela, and served as an emancipatory beacon for South and Central America in the nineteenth century.[59]

Latin Americans saw only America's reactionary, postwar face, not the buried history of the second revolution. Yet the first revolution influenced others, even in Sierra Leone, and its natural connection with the second still surrounds it like a penumbra. The vision of equality entertained by people such as John Laurens, the 1779 resolution of the Continental Congress to recruit and free three thousand southern blacks, the rivalry with Britain over the pace of emancipation, the contributions of blacks on both sides of the Revolutionary War, and the struggles of blacks for freedom on both sides afterward all foreshadowed the possibility of emancipation, even in the American South. Any of those who participated in that struggle might have spoken the words delivered by the leader of the American slave insurrection, Gabriel, at his trial in Richmond, Virginia, in 1800: "I have nothing more to offer than what George Washington would have had to offer, had he been taken by the British and put on trial by them. 'I have adventured my life in endeavouring to obtain the liberty of my countrymen, and I am a willing sacrifice in their cause.'"[60] In the cause of the two revolutions, emancipation and independence, many already had. In the cause of emancipation and independence, many more would sacrifice as well.

Notes

In citing works in the notes, I have used short titles. The full titles and sources are listed in the bibliography. The following abbreviations have been used in the notes and bibliography.

Research Libraries and Collections

AL-UV	Alderman Library, University of Virginia, Charlottesville
CHS	Connecticut Historical Society, Hartford
GDAH	Georgia Department of Archives and History, Morrow, GA
LOC	Library of Congress, Washington, DC
MHS	Massachusetts Historical Society, Boston
NA	National Archives, Washington, DC
NYHS	New-York Historical Society, New York
NYPL	New York Public Library, New York
PAC	Public Archive of Canada, Ottawa
PANS	Public Archive of Nova Scotia, Halifax
PHS	Pennsylvania Historical Society, Philadelphia
PRO	Public Records Office, London
RIHS	Rhode Island Historical Society, Providence
SCDAH	South Carolina Department of Archives and History, Columbia
SCHS	South Carolina Historical Society, Charleston
SCL-USC	South Caroliniana Library, University of South Carolina, Columbia
TWML-UV	Tracy W. McGregor Library, University of Virginia, Charlottesville
WLCL-UM	William L. Clements Library, University of Michigan, Ann Arbor

Documents and Papers

DAR	*Documents of the American Revolution*
DHAR	*Documentary History of the American Revolution*
PGM	*Papers of George Mason*
PGW-CS	*Papers of George Washington, Confederation Series*
PGW-RS	*Papers of George Washington, Revolutionary Series*
PGW-RWS	*Papers of George Washington, Revolutionary War Series*
PHL	*Papers of Henry Laurens*
PNG	*Papers of Nathanael Greene*
PPAS	*Papers of the Pennsylvania Abolition Society*

1. C. L. R. James wrote the pathbreaking but neglected *The Black Jacobins* in 1938. Robin Blackburn's *The Overthrow of Colonial Slavery* (1988) restored the centrality of the Haitian and Venezuelan Revolutions.

2. Some might balk at the term "social revolution" to capture this second revolution, although Gary Nash, in the *Forgotten Fifth*, 39, also uses the term "social revolution" for the black uprising in the South. Blacks, some might point out, staged no insurrection comparable to the one in Saint Domingue that created Haiti. They did not torch the mansions and slay the slave owners. But this incendiary image reflects only one prototype—in this case, a stereotype—about social revolution. First, during the war, somewhere between twenty thousand and one hundred thousand blacks escaped from their owners and found freedom with the Crown. That number is roughly one-twentieth to one-quarter of all slaves at the time. Second, many owners also fled, leaving blacks to remain on plantations in South Carolina and Virginia, where they ran their own lives to an unusual extent. These blacks were widely known as "Torified," and they hoped for freedom from a victorious "King." This magnitude of revolt against bondage was a social revolution. Third, many thousands of blacks fought or worked for the redcoats. Fourth, in competition, Patriots recruited a large number of blacks and freed many. With the Continental Congress's passage of the Laurens proposal in 1779, the possibility dawned of gradual emancipation even in the South. Trading soldiering for freedom marked a revolutionary change in the elites, provoked by massive escape to the Crown. In the reality of social revolution, blacks were fighters and free. The American Revolution achieved vigor, honor, and consistency through relying on black soldiers. Fifth, Tory blacks appeared as leaders of multiracial and all-black guerilla bands. As we will see, Colonel Tye in New Jersey and the Black Dragoons in South Carolina killed plantation owners in their homes and fields. These forces incarnated armed insurrection against Patriot slave-owning. In the postwar period, these five factors propelled gradual emancipation in the North; during the war, they pushed heavily even in the South. If this was not a social revolution, what would be? Conversely, independence led to a reassertion of bondage. Memories of social rebellion were repressed on both sides of the Atlantic. A failed social revolution, however, is still a social revolution. The thirteen-year insurrection that created Haiti was, after all, the only *successful* slave insurrection in history. To rule out other candidates, including ones that did achieve significant freedom—for instance, gradual emancipation in the North—seems bizarre.

3. Gary Nash, *Race and Revolution*, 60. As we will see, whole families fled to the Crown together.

4. Nash, *Forgotten Fifth*, 74–75, adds this thought.

5. Some of these causes do not undermine bondage. Slave owning was still profitable. The Haitian Revolution struck fear into slave owners such as Jefferson and gave many an elective affinity for biological racism.

6. To justify exploring a particular counterfactual, scholars of the comparative social history of revolutions must make an alternate outcome such as the ones sketched

here causally possible, even palpable. The analysis of "possible worlds" among philosophers, as in the work of David Lewis or Simon Blackburn, is abstract—too loose to be interesting to historians, who want the facts about what happened in this world, not what might have happened in a possible, but distant one. Yet in history, some facts point to what nearly happened. For instance, military competition between the Crown and the Patriots to recruit and free blacks did generate gradual emancipation in the northern states by the turn of the nineteenth century. Such causes had a strong effect in the South as well. Furthermore, other independence revolutions in the hemisphere were either launched by slaves (Haiti) or resulted in gradual emancipation (Venezuela). That gradual emancipation did not occur in southern states needs explanation.

In addition, egalitarian sailors and artisans in the port cities had forceful abolitionist spokesmen such as James Otis and Thomas Paine. In both Massachusetts and Pennsylvania, Otis's and Paine's views achieved mass influence, but they did not become the main political leaders. In a comparative context, however, one might imagine such figures, analogous to Jacobins, leading a stronger radical push from below. The decentralization of American state legislatures limited the influence of democratic radicalism. As Shays's Rebellion revealed, such legislatures were open to democratic pressure from below. But as Nash stresses, sailor-artisan movements were not as unified and powerful as the Montagnards became. Still, had leaders like Otis and Paine come to power in the ports of the South, including Charlestown, they, too, might have instigated gradual emancipation throughout the United States.

7. Samuel Johnson, "Taxation No Tyranny," in Samuel Johnson, *Works*, 14:93–144.

8. Christopher Brown, *Moral Capital*, chaps. 3–4, p. 461. In *Must Global Politics Constrain Democracy?* I name this the democratic feedback of revolutions from below.

9. Nash published *Race and Revolution* in 1993 but sees the issue anew in *The Forgotten Fifth* in 2006. Woody Holton published *Forced Founders* in 1999; Cassandra Pybus, *Epic Journeys of Freedom* in 2005; Simon Schama, *Rough Crossings* in 2006; Brown, *Moral Capital* in 2006; and Douglas Egerton, *Death or Liberty* in 2008.

10. Indeed, among American high school and college students today, blacks are often still not seen as central to the Revolutionary War. But black soldiers were the secret of the imperial army in North America.

11. After James's *Black Jacobins* in 1938, the next full-length work is Elizabeth Fick, *The Making of a Nation* (1990).

INTRODUCTION

1. Aristotle, *Politics* 1269a36–39.

2. See Peter Wood's insightful *Black Majority*.

3. Cheryl A. Wells, "New York City Slave Rebellion (1712)," 349–51.

4. Gary B. Nash, *The Unknown American Revolution*, 37.

5. An eighteenth-century Charlestown newspaper reported examples of individual resistance. A black "took an opportunity and killed an overseer with an axe." Another "desperate villain the Negro Cain attacked and dangerously wounded his master,

Mr. Isaac McPherson and several of his family . . . and made his escape." In the reporter's fantasy of a murderous brotherhood between whites and blacks, this case involves a rarely mentioned biblical name, the dark *"Cain"* who slew the fair Abel. But John Cuffe, a former slave in Charlestown, describes the practices of the sadistic McPherson, who turned "a thin screw" into the nails of blacks until blood flowed profusely. In another story, the colony of South Carolina accused a woman of poisoning "her mistress." On a Charlestown green, it burned the accused at the stake. Authorities routinely confined blacks, hanging in cages, to die of thirst, the bodies to rot. See Robert A. Olwell, *Masters, Slaves and Servants*, 23–24.

6. Jill Lepore, *New York Burning*, 188–89.

7. Daniel Horsmanden, preface to a *Journal of the Proceedings in the Detection of the Conspiracy*.

8. Lepore, *New York Burning*, 122.

9. Ibid., 143–44.

10. Graham Russell Gao Hodges, *Slavery, Freedom and Culture among Early American Workers*, 88–89.

11. Lepore, *New York Burning*, 54.

12. In 1709 the Crown overturned New Jersey's 1704 "Act for Regulating Negro Indians and Mulato Slaves," modeled on the New York law, because "the Punishment to be inflicted on Negroes &ca is such as never was allowed by or known in the Laws of this Kingdom." Ibid., 59.

13. Ibid., 57.

14. Alan Singer, *New York and Slavery*, 59.

15. Johann Hinrichs, *Diary*, 322–23.

16. Robert A. Olwell, "Domestick Enemies," 24. Blacks indeed outnumbered whites, but except in the "low country," Glen exaggerates the number.

17. Ibid., 27.

18. *American Weekly Mercury*, February 26–March 5, 1733.

19. The *Weekly Mercury* editorial (ibid.) also depicts a sharp exchange between a black man, identified only as "Hall's Negro," and Rennalds, a white Philadelphian: "Rennalds surprised at the Freedom of this Fellow, told him he was a very great Raskal to talk in that manner; the Negro answered that he was as good a Man as himself, and that in a little Time he would be convinced." As a result, Rennalds informed on him to the authorities. "Hall's Negro" and another were "Try'd"—a loose term for a judicial procedure generally relying on the word of one white—and one was "Hang'd." But "Hall's Negro," who had spoken so forcefully of freedom, escaped.

20. Mark Stegmaier, "Maryland's Fear of Insurrection at the Time of Braddock's Defeat," 468, 479n5.

21. Ibid., 477–79. Woody Holton, *Forced Founders*, 138–39, details threats of revolt during the French and Indian War and the official brutality in suppressing them.

22. *Archives of Maryland*, 52:160, cited in Stegmaier, "Maryland's Fear," 479.

23. Cited in Marcus Rediker, "Motley Crew of Rebels," 174.

24. Ibid., 174–75.

25. Ibid., 178–79.

26. Winthrop Jordan, *White over Black*, 112.

27. *American Weekly Mercury*, February 26–March 5, 1733.

28. Ray Raphael, *People's History of the American Revolution*, 251; Olwell, *Masters, Slaves and Servants*, 233.

29. See Bernard Bailyn, *Ideological Origins of the American Revolution*, 232–46.

30. Alfred Blumenrosen and Ruth Blumenrosen, *Slave Nation*, 277.

31. Christopher L. Brown, *Moral Capital*, 167.

32. Lord Mansfield, Somersett v. Stewart, June 22, 1772, 79–82.

33. Chapter 8 describes Sharp's thinking. Christopher Brown's *Moral Capital*, chapter 3, emphasizes his contribution to the abolitionist movement. Also see James Oldham, "New Light on Mansfield and Slavery," 5–6.

34. Blumenrosen and Blumenrosen, *Slave Nation*, 13.

35. Oldham, "New Light on Mansfield and Slavery," 47.

36. Sharp cited in F. O. Shyllon, *Black Slaves in Britain*.

37. Blumenrosen and Blumenrosen, *Slave Nation*, 12.

38. Riddell to Stewart, July 10, 1772, in Oldham, "New Light on Mansfield and Slavery," 65.

39. David Brion Davis, *Problem of Slavery*, 303.

40. Blumenrosen and Blumenrosen, *Slave Nation*, 24–25.

41. Herbert Aptheker, ed., *Documentary History of the Negro People*, 9–10; Montesquieu, *De l'esprit des lois*, bk. 15.

42. Sidney Kaplan, "The 'Domestic Insurrections' of the Declaration of Independence," 253–54; Sylvia R. Frey, *Water from the Rock*, 53.

43. The text of the Dunmore Proclamation is available online at www.upa.pdx.edu/IMS/currentprojects/TAHv3/Content/PDFs/Dunmore_Proclamation_1775.pdf.

44. Bradford to Madison, January 4, 1877, in Peter H. Wood, "Dream Deferred," 171.

45. Rediker, "Motley Crew," 179, 182.

46. Ibid., 184–85.

47. Ibid., 179–80.

48. For an analysis of elite efforts to forge division, see Theodore Allen, *The Invention of the White Race*, chaps. 1–2.

49. Rediker, "Motley Crew," 185.

50. John Allen, "Oration on the Beauties of Liberty," in Roger Bruns, ed., *Am I Not a Man and a Brother*, 258–59.

51. Gary B. Nash, *The Forgotten Fifth*, 15–16, suggests that news of natural liberty spread along the black network like "cognitive shrapnel."

52. *Savannah (GA) Gazette*, December 7, 1774, in U. B. Phillips, ed., *Plantation and Frontier Documents*, 2:118–19; Herbert Aptheker, *American Negro Slave Revolts*, 201.

53. Frey, *Water from the Rock*, 54.

54. Report of Dorchester County Committee of Inspection, Fall 1775, Gilmor Papers, 1689–1855, ms. 387.1, Maryland Historical Society.

55. First names are often all that survive in reports of blacks. Laurens to Gervais,

January 29, 1766, in Peter H. Wood, "Taking Care of Business," 276; Wood, "Dream Deferred," 170, 172–75; Aptheker, *American Negro Slave Revolts*, 87, 200–2.

56. Janet Schaw, *Journal of a Lady of Quality*, 195.

57. *Sic*: the "court" should have recorded the "owner's" name.

58. Thomas Hutchinson to Henry Laurens, July 5, 1775, in Raphael, *People's History of the American Revolution*, 251.

59. Rediker, "Motley Crew," 198.

60. David McCullough, *John Adams*, chap. 3.

61. Emma Nogrady Kaplan and Sidney Kaplan, *Black Presence*, 9–10. In contrast, the frontispiece of William Nell's 1855 abolitionist book *The Colored Patriots of the American Revolution* depicts the British firing on "Crispus Attucks, the First Martyr of the American Revolution, King (now State) Street, Boston, March 5th, 1770." Along with the works of Livermore (*Historical Research Respecting the Opinions of the Founders*, 1862) and Moore (*Historical Notes on the Employment of Negroes*, 1862), this work by a black abolitionist is still a striking, often overlooked source on the Revolution. On the eighty-eighth anniversary of Attucks's death, March 5, 1858, Boston abolitionists inaugurated Crispus Attucks' Day. In abolitionist lawyer and orator Wendell Phillips's words at the celebration, "Emerson said the first gun heard round the world was that of Lexington. Who set the example of guns? Who taught the British soldier that he might be defeated? Who dared look into his eyes?" (Kaplan and Kaplan, *Black Presence*, 9–10). In the silence of the post-Revolutionary era, however, it took nearly a century for Attucks to be celebrated as an American hero.

62. Jefferson added this passage to the revised draft. In what was an act of calculated propaganda for Jefferson, who otherwise admired Native Americans, the Declaration denounces Indians as "merciless savages." This stereotype encouraged American genocidal tendencies toward indigenous people. (A conqueror's projection, the word "*indio*" in Spanish or "Indian" derives from Columbus's illusion that he had stumbled onto Asia. But along with "Native American," "indigenous person" and anglicized names of tribes, I occasionally employ it for stylistic variety.) Though the Declaration warned "of merciless savages who would engage in an undistinguished destruction of all ages, sexes and conditions," the future American government would mercilessly slaughter Native Americans of all ages, sexes, and conditions. They would cordon their remnants on reservations. Yet despite Patriot scorn, many indigenous people fought heroically for independence. Every northern state recruited significant numbers. After the war, however, the new government would traduce Native American Patriots even more than it did blacks. Blacks were freed, but not paid.

63. This chapter illustrates the power of contextualism, of discovering whom political theorists were arguing against and the exact, often limited, bearing of seemingly global formulations. See Alan Gilbert, *Marx's Politics*, chap. 13.

64. Staughton Lynd, *Class Struggle, Slavery and the United States Constitution*, 159.

65. James Iredell, "Causes of the American Revolution," June 1776, in *Papers of James Iredell*, 1:409.

1. I have benefited from Woody Holton, *Forced Founders*, chap. 5.

2. Emma Kaplan and Sidney Kaplan, *Black Presence*, 72–73.

3. In May 1774, for example, the House of Burgesses had opposed the British Port Bill, which, in response to the Boston Tea Party, would close Boston harbor. For June 1, the prospective date of the closing, eighty-four burgesses, including Patrick Henry, Richard Henry Lee, Francis Lightfoot, and Thomas Jefferson, called for a "day of general fasting and prayer." On May 26, 1774, Dunmore dissolved the House of Burgesses. Patriots then met at Raleigh Tavern in Williamsburg and called for an "association" of representatives of the colonies to be held in September. Joining Patriots in Boston, Philadelphia, and Maryland, these Virginians demanded that "all commercial intercourse with Britain be avoided." Peyton Randolph, "Proclamation of the House of Burgesses," called the "McGregor Broadside," May 31, 1774, AL-UV.

4. *Purdie's Virginia Gazette*, April 21, 1775, *Naval Documents of the American Revolution*, 1:204–5, www.revwar75/battles/primarydocs/williamsburg.htm.

5. *Dixon and Hunter's Virginia Gazette*, April 22, 1775, in ibid., 207–8.

6. Dunmore to the Earl of Dartmouth, May 1, 1775, in K. G. Davies, ed., *Documents of the American Revolution* (cited hereafter as *DAR*), 9:108.

7. Ibid.

8. Henry Collins, *Journal of His Majesty's Schooner Magdalen*, April 20, 1775, in *Naval Documents of the American Revolution*, 1:204.

9. Fredericksburg officers to Captain William Grayson, April 24, 1775, in ibid., 214–15.

10. Eppes to Jefferson, June 3, 1776, Jefferson Papers, LOC.

11. Woody Holton, "'Rebel against Rebel,'"185, 187.

12. Peyton Randolph, April 27, 1775, AL-UV.

13. Dunmore to Dartmouth, May 1, 1775, in Davies, *DAR*, 9: 109.

14. But Randolph misinterpreted Dunmore's provocation: "So far as we can Judge from a Comparison of all Circumstances, the Governor considers his Honor as at Stake; he thinks that he acted for the best and will not be compell'd to what we have abundant Reason to believe he would cheerfully do were he left to himself." Dunmore did not intend to return the powder. As a Patriot and threatened slave owner, Randolph noted gratefully, neighboring communities had offered to defend Williamsburg with arms. Fearing unforeseen consequences of further "violent measures," however, Randolph urged "quiet." Randolph, April 27, 1775, Al-UV.

15. Benjamin Quarles, "Dunmore as Liberator."

16. Dunmore to Dartmouth, May 1, 1775 in Davies, *DAR*, 9:108.

17. Ibid., 109.

18. Gage to Dartmouth, May 15, 1775, in ibid., 132.

19. Address of the House of Burgesses to Dunmore, June 19, 1775, in ibid., 184.

20. Ibid.

21. Ibid.

22. Ibid.

23. Ibid.

24. Ibid., 185.

25. Dunmore to Dartmouth, May 15, 1775, in ibid., 133.

26. Dunmore to Dartmouth, June 1775, in ibid., 205.

27. Ibid., 204.

28. Campbell to Dartmouth, August 31, 1775, in ibid., 94.

29. Kenny to Marshall, April 25, 1775, Marshall Papers, WLCL-UM.

30. Sip Wood, Memorial to Gen. Assembly [Hartford, CT.], May 20, 1772, African-American History Collection, WLCL-UM.

31. Kenny to Marshall, April 25, 1775, Marshall Papers.

32. Gage to Barrington, Boston, June 12, 1775, Gage Papers, WLCL-UM.

33. Ibid.

34. Sylvia R. Frey, *Water from the Rock*, 67.

35. Ibid.

36. Though Dunmore was offshore, the Patriots did not control the territory; Dunmore could still organize the recruits for battle.

37. James W. St. G. Walker, *Black Loyalists*, 53.

38. Ibid.; Page to Jefferson, November 24, 1775, *Papers of Thomas Jefferson*, 1:265; Quarles, "Dunmore as Liberator," 498, 501; *Virginia Gazette*, November 30, 1775, cited in Peter H. Wood, "Dream Deferred,"178.

39. Richard Shannon Moss, *Slavery on Long Island*, 143.

40. Ronald Hoffman, *Spirit of Dissension*, 148.

41. "Liberty to Slaves," *Maryland Gazette*, December 14, 1775, Maryland Historical Society.

42. Ibid.

43. "Declaration of the General Assembly of Virginia," December 15, 1775, John Brown Carter Library, Brown University.

44. Ellen Gibson Wilson, *Loyal Blacks*, 26.

45. Brent, advertisement, *Virginia Gazette*, November 16, 1775, LOC.

46. Benjamin Quarles, *Negro in the American Revolution*, 27.

47. Ira Berlin, *Many Thousands Gone*, 257.

48. Holton, 'Rebel against Rebel,' 186.

49. Simon Schama, *Rough Crossings*, 72, mistakenly infers that they all reached British lines.

50. *Virginia Gazette*, July 1775, http://research.history.org/DigitalLibrary/Virginia Gazette/VGbyIssueDate.cfm?year=1775/pPrinter=Dixon%and%20Hunter.

51. Deposition of George Gray, September 4, 1775, in Holton, "'Rebel against Rebel,'" 105, 158.

52. John Page to Thomas Jefferson, November 11, 1775, *Papers of Thomas Jefferson*, 1:257.

53. Lund to George Washington, November 5, 1775, in W. W. Abbot and Dorothy Twohig, eds., *PGW-RWS*, 2:306.

54. Handwritten letter, W. Brown Wallace to Michael Wallace, accession no. 38–150, TWML-UV.

55. Jean Butenhoff Lee, *Price of Nationhood*, 139–40.

56. Kaplan and Kaplan, *Black Presence*, 76–78. As the American Revolution developed from a series of local and regional skirmishes into a full-fledged revolt in 1776, the Crown, according to Lieutenant Colonel Archibald Campbell of the Seventy-First Highlanders, could bolster its strength by recruiting a "Regiment of Stout Active Negro's," perhaps fourteen hundred, from the West Indies; see ibid., 69. On this regiment's landing, he hoped, "90%" of American blacks would desert their "masters." Yet, in what was a bizarre idea, he surmised that this force could involve many slaves. How would this inspire blacks to rise up? Nonetheless, the idea recalled Dunmore's Royal Ethiopian Regiment. Campbell to Germain, January 16, 1776, Germain Papers, WLCL-UM; Frey, *Water from the Rock*, 69. And in January 1776, imperial warships put down anchor at the mouth of the Savannah River. The British sought to find provisions, not to free blacks. Nonetheless, the ships engendered a mass of "desertions" of slaves from Georgia's plantations. Archibald Bullock and John Houston, delegates to the Continental Congress, reported to John Adams: "If one thousand regular troops should land in Georgia, and their commander be provided with arms and clothes enough, and proclaim freedom to all the Negroes who would join his campaign, twenty thousand would join it from [Georgia and South Carolina] in a fortnight" (cited in Frey, *Water from the Rock*, 68). Observing the thousands of not yet organized blacks who trailed every Royal regiment, John Andre, the English spy, would note, "Their Property in Slaves we need not seek; it flyes to us and Famine follows." Kaplan and Kaplan, *Black Presence*, 78.

57. Schama, in *Rough Crossings*, summarizes Dunmore's character: rather than a "Machiavel," he was "in reality no more than a standard issue Scots-Hanoverian imperialist, handicapped by a rigid sense of duty, a political tin ear, and, as events would show, a fatally imperfect grasp of military tactics" (70). For good measure, he sneers at "a pink-cheeked time-server" (74). Dunmore did have a tin ear and was no tactician. Yet one would not guess from this portrayal that Dunmore's initiative would provoke southern secession for bondage. Instead, Schama says, Dunmore's strategy "backfired as it did throughout the South" (67). He is right that Dunmore did not cow the Patriots. But he did enlist thousands of blacks and made the redcoats fearsome. Even though Schama briefly addresses this central point—"this was a revolution mobilized first and foremost to protect slavery" (67)—he labels Dunmore's initiative simultaneously a "backfire" and hurries away from his insight; Schama suggests that George Washington's fear—Dunmore would gain strength among blacks like "a snowball in rolling"—was unmotivated (74). On the contrary, Dunmore unleashed the military rivalry for black recruitment that shaped the first revolution and, unintentionally, nearly resulted in fusing the two revolutions. Dunmore was thus unique, not "standard issue." Schama also ignores the difficulties of his circumstances, in particular, the smallpox that ravaged his forces. Listening to Schama, one would not imagine Quarles's apt title: "Dunmore as Liberator."

58. Dunmore to Dartmouth, December 6, 1775–February 18, 1776, in Davies, *DAR*, 12:58.

59. Ibid., 59.

60. Ibid.

61. Peter Jennings Wrike, *Governor's Island*, 8.

62. Johnston to Johnston, December 9, 1775, William Johnston and Family Papers, Miscellaneous Manuscript Collection, LOC.

63. Ibid. Perhaps Patriot reinforcements arrived after the deserter fled.

64. Ibid.

65. *PGW-RWS*, 2:572n9.

66. Ibid., 571. The empire had repeatedly suppressed Scottish rebellions for independence. As Richard Henry Lee noted, Dunmore's threats to free the slaves did not frighten Scots, who admired liberty. In January 1775, in a republican vein, Scottish Patriots meeting in Darien, Georgia, indicted bondage and its tainting of the revolutionary cause: slavery is "an unnatural practice . . . founded in injustice and cruelty, and highly dangerous to our liberty (as well as our lives), debasing part of our fellow creatures below men, and corrupting the virtues and morals of the rest" (Alton Hornsby Jr., *Negro in Revolutionary Georgia*, 3).

67. Dalrymple to Howe, 1775, in Germain Papers NLCL-UA.

68. Ibid.

69. Ibid.

70. Ibid.

71. Ibid.

72. Joseph Galloway, "Plan for Reducing the Colonies in the Most Expeditious Manner and at the Least Expense," to Germain, Germain Papers, vol. 17.

73. Ibid.

74. Eno, "Strange Fate of the Black Loyalists," 162, 166.

75. Kaplan and Kaplan, *Black Presence*, 82.

76. Henry DeSaussure Bull, "Ashley Hall Plantation," in Robert Olwell, *Masters, Slaves and Servants*, 258.

77. Thus, the Patriots initiated a tradition of such provocations, rumors, and lies. Some examples of lies are, for instance, "Remember the Maine!" in the Spanish-American War, the Gulf of Tonkin incident in Vietnam, and the supposed Iraqi dumping of fetuses on the floor of a Kuwaiti hospital in the First Gulf War.

78. Wrike, *Governor's Island*, 12–13.

79. Ibid., 8.

80. The total of ninety-one men listed in the regiment included three white officers.

81. Wrike, *Governor's Island*, 121–35, compiled the list from surviving records. The numbers, however, are mine.

82. This list does not have detailed information.

83. Four men (Arculls, Glasgow, Peter. and Robert) and ten women (Abby, Dinah,

Elizabeth, Esther, Jenny, Judith, Kate, Lettice, Manda, and Mary) came from the Willoughby plantation.

84. Wrike, *Governor's Island*, 14.

85. Ibid., 13.

86. Hamond to Stanley, February 1776, Hamond Naval Papers, 1766–1825, TWML-UV.

87. Ibid., August 5, 1776. This letter told the tale after they had left Virginia.

88. Ibid.

89. Wrike, *Governor's Island*, 14.

90. Johnston to Johnston, June 15, 1776, William Johnston and Family Papers.

91. Ibid., June 21, 1776.

92. Abigail Adams described the vaccination's impact on her family: "The little folks are very sick then and puke every morning, but after that they are comfortable. . . . Nabby has enough of the smallpox for all the family beside. She is pretty well covered, not a spot of what is so sore that she can neither walk, sit, stand, or lay with any comfort" (McCullough, *John Adams*, 143).

93. Wrike, *Governor's Island*, 30.

94. Hamond to Stanley, May 16, 1776, Hamond Naval Papers.

95. Johnston to Johnston, June 21, 1776, William Johnston and Family Papers.

96. Eppes to Jefferson, May 27, 1776, Edgehill-Randolph Papers, LOC.

97. Ibid.

98. Hamond to Stanley, June 10, 1776, Hamond Naval Papers.

99. Ibid., July 9, 1776.

100. Ibid., July 14, 1776.

101. Ibid., July 24 and August 5, 1776.

102. Lee to Washington, April 5, 1776, *PGW-RWS*, 4:43–44.

103. Ibid., May 10, 1776, *PGW-RWS*, 4:257, 259n1.

104. In May 1776, a North Carolina committee urged that all masters "on the south side of Cape-Fear River remove such male slaves as are capable of bearing arms, or otherwise assisting the enemy, into the country, remote from the sea" (Kaplan and Kaplan, *Black Presence*, 79).

105. *PGW-RWS*, 4:412–13.

106. Johnston to Johnston, May 22, 1776, William Johnston and Family Papers.

107. Ibid.

108. Ibid., March 22, 1776.

109. Ibid., June 15, 1776.

110. Ibid.

111. Peter Minor to Garrett Minor, August 9, 1776, Minor Papers, 2 vols., microfilm, LOC.

112. Ibid.

113. Ibid.

114. Wrike, *Governor's Island*, 86.

115. Ibid., 105.

116. Christopher Gadsden, Raws. Lowndes, Isaac Mazyck, David Oliphant, Thos. Lynch, Thos. Wright, Jas. Parsons, Thos. Bee, Chas. Pinckney, J. Rutledge, and Eben Simmons, "Remonstrance from South Carolina against the Stamp Act," September 4, 1764, SCHS, in Gibbes, *Documentary History of the American Revolution*, 1:1–6.

117. Ibid.

118. Ibid.

119. Frey, *Water from the Rock*, 56. "Common talk" among blacks, refers, once again, to a web of slave communication connecting mansion and field across hundreds of miles. The owner's table or bed held no secrets from blacks who served the meals, washed the sheets, and listened to fervent talk of the natural rights of each individual. "What about my natural rights?" each must have thought. In Virginia, the layout of Thomas Jefferson's Monticello shows how communication among slaves escaped the attention of owners. Craving social distance, Jefferson placed the kitchen far below the dining room and connected the two only by a dumbwaiter. But blacks could have heard him talking with family or visitors on other occasions. Communication among slaves occurred without his knowledge. Yet relations could also be intimate. Stories long survived among blacks about Jefferson's paternity of Sally Hemings's children. Given DNA evidence, the Jefferson family cemetery now includes one of the offspring. Of the despised, however, as a class, the masters suspected everything and saw nothing. (See Douglas R. Egerton's description [*Gabriel's Rebellion*, chaps. 4–5, 8–9] of how word passed among blacks in Gabriel's revolt in 1800 and Sancho's in 1802 in Virginia and how whites got a glimmer of these "conspiracies.") Among the despised, the idea of natural rights spread like wildfire.

120. Davies, *DAR*, 9:144.

121. Ibid., 11:94.

122. Ibid. In the epilogue to *The World of Thomas Jeremiah*, William Ryan thinks it is an open question whether Campbell instigated black insurrection parallel to, though less openly than, Dunmore. Unless Campbell was secretly bent on deceiving his superiors (with the example of Dunmore already threatening such insurrection since 1772, there is no reason why he needed to), his letters show decisively that nothing of the kind was the case.

123. *Papers of Henry Laurens* (cited hereafter as *PHL*),10:320.

124. Kaplan and Kaplan, *Black Presence*, 76–77; Frey, *Water from the Rock*, 57–58.

125. Campbell in Davies, *DAR*, 11:96.

126. Henry to John Laurens, August 20, 1775, *PHL*, 10:320. The two ministers were Robert Smith of St. Philip's and Robert Cooper of St. Michael's.

127. *PHL*, 10:320–21.

128. That Reverend Smith, who was a Patriot, repeatedly questioned and found Jeremiah innocent suggests that Ryan's (*World of Thomas Jeremiah*, 158–59) surmise about Jeremiah's possible guilt is unlikely and, more important, unproven.

129. *PHL*, 10:320.

130. Ibid., 321.

131. Henry Laurens to John Laurens, August 17, 1775, *PHL*, 10:331.

132. Ibid., 332.

133. Ibid., August 20, 1775, 321.

134. The fact that some American historians treat the Jeremiah case uncritically, as a matter of legality because a so-called court reached "a decision," testifies to startling racism. Even the cautious Ryan (*World of Thomas Jeremiah*), does not attend sufficiently to the rule of law and thus speculates that Lord Campbell might have instigated revolt, that Jeremiah might—glossing over Whig reverend Smith's testimony from a legal point of view (59)—have been guilty. *As if* there must be some plausible evidence that Jeremiah "plotted" revolt, he extenuates the Patriots (56). For instance, Ryan notes that Jeremiah may have committed perjury about knowing Jemmy. But if innocent, why would he not have been frightened for his life before that "court" and tried to put them off as best he could? Ryan presents the deliberate misreading of the slave law of 1740 by one judge, Coslett, as if it was significant from a legal point of view. But there never should have been such a "trial" for a free citizen. The fact of "our" Revolution trumps the principle that made it great.

135. *PHL*, 10:321.

136. Ibid.

137. Campbell to Laurens, August 17, 1775, *PHL*, 10:334. Schama, *Rough Crossings*, describes this appeal as made "rather pathetically" (62). On the contrary, it is a sign of Campbell's honor and decency.

138. Campbell to Dartmouth, August 31, 1775, in Davies, *DAR*, 11:93.

139. Davies, *DAR*, 11:95.

140. Ibid., 96. For an account of Patriot tarrings and featherings at that time, see Ryan, *World of Thomas Jeremiah*, 56–57.

141. Davies, *DAR*, 11:95.

142. Ibid.

143. What had once been colonial bodies reconvened as independent decision makers.

144. Davies, *DAR*, 11:95.

145. *PHL*, 10:321–22. Schama, *Rough Crossings*, 59–65, does a journalistic "he said, she said" account of this material. Noting Campbell's horror, he concludes with Henry Laurens, whom he says was unconvinced by the "evidence" that swayed Campbell. Schama believes that the dangers of slave revolt mandated preemptive actions by slave owners (65). In one passage, he even says: "When he [Jeremiah] got into a fight with a white captain he had been put in the stocks, a serious ordeal in a place like Charleston, where delivering salutary correction to an uppity nigger would qualify as civic duty. In the circumstances Jerry was just a disaster in the offing. He had been conspicuous in helping to put out Charleston's many fires; why then should he not, when time and occasion presented itself set them?" (62–63). Here, in a racist vein, Schama empathizes with hysterical slave owners and loses himself. Whites should not be grateful that Jeremiah put out fires, he seems to say; instead, they should hang and burn Jeremiah because they imagine he *might* plan to set them. Schama alludes

to Henry Laurens's "decency as always" (85), though the actions he describes are murderous. Instead, he trusts Laurens's description of Jeremiah as a "silly coxcomb" (62); Patriot reverend Smith's letters to Campbell reveal Laurens's description as nothing but bigotry. The rule of law—the fundamental issue in the lynching—does not interest Schama.

146. *PHL*, 10:322.

147. John Laurens to Henry Laurens, October 4, 1775, *PHL*, 10:450.

148. Compare Ryan, *World of Thomas Jeremiah*, 159.

149. The international term "maroon" in English mirrors "*marron*" in French and derives from the Spanish "*cimarron*." In Hispaniola, the first island Europe conquered in the New World, the word initially referred to escaped cattle. It later indicated indigenous escapees. Columbus required of each Arawak a hawksbell of gold every three months or have a hand cut off. Because there was no gold on Hispaniola, his psychotic practices resulted in the eradication of roughly half a million indigenous people by 1520.

By the 1530s, the Spanish term referred to imported slaves from Africa and had acquired resonances of "fierce," "wild," and "unbroken." The existence of maroon settlements internationally manifests the depth of black enmity to bondage. Hispaniola later became the French colony Saint Domingue. In 1791 slaves launched a thirteen-year uprising to create the greatest *maroon regime*: Haiti.

150. Herbert Aptheker, "Maroons within the Present Limits," 152; Jeffrey Crow, *Black Experience*, 89–90.

151. Bull to Laurens, March 14, 1776, *PHL*, 11:163.

152. William Willis, "Divide and Rule," 158.

153. Aptheker, "Maroons within the Present Limits," 165.

154. Willis, "Divide and Rule," 161.

155. Ibid.

156. *PHL*, 11:164.

157. Laurens to Stephen Bull, March 16, 1776, *PHL*, 11:172

158. Ibid., 172–73.

159. Ibid., 172.

160. Ibid; Kaplan and Kaplan, *Black Presence*, 78.

161. Ryan, *World of Thomas Jeremiah*, 142–44,

162. *PHL*, 11:172.

163. Ryan, *World of Thomas Jeremiah*, 111–12.

CHAPTER 2

1. John Locke, *Second Treatise*, par. 4.

2. J. Philmore, *Two Dialogues on the Man-Trade*, 6–7.

3. Ibid., 7.

4. Montesquieu, *De l'esprit des lois*, 1.15, chap. 5.

5. Philmore, *Man-Trade*, 7.

6. Ibid., 10.

7. Ibid., 23, 24.

8. Ibid., 25.

9. By emphasizing the coercion for "subjects" involved in armies, Philmore improves this point from Montesquieu, *Esprit des lois*, 1.15, chap. 5.

10. Philmore, *Man-Trade*, 28.

11. In an idiom of his own, Philmore refers to Africa as "Negroland." Ibid., 29.

12. Ibid., 29–30. Aristotle mistakenly defended "natural" slavery. See Alan Gilbert, *Democratic Individuality*, chap. 1. Having corrected Locke's vision of the state of nature, however, Philmore inconsistently defends a Lockean claim about murderers. Locke declared that in cases of capital punishment, a prisoner may be enslaved, "for if he should think this a greater punishment than death, if he should chuse to die, rather than live all his days in that miserable state of slavery, it would be in his own power to deliver himself out of that state, by putting an end to his life" (Locke, *Second Treatise*, par. 4). (Following Locke, Philmore is not sure that suicide is "lawful"; Philmore, 30–31.) Philmore echoes this point. On the contrary, to execute or lock up a murderer is different from enslaving him. The former is a punishment for a crime committed by a free man; the latter is inconsistent with his human capacities, sabotages freedom in a regime, and breeds, as Montesquieu suggests, despotic mores in owners. In democratic theory, slavery corrupts the equal freedom of citizens; there can be no *right* to enslave another.

13. Philmore, *Man-Trade*, 34–35.

14. Technically, one might say that a trader lacks a "mens rea" for murder, but is guilty of kidnapping and torture in the course of which many die and, hence, murder.

15. Philmore, *Man-Trade*, 37.

16. Ibid., 41–42.

17. Ibid., 45.

18. Locke, *Second Treatise*, par. 176. Locke continues: "He that troubles his neighbor without a cause is punished for it by the justice of the court he appeals to. And he that appeals to Heaven must be sure he has right on his side; and a right too that is worth the trouble and cost of the appeal, as he will answer at a tribunal, that cannot be deceived, and will be sure to retribute to every one according to the mischiefs he hath created to his fellow-subjects."

19. Philmore, *Man-Trade*, 51.

20. Ibid., 55.

21. Ibid., 55–56.

22. Ibid., 56.

23. Marcus Rediker, "Motley Crew," 178.

24. Ibid.

25. James Otis, *The Rights of the British Colonies Asserted and Proved*, 56.

26. Ibid., 43.

27. Ibid., 57, 58.

28. Ibid., 43–44. On pp. 44–45, Otis repeatedly invokes Locke's words.

29. Ibid.

30. Ibid., 45.

31. Ibid., 46.

32. Louis Hartz, *The Liberal Tradition in America*, 6, 8, 10, 26, 59, 136.

33. George Mason, *The Papers of George Mason, 1725–1792* (cited hereafter as *PGM*), 1:61–62.

34. Ibid., 173.

35. Montesquieu, *Esprit des lois*, 1:389.

36. Mason, *PGM*, 1:173.

37. Though an opponent of the slave trade, Mason kept slaves.

38. Levi Hart, *Liberty Described and Recommended*, 9, 23; Joseph A. Conforti, *Samuel Hopkins and the New Divinity Movement*, 127.

39. Hart, *Liberty*, v, 16, 20; Arthur Zilversmit, *First Emancipation*, 107–8.

40. David Brion Davis, *The Problem of Slavery in the Age of Revolution*, 302.

41. Phyllis Wheatley, "Letter to the Native American Preacher Samuel Occom"; Sidney Kaplan, "The 'Domestic Insurrections' of the Declaration of Independence," 254.

42. Roger Bruns, ed., *Am I Not a Man and a Brother*, 397.

43. Conforti, *Samuel Hopkins*, 126–27.

44. Samuel Hopkins, *Dialogue concerning the Slavery of the Africans*, in Bruns, *Am I Not a Man and a Brother*, 397.

45. Ibid., 398.

46. Ibid., 413.

47. Ibid., 397.

48. Ibid., 399.

49. Ibid., 399, 414.

50. Ibid., 417–18.

51. Ibid., 401–2.

52. Ibid., 402.

53. Ibid.

54. These republican and abolitionist movements, once again, contradict Max Weber's thesis of a unique link between Protestantism and capitalism.

55. Bruns, *Am I Not a Man*, 407.

56. Ibid., 418–19.

57. Ibid., 422–23.

58. Ibid., 417, 405–6.

59. George Livermore, *An Historical Research Respecting the Opinions of the Founders*, 98.

60. Ibid.

61. Conforti, *Samuel Hopkins*, 130.

62. Livermore, *Historical Research*, 98.

63. Ibid.

64. John Woolman, *Journal*, 195–96.

65. Ibid., 186.

66. Ibid., 201–2.

67. In his first essay, "Some Considerations on the Keeping of Negroes" (1754), in Bruns, *Am I Not a Man and a Brother*, p. 71, Woolman contrasted the pride (hubris) that inspires men to dominate others with humility and equality: "When we remember that all Nations are of one Blood, *Gen*. iii. 20. that in this World we are but Sojourners, that we are subject to the like Afflictions and Infirmities of Body, the like Disorders and Frailties in Mind, the like Temptations, the same Death, and the same Judgment . . . it seems to raise an Idea of a general Brotherhood, and a Disposition easy to be touched with a Feeling of each others Afflictions; But when we forget those Things, and look chiefly at our outward Circumstances . . . our Breasts being apt to be filled with fond Notions of Superiority; there is Danger." Alan Gilbert, *Must Global Politics Constrain Democracy*, chap. 4, distinguishes between the Greek term "hubris," recognizing a moderation that characterizes love of self, and a Christian "pride" pitted against selfless "humility" and altruism. Invoking Sodom, Elhanan Winchester, the Calvinist minister, remarked in 1774, "Pride is another of the baleful effects of the [slave] trade; or whether it is not in some measure a cause, I shall not positively determine, but there is not the smallest doubt of their close connection" (Bruns, *Am I Not a Man*, 361).

68. Woolman, *Journal*, 214–15.

69. Ibid., 211.

70. He might have invoked the slaves in Egypt, but lacked a comparable compassion for Jews.

71. Woolman, *Journal*, 211.

72. Ibid., 212.

73. Ibid., 211–12.

74. Ibid., 215–16. The defiant phrase "no respecter of persons" would recur in John Brown's speech to the court after his capture at Harpers Ferry on November 2, 1859.

75. Bruns, *Am I Not a Man*, 68.

76. Amelia M. Gummere, ed., *The Journals and Essays of John Woolman*, 234–37.

77. "Historical Note," Papers of Moses Brown, Rhode Island Historical Society.

78. Bruns, *Am I Not a Man*, 311. The story may illustrate Quaker narrow-mindedness; the couple could have been in love.

79. Ibid.

80. Zilversmit, *First Emancipation*, 106.

81. Ibid., 107.

82. Washington to Reed, December 15, 1775, *Papers of George Washington, Revolutionary War Series* (cited hereafter as *PGW-RWS*), 2:553.

83. George Quintal's *Patriots of Color*, 39–44, enumerates 103, though this number, referring only to references in the records to "a man of color," is probably low.

84. "Proceedings of the Committee of Conference," October 18–24, 1775, *PGW-RWS*, 2:125.

85. Washington to Richard Henry Lee, December 26, 1775, PGW-RWS, 2:611.

86. Ibid.

87. Ibid., 620.

88. Nathanael Greene, *Papers of Nathanael Greene* (cited hereafter as *PNG*), 1:259.

89. Mark M. Boatner III, *Encyclopedia of the American Revolution*, 647–57.

90. Phillip Foner, *Blacks in the American Revolution*, 186.

91. Ron Chernow, *Alexander Hamilton*, 78.

92. David McCullough, "What the Fog Wrought," 197.

93. Henry Wiencek, *An Imperfect God*, 217.

94. Ibid.

CHAPTER 3

1. See Winthrop Jordan, *White over Black*, xii.

2. Laurens to Grant, November 1, 1765, *PHL*, 5:39–40.

3. Ibid., 31.

4. Ibid. In his November 1 letter to Grant, Laurens speaks more charitably of the sailor-"jacks": "The Mob consisted of about 60 or 80 nearly an equal number of Honest hearted Jacks & Townsmen, the former not knowing me & dreading no body were zealous to execute the business on which they were sent" (*PHL*, 5:39–40).

5. Pauline Meier, *From Resistance to Revolution*.

6. Laurens, *PHL*, 5:31n9.

7. Karl Marx and Friedrich Engels, *Collected Works*, 11:142; Alan Gilbert, *Marx's Politics*, chaps. 2, 9, and 12. In 1791 the same dynamic affected the outlook of mulattoes and blacks in Saint Domingue.

8. Sylvia R. Frey, *Water from the Rock*, 51; R. Palme Dutt, *Fascism and Social Revolution*.

9. *PHL*, 5:53–54.

10. Ibid., 54n9.

11. Henry Laurens to John Laurens, August 14, 1776, in *PHL*, 11:224.

12. Ibid., 225.

13. Ibid.

14. Ibid., 224–25.

15. Ibid., 225.

16. Laurens to Ettwein, March 19, 1763, in David Duncan Wallace, *Henry Laurens*, 445.

17. Cited in Sara Townsend, *An American Soldier*, 119.

18. Ibid.

19. Benjamin Franklin, *Autobiography of Benjamin Franklin*, 44. Emphasis added.

20. Townsend, *An American Soldier*, 119.

21. *PHL*, 11:50.

22. Ibid., 154.

23. Ibid., 55.

24. Ibid., 160.

25. Ibid., 174.

26. Ibid., 224, 227, 242, 346, 350–51, 354, 405–6.

27. Ibid., 464.

28. Ibid., 5.

29. Ibid., 28n, 39–40, 74, 155, 163,164, 172, 173n, 265, 350, 386, 410, 411–12, 414, 565.

30. Ibid., 199, 250.

31. Ibid., 271.

32. Ibid., 153, 174, 177.

33. Henry to John Laurens, March 16, 1776, ibid., 174.

34. Henry to John Laurens, August 14, 1776, ibid., 224.

35. *PHL*, 11:269.

36. Ibid., 487.

37. Ibid., 189.

38. Ibid., 224n4.

39. Ibid., 264.

40. Oddly, today's historians, such as Massey, Wiencek and Schama, often praise Henry Laurens at the expense of his son. They miss the psychological dynamic between hypocritical father and sincere son. More deeply, they do not appreciate the fundamental role of John Laurens in fighting for American abolition.

41. *PHL*, 11:275.

42. Ibid., 276–77.

43. For instance, Hamilton supported abolition, yet no trace of Rousseau shows in his writing.

44. Jean Jacques Rousseau, *Du contrat social*, bk. I, chap. 4, p. 37. Laurens also learned about emancipation from a poem by Thomas Day and John Bicknell, British abolitionists who supported the American Patriots. A May 1773 London newspaper story about the suicide of an unnamed "servant" of one Captain Ordington moved them. The servant had escaped, been christened, and intended to marry a white woman. Recaptured and returned to a ship in the Thames, he obtained a gun and committed suicide. These insights about Day and Bicknell are the best discovery in Gregory Massey's *John Laurens and the American Revolution*, 47, 62–63. In contrast, Schama, *Rough Crossings*, demeans Day as a "future moralizing novelist and utopian educator" and says, "What Day and Bicknell undoubtedly lacked in poetic talent they more than made up for with a flair for high-strung sentimental melodrama of the kind that struck directly at the post-Somerset generation's hearts" (56). In the British press's racist and sexist conventions of the time, only Ordington, not the black man or the white woman, is named. Thus, Day and Bicknell title their poem "The Dying Negro" and invoke the man: "Myself become a thing without a name." They conjure the fate of slaves: "Salute with groans unwelcome morn's return." Day and Bicknell, "The Dying Negro," pp. 9, 4.

The return of a black man to a ship in London harbor indicates that Chief Justice Mansfield's *Somersett* decision, reached but a year before, was enforced only by lawsuits brought against masters by slaves. Day and Bicknell hoped to instigate further abolitionist action in Britain. In an introduction to a second edition, despite their support for independence, they rightly criticized the incompleteness of an American freedom that failed to eliminate slavery: "Such is the inconsistency of mankind! these are the men whose clamours for liberty and independence are heard across the Atlantic" (ibid., ix). Laurens had joined the Chancery Lane chambers of Charles Bicknell, brother of John Bicknell. See Schama, *Rough Crossings*, 428n19. From John Bicknell, Laurens learned of Granville Sharp. Schama is surprised that Bicknell, Day, and Sharp sympathize with the American cause, yet decry the Patriots' slaveholding; their introduction, Schama says, "harangued American hypocrisy—notwithstanding the fact that Day thought of himself, as did Sharp, as the friend of America against the coercion of Lord North's government" (56). Schama has no name for a second revolution that initially challenged, but could also reinforce the first. At the end of this passage, Schama suggests, with some exaggeration, that the crusade of his hero Granville Sharp "changed [Laurens's] life, and five years later it almost changed America." Once again, he quickly turns away from this insight.

45. The general will aims at a common good, a will of all at a particular interest. A general will, for instance, upholds the right of each to vote. Without underlying basic rights, we might imagine a series of steadily contracting majority wills, wills of all, disenfranchising most voters. In *Must Global Politics Constrain Democracy*, I name this "self-undermining majority rule" (266n17).

46. Montesquieu, *Esprit des lois*,1.15, chap. 9.

47. Rousseau, *Du contrat social*, bk. 1, chap. 2, p. 4.

48. *PHL*, 11:277.

49. Ibid.

50. Ibid.

51. Ibid.

52. Curiously, in *An Imperfect God*, Wiencek imagines that Laurens could not have learned from Geneva and France. Instead, he *must* concur mainly with Locke. "As a student in England, Laurens had read the works of John Locke whose philosophy of innate human liberty underpinned the thinking of many American revolutionaries" (238). But only a Locke reshaped by J. Philmore and James Otis was antislavery. Furthermore, Locke did not emphasize egalitarian, small property-holding for citizens as did many American revolutionaries, notably John Laurens, who had learned from Rousseau. In addition, many of the Founders, including Laurens, profoundly studied Montesquieu.

53. Laurens to Kinloch, November 6, 1774, Myers Collection, microfilm, reel 3, Manuscripts and Archives Divisions, NYPL.

54. Laurens to Kinloch, May 28, 1776, Emmet Collection, NYPL.

55. Ibid.

56. Laurens to Kinloch, September 30, 1776, in ibid. Rawls adopts the "veil of ignorance" in the original position not only to rule out such interested judgments but also to bar slavery as a rational choice for a free and equal deliberator.

57. Looking to an egalitarian peasant republic, Rousseau was not a revolutionary and did not hope for the political transformation of France.

58. Historians have not previously recognized how decidedly Laurens took up Rousseau's vision.

59. Kinloch as reported in Laurens to Kinloch, June 16, 1776, Chamberlain Collection, Boston Public Library.

60. Ibid.

61. Kinloch to Laurens, July 1, 1776, in private hands, cited in Gregory D. Massey, *John Laurens and the American Revolution*, 60, 253n47.

62. Laurens to Kinloch, summer 1776, Emmet Collection.

63. The term "corruption," the destruction of a common good through mere pursuit of wealth (oligarchy) or democratic imperialism (Athens), emerges in Thucydides. Modern republican theorists, such as Machiavelli, Montesquieu, and Rousseau, sharpen this critique of oligarchic luxury. Marx's vision of the state as, in part, a tool of the capitalist class extends this older republican vision. Gilbert, *Marx's Politics*, chap. 12.

64. Laurens to Kinloch, June 16, 1776, Chamberlain Collection.

65. Laurens to Kinloch, September 30, 1776, and spring 1776, Emmet Collection.

66. Jean Jacques Rousseau, *Discourse on Political Economy*, 40.

67. Laurens to Kinloch, June 16, 1776, Chamberlain Collection.

68. Ibid.

69. Ibid.

70. Laurens to Kinloch, spring 1776, Emmet Collection.

71. Laurens to Kinloch, summer 1776, in ibid.

72. Ibid. To repair the friendship, Laurens also speculated happily on a potential romance of Kinloch with "the fair Miss Stephens."

73. John Laurens to Henry Laurens, *PHL*, 12:305.

74. John Laurens, PHL, 12:391.

75. Henry Laurens to John Laurens, January 22, 1778, *PHL*, 12:328–29.

76. John Laurens, *PHL*, 12:390.

77. Ibid., 391.

78. Ibid.

79. Ibid., 392.

80. Ibid.

81. Ibid.

82. Ibid.

83. Henry Laurens to John Laurens, February 6, 1778, ibid., 412.

84. Ibid.

85. In *Rough Crossings*, Schama reproduces Henry Laurens's position uncritically: "Military service [John] thought, was the perfect way to fit such men, accustomed only to servitude, for liberty. Henry Laurens, who owned three hundred slaves, unsurprisingly, thought differently" (101).

86. *PHL*, 12:413.

87. Benjamin Quarles, *Negro in the American Revolution*, 61.

88. *PHL*, 12:413. Even Quarles, *Negro in the American Revolution*, 61, emphasizes only this side of Henry Laurens and the subsequent attacks on him in South Carolina.

89. John to Henry Laurens, March 9, 1778, *PHL*, 12:532.

90. John to Henry Laurens, May 1779, handwritten letter in the Papers of Henry Laurens/John Laurens, LOC, 12 (the numbers were handwritten by the file's compiler).

91. Ibid., 8.

92. Ibid.

93. Ibid., 10.

94. Ibid.

95. John Laurens, March 10, 1779, in ibid.

96. Ibid. Laurens here prefigures the heroism of Robert Gould Shaw, commander of the Massachusetts Fifty-Fourth Regiment, composed of black soldiers who fought bravely in the Civil War. Due to their example, the North would enroll 184,000 blacks in that conflict. Patriots recruited blacks on a smaller scale. Still, in the American Revolution, Laurens and the First Rhode Island Regiment had the potential for a broadly similar role.

97. Ibid.

98. John Laurens, March 16, 1779, in ibid.

99. Schama, *Rough Crossings*, speaks derisively "of an improbable surge of idealism" in Henry Laurens (102). He demeans the son as "young Laurens" (it seems a preoccupation: on page 100, he describes him as "25" years old and on page 101, referring to an event two years earlier, as "23"). Yet he notices a reason why South Carolinians might have gone along: "Ironically, then, young Laurens's proposal could be promoted as a way of actually controlling black violence by harnessing it against the enemy rather than risking it being turned on the masters" (102). Otherwise, Schama makes dismissive judgments without giving counterarguments.

100. John Laurens to Henry Laurens, March 16, 1779, Papers of Henry Laurens/John Laurens.

101. Ibid., 12.

102. David Duncan Wallace, *Henry Laurens*, 449.

103. Henry Laurens to Washington, March 16, 1779, http://memory.loc.gov/cgi-bin/ampage?collId=mgw48fileName=gwpage056.dlb&recNum=911.

104. Washington to Henry Laurens, March 20, 1779 in Saul Padover, ed., *The Washington Papers*, 176.

105. Wiencek, *Imperfect God*, 230.

106. Ibid.

107. In *The Forgotten Fifth*, 12–13, Nash says that Washington opposed the Laurens proposal. But no proposal rejected by Washington would have passed the Continental Congress. Schama, *Rough Crossings*, rightly notes the meaning of Laurens's proposal: "This would have been a revolution indeed, and at a stroke would have disposed of British accusations of hypocrisy" (103). But he investigates the possibility no further.

108. Washington to Henry Laurens, March 20, 1779, in Padover, *Washington Papers*, 176.

109. Ibid.

110. Continental Congress, March 29, 1779, http://memory.loc.gov/cgi-bin/query/

r?ammem/hlaw:@field(DOCID+@lit(jc01380)); George Livermore, *Historical Research*, 133–34.

111. Without illustrations, Schama in *Rough Crossings* introduces John Laurens with the phrase "enough to stir his always restive conscience to action" (101) and adds "thirsty for action as always" (103). For Schama, there is no reason why anyone should fiercely oppose slavery or fight for revolution against an empire. Many of the rest of us, however, might honor Laurens and try to discern his reasons for standing out in these ways.

112. Wallace, *Henry Laurens*, 476–77.

113. Ibid.

114. Ibid., 478.

115. John Laurens to Henry Laurens, June 1, 1778, cited in ibid., 490.

116. As a result, historians have often added his name to Laurens's proposal.

117. Hamilton to Jay, March 14, 1779, in Alexander Hamilton, *Works of Alexander Hamilton*, 9:160.

118. Ibid.

119. Ibid., 161.

120. Ibid., 162.

121. Hamilton and Laurens became dear friends as well as comrades. They shared the masculine ethic of honor that makes them, in Aristotle's terms, magnanimous. (Gregory Massey, *John Laurens*, 82, invokes Aristotle on "honor." But magnanimity, the actions of a great-souled man—*megalopsuche*—has an arrogance toward others, a sense that one gives from superiority and that it is necessary to do favors but not accept them, which differs from honor. Aristotle, *Nicomachean Ethics*, bk. 4.) Ironically, that sense of honor also sealed their fates: Laurens died at the Combahee River in a meaningless skirmish in 1782 and Hamilton, years later, in a duel at the hand of Aaron Burr. Yet this ethic—as well as affection—inclined Hamilton to fight for a common good, the genuine republicanism of Laurens. As a disappointed older man, Hamilton would coauthor the antidemocratic *Federalist Papers*, which celebrate commerce at the expense of revolutionary soldier/farmers. He would also support the Alien and Seditions Acts. These reactionary stands overshadow his radiant, youthful republicanism.

Hamilton found himself deeply attracted to Laurens. In September 1779, he sent back a curious missive as a "jealous lover." Laurens apparently did not fully reciprocate Hamilton's ardor. In perhaps a defensive stratagem, Laurens had not responded, Hamilton complained, to "five or six letters." (Several of Laurens's letters to Hamilton are missing.) "When I thought you slighted my caresses," Hamilton urged, "my affection was alarmed and my vanity piqued." After coquetting with Laurens, Hamilton took up abolition. In what would for the later Hamilton be a shockingly republican vein, he even invoked the corruption—"the lethargy of voluptuous indolence"—of commerce and slaveholding: "even the animated and persuasive eloquence of my young Demosthenes will not be able to rescue his countrymen from the lethargy of voluptuous indolence or dissolve the fascination[s—word missing] of self-interest." Hamilton to John Laurens, September 1779, Papers of Henry Laurens/John Laurens. This handwritten letter has holes in it, sometimes removing vital words. Oddly, this letter does not appear in Hamilton's *Papers*.

122. Hamilton to Jay, March 14, 1779, in Hamilton, *Works of Alexander Hamilton*, 9:161.

123. Robert A. Hendrickson, *Hamilton*, 1:12–13.

124. Ron Chernow, *Hamilton*, chap. 1.

125. Hamilton, *Works of Alexander Hamilton*, 9:161.

126. Ibid.

127. Ibid., 160–61.

128. Ibid., 2:52.

129. Ibid.

130. Ibid., 53.

131. Massey, *John Laurens*, 6, 30, 60, 100, invokes, but does not spell out, Montesquieu's influence on Laurens.

132. Montesquieu, *Esprit des lois*, 1:157–58.

133. John Rutledge to John Laurens, May 26, 1779, Papers of Henry Laurens/John Laurens.

134. Washington later sent Lincoln to accept the British surrender at Yorktown.

135. Lincoln to Washington, November 7, 1779, http://www.familytales.org/db Display.php?id=ltr_bel3205&person=bel.

136. Livermore, *Historical Research*, 133–34.

137. Ibid., 134.

138. Ibid.

139. Ibid.

140. Quarles, *Negro in the American Revolution*, 64–65.

141. John Laurens to Washington, May 19, 1782, http://www.familytales.org/db Display.php?id=ltr_jol3703&person=jol.

142. Ramsay to Drayton, Charlestown, September 1, 1779, SCHS, in Gibbes, *DHAR*, 2:121.

143. Quarles, *Negro in the American Revolution*, 67.

144. In 1798 Jefferson and Madison wrote the Virginia and Kentucky Resolutions, which defended the rights of immigrant and citizen against the Alien and Sedition Acts, a unique, liberty-affirming instance of "states' rights."

145. Henry Laurens to John Laurens, September 21, 1779, in Wallace, *Henry Laurens*, 450–51.

146. John Laurens to Hamilton, July 14, 1779, *PAH*, 2:102, 103.

147. Ibid., 103.

148. Ibid.

149. See "Going Down: On a Democratic Interpretation of Plato," Democratic-individuality.blogspot.com/2010/08/going-down-on-democratic-interpretation.html. Despite capture in the temple at Calauria, Demosthenes secretly took poison. He said

to Archias, a confidant of Antipater, "'Now, as soon as you please you may commence the part of Creon in the tragedy [Sophocles, *Antigone*], and cast out this body of mine unburied. But . . . I, for my part, while I am yet alive, arise up and depart out of this sacred place; though . . . the Macedonians have not left so much as the temple unpolluted.' After saying these words, he passed by the altar, fell down and died" (Plutarch, "Demosthenes").

150. John Laurens to Hamilton, July 14, 1779, *PAH*, 2:103

151. Hamilton to Laurens, September 1779, Papers of Henry Laurens/John Laurens. In April 1779 (*PAH*, 2:34), Hamilton wrote to Laurens of "the favorable omens that precede your application to the Assembly," underlining how little the proposal appeared to him a joint effort.

152. If Laurens had survived the war and become a force in national politics, perhaps even president, he might have led America toward gradual emancipation.

153. Wallace, *Henry Laurens*, 451n2.

154. A Department of Education curriculum on *Teaching American History in South Carolina*, which provides summer institutes for teachers (last grant from the US Department of Education in 2007) includes only Henry Laurens's imprisonment in the Tower of London and no mention of John Laurens. In 2000, the University of South Carolina Press published Gregory Massey's *John Laurens and the American Revolution*. Startlingly, Massey downplays Laurens's role in converting Washington and the Continental Congress to emancipation in South Carolina and concludes, "He did not live to see his country win independence, nor did his espousal of emancipation even dent an institution to which his fellow Carolinians were committed universally" (240). See also Massey, *John Laurens*, 72–74, 194, 130–34. But black and white crowds, often antislavery, protested British press-gangs in Charlestown before the Revolution. In addition, with Thoreau and John Brown, there is something noble in being "a majority of one."

CHAPTER 4

1. In the twentieth and twenty-first centuries, such substitution occurs indirectly: through the 2-S–student—deferment during Vietnam or, more recently, poverty and a "volunteer army."

2. Benjamin Quarles, *Negro in the American Revolution*, 59.

3. Ibid., 59–60; Herbert Aptheker, ed., *Documentary History*, 14.

4. Lorenzo Greene, "Some Observations on the Black Regiment," 150.

5. George H. Moore, *Historical Notes*, 17; Charles Knowles Bolton, *Private Soldier*, 22.

6. Phillip Foner, *History of Black Americans*, 327–28; Fritz Hirschfeld, *George Washington and Slavery*, 156.

7. *Sic*—the actual number was 755; Frank Landon Humphreys, *Life and Times of David Humphreys*, 1:191–92.

8. Recruitment of free blacks in Virginia also reveals this embryonic trend as well as how limited it was.

9. Emma Kaplan and Sidney Kaplan, *Black Presence*, 4.

10. Ibid.

11. "The Memorial of Benjamin Whitecuff, a Black," June 3, 1784, AO 12119/1227061, PRO; Kaplan and Kaplan, *Black Presence*, 71.

12. For instance, for the National Archive, Debra L. Newman, "List of Black Servicemen," 1974, 2, counts several hundred black soldiers in the revolutionary army. She based her estimate on four categories. The first includes African names or words: Juba, Cudjo, Quok, Mingo, and Cuffee. Second, in an ugly parody of their ostensible republicanism, slave owners often named blacks for Roman and Greek politicians, tyrants, gods, or philosophers: Caesar, Cato, Scipio, Nero, Jupiter, and Plato. The third category is geographical names: Africa, Congo, London, Boston, and York. The fourth recognizes black adoption of the names of freedom: Free, Liberty, Freedom, and Freeman. Owners fecklessly used the blanket surname "negro," however. Newman also includes such names under the heading "status." As she rightly notes, however, no more than 5 percent of all blacks had names in these categories.

On a list of blacks who escaped to the British from Rhode Island, a list drawn up for Congress in 1786, five of thirty-eight had such names: around 12 percent. Original document in the RIHS. Only Louis Wilson's careful study ("List of Black and Narragansett Patriots in Rhode Island," RIHS, 1990) of 649 blacks and Narragansett Indians begins to depict the numbers on the Patriot side.

13. Washington Papers, microfilm, series 4, reel 46, LOC; Hirschfeld, *George Washington and Slavery*, 148.

14. *PNG*, 2:249n7. Greene and Olney would command the regiment.

15. George Livermore, *Historical Research*, 118–19; Arthur Zilversmit, *First Emancipation*, 119, surprisingly misses that the First Rhode Island Regiment fought throughout the war.

16. Zilversmit, *First Emancipation*, 119; Livermore, *Historical Research*, 120–21.

17. Livermore, *Historical Research*, 118–19. Theodore Ayrault Dodge, a nineteenth-century military historian, wrote on this theme.

18. Colonists also enslaved some Narragansetts. Rhode Island had already enlisted free blacks and Narragansett Indians, but analysis of black and Native American recruits from Rhode Island shows that just 11 percent were ex-slaves for whose liberty the state had paid.

19. Livermore, *Historical Research*, 118–19.

20. Greene, "Some Observations," 156.

21. John Russell Bartlett, ed., *Records of the State of Rhode Island*, 8:360.

22. Governor Nicholas Cooke to General Washington, Providence, January 19, 1778, in Greene, "Some Observations," 153. I am indebted to Greene's work.

23. Greene, "Some Observations," 153.

24. Cooke to Washington, February 23, 1778, in *PGW-RWS*, 13:646.

25. Greene, "Some Observations," 162.

26. Residence not reported.

27. *PNG*, 2:346, 347n6.

28. Greene, "Some Observations," 156–57.

29. Ibid., 162–63.

30. Ibid., 163.

31. In a letter to Governor Cooke, William Ellery indicated that the regiment consisted of "eight sergeants, nineteen corporals and one hundred and thirty-nine privates." In the State Treasurer's Reports for 1778, Rhode Island paid 93 owners for the recruitment of 110 blacks. See Ellery to Governor Cooke, Philadelphia, March 1, 1778, in Greene, "Some Observations," 163–64, 165n1.

32. *PNG*, 2:458.

33. Greene, "Some Observations," 163, 165.

34. Blacks often escaped to or intermarried with Narragansetts. Twenty-five members of the regiment had been born to black and Narragansett parents; none were slaves. I developed this number and others on the basis of Louis Wilson's list, RIHS.

35. Greene, "Some Observations," 165.

36. Kaplan and Kaplan, *Black Presence*, 70; Douglas R. Egerton, *Death or Liberty*, 256, corrects this story to be of Prince Whipple and owner William Whipple.

37. Samuel Greene Arnold, *History of Rhode Island*, 2:427–28. This premonition prefigures the widespread practice of American soldiers "fragging," that is, rolling a grenade into the tent of their officers in Vietnam. They responded especially to the racism that pushed blacks disproportionately to the front in a war largely conducted against civilians.

38. *PNG*, 2:503n7; Rita Elaine Souther, *Minority Military Service*, v.

39. Souther, *Minority Military Service*, v.

40. These prisoners represented 2.6 percent of the regiment.

41. The seven were 1 percent of the regiment.

42. The precise figure was 12.7 percent.

43. This represented 4.2 percent.

44. The festival displayed a letter of Captain Perkins to Brigadier General [Nathanael] Greene, Long Island, July 11, 1776, in the *Liberator*, March 12, 1858.

45. Livermore, *Historical Research*, 154.

46. Foner, *History of Black Americans*, 327.

47. Elleanor Eldridge's *Memoirs*, pp. 11–21, are in the RIHS, RHI(x3)4807.

48. Ibid.

49. Ibid.

50. Ibid.

51. Ibid.

52. Greene, "Some Observations," 171.

53. They were forced to serve as apprentices until those ages. In addition, the owners could free the mothers and require the state to support them. See Peter P. Hinks, John R. McKivigan, and R. Owen Williams, *Encyclopedia of Antislavery and Abolition*, 305.

54. Greene, "Some Observations," 172.

55. A 1777 return shows Burrough[s], along with Jack and York Champlin, to be the initial three recruits. The roster is in the RIHS.

56. Olney to Arthur Fenner, May 18, 1791, Jeremiah Olney Papers, RIHS.

57. On this list, only Cato Bannister would be otherwise identified as black.

58. Olney to Wolcott, April 2, 1794, Jeremiah Olney Papers.

59. Mary H. Mitchell, "Slavery in Connecticut," 302, does not name the woman.

60. Zilversmit, *First Emancipation*, 108.

61. Livermore, *Historical Research*, 113–14.

62. Ibid., 114–15.

63. Ibid.

64. Four certificates concern the military service of Prince Dupleix; see Dupleix File, Manuscript Division, LOC.

65. Heart's first name is unclear; perhaps it was Selah.

66. David O. White, *Connecticut's Black Soldiers*, 56–64.

67. Ibid., 60–62.

68. At a celebration of Crispus Attucks's Day in Boston in 1858, organizers displayed this certificate.

69. White, *Connecticut's Black Soldiers*, 25.

70. In Massachusetts, only Jupiter Free changed his name; see Quarles, *Negro in the American Revolution*, 51–52.

71. Livermore, *Historical Research*, 116–17.

72. Ibid.

73. Humphreys, *Life and Times of David Humphreys*, 1:191–92.

74. Washington freed William Lee in his will.

75. Hirschfeld, *Washington and Slavery*, 151.

76. White, *Connecticut's Black Soldiers*, 8, 56, 57–64.

77. Kench to the House of Representatives, in Livermore, *Historical Research*, 125.

78. Ibid.

79. Ibid.

80. Kench, "To the Honorable Council in Boston," April 7, 1778, in Livermore, *Historical Research*, 126.

81. Ibid.

82. Reverend Theodore Parker suggested that the initials are of Washington and Hancock. In an unpublished manuscript, the historian Anne Bentley speculates that the initials may be of Hancock's infant son, John George Washington Hancock, who died in February 1787. In *Colored Patriots*, 24–25, abolitionist historian William Nell interviewed Mrs. Margaret B. Kay of Boston, daughter of the ensign who received the flag, and reports that Hancock and his son presented the company with the flag. Nell purchased it from Kay and eventually gave it to the Massachusetts Historical Society. The society also possesses a silver badge with many of the same inscriptions; the initials "M. W.," differ. Nell's research on black Patriots kept many stories alive.

83. Livermore, *Historical Research*, 93–95.

84. William Cooper Nell, *Services of Colored Americans*, 13.

85. At a ceremony in 1858 at Faneuil Hall, Reverend Theodore Parker described the Bucks as "the first company, I think it was, of colored persons ever organized in Massachusetts." He contrasted them to the "association of colored men called 'The Protectors' who guarded the property of Boston merchants during the Revolutionary War." Most likely, the Bucks fought alongside the Continental army. Four witnesses, Mrs. Kay, a Mrs. Brown (daughter of Cornelius Haskell, killed at Bunker Hill), Grandmother Boston (age 105), and Father Vassall (age 88), all of whom had direct ties to the soldiers or lived through the period, attended the celebration. See *Liberator*, March 12, 1858.

86. Child was a Swedenborgian. Tisa Anders, "Religion and Advocacy Politics in L. Maria Child."

87. Nell, *Colored Patriots*, 25.

88. Ibid., 26. This patronizing phrase possessed her. All democrats should celebrate this day, white as much as black. Perhaps the election of Barack Obama as president finally indicates this.

89. Ibid.

90. Ibid.

91. Karl Marx, *Capital*, 1:301.

92. Nell, *Colored Patriots*, 87–88.

93. Ibid., 89–90.

94. Paul Cuffe and John Cuffe, February 18, 1781, draft of petition, in Cuffe, *Papers*, LOC.

95. Nell, *Colored Patriots*, 90.

96. The first clause of the Vermont Bill of Rights, July 8, 1777, states: "That all men are born equally free and independent, and have certain natural, inherent and unalienable rights. . . . Therefore, no male person, born in this country, or brought from over sea, ought to be holden by law, to serve any person, as a servant, slave, or apprentice, after he arrives to the age of twenty-one years, nor female, in like manner, after she arrives to the age of eighteen years." See http://faculty.cua.edu/pennington/law111/VermontBillRights.htm.

97. Gary B. Nash and Jean R. Soderlund, *Freedom by Degrees*, 80.

98. Ibid., 79–80.

99. Ibid., 81.

100. Ibid., 95.

101. Ibid., 84, 89.

102. Zilversmit, *First Emancipation*, 126.

103. Ibid.

104. Ibid.

105. Pitting blacks and Native Americans against whites, anti-"miscegenation" legislation would characterize racial relations in the United States from colonial times though the mid-twentieth century. Such alliances broke down divisions crucial to elite rule.

106. Zilversmit, *First Emancipation*, 127; *Pennsylvania Packet*, March 4, 1779.

107. *Pennsylvania Packet*, December 23, 1779; Zilversmit, *First Emancipation*, 129.

108. Zilversmit, *First Emancipation*, 129; *Pennsylvania Packet*, December 25, 1779, January 1, 1780; Burton Alva Konkle, *George Bryan*, 190.

109. Kaplan and Kaplan, *Black Presence*, 30–31.

CHAPTER 5

1. General Order Book for the British Troops under Genl. Howe, 1776–78, Headquarters, Philadelphia, March 22, 1778, Howe Papers, WLCL-UM.

2. Ira Berlin, *Many Thousands Gone*, 258.

3. Return of Persons Who Came Off from Virginia with General Matthews in the Fleet the 24th of May, 1779, PRO 30/55/95.

4. Kirkland to His Majesty's Commissioners, Clinton Papers, vol. 43, no. 38, WLCL-UM.

5. Ibid.

6. Robert Olwell, *Masters, Slaves and Subjects*, 249n115; Alton Hornsby Jr., *Negro in Revolutionary Georgia*, 11.

7. Bernhard A. Uhlendorf, ed., *Siege of Charleston*, 193, 184, 379.

8. Boston King, "Memoirs of the Life," 354.

9. Ibid.

10. Emma Nogrady Kaplan and Sidney Kaplan, *Black Presence*, 79.

11. Archibald Campbell to Unknown, January 9, 1779, Prioleau Papers, SCHS; Olwell, *Masters, Slaves and Subjects*, 250.

12. "South Carolina Prisoners of War," in Olwell, *Masters, Slaves and Subjects*, 257.

13. Thomas Jefferson, *Thomas Jefferson's Farm Book*, 48, 232n23.

14. Jefferson to Gordon, in George Livermore, *Historical Research*, 137.

15. In an example of wish fulfillment, Jefferson also exaggerated: twenty-seven thousand killed by disease. Both numbers add three zeroes to his report from his own plantation. Nonetheless, such guesses indicate a rough magnitude. Jefferson meant, "I lost every slave, my neighbors lost every slave, most owners lost every slave." To Gordon, he wrote: "From an estimate I made at the time . . . I supposed the state of Virginia lost, under Lord Cornwallis's hand, that year, about thirty thousand slaves; and that, of these, twenty-seven thousand died of the small-pox and camp-fever; and the rest were partly sent to the West Indies, and exchanged for rum, sugar, coffee, and fruit; and partly sent to New York, from whence they went, at the peace, either to Nova Scotia or to England. From this last place, I believe, they have been lately sent to Africa. History will never relate the horrors committed by the British Army in the Southern States of America." See Jefferson to Gordon, in Livermore, *Historical Research*, 137–38.

16. Kaplan and Kaplan, *Black Presence*, 73–74.

17. Benjamin Quarles, *Negro in the American Revolution*, 113.

18. James W. St. G. Walker, *Black Loyalists*, 57.

19. Kaplan and Kaplan, *Black Presence*, 78.

20. Thirty-nine scouts and eight waggoners; see Clinton Papers, vol. 37, no. 39.

21. Sixty-two men (sixty scouts and two "waggoners"), twenty women, and fourteen children; Clinton Papers, vol. 37, no. 18.

22. Forty-two men (forty-one scouts and one "waggoner"), nineteen women, and eight children; Clinton Papers, vol. 54, no. 20.

23. Forty-three men, thirty-two women, and twenty-eight children; Clinton Papers, vol. 66, no. 36.

24. One man and three women had joined; Clinton Papers, vol. 69, no. 17.

25. Order concerning Virginia Refugees, June 18, 1779, vol. 52, no. 62, item no. 10235, summarized in *Report on American Manuscripts in the Royal Institution*, 1:451.

26. Each company had three white officers, six black sergeants and corporals, thirty "fit for duty," four sick in barracks and the hospital, and six who had "deserted since they came from Philadelphia." But the companies had varying numbers of casualties: one, three, and three, respectively, who had been discharged by order of Lord Rawdon, as well as ten, twenty-eight, and twenty dead, respectively. Each unit had since recruited twelve; the soldiers were supposedly accompanied by exactly sixteen women and fifteen children for each unit.

27. Clinton Papers, vol. 41, no. 29.

28. Seventy-four black men, sixteen women, and fifteen children.

29. Ibid.

30. On the ship *Margery*, three are listed as servants (who were probably not slaves); the rest are soldiers/sailors and their families.

31. Return of Those Who Came Off from Virginia with General Matthews in the Fleet, May 24, 1779, PRO 30/55/95.

32. Once again, even among whites, the ratio is forty-six men to forty-four women and children.

33. Return of the Number of Men, Women, and Children of the British and Foreign Regiments New Levies Civil Departments &c Victualled at New York and the Different Out Posts between 14th & 21st November, 1779, signed by Daniel Wier, Clinton Papers, vol. 76, no. 21. Four other returns survive for this period: for March 16 to 24, July 23 to 29, August 22 to 29, and September 19 to 26.

34. Fifty-six men, twenty-five women, and twenty children; ibid.

35. Ibid. For March 16–24, Wier indicates a greater number: 29,630 men, 3,386 women, and 3,096 children. "Stuart's Black Company" included a smaller number than the later report: 41 men, 19 women, and 8 children, for a total of 68. Clinton Papers, vol. 54, no. 20.

36. Ibid.

37. In the South, large numbers of blacks worked in the artillery and engineers. The Royal Regiment of Artillery lists 505 men, 117 women, and 103 children; the Engineers Department includes 314 men but only 12 women and 25 children.

38. Memorial of the Officers, Emmerich's Chasseurs, June 22, 1779, Clinton Papers, vol. 61, no. 20.

39. Return of the Number of Men, Women & Children . . . Victualled at New York . . . between the 19th and 26th September, 1779, Clinton Papers, vol. 69, no. 17.

40. An Abstract of the Number of Men, Women, and Children, Negroes, and Prisoners Victualled at Savannah from 11th to 20th October, 1779, Clinton Papers, vol. 72, no. 10.

41. Ibid.

42. One heroic black soldier, Austin, fought for Georgia.

43. An Abstract of the Number of Men, Women and Children, Negroes and Prisoners Victualled at Savannah from 11th to 20th October, 1779.

44. *Charlestown Royal Gazette*, April 24, 1782; Olwell, *Masters, Slaves and Subjects*, 257.

45. Or 608 if the small numbers are subtracted as servants.

46. Clinton Papers, vol. 72, no. 10.

47. Archibald Campbell, *Journal of an Expedition*, 86.

48. Todd W. Braisted, "Black Pioneers and Others," 20–21.

49. Abstract of Men Victualled at Gibb's Landing, Camp Charlestown Neck from April 7 to 9, 1780, MacKenzie Papers, WLCL-UM.

50. Return of Clerks, Storekeepers, Waggon Masters, Conductors, Artificers, Boatmen & Labourers Employed in the Quarter Master Generals Department in South Carolina, 1st June, 1780, signed John McKinnon, Clinton Papers, vol. 102, no. 47.

51. Muster Roll of the Civil Branch of Ordnance Attending His Majesty's Field Train of Artillery, Charlestown So. Carolina, 30th June, 1780, signed George Wray, Wray Papers, WLCL-UM.

52. The four first names may be after Alexr McBride and, also, be McBrides. But the large group and the absent last names (or assumed recurring ones) suggest blacks. The *Book of Negroes* often lists families of the same master in this way; it is unlikely that four brothers enlisted from Britain in a company of thirty. Peleg Carr may be a name for a white or black (as may many others on the list). Muster Roll of the Civil Branch of Ordnance Attending His Majesty's Train of Artillery at Rhode Island, 1 July, 1779, signed George Wray, Wray Papers.

53. A Return of Negroes for the Royal Artillery Department, Lenings Landing, April 28, 1780, signed by P. Traille, Clinton Papers, vol. 95, no. 27.

54. The lists, signed William Wilson, Royal Artillery, are in the Wray Papers, vols. 6 and 7.

55. Lisbon, Dick, Peter, Plenty, Bob, and Catto Smith; Sanco, Cyfax, and Clark Bee; Cipio and Liewe Black; Bob and Catto Tines; Quash, George, and Harvey Wilkinson; Dick and Bob White; Paul and Tom Coal; Joe and Will Devant; Monday, Tom, Titus and Winter Stone; and Tom and Jesse Shigalton.

56. General List of Negroes Employed in the Royal Artillery Department for the Month of November (and December), 1781, Wray Papers, vol. 7.

57. Olwell, *Masters, Slaves and Subjects*, 248.

58. "John Ball's Planting Book for the Year 1780," Ball Family Papers, William Perkins Library. Olwell, *Masters, Slaves and Subjects*, 251, says one "returned to work" which is a slave owner's description; the person briefly returned to bondage.

59. Samuel Mathis, *Journal*, March 26, 1781, SCL-USC; Olwell, *Masters, Slaves and Subjects*, 251.

60. Sylvia Frey, *Water from the Rock*, 140, 165.

61. Johann Ewald, *Diary of the American War*, 298 (April 17, 1781).

62. Ibid., 183 (June 29, 1779); Gilbert, *Must Global Politics Constrain Democracy*, chap. 4.

63. Ewald, *Diary*, 183–86.

64. Ibid., 203 (March 4, 1780).

65. Ibid., 221 (April 1, 1780); see also 278.

66. Ewald notes that near Portsmouth, Virginia, "the Negroes and the entire garrison were put to work." But the British had neither brought the right tools from New York nor requisitioned them in the countryside. Ibid., 289 (March 17, 1781).

67. Ibid., 219–20 (March 31, 1780).

68. Olwell, *Masters, Slaves and Subjects*, 251–52.

69. Ewald, *Diary*, 305 (April 30, 1781).

70. Ibid.

71. Ibid.

72. Quarles, *Negro in the American Revolution*, 27.

73. Ibid., 63n51.

74. Olwell, *Masters, Slaves and Subjects*, 252–53.

75. Clinton to Cornwallis, May 20, 1780, in Frey, *Water from the Rock*, 119.

76. Patterson to the Board of Police, June 13, 1780, "Proceedings of the Board of Police," CO 5/520/2, PRO.

77. Proceedings of the Board of Police, July 14, 1780, CO 5/520/7, PRO; Olwell, *Masters, Slaves and Subjects*, 253.

78. John W. Pulis, "Bridging Troubled Waters," 187–88.

79. Campbell, *Journal of an Expedition*, 33–34.

80. Ibid., 53.

81. Ibid., 56.

82. Particularly at the battle of Charlestown, black soldiers were vital to British victory. Yet Campbell made no favorable comment about this. On February 11, 1779, he planned a surprise attack on Lytell's post. But in the middle of the night, "a very great Noise and scattered Firing" took place all across the swamp along his planned route. As he wrote later in his *Journal*: "Four Negroes on Horseback [swam] toward the Bank; These Fellows surrendered their Arms and informed [the Soldiers] that they had stolen their Master's Horses and made the best of their Way to our Army" (ibid., 65). In hot pursuit, Patriots wrecked Campbell's plan for surprise.

83. Cruden to Dunmore, January 5, 1782, in Livermore, *Historical Research*, 142.

84. Ibid., 142–43.

85. Ibid., 144.

86. Ibid., 143.

87. Ibid., 144–45.

88. Ibid., 143–44.

89. Dunmore to Clinton, February 2, 1782, in ibid., 146.

90. Ibid., 147.

91. Dunmore to Germain, February 5, 1782, in K. G. Davies, ed., *Documents of the American Revolution*, 21:37.

92. Ibid., 36–37.

93. Dunmore to Germain, in Livermore, *Historical Research*, 147–48.

94. Ibid., 148.

95. Peter Jennings Wrike, *Governor's Island*, 166–67.

96. Leslie to Clinton, March, 1782, vol. 23, no. 106, item no. 4331, summarized in *Report on American Manuscripts in the Royal Institution*, 2:438.

97. Peter Kolchin, *Unfree Labor*, 320.

98. Cited in Berlin, *Many Thousands Gone*, 294, 301.

99. Olwell, *Masters, Slaves and Subjects*, 250.

100. Rutledge to Garden, March 2, 1780, SCHS, in Robert Wilson Gibbes, ed., *DHAR*, 2:139.

101. Gervais to Henry Laurens, March 29, 1780, Henry Laurens Papers, SCL-USC.

102. David George, "An Account of the Life of David George."

103. Kolchin, *Unfree Labor*, 286.

104. Ibid., 288–89.

105. Berlin, *Many Thousands Gone*, 263.

106. Olwell, *Masters, Slaves and Subjects*, 243–50, 260–65.

107. This is one of Pulis's themes in *Moving On*; see xiii, xxin1, 183.

108. William R. Ryan, *World of Thomas Jeremiah*, 115–18, 129, 190–91, reproduces another Audit Office document: AO 12/147/17.

109. Scipio Handley, Petition, Audit Office, class 13, vol. 119, folio 431, PRO.

110. Ibid.

111. John Wright, "Notice of Rent," Savannah, December 11, 1779, PANS, RG 1, 170:332–33.

112. Edward Cooper, certificate for David George, ibid.

113. George, "An Account of the Life," 336.

114. Ibid.

115. Pulis, "Bridging Troubled Waters," 194.

116. Ibid.

117. Ibid., 195; George Liele, "An Account of Several Baptist Churches," 327.

118. Pulis, "Bridging Troubled Waters," tables on 185–86. Indentures lasted from three to seven years. Pulis estimates that 200 free blacks came to Jamaica in the mid-1780s, of whom 133, for the towns of Kingston and St. Catharine's, are recorded in archives. Pulis's figures do not include, however, a probably sizeable number of indentured servants, including Liele.

119. Hornsby, "Negro in Revolutionary Georgia," 5.

120. Pulis, "Bridging Troubled Waters," 207–8.

121. Letter from Monmouth County, *New Jersey Gazette*, April 24, 1782, reel 2, Ameri-

can Antiquarian Society. Schama, *Rough Crossings*, 121, mentions Captain Tye but does not understand the significance of irregulars.

122. Graham Russell Gao Hodges, *African-Americans in Monmouth County*, 15.

123. In 1778 they finally ostracized Corlis: "After a considerable Deal of Labour bestowed on him Respecting his keeping Negroes in Slavery, he still continues to decline complying with the yearly meeting.... Therefore there is the necessity to disown him" (ibid., 18n40).

124. Larry R. Gerlach, ed., *Documentary History of the American Revolution in New Jersey*, 147–49.

125. Henry Melchior Muhlenberg, *Journals of Henry Melchior Muhlenberg*, 3:105.

126. Hodges, "African-Americans," 18n54. I am indebted to Hodges's work on Tye.

127. Ibid., 18n56.

128. Hodges (ibid., 35) sees the causality going the other way. But Tye began his raids a year before Franklin's proposal, which does not mention blacks.

129. William Franklin was the son of Benjamin Franklin, who opposed bondage and would become, after the Revolution, president of the burgeoning Pennsylvania Abolition Society. In an unusual competition, William, who on the imperial side stood with Tye, spurred on his father.

130. Franklin to Andre, May 29, 1779, Clinton Papers; Sheila Skemp, *William Franklin*, 235.

131. Skemp, *William Franklin*, 235–36; Tryon to Clinton, July 20, 1779, C05/82/46–48, PRO.

132. Graham Russell Gao Hodges, "Black Resistance," 16.

133. Hodges, "African-Americans," 18n54; Africans in America, Narrative, Revolution, Colonel Tye, www.pbs.org/wgbh/aia/part2/2narr4.html.

134. Shrewsbury was where Titus had been enslaved. Graham Russell Gao Hodges, "Black Revolt in New York City," 35.

135. Ibid. Hodges recognizes that a much larger picture of black efforts in the American Revolution would yield startling conclusions. This book hopes to paint such a portrait.

136. Interview with Professor Margaret Washington, Department of History, Cornell, in Africans in America, Narrative, Revolution, Colonel Tye, www.pbs.org/wgbh/aia/part2/2:1632.html.

137. Letter from Trenton, April 12, 1780, published in the *Pennsylvania Evening Post* (Philadelphia), June 30 1780, in *Early American Newspapers: Pennsylvania Evening Post*, October 23, 1777–October 26, 1784, Yale University. microfilm, reel 2.

138. Kaplan and Kaplan, *Black Presence*, 81.

139. This appearance of slaves in arms at their homes gave many in the North reason to fear bondage and liberate blacks. Along with the positive logic of freedom—if whites were, by nature, free, why not blacks?—and the small number of slaves, fear of this kind of insurrection contributed to gradual emancipation in the northern states from 1780 to 1804. There, emancipation and independence were linked. Only for the South does the question remain: Why didn't independence lead to emancipation?

140. Hodges, "Black Revolt in New York City," 21,

141. Forman to Governor Livingston, June 9, 1780, in Livingston, *Papers of William Livingston*, 3:423n3

142. Ibid., 323.

143. Livingston, "To the Assembly," Trenton, June 6, 1780, in ibid., 421.

144. Ibid., 323n4.

145. Kaplan and Kaplan, *Black Presence*, 81–82

146. Hodges, *African-Americans in Monmouth County*.

147. Letter from Monmouth County, June 22, 1780, *Pennsylvania Evening Post*, June 30, 1780, microfilm, reel 2.

148. Skemp, *William Franklin*, 257 and n. 44.

149. Letter from Monmouth, October 3, 1778, *Pennsylvania Packet*, January 7, 1778–December 30, 1780, American Antiquarian Society, reel 2.

150. Varick to Philip Van Rensselaer, October 30, 1778, Varick Papers, NYHS.

151. Hodges, "Black Resistance," 16–17.

152. In a typical racist listing, however, the British note 92 officers and men "(+) 20 Negroes." See Braisted, "Black Pioneers," 24.

153. Abraham Cuyler to Major John Andre, August 1, 1780, Clinton Papers, vol. 114, no. 21.

154. Letter from Monmouth County, *New Jersey Gazette*, April 24, 1782, reel 2, American Antiquarian Society.

155. Interview with Professor Margaret Washington.

156. Kaplan and Kaplan, *Black Presence*, 81.

157. Romeyn to Varick, July 20, 1782, Varick Papers.

158. Hodges mistakenly calls them "black mobs," as does Paul Gilje in *The Road to Mobocracy*, 147–53. In fact, they are freedom fighters, as worthy as the integrated participants in the Boston Tea Party.

159. Romeyn to Varick, July 20, 1782, Varick Papers.

160. *Pennsylvania Packet*, October 28, 1783.

161. Letter from Freehold, Monmouth County, in *New Jersey Gazette*, April 24, 1782, reel 2, American Antiquarian Society.

162. Skemp, *William Franklin*, 343n44, 257–58.

163. Ibid., 257n42.

164. Hodges, "Black Revolt in New York City," 38.

165. Letter from Monmouth County, *New Jersey Gazette*, April 10, 1782

166. Clinton to Franklin, April 20, 1782, Washington Papers at the Library of Congress, Series 4, General Correspondence, image 390–91 (memory/locgov/search: William Franklin), http://memory.loc.gov/cgi-bin/query/P?mgw:7:./temp/~ammem_GSkB::.

167. Clinton to Franklin, April 26, 1782, image 618, ibid.

168. Braisted, "Black Pioneers," 25.

169. Cited in ibid., 25–27; Court Martial Proceedings against Samuel Doremus

et al., War Office Papers 71/96/126–307, PRO. For Ward's Blacks, see Hodges, "Black Resistance," 16.

170. Braisted, "Black Pioneers," 27.

CHAPTER 6

1. "List of the Names of the Negroes belonging to Capt Martin's Company," 1778, Clinton Papers, WLCL-UM. "Lookouts Folly" and "Rock fish" are in North Carolina.

2. Jill Lepore, "Goodbye Columbus," 1.

3. Statement of Lieutenant Murphy Steele, August 16, 1781, Clinton Papers.

4. Ibid.

5. Though Steele did not know the background, the idea was not new. Among political philosophers, Machiavelli and Rousseau had advised legislators to use divinity to make strange laws convincing. In Machiavelli's words, "Nor in fact was there ever a legislator who in introducing extraordinary laws to a people, did not have recourse to God, for otherwise they would not be accepted, since many benefits of which a prudent man is aware, are not so evident to reason that he can convince others of them" (Machiavelli, *Discourses*, 1:11). He got this idea from Plato's *Laws*. See Alan Gilbert, "Do Philosophers Counsel Tyrants," *Constellations* (March 2009). To enact laws for a common good, Rousseau recommended speaking in God's voice: "This is what has always forced the fathers of nations to have recourse to the intervention of heaven, and to attribute their own wisdom to the Gods so that the people might obey with freedom and bear with docility the yoke of public felicity." But men who lack strategic wisdom, Rousseau suggests, cannot make the Lord speak: "Any man can engrave stone tablets, buy an oracle, pretend to have a secret relationship with some divinity, train a bird to talk in his ear, or find other crude ways to impress the people. One who knows only that much might even assemble, by chance, a crowd of madmen, but he will never found an empire, and his extravagant work will die with him" (Rousseau, *Social Contract*, 69).

6. Simon Schama, *Rough Crossings*, 120–21, cites Steele's words, but only as a "straight man" to his own cynicism about Cornwallis: "God must have been joking, for he let Cornwallis march or stagger into the trap carefully laid by Washington and Rochambeau, whilst Clinton let him stay there." The rare words of a black man are here ignored to mock "the great." Steele's strategic wisdom escapes Schama.

7. Leslie to Clinton, December 27, 1781, in K. G. Davies, ed., *DAR*, 20:287.

8. Eliza Wilkinson, *Letters of Eliza Wilkinson*, 29; Robert Olwell, *Masters, Slaves and Subjects*, 258. White soldiers also "plundered."

9. Lincoln to Marion, Charlestown, December 30, 1779, SCHS, in Gibbes, *DHAR*, 3:6.

10. Benjamin Franklin Hough, *The Siege of Savannah*, cited in Olwell, *Masters, Slaves and Subjects*, 257.

11. *Royal Georgia Gazette*, November 18, 1779, http://www.loc.gov/rr/news/18th/84.html; Todd W. Braisted, "The Black Pioneers," 21.

12. Gervais to Henry Laurens, April 28, 1780, Henry Laurens Papers, SCL-USC; Olwell, *Masters, Slaves and Subjects*, 257.

13. Matthews to White, April 26, 1782, White Collection, PANS, no. 130.

14. Ibid.

15. Letter 3 in Wilkinson, *Letters of Eliza Wilkinson*, 28–29. Cf. 9–10.

16. Letter 3, ibid., 29.

17. "We were crossing a place they call the Sands, when one of the enemy's Negroes came out of the woods. He passed our advance guard with nothing but the loss of his smart Jocky cap, which was snatched from his head. He turned round and muttering something, then proceeded on; when, attempting to pass our rear-guard, he was immediately leveled to the earth; he arose, and attempted to run off, when he received another blow, which again brought him down. I could not bear the sight of the poor wretch's blood, which washed his face and neck. . . . 'Enough, Joe! enough,' cried I; 'don't use the creature ill, take him at once, I wont have him beaten so.' 'Let me alone, Mistress, I'll not lay hand on him till I have stunned him; how do I know but he has a knife, so some such thing under his clothes, and when I go up to him, he may stab me. No, no,—I know Negroes' ways too well.' With that he fetched him another blow. I was out of all patience; I could not help shedding tears. I called out again, 'Inhuman wretch, take the Negro at once, he cannot hurt you now if he would; you shall not—I declare you shall not beat him so.'" Wilkinson heard a commotion. She feared capture by the British with her bloodied prisoner and being put to death. Still, she opposed Joe's proposal to drag the prisoner into the bushes and murder him. She called another black to take the captive away. The noise, however, did not turn out to be redcoats. See letter 6, ibid., 67–68, 70 and letter 7, 72–74. The noise came from slaves quarreling about carrying her baggage.

18. Sumpter to Marion, February 20, 1781, SCHS, in Gibbes, *DHAR*, 3:23.

19. Treaty between General Marion and Major Ganey, June 17, 1781, SCHS, in ibid., 98.

20. Rutledge to Marion, September 2, 1781, SCHS, in ibid., 131.

21. Marion to Horry, March 10, 1782, SCHS, in ibid., 267.

22. John Matthews to Marion, October 6, 1782, SCHS, in ibid., 2:232–33.

23. Jno. McKinnon, "Certificate on the Death of Harry," Audit Office, class 13, vol. 4, folio 321, PRO.

24. Robert Andrews, "Abstract of Pay to Black Dragoons," July 1–September 30, 1782, Treasury Office, class 50, vol. 2, folio 372, PRO.

25. Jim Piecuch, *Three Peoples, One King*, 317.

26. March Kingston, "Memorial to the Honorable Commissioners Appointed by Act of Parliament for Enquiring into the Losses of Services of the American Loyalists," Audit Office, class 13, vol. 30, folio 293, PRO.

27. William Matthews to White, April 26, 1782, White Collection, MG 1, Vo1.947, folio 130, PANS.

28. *Book of Negroes*, document 10427, PRO 30/55/100.

29. The list of émigrés on the *L'abondance* includes two John Jacksons. But the second would only have been eighteen in 1782.

30. The entries for John and Hannah Jackson are also in Graham Russell Gao

Hodges, ed., *The Black Loyalist Directory*. After doing research on two versions of the *Book*, I learned of this volume in 2003.

31. Piecuch, *Three Peoples, One King*, 317.

32. Pinckney to Middleton, August 13, 1782, in Joseph W. Barnwell, ed., "Correspondence of Hon. Arthur Middleton," *South Carolina Historical Magazine* 28 (1926): 64; Olwell, *Masters, Slaves and Subjects*, 259.

33. "Extracts from the Journal of Lt. John Bell Tilden," 225; Olwell, *Masters, Slaves and Subjects*, 259.

34. John Matthews to Marion, August 29, 1782, SCHS, in Gibbes, *DHAR*, 2:215–16.

35. Marion to John Matthews, August 30, 1782, 38–43-6, Middleton Papers, SCHS; Sylvia R. Frey, *Water from the Rock*, 138.

36. Bee to Governor Benjamin Matthews, December 9, 1782, Bee Papers, SCL-USC; Olwell, *Masters, Slaves and Subjects*, 259n161. I am indebted to Olwell's research on the Black Dragoons.

37. Africans-in-America teacher's guide, www.pbs.org/wgbh/aia/part2/2p50.html.

38. In 1800 the near miss of Gabriel's revolt in burning the wooden city of Richmond underlined that resistance would but temporarily subside. Peter H. Wood, "Dream Deferred," 167–68.

39. Henry Wiencek, *Imperfect God*, 214, 217.

40. At Cowpens, Morgan noted, the Americans killed, wounded, and captured eight hundred British soldiers. In the usual racial division, he listed "seventy Negroes" separately as casualties. (No breakdown is given for those killed and wounded. Thus, the total figure for blacks is probably higher. Morgan to Greene, January 19, 1781, Cowpens Papers, Theodorus Bailey Myers Collection, 24–28, SCHS.) The proportion of blacks to whites probably mirrored that of the troops as a whole. If so, at the Battle of Cowpens, blacks made up roughly 9 percent of the imperial forces. Morgan did not consider freeing South Carolina's blacks to fight.

41. Nathanel Greene, *Papers*, 10:22.

42. Ibid.

43. This comment could suggest that better clothes were needed or that "field slaves" often worked naked in South Carolina.

44. Greene to Rutledge, December 9, 1781, Greene Papers, WLCL-UM.

45. Greene, *Papers*, 10:74.

46. Rutledge to Greene, December 18 and 24, 1781, Greene Papers.

47. Greene, *Papers*, 10:130–31.

48. Laurens to Washington, January 28, 1782, in ibid., 101n3.

49. Governor's Message to the South Carolina Assembly, January 18, 1782, SCHS, in Gibbes, *DHAR*, 3:233.

50. "Master Tarleton" was the British colonel Banastre Tarleton.

51. Rutledge to Morgan, January 25, 1781, Cowpens Papers.

52. Greene to Governor Rutledge, January 21, 1782, Greene, *Papers*, 10:228.

53. Ibid., 228, 229.

54. Ibid., 229, 229n3.

55. Ibid., 228–29

56. Ibid.

57. Ibid., 305–6.

58. Greene to Washington, January 24, 1782, ibid., 256.

59. Ibid, 257.

60. David Duncan Wallace, *Henry Laurens*, 452.

61. Greene to Martin, February 2, 1782, Greene, *Papers*, 10:304.

62. Greene, *Papers*, 10:257.

63. Burke to Arthur Middleton, January 25, 1782, in "Correspondence of Arthur Middleton," 194.

64. Mordecai Gist to Richard Henry Lee, February 10, 1782, in "Letters, Colonial and Revolutionary," 82; Benjamin Quarles, *Negro in the American Revolution*, 66.

65. General Lewis Morris to Major Jacob Morris, February 7, 1782, in Letters to General Lewis Morris, NYHS.

66. Josiah Smith to George Appleby, March 15, 1781, Josiah Smith Jr. Letterbook, Southern Historical Collection, University of North Carolina; Olwell, *Masters, Slaves and Subjects*, 266.

67. Memorial of John Hopton, 1786, Loyalists, microfilm, SCDAH, 54:513; Olwell, *Masters, Slaves and Subjects*.

68. John Peebles, *Diary*, May 25, 1780, SCL-USC; Olwell, *Masters, Slaves and Subjects*, 266–68.

69. Matthews to Greene, February 6, 1782, Greene Papers.

70. Greene to Matthews, February 11, 1782, ibid.

71. Matthews to Legislature, February 12, 1782, SCHS, in Gibbes, *DHAR*, 3:251.

72. Washington to Laurens, July 10, 1782, http://memory.loc.gov/cgi-bin/query/P?mgw:1:./temp/~ammem_OYDb::.

73. Ibid.

74. Laurens to Washington, June 11, 1782, http://memory.loc.gov/mss/mgw/mgw4/085/0700/0720.jpg.

75. Forgetting himself, Schama in *Rough Crossings* trivializes Laurens as a "gallant fool." He imagines details—"Suddenly aware that his force of fifty men were outnumbered three to one and faced with the choice of waiting for reinforcements or taking action, John Laurens did what he always did: he charged the guns" (136). Laurens was surprised by an ambush; whether he could have estimated the British forces present or called for reinforcements is unlikely. Laurens had the general policy—probably a plausible one for a soldier—of disregarding fear and daring danger in battle. He had been wounded before. Brave soldiers often get killed . . .

76. See also Laurens to Drayton, February 15, 1783, in Wallace, *Henry Laurens*, 454. Sadly, Laurens opposed intermarriage and wanted restrictive laws so that "they may continue a separate people."

77. Ibid., 455, 456.

78. See also Henry Laurens to William Drayton, February 15, 1783, in *PHL*, 16:156–57.

79. Alluding to Henry Laurens's illness, Schama, *Rough Crossings*, talks around this betrayal: "None of his infirmities, however, explains quite why Henry Laurens should have wanted to include, in a treaty he had little business in drafting, an article so decidedly uncharacteristic of his dead son. Perhaps the old planter, who had built his own fortune on slave labour, had reverted to type? " (137–38). Given this last recognition, it is curious how decisively Schama allies himself with Henry against John, "the idealist" (137).

80. Henry Laurens to the Speaker of the South Carolina House of Representatives, January 31, 1785, Ford Collection, NYPL.

81. Hamilton to John Laurens, August 15, 1782, in Alexander Hamilton, *Papers*, 9:280.

82. Hamilton to Greene, October 12, 1782, in ibid., 301.

83. Wallace, *Henry Laurens*, 489.

84. Ibid. Nathanael Greene survived the Revolution and afterward accepted a plantation from South Carolina. In this, he emulated many of the Revolution's tactical abolitionists, notably Washington. They not only betrayed the second revolution but transformed the first into a commercial oligarchy and in 1787 suppressed Captain Daniel Shays and other farmer and artisan revolutionaries whose sacrifices had brought them to victory. When it came to the second revolution, many white southerners were even worse. As historian Donald Robinson notes, Charles Cotesworth Pinckney justified Article 1, section 9 of the proposed Constitution, which licensed the slave trade until 1808, "on the ground of necessity. . . . Without slaves, he said, 'South Carolina would soon be a desert waste'" (Robinson, *Slavery in the Structure of American Politics*, 242). Cognizant of Greene's venality in accepting a plantation and slaves from South Carolina, but nonetheless hoping to enlist him against traffic in humans, Benjamin Rush urged in a letter, "For God's sake, do not exhibit a spectacle to the world of men just emerging from a war in favor of liberty, with their clothes not yet washed from the blood which was shed in copious and willing streams, fitting out vessels to import their fellow creatures from Africa to reduce them afterward to slavery" (Ellen Gibson Wilson, *Loyal Blacks*, 36).

85. Emancipated blacks were mulatto children of white women who had worked as servants (relations between servants were probably mostly voluntary), individuals manumitted in an "owner's" will (sometimes his own mulatto children), and descendants of black indentured servants who came between 1619 and 1660. After 1660, indenture became a "privilege" offered to white immigrants, but not to blacks, in order to pit one against the other. Lerone Bennett, *The Road Not Taken*, is particularly good on divide and rule.

86. Luther Jackson, *Virginia Negro Soldiers and Seamen*, vi.

87. Ibid. His own figure, 158 free, is greater by 4 than his other figure—179 total minus 25 slaves.

88. Ibid.

89. Ibid., 10–11.

90. Ibid., 21–22.

91. Ibid., 37.

92. Ibid., 16, 18.

93. Ibid., 24–27

94. Ibid.

95. Brandum to Cols. John and Charles Tucker, Esqs., December 11, 1824, item no. 3307, Special Collections, AL-UV.

96. Ibid.

97. George Livermore, *Historical Research*, 127.

98. Madison to Jones, November 28, 1780, in Madison, *Writings of James Madison*, 1:107.

99. Jones to Madison, December 8, 1781, in ibid., 1:106.

100. Ibid.

101. Ibid.; Joseph Jones, *Letters*, 48, 63, 64.

102. Great Britain Army, *Orderly Book*, June 5, 1781, LOC.

103. Ibid.

104. Brigade Order, Portsmouth, June 10, 1781, ibid.

105. Ibid., June 10 and June 11, 1781.

106. Ibid., May 21, 1781.

107. Ibid.

108. Evelyn Acomb, ed., *The Revolutionary Journal of Baron Ludwig von Closen*, 89, 91–92.

109. Stephen Olney, "Memoir," in Catherine Read Williams, ed., *Biography of Revolutionary Heroes*, 276; Wiencek, *Imperfect God*, 245.

110. There were precursors in New England even before independence, as the British murder of Crispus Attucks reveals, as well as the role, in many battles, of the First Rhode Island Regiment. But Patriot reliance on black soldiers at Yorktown was at its height.

111. Robert Selig, "Revolution's Black Soldiers," 12–13.

112. Robert Selig, "German Soldier in America," 583.

113. With his back to the sea, Cornwallis had no place to shield these followers and did not have ships to help them.

114. Ewald, *Diary of the American War*, October 17, 1781, 335–36.

115. Cornwallis has gone down in history far too kindly.

116. Ewald, *Diary of the American War*, October 17, 1781, 335–36.

117. Ibid.

CHAPTER 7

1. See Colonial National Historical Park–Yorktown Battlefield, http://www.nps.gov/york/index.htm.

2. Cited on the first page of hearings in the *Book of Negroes*, PRO.

3. Ibid.

4. Simon Schama, *Rough Crossings*, 144–49.

5. Clarke to Cornwallis, July 10, 1780, CO 217/56, 57, PRO; James W. St. G. Walker, *Black Loyalists*, 8.

6. Leslie to Carleton, June 27, 1782, vol. 23, no. 188, item no. 4916, summarized in *Report on American Manuscripts*, 2:544. As rephrases of the letters, the summaries are often less colorful than the originals.

7. Leslie to Carleton, October 18, 1782, PRO 30/55/52, item no. 5925, 3.

8. In *Roll Jordan Roll*, Eugene Genovese claims otherwise, but I am skeptical

9. Alexander Innes, "Aid de Camp to His Excy the Commr. in Chief," Audit Office, class 13, vol. 98, folio 330, PRO.

10. Lowndes to Carleton, August 8, 1782, vol. 23, no. 216, item no. 5243, *Report on American Manuscripts*, 3:59–60

11. Ibid.

12. Leslie to Carleton, October 18, 1782, vol. 17, no. 139, item no. 5924, ibid., 175–76.

13. Ibid.

14. The fate of black Loyalists occupied the thoughts of Leslie, a racist imperial officer, less than did that of white Tories. Noting, however, that Patriot general Nathanael Greene disagreed about the "value" of blacks previously enslaved to supporters of the Revolution, he remarks angrily of Greene's continuing attacks while Leslie was negotiating with American "commissions": "If Mr. Greene continues to insult our front, while their commissions are here, I shall break off the business[.] [A] letter is gone out on that head." Ibid.

15. Butler to Carleton, September 16, 1782, vol. 17, no. 143, item no. 5604, ibid., 118.

16. Such certificates did not mention employment. And though a primary way for slaves to gain their liberty with the British was to join the military, many were not soldiers. For example, on July 1, 1781, in Savannah, a W. Jones, justice of the peace, and one Alexander Whiley recertified that Thomas Williams and his wife, Hannah, were free. They described how, in immigrating from "tibe" (Tybee Island) to Savannah, the Williamses "got cast away, lost every thing they had." Those possessions included "the free pass," which Jones "saw them with before." Jones and Whiley, Certificate for Thomas Williams, Savannah, July 1, 1781, PANS.

17. For instance, Rt. Ballingall, "Certificate for Phyllis Thomas," October 12, 1782, Charlestown, and Augustine Prevost and Allured Clark, "Certificate for the Thomas Family," July 24, 1780, PANS, RG 1, vol. 170, p. 338.

18. Metland, "Certificate for Ned and Family," Savannah, November 19, 1779, and R. Ballingall, "Permission for Ned and Family to go to Canada," October 14, 1782, PANS, RG 1, vol. 170, pp. 336, 333.

19. How would "slaves," unless they had escaped, "attach themselves" to his department and with what right or expectation look to Moncrief for "protection," in case of British defeat, from Patriot masters? Why, unless they were free, would this expectation cause any practical or moral concern to an imperial officer? Perhaps if some had escaped or been commandeered from Tories and if Moncrief valued their contribution and understood their fears, this might have caused his concern. But because

most answered British emancipation proclamations, Moncrief probably referred to them inaccurately.

20. Moncrief to Clinton, March 13, 1782, vol. 53, no. 129, item no. 9955, *Report on American Manuscripts*, 2:419.

21. Leslie to Carleton, June 27, 1782, vol 23, no. 190, item no. 4915, ibid., 543–44.

22. British East Florida had emancipated black soldiers, and in 1781 the assembly voted to furnish any slave who would fight for the empire freedom, a red coat, and a silver badge. See Sylvia R. Frey, *Water from the Rock*, 69. Although the badge did not equal Dunmore's famous inscription "Liberty to slaves," its possession nonetheless attested to the dignity of black Loyalists there. On October 11, 1782, Florida governor Patrick Tonyn informed Carleton: "I am authorized by an Act of the Assembly to arm every male Inhabitant within the Province, and I apprehend about five hundred Negroes might be trusted with arms." Tonyn to Carleton, October 11, 1782, vol. 48, no. 29, item no. 5850, *Report on American Manuscripts*, 3:163–64.

23. Tonyn to Carleton. October 11, 1782.

24. Return of South Carolina Loyalists, signed by Charles Ogilvie and Gideon Dupont Jr., August 29, 1782, vol. 52, no. 36, item no. 10316, *Report on American Manuscripts*, 3:97–98.

25. Commentators such as Emma Nogrady Kaplan and Sidney Kaplan (*Black Presence*, 82–83) and Hugh Thomas (*Slave Trade*, 481), who estimate, respectively, that 23,500 and 50,000 free blacks emigrated with the Crown mostly from southern ports, overstate the number.

26. Given British efforts to secure counts, the return from St. Augustine is probably precise.

27. McArthur to Carleton, January 9, 1783, item no. 6728, *Report on American Manuscripts*, 3:321.

28. McArthur to Carleton, May 23, 1783, item no. 6842, ibid., 4:97–98. McArthur noted that Governor Tonyn "will furnish us Negroes (we feeding them) to make an abbatis across the Neck; this will be an arduous task, the space being at least twelve hundred yards." On January 31, he reported to Carleton that "the Assembly" had assigned him a large group. See vol. 30, no. 198, item no. 6842, ibid., 4:344. Whether these blacks were free or slave is unclear.

29. Georgia Refugees to Carleton, July 31, 1782, vol. 53, no. 118, item no. 10002, ibid., 3:44–45. The tone of such requests as this, with their assumption that slavery must endure as an institution, differs markedly from the attitude of soldiers, for example Leslie, and certainly of Carleton himself. In Leslie's worst moment, however, he asked Carleton in October 1782, "Quere—if an officer takes a negroe belonging to the enemy in action, with his master's horse, is that negroe looked on to be the property of the officer who took him or not?" Leslie to Carleton, October 1782, vol. 53, no. 42, item no. 10025, ibid., 221–22.

30. Technically, these employees might have been slaves, "rented" as it were. But there were few slaves in British New York. And the workers were to be paid directly. Probably, the Crown recruited free laborers.

31. Mayhew to Henry White, July 2, 1782, vol. 12, no. 198, item no.498, *Report on American Manuscripts*, 3:3.

32. Carleton to Mayhew, August, 1782, vol. 32, no. 195, item no. 5506, ibid., 100.

33. Carleton to Leslie, vol. 17, no. 147, item no. 5575, ibid., 112.

34. Saundra Riley, *Homeward Bound*, 140–41, 142.

35. Kaplan and Kaplan, *Black Presence*, 82.

36. Some historians' estimates are guesses, wildly at variance. Ira Berlin (*Many Thousands Gone*, 263) suggests that nearly all blacks who emigrated from the South were slaves, Kaplan and Kaplan (*Black Presence*, 82) and Thomas (*Slave Trade*, 481) that all were free. Recently, John Pulis, "Bridging Troubled Waters," has tried to construct from Jamaican records a more exact picture for part of one island.

37. George Tyson, "The Carolina Black Corps," 663–64.

38. Leslie to Carleton, October 18, 1782, vol. 17, no. 139, item no. 5924, *Report on American Manuscripts*, 3:175–76.

39. Leslie to Carleton, July 19, 1782, vol. 23, no. 208, item no. 5704, ibid., 28–29.

40. The latter number is for two towns, Kingston and St. Catharine's. The comparable figure for the free is 133.

41. Pulis, "Bridging Troubled Waters," 187.

42. Ibid., 210n12.

43. Pulis notes this figure. But it would rapidly lead to the registration of more than his total of two hundred free blacks from the United States.

44. Pulis, "Bridging Troubled Waters," 210n12.

45. Blacks are listed in the same way as whites. Pulis infers they are all slaves. But nothing indicates that the blacks might be slaves or even indentured servants—again, like Liele, to be freed after a definite period—of white Tories. See CO 5/561/409, 410, PRO.

46. Pulis, "Bridging Troubled Waters," speculates that he left with other volunteers. He may, however, have faded into the island population.

47. Ibid., 187, 188.

48. Ibid., 188.

49. Campbell to Carleton, December 6, 1782, vol. 12, no. 191, item no. 6341, *Report on American Manuscripts*, 4:251. Pulis's estimates include no record of this battalion.

50. In 1789, with certificates signed by Richard Buckley, Hannah Freeman, Edward Freeman, and their sons, John and Joseph, would arrive from Halifax, Nova Scotia. Note the choice of liberty in their names. Chole, a woman, came to Halifax from New Providence in the Bahamas. See Pulis, "Bridging Troubled Waters," 190.

51. Cruden to Majr. C. Nesbit, Tortola, March 25, 1783, PRO 30/55/65, item N, 7213, 1.

52. Walker, *Black Loyalists*, 64–65.

53. Whitecuff, "To the Commissioners," Audit Office, class 13, vol. 56, folio 628, PRO.

54. PRO 30/55/100, document 10427.

55. Boston King, "Memoirs of the Life," 355.

56. Ibid.

57. King's estimate is one thousand less than those who emigrated on ships with the Crown from New York in 1783. Ibid., 356.

58. Schama, *Rough Crossings*, 144–49, offers an interesting account of this meeting, with perhaps overly keen attention to Carleton's imagined patronizing attitude, as if still higher in the British hierarchy, to the victorious general, and too much patriarchal empathy for Washington's imagined outrage: "And now, it seemed the man [Carleton] was concerned with the fate of negroes, *our* negroes, *my* negroes!" (145).

59. Among imperial officers, hierarchy ordinarily squelched imagination and initiative, but in far-flung colonial enterprises, London's decisions rarely determined what transpired in the field, and that included enforcement of the provision of the peace treaty reenslaving freed blacks. In his *History of New York during the Revolutionary War*, Thomas Jones, a Tory judge, agreed with Washington on the legality of the Henry Laurens clause. But Jones raged at British negotiators for their willingness to turn freed blacks over to the Americans. They mistakenly "thought the sacrifice of 2,000 negroes a mere bagatelle." In contrast. he celebrated Carleton's nobility: "Sir Guy possessed the honor of a soldier, the religion of a Christian and the virtue of humanity. He shuddered at the article that gave up the blacks, and at once resolved to apply a substitute." See Jones, *History of New York*, 256–57.

60. Carleton to North, June 6, 1783, in Davies, *DAR*, 21:178.

61. King, "Memoirs of the Life," 356.

62. Carleton, New York, May 12, 1783, Miscellaneous Papers of the Continental Congress, NA, microcopy 247, roll 66, 164.

63. Ibid.

64. In his April 14 letter to Lord North, Carleton remarked that he had set up a commission of Americans and Englishmen to "oversee" the creation of the *Book of Negroes*. The commission included imperial captains Armstrong, Gilfillan, and Cook and Major of Brigade Phillips of the Thirty-Seventh Regiment, as well as Patriots Egbert Benson, Lieutenant Colonel William Smith, and Daniel Parker. See *Book of Negroes*, PRO 30/55/100, document 10427, pp. 2–3. Oddly, British officers are listed only by surname, Americans with full names. The British officers had interviewed and collected information on all the émigrés for the *Book of Negroes*. Furthermore, they controlled the hearings. But the commission's composition foreshadowed coming American power in New York.

65. Berlin, *Many Thousands Gone*, 294.

66. John Beckley, Extract from the Journal of Assembly, NA, microcopy, roll 66, p. 87.

67. Ibid.

68. Ibid., 88, 89.

69. The Library of Congress also has copies.

70. PRO 30/55/100, document 10427, 3.

71. Ibid., 4.

72. Ibid.

73. Ibid., 5.

74. Ibid., 5–7.

75. In addition, this is hopeful rather than conclusive evidence. The inspectors might have made the entry about Francis before he was brought back for a hearing. Alternately, however, transport to Canada could have preceded Francis setting off to join Thelwall's unit in Jamaica.

76. PRO 30/55/100, document 10427, 7–10.

77. See the testimony for the next case.

78. PRO 30/55/100, document 10427, 10.

79. Ibid., 10–11.

80. Ibid., 11–12.

81. The *Book of Negroes* records the logs of blacks on specific ships and their destination. Another possibility is that she is listed as Judith Johnson, 18, who left Samuel Elliot of Norfolk, Virginia, five years before and sailed on the ship *Clinton* bound for Annapolis and St. John's.

82. Dinah Archey, "To His Excellency Sir Guy Carleton," August 2, 1783, WLCL-UM.

83. PRO 30/55/100, document 10427, 12.

84. Ibid.

85. Ibid., 13–15.

86. No separate evidence exists, however, that blacks on the ships, listed in the *Book of Negroes* but taken back for hearings, in fact departed with the British.

87. Wilson, *Loyal Blacks*, 56.

88. Ibid.

89. North to Carleton, August 1783, in Davies, *DAR*, 21:202.

90. Walker, *Black Loyalists*, 61.

91. Wilson, *Loyal Blacks*, 54–55.

92. Most investigations at the British Public Records Office focus on genealogies. The office offers no clear way to track ship manifests.

93. The report listed 102 men, 59 women, 21 children over age ten, and 40 under age ten.

94. The report listed 171 men, 145 women, 60 children over age ten, and 54 under age ten.

95. Slaves were 14.2 percent of those listed with a status, 13.6 percent of all who were listed in the *Book*. The figures given in the text are rounded off and specify only the percentage of those listed with an age, for example, as opposed to the total. Of 2,679 blacks in the *Book*, 2,612 had ages indicated.

96. In his first roster to Lord North, Carleton provides no listing of individuals. If a separate group, they would be a component of the much larger number of blacks who escaped to Canada with the British than those listed in the *Book of Negroes*.

97. Gilbert Harman, "Inference to the Best Explanation," 88–95. The National Archives copy of the *Book of Negroes* enumerates 2,679 émigrés. The Public Records Office in London, however, holds one of exactly three thousand. The Washington copy

includes most of those whom the British copy lists as 2,714 émigrés. The Public Records Office version includes an additional 286. For a year, I had only the National Archive list. The statistics below are based on it.

98. PRO 30/55/100, document 10427. Two others report being born free at St. Augustine.

99. Charles Halstead (50) escaped from Rye, Connecticut.

100. PRO 30/55/100, document 10427.

101. Phyllis R. Blakely, *Boston King*, 1; Cato Hamanday, "Certificate of Freedom," Canadian Digital Collections, http://collections.ic.gc.ca/blackloyalists/documents/official/order_of_general_birch.htm.

102. Certificates of Freedom of John Williams, PANS, RG 1, vol. 170, p. 350. Williams worked for the Royal Department of Engineers and carried a second certificate from William Fyers, lieutenant of engineers.

103. Walker, *Black Loyalists*, 64.

104. Of those listed with a place of origin.

105. In the *Book of Negroes*, the Winslows and Mary Thompson are listed with certificates of service from General Musgrave or General Birch. The certificates no longer survive but would have mentioned the commanders with whom they fought. From the time—1775—one may infer that they answered Dunmore's Proclamation.

106. Graham Russell Gao Hodges, "Black Revolt in New York City," 20–21. She immigrated to Canada with her daughters May (25), Polly (10), Rachel (3), and Sally (1). Perhaps May was the mother—and Mary the grandmother—of the youngest children.

107. On a single page, 21 blacks who came mainly from New Jersey and Virginia enlisted with General Howe: William Fortune (aged 40) formerly enslaved at Harrington, Simsa Herring (26) of Taunton, Thomas Smith (25 [unusual on the list, he reports a status as an artisan, a "brickmaker"]), Susanna Herring (22), William Bogert (20), Dinah Blavelt (20) and William Dussel (32) of Tappan, Charles Francis (20) of South Tappan, Thomas Browne (40) of Hackinsack, Sarah Berrigan (27) of Cacute, Mary Brown (30) of Bergen, Phillip Sparrow (20), along with 3 young children, Ninnas (11), Sukey (9), and John (3), of Brunswick. From Virginia, Isaac (21) came from Williamsburg, John Simonsbury (43) from Fredericksburgh, Dick Richards (22) from White, Isaac Connors (49) and Ben Broughton (30) from Norfolk, and Samuel Martin (16). The first responded to "Howe's Proclamation"; the others refer to "on the strength of proclamation," "in consequence of Proclamation," and so forth.

108. Age 47.

109. Age 34.

110. The liberators are listed in the *Book* by surname only.

111. I have left abbreviations as they appear in the *Book*.

112. If, as historian Herbert Gutman (*Black Family in Slavery and Freedom*, 241–44) fails to recognize, these ex-slaves had not joined specific companies to obtain freedom, why would they be with the Crown? If Carleton had merely helped "outlaw" maroons, why would he have written to Lord North with such a pang, saying, "I found them free"?

113. James Watson (aged 30) escaped from Cheermas, South Carolina. Ab Marrion (26) was listed as "formerly property of General Marrion." Six others also came from South Carolina. Edmund Hill (21) hailed from Somerset County and Pompey Brown (21) from Back Society in New Jersey. And Hilton (22) lived in Benedict County, Maryland; Geo Dickenson (22) North Castle, New York; Thos Morgan (21) Hillingsworth, Connecticut; Cha Allen (23) Sussex County, Maryland; Jos Williams (23) North Carolina; Cha Terrill (21) Richmond, Virginia; and William and Nancy Butler and child, Georgia. The page also includes Geo Roberts (20), free born but "ignorant of the place of his birth," Hannah Roberts (30), born free at Bermuda, and Daniel Green awarded freedom by Captain Williams, master of an English transport.

114. I list ages in parentheses because the information helps underline both the diversity of the émigrés and the determination of the young to become free.

115. PRO 30/55/100, document 10427.

116. The next two people mention only that they had escaped "7 years" and "6 years past."

117. Later in the *Book*, the insistence of thirteen blacks on fighting again supersedes the inspectors' routine notations of "GBC" or "GMC." In 1781, Jerry Miller (22) of Prince George, Samuel Johnson (16) of Williamsburgh, Will Hollyday (33) of Nancomond, George (17) enslaved to Landon Carter, London (17) in bondage to the Quaker Robert Pleasants, and Nathaniel (16) to Colonel Bannister, all of Virginia, joined General Arnold. Paul Moore (36) escaped from John Taylor of Richmond and became an English soldier, probably with General Howe, in 1777. John Fortune (20) of Norfolk joined the Crown in 1779, probably with General Clinton. Michael Beacon (25) of New Kent, Virginia, left with General Cornwallis in 1780. Formerly in bondage at Charlestown, Chloe (19) responded to Clinton's proclamation, at Johns Island in 1780. To enlist in 1781 with Clinton, Ned Husted (22) left John White of Camden, South Carolina. After the Battle of Charlestown, Prince Blake (16) joined the British. Ned Ugee (30) left General Hugee and enlisted with the Crown before the siege. Ned probably had his "owner's" last name, actually Huger, which the inspector misspelled. In addition, at Savannah in 1780, Chris Wyher (28) of (British) East Florida joined the Royal troops and Silvia (no last name) (20) of New Brunswick, New Jersey, left "with the British troops" in 1776.

118. Berlin, *Many Thousands Gone*, 260, is an exception.

119. PRO 30/55/100, document 10427.

120. No last name; age 30.

121. PRO 30/55/100, document 10427.

122. Ibid.

123. Once again, of those listed with a status.

124. A figure of 35 or 50 percent of those from the Caribbean.

125. This figure is probably low. Some of the sixty-seven who enlisted from Canada, 3.4 percent of those reporting a place of origin, and the nine from Europe may also have been free.

126. Walker, *Black Loyalists*, 57.

127. On this list the number of men was 10 percent below that of women and children.

128. On the National Archive list, 1,442 (57 percent) were male and 1,069 (43 percent) were female (26 percent were fifteen years old or younger).

129. A total of 50 of 2,612 or 2 percent of those reporting an age at 16; 35 or 1 percent at 17; 45 or 2 percent at 18, 58 or 2 percent at 19, 124 or 5 percent at 20, 92 or 4 percent at 21; 107 or 4 percent at 22, 104 or 4 percent at 23, 104 or 4 percent at 24, 151 or 6 percent at 25, 111 or 4 percent at 26, 61 or 2 percent at 27, 63 or 2 percent at 28, 30 or 1 percent at 29, 170 or 6 percent at 30. The larger numbers entered for age 20 and 30 (for 30, three to six times greater than the surrounding figures) probably stem from rounded-off or estimated ages by inspectors.

130. For age 40, 108 or 4 percent escaped, compared with 12, 0.5 percent, at 39 and 10, 0.4 percent, at age 41. For age 50, 43 or 2 percent came, contrasted with 9 or 0.3 percent at 49 and 2 or 0.1 percent at 51. A similar disparity occurs for age 60. For small numbers of the aged, however the rounding off ends: only three escapees are reported at age 70, the same as for 69; two joined the British at age 71. That people of such ages escaped again casts remarkable light on the horrors of slavery. One escaped to the British at age 80 and another at age 93.

131. Gutman, *Black Family in Slavery and Freedom*, 241.

132. Those aged 2 and 12 are nonetheless roughly equivalent.

133. King, "Memoirs of the Life," 353. Eighty-two or 3 percent of the 2,612 reported with ages were 1 year or less; 51 or 2 percent 2 years or less; 36 or 1 percent 2 years; 34 or 1 percent 3 years; 34 or 1 percent 4 years; 40 or 2 percent 5 years; 34 or 1 percent 6 years; 31 or 1 percent 7 years; 23 or 1 percent 8 years; 31 or 1 percent 9 years, 42 or 2 percent 10 years; 38 or 1 percent 11 years, 52 or 2 percent 12 years; 29 or 1 percent 13 years; 43 or 2 percent 14 years, and 43 or 1 percent 15 years.

134. Mary Sheppard (40) escaped with Priscilla (8). Rachel Jackson (30) left with Dampre (11) and Judy (9).

135. Randy Kennedy, "Journals of 2 Former Slaves Draw Vivid Portraits," *New York Times*, June 14, 2004, A1–12.

136. Gutman, *Black Family*, 242.

137. "Return of Steward's Company," September 13, 1783, PRO; "Negroes, Belonging to Captain Martin's Company," 1778, Clinton Papers, WLCL-UM.

138. PRO 30/55/100, document 10427.

139. "Return of Captain Martin's Company," 1778, Clinton Papers; "Return of Stewart's Black Pioneers," September 13, 1783, PRO.

140. Report to Congress, 1786, Rhode Island Legislature, handwritten document, RIHS.

141. Shadrack Furman, "Petition," Audit Office, class 13, vol. 29, folio 658–59, PRO. Furman requested £146, 19s, 9d, for which a witness, John Williams, also signed an affidavit.

142. Ibid.

143. Ibid.

144. The document alternately refers to him as Doctor Hungerford. Furman appended affidavits from Huggeford, John Blair, and Edward Rice.

145. Furman, "Petition."

146. Cited in Wilson, *Loyal Blacks*, 47.

147. Walker, *Black Loyalists*, 56; Benjamin Quarles, *Negro in the American Revolution*, 115.

148. Cassandra Pybus ("Jefferson's Faulty Math") does a fine and careful job deflating earlier accounts. To preserve British honor, she suggests the number of blacks who escaped may be more like twenty thousand (264). But of course, Carleton and some other officers aside, the British were also often dishonorable, notably Prime Minister North, who signed the infamous Article VII of the peace treaty and whom Carleton had to defy, and Cornwallis at Yorktown. She is not aware of or downplays important evidence, for instance, that blacks were the main fighters on both sides as well as most of the dead at Yorktown, or that in the *Book of Negroes*, other units than Dunmore's (248), particularly General Howe's, were the ones most signed on to by blacks, or that a vast array of minor British officials freed blacks, or that black guerilla fighters were very important and present in South Carolina until 1786, and the like. She also fails to see the importance of how many blacks escaped into America, a point she nonetheless makes well at the very end (264, 264n38). While she wonderfully describes the heroism of individual escape in *Epic Journeys of Freedom*, this influential essay mistakenly deemphasizes the strong collective push for emancipation from below by black loyalists as well as black patriots and their allies. Thanks to Gary Nash for helpful correspondence on this issue.

149. Frey, *Water from the Rock*, 193–94.

150. Gretchen Holbrook Gerzina, "Black Loyalists in London," 85.

151. Kaplan and Kaplan, *Black Presence*, 82.

152. Smaller numbers went to Abaco: 97 or 4 percent; Spithead: 63 or 2 percent; Halifax: 48 or 2 percent; Quebec: 32 or 1 percent; and Cat Island: 25 or 1 percent. In the *Book*, only two went to England and none to the Caribbean.

153. Kaplan and Kaplan, *Black Presence*, 83. The three thousand from New York is a person-by-person count. The count of those who left East Florida in 1786 is also exact. Other figures are estimates.

154. CO 5/561/817 in the PRO. I found this return, but there may well be others. The collection has vast records, but not, despite some indexes to documents, breakdowns of relevant topics. This disorganization contributes to an explanation of why English authors have written so little over two hundred years about imperial emancipation during the Revolution.

CHAPTER 8

1. Cassandra Pybus has discovered that some of those listed as "slaves" of Tories in the *Book of Negroes* were, in fact, free in Canada (personal correspondence, August 21, 2011). Sympathetic officers could perhaps occasionally have claimed some to make attempts at reenslavement more difficult and/or freed them upon arrival. This is consistent with my account of the hearings in New York as a ruse to get most freed blacks out.

2. Annapolis, Muster 1784, Canada's Digital Collections, http://collections.ic.gc.ca/blackloyalists/documents/official/annapolis_muster.htm. I am grateful to historians such as Todd Braisted, working with the Canadian government, for posting extensive materials about black Loyalists online.

3. Muster Book of Free Blacks, Settlement of Birchtown 1784, Canada's Digital Collections, http://collections.ic.gc.ca/blackloyalists/documents/official/muster_book_free_blacks.htm.

4. The total from the *Book of Negroes* who settled in Birchtown and Annapolis was 253 heads of families (and, thus, probably 750 people for Birchtown plus for Annapolis 163 equals 913, 31 percent of the total). That leaves some 1,680 other free blacks from the ships who settled in Nova Scotia. The inference from ratios of immigrants by alternate means to those accompanying Carleton drawn from these two communities to other communities is likely, but not conclusive.

5. As Cassandra Pybus notes carefully in "Jefferson's Faulty Math," "In New York, the *Book of Negroes* listed the names and some distinguishing details of 2,744 people evacuated as free people on evacuation ships that were inspected by American and British commissioners from April to November 1783. As Congress complained, many more runaways left New York than were acknowledged in that document, which covered only a short period and included neither merchant vessels nor troop ships. Once again it is a conservative estimate to agree with Quarles that at least four thousand free black people were evacuated from New York" (263).

She suggests that 8,000 to 10,000 free blacks immigrated with the British, including three thousand free sailors (263–64). As my comparison of the musters of Birchtown and Annapolis to the *Book of Negroes* shows, however, a far larger number came to Canada, and so the adjusted total, based on her estimates, of freed blacks who immigrated should be at least 14,500 to 15,800. She is certainly right, however, that the British during and at the end of the war carried out " the most significant act of emancipation in early American history"(264).

6. R. D. Eno, "Strange Fate of the Black Loyalists," 167–68.

7. Morse to Fox, August 23, 1783, vol. 49, no. 195, item no. 8800, *Report on American Manuscripts*, 3:298.

8. Howe to W. D. Quarrel, August 9, 1797, CO 217/68, PRO, cited by James Walker, "Land and Settlement in Nova Scotia," 51.

9. Eno, "Strange Fate," 167.

10. Walker, "Land and Settlement," 53.

11. Ellen Gibson Wilson, *Loyal Blacks*, 70, 85, 87, 101, 102.

12. Wesley to Barry, July 3, 1784, cited in ibid., 96. Wesley's striking abolitionism mirrors that of many Christians. In contrast, E. P. Thompson, *Making of the English Working Class*, traces the mainly dark impact of Wesleyanism on English workers.

13. Benjamin Marston, *Journal*, Canada's Digital Collections, http://collections/ic/gc/ca/blackloyalists/documents/diaries/marston_journal.htm.

14. Canadian research about Blucke can be found at http://www.blackloyalist.com/canadiandigitalcollection/people/secular/blucke.htm.

15. William Booth, Diary, March 14, 1789, http://www.blackloyalist.com/canadian digitalcollection/document/diaries/booth_diary.htm.

16. William Dyott, Diary, October 1788, http://www.blackloyalist.com/canadian digitalcollection/.

17. Simon Schama, *Rough Crossings*, sees only Blucke's pretensions, not what he was able to organize. His followers succeeded with the British in Canada.

18. Nova Scotia court document, Canada's Digital Collections, http://www.black loyalist.com/canadiandigitalcollection/documents/official/court_case_gjohnston.htm.

19. Stephen Blucke, "Petition," 1792, http://www.blackloyalist.com/canadiandigital collection/documents/official/blucke_petition-1791.htm.

20. The 1784 Birchtown *Muster Book* records the following professions for 317 blacks: carpenters 29, sawyers 25, farmers 22, seamen 14, ship carpenters 9, caulkers 8, coopers 7, blacksmiths 6, tailors 5, shoemakers 4, cooks and bakers 4, chimney sweeps 2, masons 1, bricklayers 1, seamstresses 1, pedlars 1, weavers 1, painters 1, millers 1, skinners 1, chair makers 1, anchorsmiths 1, sailmakers 1, "gardiners" 1, butchers 1, doctors 1, barbers 1, and tanners 1 for a total of 151 skilled workers. Roughly the other half, unskilled laborers, numbered 166.

21. William Jessop, Diary, March 8, 1786, Ref MG 106, vol. 169, p. 27, PANS.

22. Boston King, "Memoirs of the Life," 360.

23. Ibid.

24. John Harris, Indenture to William Stone, May 1, 1786, Canada's Digital Collections, Collections.ic.gc.ca/black loyalists/documents/official/indenture/_jharris.htm.

25. Herman Horton Indenture, Canada's Digital Collections, www.blackloyalist .com/canadiandigitalcollection/documents/official/indenture_heman_deinstadt.htm.

26. James Cox, foreman, Hand Jury, April 22, 1794, Canada's Digital Collections, http://www.blackloyalist.com/canadiandigitalcollection/.

27. Eno, "Strange Fate," 167; Robin W. Winks, *Blacks in Canada*, 38.

28. King, "Memoir of the Life," 360.

29. Marston, *Journal*, May 8, 1783.

30. Alan Gilbert, *Marx's Politics*, 119–20.

31. Marston, *Journal*, May 16, 1783.

32. Ibid., May 14 and May 16, 1783.

33. Ibid., May 24, 1783.

34. Ibid., July 26, 1783.

35. As we have seen, this was more evident on the American side because the Patriots recruited white militiamen for ten months, but blacks served throughout the war. Yet on the British side, blacks still fought for freedom and had motives to prove themselves far beyond those of whites. The imperial officers and mercenaries who have left diaries were professionals, white redcoats part of the long-term army. Only some of the officers took in, gradually and insufficiently, the resource they had squandered.

36. Marston, *Journal*, July 27, 1783; Phyllis R. Blakely, *Boston King*, 3.

37. James W. St. G. Walker, *Blacks Loyalists*, 49.

38. Gibson, *Loyal Blacks*, 109.

39. An artisan and sailor, King referred to bosses as "masters."

40. King, "Memoir of the Life," 362.

41. Eno, "Strange Fate," 167.

42. Walker, *Land and Settlement*, 53–54.

43. David George, "An Account of the Life of David George," 338; Walker, *Black Loyalists*, 53.

44. Max Weber, *Economy and Society*, vol. 2, chap.6.

45. King, "Memoir of the Life"; Blakely, *Boston King*, 2.

46. Wilson, *Loyal Blacks*, photograph following p. 226.

47. Nash, "Thomas Peters," 274. The *Book of Negroes* lists them disparately under the name Petters. Only Peters himself would later be listed as an immigrant to Sierra Leone.

48. Peters is also listed as "Sgt. Petters" in "A Return of Steward's Company of Black Pioneers," September 13, 1783, PRO.

49. Steele is listed "with Petters" on the Rosters of Steward's Company, PRO, and Martin's Company, WLCL-UM.

50. Peters, "To His Excelency Thomas Carleton," New Brunswick Land Petitions, 1790, RS 108, reel F1037, PANS.

51. Walker, *Black Loyalists*, 94. Walker has done fine comparative research on the Canadian and Sierra Leonean experience.

52. "Nomination of Thomas Peters," New Brunswick Land Petitions, 1790, RS 108, reel F1037, Public Archives of New Brunswick.

53. Simon Adam, Wllm Solly, Cato Charles, Josh Willmot, Henry Smunna, Saml Carter, Anty Stevenson, Stephn Saunders, Willm Taylor, Wllm Waterbury, Nal Lad, Toney Zingar, John Brown, Saml Wright, and Robt Stafford.

54. Perhaps his owner permitted Peters some instruction as well as whipping him. No evidence survives, however.

55. Eno, "Strange Fate," 167.

56. Walker, *Black Loyalists*, 95.

57. Cited in Wilson, *Loyal Blacks*, 179.

58. The painting can be found at http://blackloyalist.com/canadiandigitalcollection/story/exodus/London.htm.

59. Christopher L. Brown, *Moral Capital*, 161–65, 170.

60. Ibid., 164–65. Brown's account of Sharp's words—chapter 3—in crystallizing an unlikely British abolitionist movement is exceptional.

61. The new abolitionist movement did not value British emancipation in exchange for recruitment. It, too, let this extraordinary historical opportunity fade.

62. Granville Sharp, *Short Sketch of Temporary Regulations*. See also Folarin Shyllon, *Black People in Britain*, 132, and Wilson, *Loyal Blacks*, 162. Brown, *Moral Capital*, chap. 3, overestimates the religious and moral force of Sharp's views rather than his originality as a democratic theorist, though he illuminates the latter as well (228–32). Ironically, Brown misses Sharp's visionary political institutional role in Sierra Leone (321).

63. Sharp was no economist. Such work would have to be a social necessary aver-

age, that is, an hour at a normal level of skill and intensity with the standard tools and land of the time and place.

64. Sharp, *Short Sketch of Temporary Regulations*, 1–8. I have benefited from the account of Sharp's vision in Wilson's *Loyal Blacks*, 161–62.

65. Eno, "Strange Fate," 167.

66. "The Humble Memorial and Petition of Thomas Peters," n.d. (received December 24, 1790), CO 217/63, PRO.

67. Ibid.; Walker, *Black Loyalists*, 95.

68. Petition of Thomas Peters, FO 4/1, p. 419, PRO; Wilson, *Loyal Blacks*, 180–81.

69. Paul Cuffe, "*A Brief Account of the Settlement*," 4.

70. Ibid.

71. Blakeley, *Boston King*.

72. "Free Settlement on the Coast of Africa," August 2, 1792, Canada's Digital Collections, collections.ic.gc.ca/blackloyalists/documents/official/free_settlement_coast _of_Africa.

73. Blakely, *Boston King*, 2.

74. Wilson, *Loyal Blacks*, 209; Nash, "Thomas Peters," 278.

75. Nash, "Thomas Peters," 278.

76. Blakely, *Boston King*, 3.

77. Wilson, *Loyal Blacks*, 205; Nash, "Thomas Peters," 278.

78. Nash, "Thomas Peters," 278.

79. Report of the Plymouth Abolition Society, The American Museum, 1791, *PPAS*, LOC, microfilm, reel 2.

80. In contrast, fourteen free black Canadian immigrants signed up for military service in the British West Indies. See Nash, "Thomas Peters," 278.

81. There were 126 girls and 128 boys.

82. Daniel Payne also escaped from Washington to Nova Scotia and apparently stayed.

83. Ned Elliott, Henry Washington, Thos. Bacchus, Norfolk Virginia—here the recorder of names failed utterly—Cato Birden, Jos Blairs, John Thomas, James Robertson, John Cooper, Cezar Bratt, Toby Castleton, Lucy Banbury—a rare female head of household—James Gordon, Frank Miller, Cato Wright, Thomas Evans, Jos. Waintrout, Charls Elliott, Step Kirkland, John Quaker, Chs Pinkins, M Cook, Thos London, Ansel Isere, Abm Croif, Stepn Williams, Thos Miles, March Jones, Jacob Collins, Henry Van, Richd Herbert, Fryday Sleek, Wm Nowles, Jms Williams, Rick Bush, Silas Williams, Frank Peters, Rick Richerson, Thos Smith, Henry Herrington, Cudgoe Francis, Robt Keeling, Bejn Brouton, Arthur Bowles, John Primus, Chs Wilkinson, Thos Caine, and John Kesel.

84. The list records 155 heads of households by place. Some brought a wife and mother. Hence the number of women exceeded that of men.

85. "Chs Town," "Ch'Town," and "Carola."

86. Because Joseph is reported to be from Charlestown, the entries from Carolina probably refer to South Carolina.

87. Inspectors identified twenty-two—14 percent—as thirty years old. Twenty-five—16 percent—were between thirty and forty, including eight listed as thirty-five. Twelve were between twenty-two and thirty.

88. CO 217/163, PRO.

89. Cited in Wilson, *Loyal Blacks*, 230.

90. Wallace Brown, "Black Loyalists in Sierra Leone," 103-4.

91. Ibid., 139.

92. Ibid. Schama, *Rough Crossings*, 90-98, has an able account of this episode.

93. Cited in Shyllon, *Black People*, 138.

94. All citations of official reports from ibid., 138.

95. Cugoano, *Thoughts and Sentiments on the Evil of Slavery*, cited in ibid., 138-39.

96. Ibid., 139.

97. Ibid.

98. AO 12/99, 359, PRO.

99. Ibid.

100. Ibid., 358-59.

101. Judith L. Van Buskirk, *Generous Enemies*, 142-43.

102. AO 12/99, 357, PRO.

103. The petition alternates the surnames Johnston and Johnson.

104. Balfour, Audit Office, class 13, vol. 70b, pt. 1, folio 303, PRO.

105. Thomas Johnson, "Petition," Audit Office, class 13, vol. 706, pt. 1, folios 301-2, PRO.

106. Nash, "Thomas Peters," 280.

107. Peters to Dundas, April, 1792, CO 267/9, cited in Wilson, *Loyal Blacks*, 232.

108. Clarkson, "Diary," 27-37; Anna Maria Falconbridge, *Narrative of Two Voyages*, 139.

109. Sierra Leone Company, "Orders and Regulations," in Colin W. Newbury, ed., *British Policy toward West Africa*, 4-6, 68-69.

110. Watt to Clarkson, April 27, 1792, Clarkson Papers, vol. 3; Additional Manuscripts 41263, British Museum; Walker, *Black Loyalists*, 149.

111. Walker, *Black Loyalists*, 245-47, explores the difficult demands on the company's budget but is overly charitable about its motives.

112. Christopher Fyfe, "Freed Slave Colonies in West Africa," 177.

113. Falconbridge, *Narrative*, 134-35, 141.

114. Even the otherwise excellent account by Walker makes this mistake.

115. Schama, *Rough Crossings*, 355, tries to consider Peters's viewpoint as well as Clarkson's. But relying on Clarkson's diary for his section titled "John," he, too, shies away from Peters and democracy.

116. Brown, "Black Loyalists," 127-29.

117. Ibid., 118.

118. Cited in Richard West, *Back to Africa*, 73; Brown, "Black Loyalists," 119.

119. Henry Thornton (chair), Philip Thornton (deputy chairman), Charles Middle-

ton, William Wilberforce, John Kingston, Samuel Parker, Joseph Hardcastle, Vickeris Taylor, William Sandford, Thomas Eldred, and George Wolf.

120. Charles A. Clegg III, "Promised Land," 140–41.

121. Ibid., 154–55.

122. The white councilors were James Cocks, John Bell, John Wakerell, Richard Pepys, James Watt, and Charles Taylor.

123. Falconbridge, *Narrative*, 134–35, 141. Falconbridge also named an idea, learned from whites, about schooling: "They seem desirous to give education to their children, or in their own way of expressing it, 'Read book, and learn to be *rogue* so well as the white man'" (ibid., 77).

124. Granville Sharp, *Memoirs*, 362; Clegg, "Promised Land," 154.

125. Wilson, *Loyal Blacks*, 388.

126. Clegg, "Promised Land," 146, 156.

127. Ibid.

128. Schama, *Rough Crossings*, startlingly cites only a passage from Clarkson that suggests that each might be lethal: "I said it was probable either one or other of us would be hanged upon that Tree before the Palaver was settled" (337). But Clarkson was governor. He alone had authority to call for "hanging." Peters had no such thought. Worse yet, Clarkson's invocation shows that he had hanging Peters in mind. Schama avoids this implication because it reveals Clarkson's madness and the weakness, relying on his diaries, of adopting his point of view.

129. Only Clarkson's description of the meeting survives. See Walker, *Black Loyalists*, 150n19.

130. Cited in Clegg, "Promised Land," 148.

131. Clarkson Papers, vol. 3, "History of Sierra Leone; Additional Manuscripts 41263, British Museum; Nash, "Thomas Peters," 280.

132. Wilson, *Loyal Blacks*, 250.

133. Ibid., 251.

134. Ibid.

135. Gordons to Clarkson, May 10, 1792, cited in Clegg, "Promised Land," 149–50.

136. Ibid., 147–48.

137. Schama, *Rough Crossings*, 342–43, echoes Clarkson.

138. E. G. Ingham, ed., *Sierra Leone*, 76, 96.

139. Colonists petition to Clarkson, June 26, 1792, cited in Wilson, *Loyal Blacks*, 253–55. The comments by Schama, *Rough Crossings*, on the petition's defense of liberty—"a chapter in the long transatlantic history of liberty" (347–48)—and Peters's influence are among the best in his book.

140. Nash, "Thomas Peters," 280–81, leaves Clarkson's story of Peters's putative disgrace at the end of his life in silence.

141. Walker, *Black Loyalists*, 167; Falconbridge, *Narrative*, 193; Wilson, *Loyal Blacks*, 283–88.

142. Falconbridge, *Narrative*, 193.

143. Ibid., 215–16.

144. Brown, "Black Loyalists," 114.

145. Anderson and Perkins spoke of settlers in the third person.

146. Falconbridge, *Narrative*, 212.

147. Ibid., 214–15.

148. Ibid.

149. Wilson, *Loyal Blacks*, 295.

150. Falconbridge, *Narrative*, 265.

151. Ibid.

152. Ibid., 256.

153. Ibid., 258; Clarkson to Anderson and Perkins, October 26, 1793, and November 3 and 11, 1793, Clarkson Papers, British Museum, Additional Manuscripts 41263; Wilson, *Loyal Blacks*, 297.

154. Anderson and Perkins to Thornton, November 20, 1793, reproduced in Falconbridge, *Narrative*, 267–68.

155. Neither was on Clarkson's list of "disorderly dangers" or even "doubtful" people; Wilson, *Loyal Blacks*, 296.

156. In a letter to Clarkson, Anderson and Luke Jordan reported that the captain had started it. He "began to threaten some of the people working at the wharf—saying in what manner he would use them if he had them in the West Indies. And some of the people told him if he came here to abuse them they would not allow it." Anderson and Jordan to Clarkson, June 28, 1794, Clarkson Papers, British Museum, Additional Manuscripts 41263; Wilson, *Loyal Blacks*, 313.

157. Wilson, *Loyal Blacks*, 314.

158. Ibid.

159. Council Minutes, August 17, 1797, CO 270/4, PRO; Claude George, *Rise of British West Africa*, 377.

160. Macaulay, *Journal*, September 30 and October 2, 1797, in Wilson, *Loyal Blacks*, 330–31.

161. Ibid.

162. Brown, "Black Loyalists," 115, 188.

163. Christopher Fyfe, *Sierra Leone Inheritance*, 124–26. I have benefited from Wilson, *Loyal Blacks*, 381.

164. To see how early this movement was, consider the nonviolent movement, led by Nkrumah, in the Gold Coast that, in 1957, became Ghana.

165. Cuffe, *Brief Account*, 4.

166. Eno, "Strange Fate," 170; Brown, "Black Loyalists," 115.

167. Brown, "Black Loyalists," 114.

168. Divide and conquer.

169. Brown, "Black Loyalists," 114.

170. Wilson, *Loyal Blacks*, 388

171. Roger Anstey, *Atlantic Slave Trade and British Abolition*, 317.

172. Ibid., 115.

173. Brown, "Black Loyalists," 117.

174. Petition of Jonathan Thorpe, February 19, 1820, CO 267/51, PRO; Brown, "Black Loyalists,"117.

175. Petition of John Kizell, March 1826, CO 267/92, PRO.

CHAPTER 9

1. Ellen Gibson Wilson, *Loyal Blacks*, 405.

2. Thompson to Castlereagh, November 2, 1808, Thompson Papers, Hull University, 1:23, in Wilson, *Loyal Blacks*, 496.

3. See Alan Gilbert, *Must Global Politics Constrain Democracy*. I have benefited from Betty Fladeland, *Men and Brothers*, chaps. 2–3, on the relation of the English and American abolitionists.

4. Quakers founded the first abolition society in England in 1773.

5. Jonathan Penrose, "Memorial," June 2, 1787, *PPAS*, LOC, reel 2.

6. Gilbert, *Must Global Politics Constrain Democracy*, chap. 1.

7. Penrose, "Memorial."

8. New York and New Jersey also only passed emancipation acts at the turn of the nineteenth century.

9. Robin Blackburn, *Overthrow of Colonial Slavery*, 124.

10. Benjamin Franklin, *Works of Benjamin Franklin*, 10:320, 321; Matthew T. Mellon, *Early American Views on Negro Slavery*, 15.

11. Benjamin Franklin, President, Philadelphia Abolition Society, to Brissot de Warville, Secretary, Les Amis des noirs, December 9(?), 1788, *PPAS*, LOC, microfilm, reel 2.

12. Lafayette is an odd Americanization of the French.

13. "To the Marquis of Fayette," 1788, *PPAS*, LOC, microfilm, reel 2.

14. Minutes of a Meeting, July 7, 1789, in ibid.

15. "A l'instant meme ou l'Amerique achevoit de briser ses fers, les amis genereux de la liberte sentirent qu'ils aviliroient leur cause s'ils autorisoint par des loix la servitude des Noirs. Un homme libre qui a des Esclaves, ou qui approuve que ses concitoyens en aient, s'avoue coupable d'une injustice, ou est force d'eriger en principe que la liberte n'est qu'une avantage saisi par la force, & non un droit donne par la nature." Condorcet to the Pennsylvania Society, February 3, 1789, in ibid.

16. Ibid.

17. Granville Sharp, "Resolutions," London, April 26, 1791, ibid.

18. Benjamin Franklin, "An Address to the Public" for the Pennsylvania Abolition Society, ibid.

19. W. Dulvoyer, Extract from a Letter, 1787, ibid.

20. Ibid.

21. Pennsylvania Abolition Society, "Memorial to the Senate and the House of Representatives of the Commonwealth of Pennsylvania," 1788, ibid.

22. In 1790, for instance, Richard Waln mentions the case of "Negro Jack," but no further information appears; ibid.

23. Richard Waln to his son, May 5 and May 7, 1790, ibid.

24. Elias Bond to Waln, May 7, 1790, ibid.

25. "State of the Case Negro Silas," ibid.

26. Richard Waln to his son, May 5 and May 7, 1790, ibid.

27. Thomas Harrison, "Extract from the Minutes for the Acting Committee," December 19, 1792, ibid.

28. The stories of Robert and Ann Massey are in Richard Waln, 1790, ibid.

29. "State of Facts Respecting Emmanuel Carpenter," ibid.

30. The meeting emblemizes how deeper thinking about emancipation would, in the mid-nineteenth century, link the fight against slavery to the liberation of women.

31. Bacon and Pemberton, "To the Monthly Meeting," September 28, 1788, ibid.

32. Ibid.

33. William Blake's poems and E. P. Thompson's *The Making of the English Working Class* illuminate this point. Franklin would not have permitted such abridgments of his enjoyments in Paris.

34. Benjamin Franklin, "An Address to the Public," November 9, 1789, *PPAS*, LOC, reel 2.

35. Ibid.

36. Benjamin Franklin, "Plan for Improving the Condition of the Free Blacks," ibid.

37. Jacques Brissot de Warville to Franklin, Paris, January 20, 1790, ibid.

38. Blackburn, *Overthrow of Colonial Slavery*, chap. 6, especially 224–25, 259–60. His chapter is the best account of this vast, revolutionary impulse to abolition.

39. James Pemberton to the Amis des noirs, August 30, 1790, *PPAS*, LOC, reel 2.

40. Granville Sharp to the Pennsylvania Abolition Society, February 20, 1790, ibid.

41. "Remarks on the Slave Trade," *American Museum*, May 29, 1789, ibid.

42. Sharp, "Statement," London, April 26, 1791, ibid.

43. "Amendment from the Rhode Island Convention to the Constitution of the United States at Newport, May 24, 1790," ibid.

44. "The Constitution of the Connecticut Society," *Pennsylvania Mercury and Universal Advertiser*, September 14, 1790, ibid.

45. Tucker to Page, March 29, 1790, ibid.

46. "The Principles of Association of the Washington Society," ibid.

47. Pemberton to the Amis des noirs, August 30, 1790, ibid.

48. Randolph to Franklin, August 2, 1788, ibid.

49. Webster to Benjamin Franklin, December 4, 1789, ibid.

50. Adams to Pemberton, February 19, 1790, ibid.

51. Graham Russell Gao Hodges, *Slavery, Freedom and Culture*, 91–92.

52. In *Le lys rouge* (The Red Lily), 1894, France said: "*La majestueuse égalité des lois, & interdit au riche comme au pauvre de coucher sous les ponts, de mendier dans les rues et de voler du pain* (The law, in its majestic equality, forbids the rich as well as the poor to sleep under bridges, to beg in the streets, and to steal bread).

53. Marx and his colleagues at the *Neue Rheinische Zeiting* put the issue this way; see Alan Gilbert, *Marx's Politics*, 183–86.

54. Ibid., chap. 10.

55. Karl Marx and Friedrich Engels, *Communist Manifesto*, 65; Gilbert, *Marx's Politics*, chap. 8.

56. Woody Holton, *Unruly Americans and the Origins of the Constitution*, 163–64, 220. Echoing his fear of blacks joining Dunmore, Washington referred to the threat of Shays's Rebellion as a "snow-ball" that must be divided: "Commotions of this sort, like snow-balls, gather strength as they roll, if there is no opposition in the way to divide & crumble them."

57. Gary B. Nash, *Race and Revolution*, 135, reprints the document.

58. The terms here are drawn from my 1999 book, *Must Global Politics Constrain Democracy*.

59. A North American cultural campaign, however, scorns Haiti as a center of voodoo and "Papa Doc" Duvalier's dictatorship. This view ignores the American guns that overthrew the republic in 1916, installed and protected the Duvaliers, and twice after the cold war struck down an elected president, Jean-Bertrand Aristide. Forgetfulness about the Haitian Revolution in the American public and academia has contributed to this campaign's success. So does the downplaying of Latin American liberators. These liberators and movements, too, are dark stars in popular and academic culture.

60. Nash, *Race and Revolution*, 79. This was perhaps the most imaginative use of democratic contractarian reasoning in the American Revolution.

Bibliography

BOOKS, ARTICLES, DISSERTATIONS, AND THESES

Abeyta, Loring. "Resistance at Cerro de Pasco." PhD diss., University of Denver, 2005.

Acomb, Evelyn M., ed. *The Revolutionary Journal of Baron Ludwig von Closen, 1780–1783*. Chapel Hill: University of North Carolina Press, 1958.

Adams, John. *Diary and Autobiography*. Cambridge, MA: Harvard University Press, 1964.

Allen, Robert S., ed. *The Loyal Americans: The Military Role of the Loyalist Provincial Corps and Their Settlement in British North America, 1775–1784*. Ottawa: National Museums of Canada, 1983.

Althusser, Louis. "Contradiction et Overdetermination." In *Pour Marx*. Paris: Maspero, 1965.

Anders, Tisa. "Religion and Advocacy Politics in L. Maria Child." PhD diss., University of Denver, 2002.

Anstey, Roger. *The Atlantic Slave Trade and British Abolition: 1760–1810*. London: Macmillan, 1975.

Aptheker, Herbert. *American Negro Slave Revolts*. New York: Columbia University Press, 1943.

———, ed. *A Documentary History of the Negro People in the United States*. New York: Citadel, 1951.

———. "Maroons within the Present Limits of the United States." *Journal of Negro History* 24 (1939): 167–84. Reprinted in Richard Price, *Maroon Societies: Rebel Slave Communities in the Americas*. Baltimore: Johns Hopkins University Press, 1996.

———. *The Negro in the American Revolution*. New York: International Publishers, 1940.

———. *"One Continual Cry": David Walker's Appeal to the Coloured Citizens of the World (1829–30)*. New York: Humanities, 1965.

Arendt, Hannah. *On Revolution*. New York: Viking, 1977.

Aristotle. *Nicomachean Ethics*. Cambridge, MA: Harvard University Press, 1975.

———. *Politics*. Cambridge, MA: Harvard University Press, 1977.

Arnold, Samuel Greene. *History of the State of Rhode Island and Providence Plantations*. 2 vols. New York: D. Appleton, 1859–60.

Bailyn, Bernard. *The Ideological Origins of the American Revolution*. Cambridge, MA: Harvard University Press, 1967.

Bartlett, John Russell. *Records of the Colony of Rhode Island and Providence Plantations in New England*. 10 vols. Providence, RI: A. C. Greene, 1860.

Bennett, Lerone. *Before the Mayflower: A History of the Negro in America, 1619–1962*. Chicago: Johnson, 1962.

———. *The Road Not Taken: Colonies Turn Fateful Fork by Systematically Dividing Races*. London: International Committee against Racism, 1976.

Bergman, Peter, and Jean McCarroll, eds. *The Negro in the Congressional Records.* 7 vols. New York: Bergman, 1937.

Berlin, Ira. *Many Thousands Gone: The First Two Centuries of Slavery in North America.* Cambridge, MA: Belknap Press, 2000.

Berlin, Ira, and Leslie M. Harris. *Slavery in New York.* New York: New Press, 2005.

Berlin, Ira, and Ronald Hoffmann, eds. *Slavery and Freedom in the Age of the American Revolution.* Charlottesville: University of Virginia Press, 1983.

Blackburn, Robin. *The Making of New World Slavery: From the Baroque to the Modern, 1492–1800.* London: Verso, 1997.

———. *The Overthrow of Colonial Slavery, 1776–1848.* London: Verso, 1988.

Blakely, Phyllis R. *Boston King.* Toronto: Dundurn, 1968.

Blumenrosen, Alfred W., and Ruth G. Blumenrosen. *Slave Nation: How Slavery United the Colonies and Sparked the American Revolution.* Naperville, IL: Sourcebooks, 2005.

Boatner, Mark M., III. *Encyclopedia of the American Revolution.* New York: David McKay, 1966.

Bobrick, Benson. *Angel in the Whirlwind: The Triumph of the American Revolution.* New York: Simon and Schuster, 1997.

Bolton, Charles Knowles. *The Private Soldier under Washington.* Port Washington, NY: Kennikat Press, 1964.

Bourdin, Henri L., ed. *Sketches of Eighteenth Century America.* New Haven, CT: Yale University Press, 1925.

Braisted, Todd W. "The Black Pioneers and Others." In *Moving On: Black Loyalists in the Afro-Atlantic World,* edited by John W. Pulis, 3–38. New York: Garland, 1999.

Brookhiser, Richard. *Alexander Hamilton, American.* New York: Simon and Schuster, 2000.

Brown, Christopher L. *Moral Capital: Foundations of British Abolitionism.* Chapel Hill: University of North Carolina Press, 2006.

Brown, Wallace. "The American Loyalists in Jamaica." *Journal of Caribbean History* 26 (1992): 121–46.

———. "The Black Loyalists in Sierra Leone." In *Moving On: Black Loyalists in the Afro-Atlantic World,* edited by John W. Pulis, 103–34. New York: Garland, 1999.

Bruns, Roger, ed. *Am I Not a Man and a Brother? The Anti-Slavery Crusade of Revolutionary America, 1688–1788.* New York: Chelsea House, 1977.

Buckley, Roger Norman. *Slaves in Red Coats: The British West India Regiments, 1795–1815.* New Haven, CT: Yale University Press, 1979.

Bull, Henry DeSaussure. "Ashley Hall Plantation." Columbia, SC: South Carolina Historical Society, 1952.

Burnett, Edmund, ed. *Letters to Members of the Continental Congress.* Boston: Greenwood, 1976.

Callahan, North. *Flight from the Republic.* Indianapolis: Bobbs-Merrill, 1967.

Campbell, Archibald. *Journal of an Expedition against the Rebels of Georgia in North America, 1778.* Darien, GA: Ashatilly, 1981.

Carretta, Vincent, ed. *Unchained Voices: An Anthology of Black Authors in the English-Speaking World of the Eighteenth Century*. Lexington: University of Kentucky Press, 1996.

Caute, David. *The Great Fear*. New York: Simon and Schuster, 1978.

Chastellux, Francois Jean, Marquis de. *Travels in North America in the Years 1780, 1781 and 1782*. Chapel Hill: University of North Carolina Press, 1963.

Chernow, Ron. *Alexander Hamilton*. New York: Penguin, 2004.

Clarkson, John. "Diary." In *Sierra Leone after a Hundred Years*, edited by E. G. Ingham. London: Cass, 1968.

Clegg, Charles A., III. "The Promised Land, Inc." In *Moving On: Black Loyalists in the Afro-Atlantic World*, edited by John W. Pulis, 135–58. New York: Garland, 1999.

Clifford, Mary Louise. *From Slavery to Freetown: Black Loyalists after the American Revolution*. Jefferson, NC: McFarland, 1999.

Coffin, Joshua. *A Sketch of the History of Newbury, Newburyport and West Newbury, from 1635 to 1845*. Boston: S. G. Drake, 1845.

Conforti, Joseph A. *Samuel Hopkins and the New Divinity Movement: Calvinism, the Congregational Ministry and Reforms in New England between the Great Awakenings*. Grand Rapids, MI: Christian University Press, 1981.

Countryman, Edward. *A People in Revolution*. Baltimore: Johns Hopkins University Press, 1981.

Cox, Joseph Mason Andrew. *Great Black Men of Masonry: 1723–1982*. New York: Blue Diamond, 1982.

Crow, Jeffrey. *The Black Experience in Revolutionary North Carolina*. Raleigh: North Carolina Historical Society, 1980.

Cushing, John D. "The Cushing Court and the Abolition of Slavery in Massachusetts: More Notes on the Quock Walker Case." *American Journal of Legal History* 5 (1961): 118–44.

Davies, K. G., ed. *Documents of the American Revolution, 1770–1783*. 21 vols. Colonial Office Series. Dublin: Irish Publishing, 1972–1981.

Davis, David Brion. *The Problem of Slavery in the Age of Revolution, 1770–1823*. Ithaca, NY: Cornell University Press, 1975

Day, Thomas, and John Bicknell. *The Dying Negro: A Poem*. London: W. Flexney, 1775.

Dodge, Steve. *The First Loyalist Settlement in Abaco: Carleton, and Marsh's Harbor*. Hope Town, Bahamas: Wyannie Malone Museum, 1979.

Dubois, Laurent. *Avengers of the New World: The Story of the Haitian Revolution*. Cambridge, MA: Harvard University Press, 2004.

Dutt, R. Palme. *Fascism and Social Revolution*. New York: Proletarian Publishers, 1936.

Egerton, Douglas R. *Death or Liberty*. New York: Oxford University Press, 2008.

———. *Gabriel's Rebellion: The Virginia Slave Conspiracies of 1800 and 1802*. Chapel Hill: University of North Carolina Press, 1993.

Ellis, Joseph. *Founding Brothers: The Revolutionary Generation*. New York: Vintage, 2002.

Eno, R. D. "The Strange Fate of the Black Loyalists." *American Heritage Magazine*, June–July 1983.

Essig, James. *Bonds of Wickedness: American Evangelicals against Slavery, 1770–1808*. Philadelphia: Temple University Press, 1978.

Ewald, Johann. *Diary of the American War*. New Haven, CT: Yale University Press, 1979.

"Extracts from the Journal of Lt. John Bell Tilden, Second Pennsylvania Line, 1781–1782." *Pennsylvania Magazine of History and Biography* 29 (1895). Reprinted in *Men and Events of the Revolution in Winchester and Frederick County, Virginia*. Winchester, VA: Winchester-Frederick County Historical Society, 1975.

Falconbridge, Anna Maria. *Narrative of Two Voyages to the River Sierra Leone during the Years 1791–93*. London: Cass, 1967

Farrand, Max, ed. *The Records of the Federal Convention of 1787*. New Haven, CT: Yale University Press, 1911.

Fenn, Elizabeth A. *Pox Americana: The Great Smallpox Epidemic of 1775–82*. New York: Hill and Wang, 2000.

Fick, Elizabeth. *The Making of Haiti*. Knoxville: University of Tennessee Press, 1990.

Finley, Moses I. *Ancient Slavery and Modern Ideology*. New York: Pelican, 1998.

Fladeland, Betty. *Men and Brothers: Anglo-American Antislavery Cooperation*. Urbana: University of Illinois Press, 1972.

Foner, Phillip. *History of Black Americans: From Africa to the Emergence of the Cotton Kingdom*. New York: Greenwood, 1975.

Force, Peter. *American Archives: Prepared and Published under Authority of an Act of Congress*. Washington, DC: Library of Congress, 1837–53.

Franklin, Benjamin. *The Autobiography of Benjamin Franklin*. Edited by Leonard W. Labaree, Ralph L. Ketcham, Helen C. Boatfield, and Helene H. Fineman. New Haven, CT: Yale University Press, 1964.

———. *Works*. Chicago: T. MacCoun, 1882.

———. *The Works of Benjamin Franklin; Containing Several Political and Historical Tracts Not Included in Any Former Edition, and Many Letters Official and Private Not Hitherto Published; with Notes and a Life of the Author*. Edited by Jared Sparks. 10 vols. Boston: Hilliard Gray, 1840.

Franklin, John Hope, and Alfred A. Moss Jr. *From Slavery to Freedom: A History of African-Americans*. New York: Knopf, 2000.

Frey, Sylvia R. *Water from the Rock: Black Resistance in a Revolutionary Age*. Princeton, NJ: Princeton University Press, 1991.

Fyfe, Christopher. "Freed Slave Colonies in West Africa." In *The Cambridge History of Africa*, vol. 5, *From c. 1790 to c. 1870*, edited by John E. Flint, 170–99. Cambridge: Cambridge University Press, 1977.

———. *Sierra Leone Inheritance*. Oxford: Oxford University Press, 1964.

———. "Thomas Peters." *Sierra Leone Studies* 1 (1953): 4–13.

Genovese, Eugene. *Roll Jordan Roll: The World the Slaves Made*. New York: Random House, 1976.

George, Claude. *The Rise of British West Africa: Comprising the Early History of the*

Colony of Sierra Leone, the Gambia, Lagos, Gold Coast, Etc. (1904). London: General Books, 2009.

George, David. "An Account of the Life of David George, from Sierra Leone in Africa." In *Unchained Voices: An Anthology of Black Authors in the English-Speaking World of the Eighteenth Century*, edited by Vincent Carretta, 333–50. Lexington: University of Kentucky Press, 1996.

Gerlach, Larry R. *Documentary History of the American Revolution in New Jersey.* New Brunswick, NJ: Rutgers University Press, 1975.

———. *New Jersey in the American Revolution, 1763–1783: A Documentary History.* Trenton, NJ: New Jersey Historical Commission, 1975.

Gerzina, Gretchen Holbrook. "Black Loyalists in London after the American Revolution." In *Moving On: Black Loyalists in the Afro-Atlantic World*, edited by John W. Pulis, 85–102. New York: Garland, 1999.

Gibbes, Robert Wilson, ed. *Documentary History of the American Revolution.* 3 vols. New York: Appleton, 1853–1857.

Gilbert, Alan. *Democratic Individuality.* Cambridge: Cambridge University Press, 1990.

———. Democratic-individuality.blogspot.com., May 2009–present.

———. "Does the American Experiment Realize Democracy?" In *The Principles of the American Political Order and Post-Constitutional Currents of Thought*, edited by Robert Utley. Lanham, MD: University Presses of America, 1992.

———. "Do Philosophers Counsel Tyrants?" *Constellations* 16 (March 2009): 106–24.

——— ."'Internal Restlessness': Social Theory and Individuality in Montesquieu." *Political Theory* 22 (February 1994): 45–70.

———. *Marx's Politics: Communists and Citizens.* New Brunswick, NJ: Rutgers University Press, 1981.

———. *Must Global Politics Constrain Democracy? Great-Power Realism, Democratic Peace and Democratic Internationalism.* Princeton, NJ: Princeton University Press, 1999.

———. "What Then?" In *History and the Idea of Progress*, edited by Arthur M. Melzer, Jerry Weinberger, and M. Richard Zinman. Ithaca, NY: Cornell University Press, 1995.

Gilje, Paul A. *The Road to Mobocracy: Popular Disorder in New York City, 1763–1834.* Chapel Hill: University of North Carolina Press, 1987.

Gilje, Paul A., and William Pencak, eds. *New York in the Age of the Constitution.* London: Associated University Presses, 1992.

Gilroy, Paul. *The Black Atlantic: Modernity and Double-Consciousness.* Cambridge, MA: Harvard University Press, 1993.

Goldfield, Michael. *The Color of Politics: Race and the Mainsprings of American Politics.* New York: New Press, 1997.

Greene, Lorenzo. "Some Observations on the Black Regiment of Rhode Island in the American Revolution." *Journal of Negro History* 37 (April 1952): 142–72.

Greene, Nathanael. *Papers of Nathanael Greene.* Edited by Dennis M. Conrad. 11 vols. Chapel Hill: University of North Carolina Press, 1976.

Gummere, Amelia M., ed. *The Journals and Essays of John Woolman*. Philadelphia: Friends, 1922.

Gutman, Herbert. *The Black Family in Slavery and Freedom, 1750–1925*. New York: Pantheon, 1976.

Hall, Basil. *Extracts from a Journal Written in the Coasts of Chili, Peru and Mexico in the Years 1820, 1821, 1822*. 2 vols. Edinburgh, Scotland: A. Constable, 1824.

Hamilton, Alexander. *Papers*. Edited by Harold C. Syrett. 27 vols. New York: Columbia University Press, 1961–87.

———. *The Works of Alexander Hamilton*. Edited by Henry Cabot Lodge. 12 vols. New York: G. P. Putnam's Sons, 1903.

Hammond, Isaac W. "Slavery in New Hampshire." *Magazine of American History* 21 (1889).

Harman, Gilbert. "Inference to the Best Explanation." *Philosophical Review* 74 (1965): 88–95.

Hartz, Louis. *The Liberal Tradition in America: An Interpretation of American Political Thought since the Revolution*. New York: Harcourt, Brace, Jovanovich, 1955.

Hegel, G. W. F. *Grundlinien der Philosophie des Rechts* [Elements of the Philosophy of Right]. Stuttgart: Reclam Verlag, 1976.

———. *Phaenomonology des Geistes* [Phenomenology of Spirit]. Hamburg: Meiner Verlag, 1952.

———. *Philosophie des Rechts: Die Vorlesung von 1819/20 in einer Nachschrift* [Philosophy of Law: The Course of 1819/20 in a Postscript], edited by Dieter Henrich. Frankfurt: Suhrkamp Verlag, 1983.

Hendrickson, Robert A. *Hamilton*. 2 vols. New York: Mason/Charter, 1976.

Hillman, James. *Dreams and the Underworld*. New York: Harper and Row, 1979.

Hinks, Peter P., John R. McKivigan, and R. Owen Williams. *Encyclopedia of Antislavery and Abolition*. Westport, CT: Greenwood, 2007.

Hirschfeld, Fritz. *George Washington and Slavery: A Documentary Portrayal*. Columbia: University of Missouri Press, 1997.

Hodges, Graham Russell Gao. *African-Americans in Monmouth County during the Age of the American Revolution*. Lincroft, NJ: Monmouth County Park, 1990.

———, ed. *The Black Loyalist Directory*. New York: Garland, 1996.

———. "Black Resistance in Colonial and Revolutionary Bergen County, New Jersey." River Edge, NJ: Bergen County Historical Society, 1989.

———. "Black Revolt in New York City and the Neutral Zone, 1775–83." In *New York in the Age of the Constitution*, edited by Paul A. Gilje and William Pencak. London: Associated University Presses, 1992.

———. *Slavery, Freedom and Culture among Early American Workers*. Armonk, NY: M. E. Sharpe, 1998.

Hoffman, Ronald. *A Spirit of Dissension: Economics, Politics and the Revolution in Maryland*. Baltimore: Johns Hopkins University Press, 1973.

Holton, Woody. *Forced Founders*. Chapel Hill: University of North Carolina Press, 1999.

———. "Rebel against Rebel: Enslaved Virginians and the Coming of the American Revolution." *Virginia Magazine of History and Biography* 105 (Spring 1997): 157–92.

———. *Unruly Americans and the Origins of the Constitution.* New York: Hill and Wang, 2008.

Hornsby, Alton, Jr. *The Negro in Revolutionary Georgia.* Atlanta: Georgia Department of Education, 1977.

Horsmanden, Daniel. *New York Conspiracy Trials of 1741: Daniel Horsmanden's Journal of the Proceedings with Related Documents.* Edited by Serena R. Zabin. New York: Bedminster, 2004.

Hough, Benjamin Franklin. *The Siege of Savannah: By the Combined American and French Forces under the Command of Gen. Lincoln and the Count D'Estaing in the Autumn of 1779.* Albany, NY: J. Munsell, 1866.

Humphreys, David. *Life of George Washington.* Athens: University of Georgia Press, 1991,

Humphreys, Frank Landon. *Life and Times of David Humphreys: Soldier, Statesman, Poet, "belov'd of Washington."* New York: G. P. Putnam's Sons, 1917.

Ingham, E. G., ed., *Sierra Leone after a Hundred Years.* London: Cass, 1968.

Iredell, James. *The Papers of James Iredell.* Edited by Don Higginbotham. Raleigh: North Carolina Division of Archives and History, 1976.

Jackson, Luther P. *Virginia Negro Soldiers and Seamen in the Revolutionary War.* Norfolk, VA: Guide Quality Press, 1944.

James, C. L. R. *The Black Jacobins: Toussaint L'Ouverture and the San Domingo Revolution.* New York: Vintage, 1938.

Jasanoff, Maya. *Liberty's Exiles: American Loyalists in the Revolutionary World.* New York: Knopf, 2011.

Jefferson, Thomas. *Papers of Thomas Jefferson.* Edited by Julian P. Boyd. 32 vols. Princeton, NJ: Princeton University Press, 1950.

———. *Thomas Jefferson's Farm Book: With Commentary and Relevant Extracts from Other Writings.* Edited by Edwin Morris Betts. Charlottesville: University Press of Virginia, 1953.

———. *Works.* Edited by Paul Leicester-Ford. 12 vols. New York: G. P. Putnam's Sons, 1904–5.

Jensen, Merrill. *The Documentary History of the Ratification of the Constitution.* Madison: State Historical Society of Wisconsin, 1943.

Johnson, Samuel. *Works.* Troy, NY: Pafraets, 1913.

Jones, Joseph. *Letters of Joseph Jones of Virginia, 1777–1787.* New York: Times Books, 1971.

Jones, Thomas. *History of New York during the Revolutionary War.* 2 vols. New York: Times Books, 1968.

Jordan, Winthrop. *White over Black: American Attitudes toward the Negro, 1550–1812.* Chapel Hill: University of North Carolina Press, 1968.

The Journals of Each Provincial Congress of Massachusetts in 1774 and 1775. Boston: Dutton and Wentworth, 1838.

Journals of the Provincial Congress of the State of New York. Albany, NY: T. Weed, 1842.

Kaplan, Emma Nogrady, and Sidney Kaplan. *The Black Presence in the Era of the American Revolution.* Amherst: University of Massachusetts Press, 1989.

Kaplan, Sidney. "The 'Domestic Insurrections' of the Declaration of Independence." *Journal of Negro History* 61 (July 1976): 243–55.

Kapur, Sudarshan. *Raising Up a Prophet.* Boston: Beacon, 1992.

King, Boston. "Memoirs of the Life of Boston King, a Black Preacher, Written by Himself, during His Residence at Kingswood School." In *Unchained Voices: An Anthology of Black Authors in the English-Speaking World of the Eighteenth Century*, edited by Vincent Carretta, 351–68. Lexington: University of Kentucky Press, 1996.

Kolchin, Peter. *Unfree Labor: American Slavery and Russian Serfdom.* Cambridge, MA: Belknap Press, 1987.

Konkle, Burton Alva. *George Bryan and the Constitution of Pennsylvania.* Philadelphia: W. J. Campbell, 1922.

Kozy, Charlene Johnson. "Tories Transplanted: The Caribbean Exile and Plantation of the Southern Loyalists." *Georgia Historical Quarterly* 75 (Spring 1991): 18–42.

Kramnick, Isaac, and Michael Foot, eds. *The Thomas Paine Reader.* New York: Penguin, 1987.

Kreinheder, Hazel Fuller. *Minority Military Service in Massachusetts, 1775–1783.* Washington, DC: Daughters of the American Revolution, 1999.

Lafayette, Marquis de. *Lafayette in the Age of the American Revolution: Selected Letters and Papers, 1776–1790.* Edited by Stanley J. Idzerda. Ithaca, NY: Cornell University Press, 1977.

Laurens, Henry. *The Papers of Henry Laurens.* Edited by David Chestnutt, Phillip Hamer, and George C. Rogers. 16 vols. Columbia: University of South Carolina Press, 1986–2000.

Lee, Jean Butenhoff. *The Price of Nationhood.* New York: Norton, 1994.

Lepore, Jill. "Goodbye Columbus: When America Won Its Independence, What Became of the Slaves Who Fled for Theirs?" *New Yorker*, May 8, 2006, 1–5.

———. *New York Burning: Liberty, Slavery and Conspiracy in 18th Century New York.* New York: Vintage, 2006.

———. "The Tightening Vise." In *Slavery in New York*, edited by Ira Berlin and Leslie M. Harris. New York: New Press, 2005.

"Letters, Colonial and Revolutionary, Selected from the Dreer Collection of the Historical Society of Pennsylvania." *Pennsylvania Magazine of History and Biography* 42 (1918).

Liele, George. "An Account of Several Baptist Churches, Consisting Chiefly of Negro Slaves Particularly of One at Kingston in Jamaica; and Another at Savannah in Georgia." In *Unchained Voices: An Anthology of Black Authors in the English-Speaking World of the Eighteenth Century*, edited by Vincent Carretta, 325–32. Lexington: University of Kentucky Press, 1996.

Lincoln, William Z. *History of Worcester, Massachusetts from Its Earliest Settlement to*

September 1836, with Various Notices Pertaining to the History of Worcester County. Worcester, MA: M. D. Phillips, 1862.

Lipset, Seymour Martin. *Continental Divide: The Values and Institutions of the United States and Canada.* New York: Routledge and Kegan Paul, 1990.

———. *The First New Nation: The United States in Historical and Comparative Perspective.* New York: Basic, 1963.

Livermore, George. *An Historical Research Respecting the Opinions of the Founders of the Republic: On Negroes as Slaves, as Citizens, and as Soldiers.* Boston: J. Wilson, 1862.

Livingston, William. *Papers of William Livingston.* Edited by Carl E. Prince. 5 vols. Trenton: New Jersey Historical Commission, 1979.

Locke, John. *Two Treatises of Government.* New York: Hafner, 1947.

Lucey, Donna. *I Dwell in Possibility: Women Build a Nation, 1600–1820.* Washington, DC: National Geographic, 2001.

Lynd, Staughton. *Class Struggle, Slavery and the United States Constitution.* Indianapolis: Bobbs-Merrill, 1968.

Madison, James. *The Writings of James Madison, Comprising His Public Papers and Private Correspondence Now for the First Time Printed.* Edited by Galliard Hunt. New York: G. P. Putnam's, 1900.

Madison, James, Alexander Hamilton, and John Jay. *The Federalist Papers.* New York: Mentor, 1999.

Maier, Pauline. *From Resistance to Revolution: Colonial Radicals and the Development of American Opposition to Britain, 1765–1776.* New York: Norton, 1991.

Mann, Barbara Alice. *George Washington's War on Native America.* Westport, CT: Praeger, 2005.

Mansfield, Lord. Somersett v. Stewart, June 22, 1772. In *Howell's State Trials,* edited by Thomas Bayly Howell, 20:79–82. London: Routledge and Kegan Paul, 1972.

Marx, Karl. *Capital.* 3 vols. New York: International, 1967.

———. *Collected Works.* 50 vols. New York: International, 1975–2005.

Marx, Karl, and Friedrich Engels. *The Communist Manifesto.* Edited by David Ryazanoff. New York: Russell and Russell, 1953.

———. *Selected Correspondence.* Moscow: Progress, 1975.

Massey, Gregory. *John Laurens and the American Revolution.* Charleston: University of South Carolina Press, 2000.

Mason, George. *Papers of George Mason, 1725–1792.* Edited by Robert P. Rutland. 3 vols. Chapel Hill: University of North Carolina Press, 1971.

McCowan, George Smith, Jr. *The British Occupation of Charleston, 1780–1782.* Columbia: University of South Carolina Press, 1972.

McCullough, David. *John Adams.* New York: Simon and Schuster, 2001.

———. "What the Fog Wrought." In *What If? The World's Foremost Military Historians Imagine What Might Have Been,* edited by Robert Cowley. New York: Putnam, 1999.

McManus, Edgar J. *Black Bondage in the North.* Syracuse, NY: Syracuse University Press, 1976.

Mellon, Matthew T. *Early American Views on Negro Slavery: From the Letters and Papers of the Founders of the Republic*. New York: Bergman, 1934,

Miller, Helen Hill. *George Mason: Gentleman Revolutionary*. Chapel Hill: University of North Carolina Press, 1975.

Mitchell, Mary H. "Slavery in Connecticut and Especially in New Haven." *Papers of the New Haven Colony Historical Society* 10 (1951): 286–312.

Montesquieu. *De l'esprit des lois*. Edited by R. Derathe. 2 vols. Paris: Gallimard, 1973.

Moore, Barrington, Jr. *The Social Origins of Dictatorship and Democracy*. Boston: Beacon Press, 1965.

Moore, Dennis D., ed. *More Letters from the American Farmer: An Edition of the Essays in English Left Unpublished by Crevecoeur*. Athens: University of Georgia Press, 1995.

Moore, George H. *Historical Notes on the Employment of Negroes in the American Army of the Revolution*. New York: C. T. Evans, 1862.

———. *Notes on the History of Slavery in Massachusetts*. New York: Appleton, 1866.

Morgan, Edmund S. *American Slavery, American Freedom: The Ordeal of Colonial Virginia*. New York: Norton, 1975.

Morgan, Phillip, and Andrew O'Shaughnessy. "Arming Slaves in the American Revolution." In *Arming Slaves from Classical Times to the Modern Age*, edited by Christopher Brown and Philip Morgan. New Haven, CT: Yale University Press, 2006.

Moss, Richard Shannon. *Slavery on Long Island: A Study in Local Institutional and Early African-American Communal Life*. New York: Garland, 1993.

Muhlenberg, Henry Melchior. *The Journals of Henry Melchior Muhlenberg*. 3 vols. Philadelphia: Lutheran Historical Society, 1982.

Nadelhaft, Jerome J. *The Disorders of War: Revolution in South Carolina*. Orono: University of Maine Press, 1981.

Nash, Gary B. *Forging Freedom: The Formation of Philadelphia's Black Community, 1720–1840*. Cambridge, MA: Harvard University Press, 1988.

———. *The Forgotten Fifth*. Cambridge, MA: Harvard University Press, 2006.

———. *Race and Revolution*, Madison, WI: Madison House Publishers, 1993.

———. *Red, White and Black: The Peoples of Early North America*. Englewood Cliffs, NJ: Prentice-Hall, 1992.

———. "Thomas Peters." In *Race, Class, and Politics: Essays on American Colonial and Revolutionary Society*. Urbana: University of Illinois Press, 1986.

———. *The Unknown American Revolution: The Unruly Birth of Democracy and the Struggle to Create America*. New York: Penguin, 2006.

———. *The Urban Crucible: Social Change, Political Consciousness, and the Origins of the American Revolution*. Cambridge, MA: Harvard University Press, 1986.

Nash, Gary B., and Graham Russell Gao Hodges. *Friends of Liberty: Thomas Jefferson, Tadeus Kosciuszko and Agrippa Hull*. New York: Basic, 2008.

Nash, Gary B., and Jean R. Soderlund. *Freedom by Degrees: Emancipation in Pennsylvania and Its Aftermath*. New York: Oxford University Press, 1991.

Nell, William Cooper. *The Colored Patriots of the American Revolution: With the Sketches of Several Distinguished Colored Persons, to Which Is Added a Brief Survey of the Conditions and Prospects of Colored Americans.* Boston: Robert F. Wallcut, 1855. Reprint, New York: Arno Press, 1968.

———. *Services of Colored Americans in the Wars of 1776 and 1812.* Boston: Robert F. Wallcut, 1852.

Nelson, William. *The American Tory.* Boston: Beacon, 1964.

Newbury, Colin W., ed. *British Policy toward West Africa.* Oxford: Clarendon Press, 1965.

Newman, Debra L. "List of Black Servicemen Compiled from the War Department Collection of Revolutionary War Records." Washington, DC: National Archives, 1974.

O'Callaghan, E. B., and Bernard Falnow, eds. *Documents Relative to the Colonial History of the State of New York.* 5 vols. Albany, NY: Weed, Parsons, 1853.

Oldham, James. "New Light on Mansfield and Slavery." *Journal of British Studies* 27 (1988): 45–68.

Olwell, Robert A. "Domestick Enemies: Slavery and Political Independence in South Carolina, May 1775–March 1776." *Journal of Southern History* 55 (February 1989): 21–48.

———. *Masters, Slaves and Subjects: The Culture of Power in the South Carolina Low Country.* Ithaca, NY: Cornell University Press, 1998.

Padover, Saul, ed. *The Washington Papers.* New York: Harper, 1955.

Palmer, R. R. *The Age of the Democratic Revolution: A Political History of Europe and America, 1760–1800.* 2 vols. Princeton, NJ: Princeton University Press, 1964.

Pennypecker, Morton. *Historical Notes Relating to Long Island.* 2 vols. New York: Long Island Historical Society, n.d.

Perdue, Charles L., Jr., Thomas E. Barden, and Robert K. Phillips, eds. *Weevils in the Wheat: Interviews with Virginia's Ex-Slaves.* Charlottesville: University of Virginia Press, 1992.

Phillips, Ulrich Bonell, ed. *Plantation and Frontier Documents, 1649–1863.* Washington, DC: Carnegie, 1909.

Piecuch, Jim. *Three Peoples, One King: Loyalists, Indians and Slaves in the Revolutionary South, 1775–1782.* Columbia: University of South Carolina Press, 2008.

Plato. *The Laws.* 2 vols. Cambridge, MA: Loeb Classical Library, 1961.

———. *Lysis, Symposium, Gorgias.* Cambridge, MA: Loeb Classical Library, 1925.

———. *The Republic.* 2 vols. Cambridge, MA: Loeb Classical Library, 1970.

Price, Richard. *Maroon Societies: Rebel Slave Communities in the Americas.* Baltimore: Johns Hopkins University Press, 1996.

Public Records of the Colony of Connecticut. 15 vols. Hartford: Brown and Parsons, 1850–90.

Pulis, John W. "Bridging Troubled Waters." In *Moving On: Black Loyalists in the Afro-Atlantic World,* edited by John W. Pulis, 183–222. New York: Garland, 1999

———, ed. *Moving On: Black Loyalists in the Afro-Atlantic World.* New York: Garland, 1999.

Pybus, Cassandra. *Epic Journeys of Freedom: Runaway Slaves of the American Revolution and Their Global Quest for Liberty*. Boston: Beacon Press, 2006.

———. http://www.blackloyalist.info. (This website supplies important details on those who emigrated with the British.)

———. "Jefferson's Faulty Math: The Question of Slave Defections in the American Revolution." *William and Mary Quarterly* 62 (April 2005): 243–64.

Quarles, Benjamin. "Dunmore as Liberator." *William and Mary Quarterly* 15 (October 1958): 494–507.

———. *The Negro in the American Revolution*. Chapel Hill: University of North Carolina Press, 1961.

Quintal, George, Jr. *Patriots of Color: 'A Peculiar Beauty and Merit.'* Boston: National Park Service, 2005.

Rael, Patrick. "The Long Death of Slavery." In *Slavery in New York*, edited by Ira Berlin and Leslie M. Harris. New York: New Press, 2005.

Raphael, Ray. *A People's History of the American Revolution: How Common People Shaped the Fight for Independence*. New York: New Press, 2001.

Rawls, John. *The Law of Peoples*. Cambridge, MA: Harvard University Press, 1999.

———. *Political Liberalism*. New York: Columbia University Press, 1993.

———. *A Theory of Justice*. Cambridge, MA: Harvard University Press, 1971.

Rediker, Marcus. "A Motley Crew of Rebels: Sailors, Slaves and the Coming of the American Revolution." In *The Transforming Hand of Revolution: Reconsidering the American Revolution as a Social Movement*, edited by Ronald Hoffman and Peter J. Albert. Charlottesville: University of Virginia Press, 1995.

Rediker, Marcus, and Peter Linebaugh. *The Many-Headed Hydra: Sailors, Slaves, Commoners and the Hidden History of the Revolutionary Atlantic*. Boston: Beacon Press, 2000.

Reynolds, David S. *John Brown, Abolitionist: The Man Who Killed Slavery, Sparked the Civil War and Seeded Civil Rights*. New York: Knopf, 2006.

Riley, Saundra. *Homeward Bound: A History of the Bahama Islands to 1850 with a Definitive Study of Abaco in the American Loyalist Plantation Period*. Miami: Island Research, 1983.

Rippon, John, ed. *Baptist Annual Register for 1798, 1799, 1800 and Part of 1801*. London: Brown and James, 1802.

Robinson, Donald. *Slavery in the Structure of American Politics*. New York: Norton, 1970.

Robinson, Marilynne. "Freed." *New York Times Sunday Book Review*, January 9, 2005.

Robinson, St. John. "Southern Loyalists in the Caribbean and Central America." *South Carolina Historical Magazine* 93 (1992): 205–20.

Rousseau, Jean Jacques. *Discourse on Political Economy*. West Valley City, UT: Waking Lion Press, 2006.

———. *Du contrat social*. Paris: Flammarion, 1992.

———. *Oeuvres completes*. Paris: Gallimard, 1964.

Royster, Charles. *A Revolutionary People at War: The Continental Army and the American Character*. Chapel Hill: University of North Carolina Press, 1979.

Rucker, William C. *The River Flows On: Black Resistance, Culture and Identity Formation in Early America*. Baton Rouge: Louisiana State University Press, 2006.

Ryan, William R. *The World of Thomas Jeremiah: Charles Town on the Eve of the American Revolution*. New York: Oxford University Press, 2010.

Salley, A. S., Jr., ed. *Journal of the House of Representatives of South Carolina, January 8, 1782–February 26, 1782*. Columbia: Historical Commission of South Carolina, 1916.

Saunders, Gail. *The Bahamian Loyalists and Their Slaves*. London: Macmillan, 1983.

Scarry, Elaine. *The Body in Pain: The Making and Unmaking of the World*. Oxford: Oxford University Press, 1987.

Schama, Simon. *Rough Crossings: Britain, the Slaves and the American Revolution*. New York: Ecco, 2006.

Schaw, Janet. *Journal of a Lady of Quality*. New Haven, CT: Yale University Press, 1921.

Schrecker, Ellen. *No Ivory Tower*. Oxford: Oxford University Press, 1986.

Selig, Robert A. "A German Soldier in America, 1780–1783." *William and Mary Quarterly*, 3rd ser., 50 (July 1993): 575–90.

———. "The Revolution's Black Soldiers." http://www.Americanrevolution.org./blk.html.

Shaffer, E. T. H. "The Rejected Laurens: A Carolina Tragedy." *Proceedings of the South Carolina Historical Society* (1934).

Sharp, Granville. *Memoirs*. London: Colburn, 1820.

Sharp, James Roger. *American Politics in the Early Republic: The Nation in Crisis*. New Haven, CT: Yale University Press, 1993.

Shklar, Judith N. *American Citizenship*. Cambridge, MA: Harvard University Press, 1991.

Shyllon, Folarin Olawale. *Black People in Britain, 1555–1833*. London: Oxford University Press, 1977.

Siebert, Wilbur. *The Legacy of the American Revolution to the British West Indies and Bahamas: A Chapter out of the History of the American Loyalists*. Boston: Gregg, 1972.

Singer, Alan J. *New York and Slavery: Time to Teach the Truth*. Albany, New York: SUNY Press, 2008.

Skemp, Sheila, L. *William Franklin: Son of a Patriot, Servant of a King*. New York: Oxford University Press, 1990.

Slaughter, Thomas P. *The Beautiful Soul of John Woolman: Apostle of Abolition*. New York: Hill and Wang, 2008.

Smith, James Morton. *Freedom's Fetters: The Alien and Sedition Acts and American Civil Liberties*. Ithaca, NY: Cornell University Press, 1956.

Smyth, Edward A. "Mob Violence in Prerevolutionary Norfolk Virginia." Master's thesis, Old Dominion University, 1965.

Sobel, Mechal. *The World They Made Together: Black and White Values in Eighteenth Century Virginia*. Princeton, NJ: Princeton University Press, 1987.

Soderlund, Jean. *Quakers and Slavery: A Divided Spirit*. Princeton, NJ: Princeton University Press, 1985

Souther, Rita Elaine. *Minority Military Service: Rhode Island, 1775–1783*. Washington, DC: Daughters of the American Revolution, 1988.

Sparks, Jared, ed. *Correspondence of the American Revolution: Being Letters of Eminent Men to George Washington*. 4 vols. Boston: Little, Brown, 1853.

Spurlin, Paul Merrill. *Montesquieu in America, 1760–1801*. University: Louisiana State University Press, 1940.

Stampp, Kenneth M. *The Peculiar Institution: Slavery in the Ante-Bellum South*. New York: Vintage, 1956.

Staples, William R. *Rhode Island in the Continental Congress: With the Journal of the Convention That Adopted the Constitution, 1765–1790*. Providence, RI: Providence Press, 1870.

Stegmaier, Mark I. "Maryland's Fear of Insurrection at the Time of Braddock's Defeat." *Maryland Historical Magazine* 71 (Winter 1976): 467–83.

Stevens, Benjamin F., ed. *Facsimiles of Manuscripts in European Archives Relating to America, 1777–1783*. 26 vols. London: Malby, 1889–95.

Stryker, William S., ed., *Minutes of the Provincial Congress and Council of Safety of the State of New Jersey, 1775–1776*. Trenton, NJ: Sharp, 1879.

Szatmary, David P. *Shays Rebellion: The Making of an Agrarian Insurrection*. Amherst: University of Massachusetts Press, 1980.

Thomas, Hugh. *The Slave Trade: The Story of the Atlantic Slave Trade, 1440–1870*. New York: Simon and Schuster, 1997.

Thompson, Edward P. *Making of the English Working Class*. London: Vintage, 1966.

Thompson, Mack. *Moses Brown, Reluctant Reformer*. Chapel Hill: University of North Carolina Press, 1962.

Townsend, Sara B. *An American Soldier: The Life of John Laurens, Drawn Largely from Correspondence between his Father and Himself*. Raleigh, NC: Edwards and Broughton, 1958.

Troxler, Carole. "The British Evacuation of East Florida." *Florida Historical Quarterly* 60 (1981): 39–58.

Tyson, George. "The Carolina Black Corps: Legacy of Revolution, 1783–98." *Revista Interamericana* 5 (1975–76): 648–64.

Uhlendorf, Bernhard A., ed. *The Siege of Charleston: Diaries and Letters of Hessian Officers from the von Jungkenn Papers in the William L. Clements Library*. Ann Arbor: University of Michigan Press, 1938.

US Bureau of the Census. "Negro Population, 1790–1915." New York: Arno, 1968.

Van Buskirk, Judith L. *Generous Enemies: Patriots and Loyalists in Revolutionary New York*. Philadelphia: University of Pennsylvania Press, 2002.

Van Cleve, George William. *A Slaveholders' Union: Slavery, Politics, and the Constitution in the Early American Republic*. Chicago: University of Chicago Press, 2010.

Van Schreeven, William James. *Revolutionary Virginia: The Road to Independence.* Charlottesville: University of Virginia Press, 1973.

Venturi, Franco. *The Roots of Revolution: A History of the Populist and Socialist Movements in 19th Century Russia.* London: Phoenix, 1991.

Wadstroem, C. B., and August Nordenskjoeld. *Plan for a Free Community upon the Coast of Africa under the Protection of Great Britain.* London: R. Hindmarsh, 1789.

Walker, Barrington, ed. *Immigration and Racism in Canada.* Toronto: Canadian Scholars, 2008.

Walker, James W. St. G. *The Black Loyalists: The Search for a Promised Land in Nova Scotia and Sierra Leone, 1783–1870.* Toronto: University of Toronto Press, 1975.

———. "Land and Settlement in Nova Scotia." In *History of Immigration and Racism in Canada: Essential Readings*, edited by Barrington Walker. Toronto: Canadian Scholars Press, 2008.

Wallace, David Duncan. *Life of Henry Laurens.* New York: G. P. Putnam's Sons, 1915.

Walzer, Michael. *Exodus and Revolution.* New York: Basic Books, 1985.

———. *Just and Unjust Wars.* New York: Basic Books, 1977.

Washington, George. *The Papers of George Washington.* Confederation Series, edited by W. W. Abbot and Dorothy Twohig. Charlottesville: University of Virginia Press, 1992.

———. *Papers of George Washington.* Revolutionary War Series, edited by W. W. Abbot and Dorothy Twohig. Charlottesville: University of Virginia Press, 1987.

———. Washington Papers. Microfilm. Series 4, reel 46. Library of Congress.

Watson, John H. "In Re Vermont Constitution of 1777." *Proceedings of the Vermont Historical Society* (1919–20).

Weber, Max. *Economy and Society: An Outline of Interpretive Sociology.* Edited and translated by Guenther Roth and Claus Wittich. 3 vols. New York: Bedminister, 1968.

Wells, Cheryl A. "New York City Slave Rebellion (1712)." In *Encyclopedia of Slave Resistance and Rebellion*, vol. 1, edited by Junius P. Rodriguez. Westport, CT: Greenwood, 2007.

West, Richard. *Back to Africa: A History of Sierra Leone and Liberia.* London: Jonathan Cape, 1970.

White, David O. *Connecticut's Black Soldiers, 1775–83.* Chester, CT: Pequot, 1973.

Wiencek, Henry. *An Imperfect God: George Washington, His Slaves and the Founding of America.* New York: Farrar, Straus and Giroux, 2003.

Wilkinson, Eliza. *Letters of Eliza Wilkinson during the Invasion and Possession of Charlestown, S.C. by the British in the Revolutionary War.* Edited by Charlotte Gilman. New York: Arno, 1969.

Williams, Catherine Read. *Biography of Revolutionary Heroes; Containing the Life of Brigadier General William Barton, and Also, of Captain Stephen Olney.* New York: Wiley and Putnam, 1839.

Williams, George Washington. *History of the Negro Race from 1619–1880.* 2 vols. New York: G. P. Putnam's, 1883.

Willis, William S. "Divide and Rule: Red, White, and Black in the Southeast." *Journal of Negro History* 48 (July 1963): 157–76.

Wilson, Ellen Gibson. *John Clarkson and the African Adventure*. London: Macmillan, 1980.

———. *The Loyal Blacks*. New York: Capricorn, 1976.

Wilson, Louis. "List of Black and Narragansett Patriots in Rhode Island." Unpublished manuscript. Rhode Island Historical Society, 1990.

Winks, Robin W. *The Blacks in Canada: A History*. New Haven, CT: Yale University Press, 1971.

Witness to America's Past: Two Centuries of Collecting by the Massachusetts Historical Society. Boston: Fine Arts, 1991.

Wood, Gordon S. "Never Forget: They Had Lots of Slaves." *New York Times Sunday Book Review*, December 14, 2003.

———. *The Radicalism of the American Revolution*. New York: Vintage.

Wood, Peter H. *Black Majority: Negroes in South Carolina from 1670 to the Stono Rebellion*. New York: Knopf, 1974.

———. "The Dream Deferred: Black Freedom Struggles on the Eve of White Independence." In *Resistance: Studies in African, Caribbean and Afro-American History*, edited by Gary Okihiro. Amherst: University of Massachusetts Press, 1986.

———. "'Taking Care of Business' in Revolutionary South Carolina: Republicanism and the Slave Society." In *The Southern Experience in the American Revolution*, edited by Jeffrey J. Crowe and Larry E. Tise. Chapel Hill: University of North Carolina Press, 1978.

———. "'Twas a Negro Who Taught Them." In *The Invisible War*, edited by Y. N. Kly. Atlanta, GA: Clarity Press, 2006.

Wright, Desmond, ed. *Red, White and True Blue*. New York: AMS Press, 1976.

Wrike, Peter Jennings. *The Governor's Island: Gwynn's Island, Virginia during the Revolution*. Richmond, VA: Brandylane, 1993.

Zilversmit, Arthur. *The First Emancipation: The Abolition of Slavery in the North*. Chicago: University of Chicago Press, 1967.

ARCHIVAL AND ORIGINAL SOURCES

Abstract of Men Victualled at Gibb's Landing, Camp Charlestown Neck from April 7 to 9, 1780. MacKenzie Papers. WLCL-UM.

An Abstract of the Number of Men, Women and Children, Negroes and Prisoners Victualled at Savannah from 11th to 20th October, 1779. Clinton Papers, vol. 72, no. 10. WLCL-UM.

Acts of the Georgia General Assembly, 1786–1789. Dr. 54, Box 51. GDAH.

Alexander Leslie, to Sir Guy Carleton, October 18, 1782. Item no. 5925. PRO 30/55/52.

Allen, John. *The Watchman's Alarm to Lord N. H.* Salem, MA: Russell, 1774.

American Weekly Mercury, Tuesday February 26 to Tuesday March 5, 1733–34. Microfilm. Fordham University Library.

Appleton, Nathaniel. *Considerations on Slavery in a Letter to a Friend*. Boston: Edes and Gill, 1767.

Archey, Dinah. "Petition to His Excellency Sir Guy Carleton," August 2, 1783. WLCL-UM.

Baker, Moses. "An Account of Moses Baker, A Mulatoo Baptist Preacher from Martha Brea, in Jamaica." *Evangelical Magazine*, September 1803, 365–71.

Ball Family Papers. William Perkins Library, Duke University, Durham, NC.

Beckley, John. "Extract from the Journal of Assembly." NA.

Board of Police. *Proceedings*. CO 5/520. PRO.

Book of Negroes, Document 10427. PRO 30/55/100.

Brandum, Margaret, to Cols. John and Charles Tucker, December 11, 1824. Item no. 3307. AL-UV.

Brown, John. "Address to the Virginia Court at Charles Town, Virginia, November 2, 1859." http://www.pbs.org/wgbh/aia/[art4/4h2943t.html.

Brown, Moses. Papers of Moses Brown. RIHS.

Clarke, Alexander, to Lord Cornwallis, July 10, 1780. PRO 30/11/2.

Clarkson Papers. British Museum.

Clinton, Sir Henry. "Philipsburg Proclamation," June 30, 1779. WLCL-UM.

Clinton Papers. WLCL-UM.

Collections of the Massachusetts Historical Society. Boston: n.p., 1877.

Continental Congress. Resolution, March 29, 1779. http://memory.loc.gov/cgi-bin/query/r?ammem/hlaw:@field(DOCID +@lit(jc01380)).

Cornwallis Papers. PRO 30/11/64, 97.

Court Martial Proceedings against Samuel Doremus et al. War Office Papers 71/96/126–307. PRO.

Cowpens Papers. Theodorus Bailey Myers Collection. SCHS.

Cuffe, Paul. *A Brief Account of the Settlement and Present Situation of the Colony of Sierra Leone in Africa*. Cuffe Papers. LOC.

Cuffe, Paul (son). *Narrative of the Life and Adventures of Paul Cuffe, a Pequot Indian during Thirty Years Spent at Sea and in Travelling in Foreign Lands*. Vernon, CT: Hill, 1839.

Cushing, William. Notes on His Cases, 1783. Microfilm P-406. MHS.

Declaration of the General Assembly of Virginia, December 15, 1775. John Brown Carter Library, Brown University, Providence, RI.

Edgehill-Randolph Papers. LOC.

Eldridge, Elleanor. *Memoirs*. Providence, RI: B. T. Albro, 1838.

Emmet Collection. NYPL.

Ford Collection. NYPL.

Gage Papers. WLCL-UM.

General List of Negroes Employed in the Royal Artillery Department for the Month of November (and December), 1781. Wray Papers, vol. 7. WLCL-UM.

General Treasurer's Accounts, 1761–81. Alphabet Book No. 6 for 1778. Rhode Island State Library, Providence.

Germain Papers. WLCL-UM.

Gilmor Papers, 1689–1855, MS. 387.1. Maryland Historical Society, Baltimore.

Greene Papers. WLCL-UM.

Hamond Naval Papers, 1766–1825. McGregor Collection, accession no. 680. TWML-UV.

Hart, Levi. *Liberty Described and Recommended.* Hartford, CT: Eben, Watson, 1775.

Hopkins, Samuel. *A Dialogue concerning the Slavery of the Africans.* Norwich, CT: Spooner, 1776.

Horsmanden, Daniel. *A Journal of the Proceedings in the Detection of the Conspiracy, 1774.* http://law2.umkc.edu/faculty/projects/trials/negroplot/prefaceplot.html.

Howe Papers. WLCL-UM.

The Humble Memorial and Petition of Thomas Peters, n.d. (received December 24, 1790). CO 217/63. PRO.

Jefferson, Thomas. Papers. LOC.

Johnston, William, and Family Papers. Miscellaneous Manuscript Collection. LOC.

Kingston, March. "Memorial to the Honorable Commissioners Appointed by Act of Parliament for Enquiring into the Losses and Services of the American Loyalists." Audit Office, class 13, vol. 30, folio 293. PRO.

Kinloch, Francis, to John Laurens, July 1, 1776. In Private Hands. Cited by Gregory D. Massey, *John Laurens and the American Revolution.* Columbia: University of South Carolina Press, 2000, 60.

Laurens, Henry. *Letterbook.* Historical Society of Pennsylvania, Philadelphia.

———. Papers. SCL-USC.

Laurens, Henry, to George Washington, March 16, 1779. http://memory.loc.gov/cgi-bin/ampage?collID=mgw4&fileName-gwpage056.dl&recNum/=911.

Laurens, Henry, and John Laurens. Papers. LOC.

———. Papers. NA.

Laurens, John, to Francis Kinloch, June 16, 1776. Chamberlain Collection. Boston Public Library.

———, May 28, 1776, and Spring 1776. Thomas Addis Emmet Collection. NYPL.

———, November 6, 1774. Theodorus Bailey Myers Collection. Manuscript and Archive Divisions. NYPL.

———, September 30, 1776. Emmet Collection, NYPL.

———, Summer 1776. Emmet Collection. NYPL.

Lee Papers. AL-UV.

Letters and Documents Relating to Slavery in Massachusetts. 5th series. Collections of the Massachusetts Historical Society, Boston.

Letters from the Governors, 1778–1779. Rhode Island Archives, Providence.

Lincoln, Benjamin, to George Washington, November 7, 1779. http://www.familytales .org/results.php?tla=bel.

Macaulay, Zachary. Diary, 1793–94. Abolition and Emancipation. Reel 2. Marlborough, Wilshire, UK: Adam Mathew Publications, n.d.

MacKenzie Papers. WLCL-UM.

Manumission Book for the Three Philadelphia Monthly Meetings, 1772–1796. Quaker Collection. Haverford College.

Marion, Francis, to John Matthews, August 30, 1782, 38–43-6. Middleton Papers. SCHS. http://www.familytales.org/dbDisplay.php?id=ltr_bel3205&person.bel.

Marion, General, to Col. Peter Horry, March 10, 1782. SCHS.

Marshall Papers. WLCL-UM.

Massachusetts Negro Petition, April 1773. Plimpton Collection. Columbia University.

The Memorial of Benjamin Whitecuff, a Black, June 3, 1784. AO 12119/1227061. PRO.

Memorial of the Officers, Emmerich's Chasseurs, June 22, 1779. Clinton Papers, vol. 61, no. 20. WLCL-UM.

Minor Papers. 2 vols. Microfilm. LOC.

Miscellaneous Papers of the Continental Congress. Microcopy 247. NA.

Morgan Daniel, to Nathanael Greene, January 14, 1781. Cowpens Papers. Theodorus Bailey Myers Collection, 24–28. SCHS.

Morris, General Lewis. Letters. Publication Fund Series 7 (1876). NYHS.

Muster Book of Free Black Settlement at Birchtown, 1784. PAC.

Muster Roll of the Civil Branch of Ordnance Attending His Majesty's Field Train of Artillery, Charlestown, So. Carolina, 30th June, 1780. Wray Papers. WLCL-UM.

Negroes, Belonging to Captain Martin's Company, 1778. WLCL-UM.

New Jersey Gazette (Burlington and Trenton), April 24, 1782. Microfilm, reel 2. American Antiquarian Society. Fordham University Library.

New York Gazette, 1733–44 (incomplete). NYPL.

Olney, Jeremiah. Papers. RIHS.

Olney, Jonathan. Papers. RIHS.

Orderly Book, Great Britain Army. LOC.

Otis, James. *The Rights of the British Colonies Asserted and Proved*. Boston: Edes and Gill, 1764.

Parish Collection. Box 16. NYHS.

Parliamentary Commission Rulings on Claims of Blacks. AO 12/99. PRO.

Patterson, James, to the Board of Police, June 13, 1780. CO 5/52012. PRO.

Payroll of Capt. Jn Dexter's Co. Military Papers, Revolutionary War. Rhode Island State Library, Providence.

Peebles, John. Diary. SCL-USC.

Pennsylvania Evening Post, October 23, 1777–October 26, 1784. Microfilm, reel 2. Early American Newspapers. Collection of Yale University.

Pennsylvania Packet, January 7, 1778–December 30, 1780. Reel 2. American Antiquarian Society, Worcester, MA.

Peters, Thomas. Nomination of Thomas Peters. New Brunswick Land Petitions, 1790, RS 108, reel F1037. Public Archives of New Brunswick.

———. Petition, December 18, 1790. PRO.

Philmore, J. *Two Dialogues on the Man-Trade*. London: Waugh, 1760.

Pinckney, Charles Cotesworth, to Arthur Middleton, August 13, 1782. In

"Correspondence of Hon. Arthur Middleton." Edited by Joseph Barnewell. *South Carolina Historical Magazine*, vol. 28, 1926.

Postell, John. Letters. Microcopy 247. NA.

Prioleau Papers. SCHS.

Randolph, Peyton. "Proclamation of the House of Burgesses," May 31, 1774. AL-UV.

Report on American Manuscripts in the Royal Institution. Dublin: John Falconer, 1906.

A Report to Congress, 1786, by the Rhode Island Legislature. Handwritten document. RIHS.

Return of the Black Pioneers Commanded by Lieutenant Colonel Allen Steward, September 13, 1783. PRO.

Return of Blacks under the Command of General Washington, Drafted by Adjutant-General Scammel. RIHS.

Return of Captain Martin's Company, undated. WLCL-UM.

A Return of the Company of Black Pioneers Commanded by Lt. Col. Allen Steward, September 13, 1783. PRO.

Returns of Loyalists. CO 5/561/409 and 5/561/410. PRO.

A Return of Negroes for the Royal Artillery Department, Lenings Landing, April 28, 1780. Clinton Papers, vol. 95, no. 27. WLCL-UM.

Return of Nova Scotians Emigrating to Sierra Leone. CO 217/163. PRO.

Return of the Number of Men, Women, and Children of the British and Foreign Regiments New Levies Civil Departments &c Victualled at New York and the Different Outposts between 14th and 21st November, 1779, signed by Daniel Wier. Clinton Papers, vol. 76, no. 21. WLCL-UM.

Return of the Number of Men, Women and Children of the British and Foreign Regiments New Levies Civil Departments &c Victualled at New York and the Different Outposts between the 19th and 26th September, 1779. Clinton Papers, vol. 69, no. 17. WLCL-UM.

Return of Persons Who Came Off from Virginia with General Matthews in the Fleet the 24th of May, 1779. PRO 30/55/95.

Return of Persons Who Emigrated to Different Parts of the British Dominions, May 2, 1786. CO 5/561. PRO.

Romeyn, Dirck, to Richard Varick, July 20, 1782. Varick Papers. NYHS.

Rush, Benjamin. *Address to the Inhabitants of the British Settlements on the Slavery of Negroes in America*. Philadelphia: J. Dunlap, 1773.

Schomburg Center for Research in Black Culture. Slavery and Abolition Collection. NYPL.

Sharp, Granville. *A Short Sketch of Temporary Regulations (Until Better Shall Be Proposed) for the Intended Settlement on the Grain Coast of Africa, Near Sierra Leone*. London: H. Baldwin, 1786.

Steele, Murphy. Statement of Lieutenant Murphy Steele, August 16, 1781. Clinton Papers. WLCL-UM.

Swan, James. *Dissuasion to Great Britain and the Colonies from the Slave Trade*. Boston: Russell, 1772.

Varick Papers. NYHS.

Wallace, W. Brown. "To Michael Wallace." Accession no. 38–150. TWML-UV.

Weekly Rehearsal (Boston), Early American Newspapers: *New England Courant* 1721–1727 and *Weekly Rehearsal*, 1731–1735. American Antiquarian Society, Worcester, MA.

White Collection. PANS.

Williams, Catherine Read, ed. *Biography of Revolutionary Heroes.* New York: Wiley and Putnam, 1839.

Woolman, John. *Journal.* http://etext.lib.virginia.edu/toc/modeng/public/WooJour .html.

Wray Papers. WLCL-UM.

Index

Aptheker, Herbert, ix
Arawaks, 272n149
Arbado, Francis, 171
Archey, Dinah, 194
Archias, 282n149
Aristide Jean-Bertrand, 319n59
Aristotle, 1, 48, 273n12, 281n121
Arms, Consider (pseud.), 256
Armstrong (captain), 199
Arnold, Benedict, 29, 120, 199
Article VII. *See* Treaty of Paris
artisans 213, 224, 248; black and white, 2,
    149; and taxes against suffrage in Mas-
    sachusetts, 112
Ashley Hall plantation sacked by British
    irregulars, 30
Associated Loyalists, 149
Attucks, Crispus, 12–13, 103, 264n61, 286n68,
    300n110
Austin, 290n42
Ayscough, William; 98

Babcock, Samuel, 100
Babeuf, 76
Bacchus, Thos, 313n83
Bacon, D., 250
Bahamas, 185, 187, 205, 206, 225
Bailley, James, 72
Bailly, Thomas, 246
Baker, Brister, 107
Baker, David, 169
Baker, Lawrence, 169
Baker, Moses, 187
Balfour, Nisbet, 132, 157
Ball (colonel), 184
Ball, John, 127–28
Ball, Richard, 223
Ballingall, Robert, 182
Banbury, Lucy, 223–24, 313n83
Bance, 225, 236
banditti, 144, 162
Bannerman, Benjamin, 113
Bannister, Cato, 105, 285n57

Baptist, John, 227
Baptists, 210, 215, 231, 233, 240
Barbados, 200–1, 210, 222
barbarism of the Patriots, 157, 159, 204,
    271n140
Barclay, Tam, 201; and Rachel, Elizabeth,
    George, Israel, Tishy, and Jane, 201
Barnes, Jonathan, 106
Barrington (lord), 21
Bartram, A., 191
Bartram, Nancy, 191
Battle of Lexington, 16
Battles, Shadrack, 170
Beacon, Michael, 307n117
Bearmore (major), 195
Beckley, John, 190
Beckwith, George, 195
Beekman, Cornelia, 193
Beekman, Gerald G., 193
Bee, Thomas, 159, 270n116
Belley-Mars, Jean-Baptiste, 222
Bell, William, 160
Benezet, Anthony, 61, 217
Bennett, Lerone, 299n85
Bentley, Anne, 286n82
Bergen County, NJ, 147
Berlin, Ira, 138, 303n6, 307n118
Bermuda, 200–1, 222
Berrigan, Sarah, 306n107
Betty, 248–49
Beverhout, Henry, 235
Beverly, Sylvester, 170
Bicknell, Charles, 277n44
Bicknell, John, 277n44
Birch, Samuel, 191, 192, 195; and Birch cer-
    tificates held by nearly 30 percent in the
    Book of Negroes, 192, 198, 199, 306n105
Birchtown, 198, 210, 211, 221, 224; and break-
    down of occupations in 1784 *Muster Book
    of Free Blacks*, 208, 311n20
Birden, Cato, 313n83
Black Brigade, 141, 148–49, 158
Blackburn, Robin, 260n1, 318n38

tion of, 132, 179–80; treatment of blacks as pawns, 131–32

Campbell, David, 192

Campbell, William, 139, 199, 270n122; and honor 42, 43, 271n137; and rumor of "14,000 weapons," 38, 39; and trying to free Thomas Jeremiah, 271n134, 271n145

Canadian archives, xii

Cape Fear, 269n104

capital punishment, 234

Carleton, Sir Guy, 137, 177, 302n22, n28, n29; and freedom, 306n112; and honor in defeat, 177–206; and ten hearings in New York, 192, 195–96; and Washington, 177–78, 304nn58–59; no "monstrous breach of the public faith," 177, 178; unique role in evading the Treaty of Paris, 189

Carleton, Thomas, 216

Carlton, Christopher, 169

Carolinas, 240

Carpenter, Emmanuel, 249–50

Carr, Job, 249

Carroll, George, 240

Carter, Francis, 126

Carter, Landon, 23, 130

Carter, Robert, 24

Carter, Saml, 312n53

Cassells (colonel), 184

Castleton, Toby, 313n83

Cato (Philadelphia), 115

centralization and abolition, 92

certificates of freedom, 142, 181–83, 189, 197, 198, 200, 204, 301nn16–18, 303n50, 306n105. *See also* Birch certificates; Musgrave certificates

Chaimett, Nancy, 199

Chaney, James, xvi

Champlin, Dick, 100

Champlin, Hazard, 101

Champlin, Jack, 100, 101, 105, 286n55

Champlin, July, 101

Champlin, Newport, 101

Champlin, Sharper, 101

Champlin, Stephen, 100, 101

Champlin, York, 101, 286n55

Channel, Scipio, 239

Charles, 23

Charles, Cato, 312n53

Charlestown, 83, 90–91, 116, 129, 161, 163, 182, 186, 187, 188, 197, 200, 223, 262n5, 291n82, 313nn84–85

Charlestown Royal Gazette, 125

Chase, Jeremiah, 4

Chebucto, 211

Chester County, PA, 115

Chestnut Hill, 98

Child, Lydia Maria, 110–11, 287n86, 287n88

Chloe, 71

Chole, 303n50

Chomsky, Noam, 12

Christianity, 215; and equality in Sierra Leone 207, 222. *See also* Baptists; Methodists; Presbyterians; Quakers

Christophe, Henri, 256

Christopher, Cathy, 200

Christopher, Saturn, 200

Cicero, 77

citizen farmers, 46

Civil War (U.S.), 94, 254, 255

Clark, Alured, 182, 186, 199

Clarke, Alexander, 178–79

Clarke, Paul, 225

Clarkson, John, 207, 221, 224, 316nn155–56; as autocrat or tyrant, 231; historians and his written account, 231, 234, 235, 314n115; racism of, 232–33, 233–34; in Sierra Leone 229–42, 315nn128–29, 315n137; threats to hang Thomas Peters, 232–33, 234

Clarkson, Thomas, 216, 217, 221, 235, 247–48

Clements, William L., Library at the University of Michigan 121

Clinton, Sir Henry, 32, 98, 133, 135, 137, 143, 150, 151, 152–53, 183, 194, 216, 295n6; "freedom and a farm," 121; 1779 Proclamation of, 120–21, 131, 140, 178, 198, 200

Cocks, James, 237, 315n122

Davis, A., 253
Dawes, John, 236
Day, Thomas, 277n44
Declaration of Independence, 94, 112, 120, 159; domestic insurrections in, 13; and racist propaganda toward Native Americans, 13, 264n62
D'Estaing, Comte, 128–29
De Lancey's Brigade, 124
Deinstadt, George, 211–12
Delaney, Stephen, 195
democracy, 287n88; dangers of, 66; from below in Canada, 213
democratic contractarianism, 61, 81; and farmers in western Massachusetts, 256; and Gabriel, 257, 319n60; and John Laurens, 81; and Montesquieu, 73; and Rawls, 278n56; and Rousseau, 73–75; and Woolman, 61
democratic feedback of international politics, 256–57; and *Must Global Politics Constrain Democracy?* (Gilbert), 261n8, 319n58
democratic imperialism, 279n63
democratic internationalism, 242, 244–48, 250, 251–52, 256–57
democratic theory, 273n12; and primacy of equal basic rights 278n45; and self-undermining majority rule 278n45. *See also* democratic contractarianism
Demosthenes, 93, 281n121, 282n149
Dent, John, 25
Devereux, Alexander, 185
Devons, Abraham, 105
Devonshire, David, 197
Dexter, David, 101
dialectic of emancipation and independence, 5, 68, 115, 255, 256–57, 293n139; of liberty, 68, 276n7, 293n139; of republicanism and communism, 68, 255
Dickenson, Geo, 307n113
Digby, 209, 211, 214, 215
Digby, Robert, 180

Dissent to the Massachusetts Convention, 255
divide and rule, 4, 13, 241, 287n85, 316n168; against democracy in Sierra Leone, 241; blacks and Native Americans, 13, 44–45; George Washington about during Shays's Rebellion, 319n56; and *The Invention of the White Race* (Allen), 263n48; as secret of British rule in America, 299n85; as secret of British rule in Canada, 213, 214
Dixon and Hunter's Virginia Gazette, 16
Dixon, Luke, 223
Dixon, Myles, 239
documents, xii
Dodge, Theodore Ayrault, 284n17
Dolly, Quamino, 118, 132
Dolphin Negro, 96
domestic or intestine insurrections, 3, 13, 29, 38, 43, 71–72
Dominica, 206
Doron, Elizabeth, 193
Doron, Peter, 193
Doron, Samuel, 192–93, 201–2
Dorset, Joseph, 146
Douglas (colonel), 184
Douglas, Rosetta, 186
Drayton, William Henry, 86, 92, 166, 167, 202
Drayton, Cathleen, 204
Duberdue, Amelia, 186
Duberdue, Solas, 186
Dublin, Mr. 8
Dubois, Peter, 187
Dufay, Louis, 252
Dulvoyer, W., 247–48
Duncan, John, 126
Dundas, Henry, 220
Dunmore, Earl of (John Murray), 1, 7, 15–37, 83, 116, 131, 133, 145, 170, 199, 205, 224, 265n3, 266n36, 268n63, 268n66; and Colonel Tye, 146; comparison with John Cruden, 134; "a guinea, a crown and

Dunmore, Earl of (John Murray) (*continued*)
freedom," 136; and indentured servants,
29; as inspirer of Southern secession, 16,
270n122; isolation at the end of the war,
137; as liberator, 18, 63; and "liberty to
slaves," 22, 63, 302n22; and mobilization
of black irregulars after Yorktown 133–37;
and moral force of emancipation, 134,
135; as opportunist, 18; Proclamation
of, 7, 9–10, 15, 25–26, 38, 116, 141, 144, 182,
198, 200, 306n105; and reducing Patriots'
"houses to ashes," 18; Royal Ethiopian
Regiment, 15, 22, 27, 142, 197, 205, 267n56,
268n80; Schama's misestimate of, 267n57;
seizing the powder at Williamsburgh,
16–18, 265n14
Dupleix, Prince, 106–7, 286n64
Durnford (captain), 180
Dussel, William, 306n107
Duvalier, "Papa Doc," 319n59
Dyott, William, 210

East Florida, 86, 181, 186, 205, 206; black
emigration from, 205–6; emancipation of
black soldiers by Assembly, 302n22
Edwards, Stephen, 145
Egerton, Douglas, xi, xv, 285n36; on Ga-
briel's Revolt, xiii
Egypt, 189
Elbeck, Jonathan, 193–94
Eldridge, Dick 103
Eldridge, Elleanor, xiii, 103–4
Eldridge, George, 103
Eldridge, Robert, 103
Elizabeth (ship), 192
Ellery, William, 285n31
Elliott, Charles, 313n82
Elliot, Ned, 313n82
Ellis, Dinah, 202
emancipated blacks before Revolution,
299n85
Emerson, Ralph Waldo, 264n61
émigré farmers in Nova Scotia, 213

Emmerich, Andreas, 123
Emmerich's Chasseurs, 123–24
Emmons, Lucretia, 145–46
Engels, Friedrich, 276n7. *See also* Marx,
Karl
engineer department, Port Roseway, 209
England, 205
Enlightenment, vii, 244, 245, 246, 247, 252
Eno, R. D., 214
equality, 241, 255
Episcopal Church of England, 216
Eppes, Francis, 17, 32, 33
Essex County, NJ, 147
Esther, 128
Ettwein, John, 69–70, 71
Eurocentrism, vi
Eutaw Springs, 169, 171
Evans, Thomas, 313n82

Fair American (ship), 192
Falconbridge, Anna Maria, 229, 231–32,
236–37, 237–38, 240; *Narrative of Two Voy-
ages to the River Sierra Leone*, 229, 231–32,
240, 315n123
Fanning (colonel), 227
Fanny (ship), 170
farmers in western Massachusetts, 256
fear, 4, 5
Federalist Papers, 93, 168, 281n121
Fenner, Arthur, 105
Ferguson, Mr., 165
Fick, Elizabeth, 261n11
Field, Samuel, 256
First Rhode Island Regiment, xii, xiii, 28,
98–105, 121, 280n96, 300n110; at Fort
Oswego and Lake Ontario, 102, 103; and
freedom as pay, 100; and Narragansetts,
101, 284n12, n18, 285n34; only 11 percent
had freedom paid for by the Assembly,
284n18; petitions for pay of members,
105; at Redbank, 103; returns of, 101; at
Yorktown, 101, 103, 174–75
Fladeland, Betty, 317n3

Houston, John, 120, 267n56

Howe, Alexander, 209

Howe, William, 28, 29, 30, 64, 113, 147, 180, 195, 227, 307n117, 309n148; and early repudiation of black recruitment, 116; most blacks in the *Book of Negroes* enlisted with, 198–99; Proclamation, 194, 198, 200, 306n107

Hubbell, Nathan, 149

hubris, 275n67

Huddy, Josiah, 146–47, 150

Huger, Isaac, 86

Huggeford, Peter, 195, 204, 309n144

Hughson's tavern, 1

Huguenots, 41, 69; St. Bartholomew's Day massacre, 90

human rights, vii

Humphrey, Joseph, 100

Humphreys, David, 108

Humphreys, Frank Landon, 108

Hunter, William, 3

Hunterdon militia, 146

Husted, Ned, 307n117

Hutchens, Phyllis, 202

Hutchinson, Thomas, 12

imperial hierarchy, 304n59

indentured servants, 29, 211–12, 217, 292n118, 299n85, 303n45

inference to the best explanation, 197, 305n97

Innes, Alexander, 41, 179

inspectors, 198–99, 222, 224, 304n64, 305n75, 307n117; and problems with returns, 122

intermarriage, 114–15, 285n34, 287n105, 298n76

international fight against slavery, vi

Iredell, James, 13

irregular or guerilla warfare, 29, 30, 117, 123, 128; black Dragoons in South Carolina, 117, 137, 154–60; Captain Tye in New York and New Jersey, 137, 141–51; and Dunmore, 133–36; and multiracial bands, 142

Isaac, 306n107

Isard, Mr., 132, 167, 227

Isere, Ansel, 313n82

Israel, 221

Jack, 147

Jackson, Hannah, 158

Jackson, John, 158

Jackson, Judith, 193–94, 305n81

Jackson, Luther, 169, 299n87

Jackson, Peter, 147

Jackson, Rachel, Dampre, and Judy, 308n134

Jackson, Rose, 200

Jacobins, 76, 131, 260n6

Jamaica, 182, 183, 184, 186, 187, 201, 205, 206, 292n118; and free black émigrés, 303n36, n40, n43, n45, n46

Jamaican maroons, 241

Jamaica Rangers, 192

James, C. L. R., 260n1, 261n11

Jefferson, Thomas, xiii, 22, 66, 68, 77, 86, 190, 227, 265n3, 270n119; and calculated propaganda toward Native Americans, 264n62; and domestic insurrections, 13; and Haiti, 256, 260n5; and sacking of his estate by Cornwallis, 119; and Shays's Rebellion, 256; and 30,000 escapees in Virginia, x,119–20, 288n15

Jemmy, 12

Jemmy (Thomas Jeremiah's brother in law), 40, 41, 271n134

Jenkins, Chas, 222

Jeremiah, Thomas, 37, 67, 139, 270n128; crown for freeing of, 39–44; as hero and martyr of freedom, 44; Patriot "trial"/ lynching of, 39–44; and rule of law, 271n134, 271n145

Jessop, William, 211

Johnson, Edward, 31

Johnson, James, 146

Johnson, Samson, 199

Johnson, Samuel, 253; and yelps for liberty, x

Johnson, Samuel (black Loyalist), 317n117

Johnson, Simon, 239

Johnson, Thomas, 228–29

Johnston, George, 26–27, 33, 35–36

Johnston, George (black Loyalist), 211

Johnston, George Milligan, 44

Johnston, William, 26, 35

Jones, Dinah, 223

Jones, John, 126

Jones, John (in *Book of Negroes*), 199

Jones, Joseph, 152, 171–72

Jones, Lucretia, 199

Jones, March, 313n82

Jones, Thomas, 304n59

Jones, Winthrop, 5

Jordan, Luke, 316n156

jubilee, 229, 231

juries, 234

justice, 178, 196

Kaplan, Emma, Nogrady, and Sidney, 302n25, 303n36

Kate, 186

Kay, Margaret, 286n82

Keeling, Robert, 239, 313n82

Kemp's Landing, 26, 35

Kench, Thomas, 109–10; and grand controversy, 109–10; offer to lead black Massachusetts company, 109

Kenny, James, 21

Kenry, William, 187

Kerry, Mary, 2

Key, John, 169

King, Boston, xiii, 188–89, 212, 214, 304n57, 311n38; and famine in Canada, 211; and freedom with the British, 118–19, 189, 201; as a minister, 188

King Jemmy, 237

King Tom, 236–37

King, John, 31

Kingston, March, 158

Kinloch, Francis, 75–79, 90, 279n72; and debates as monarchist with John Laurens, 76–79

Kinsey, James, 249

Kirby, Lewis, 239

Kirkland, Moses, 116, 117

Kirkland, Step, 313n82

Kitchen, William, 96

Kitt, William, 187

Kizell (Kesel), John, 242, 313n82

Knight, Jack, 169

Knowles riot, 10

Knyphausen, Wilhelm, 195

Kolchin, Peter, 138

Lad, Nal, 312n53

Lafayette, James Armistead, 169–70

Lafayette, Marquis de, 170, 245, 317n12

Lake Ontario, 102

Lampert, Frances, 186

Lampert, John, 186

land for white and black Loyalists in Nova Scotia, 209–10

Laurens, Henry, 3, 12, 66–94, 145, 154, 276n4, 279n85, n88; and Article VII in the peace negotiations, 167; on equal farmers *vs.* the parasitism of the slave-owning few, 166; and George Washington concerning John Laurens's proposal, 85–86; and Guinea trade, 70; historians' odd preference for, 277n40; and honor, 67; and John Laurens, 79–85, 167–68, 277n40, 299n79; and lynching of Thomas Jeremiah, 37, 40–43, 271n145; and Moravians, 69–70, 166; and opposition to intermarriage, 298n76; and protestors against the Stamp Act, 67; and Tybee massacre, 37, 43–44

Laurens, James, 70, 71, 72

Laurens, John, xiii, 66–94, 115, 154, 160, 175, 257, 279n85, 283n152, 283n154; as aide-de-camp to Washington, 80; as an American Rousseauean, 76, 168, 246–47, 278n52, 278n58; and black levy in South Carolina, 161–62, 164; as citizen, 84, 93, 168; death

Primus, John, 313n82

Prince, Great, 107

Prince, Little, 107

prophetic religion and antislavery, 53–62

"Protectors," the 287n85

Protestantism, 231, 244. *See also* Sierra Leone

Province of Freedom, 217

Prue, 107

public or common good, 76, 81, 82, 90, 93, 195–96

Public Records Office, 121, 186, 191, 305n92; and hearings in New York in the PRO version of the *Book of Negroes*, 191–95

Pulis, John, 139, 186, 292n107, 292n118, 303n36, 303n40, 303n43, 303nn45–46, 303nn49–50

Pybus, Cassandra, ix; deflationary estimates that 20,000 total escaped to the British and 10,000 free blacks emigrated with the Crown, 309n148, 310n5; discovery that some listed as slaves of Tories in *Book of Negroes* were free, 309n1; and "Jefferson's Faulty Math," 309n148, 310n5; and most sweeping act of emancipation in early American history by the British, 310n4; on numbers of free blacks in Nova Scotia, 310n5; 3,000 free black sailors in London, 310n5; underestimate of collective push for emancipation among blacks, 309n148

Quaker, John, 313n82

Quakers, 53–54, 113, 115, 141, 220, 248, 275n78, 293n123; against slavery, 50–51, 317n4; antiradical baiting against, 65; Loyalism of, 4; men and women Friends of Philadelphia, 250; in New England, 62; and paternalism of toward blacks, 251; 1758 Meeting's barring slave-owners from future meetings, 61; Shrewsbury Friends Meeting, 141. *See also* John Woolman; Colonel Tye

Quarles, Benjamin ix, 310n4; on Dunmore as Liberator, 18

Quarter Master General's Department, 1 June 1780, South Carolina, 126

Quash, 203

Quince, Bob, 203

Quintal, George, 275n83

quitrents, 230–31, 240

racism, 179–80, 185, 187, 219–20, 227, 234, 271n134, 285n37, 290n58; of British, 160, 192, 202, 205, 209–10; of British abolitionists, 225, 230–32; and divide and rule, 4, 13, 213, 214, 241, 287n85; and North American cultural campaign toward Haiti, 319n59; of Patriots, 162, 193, 204–5, 248–52; of white Loyalists toward blacks in Canada, 211, 212, 214, 221; toward Thomas Jeremiah, 271n145

racist distinction between Negroes and other soldiers: among the British, 123–24, 129, 174, 185, 294n152, 301n14; and British distribution of land in Nova Scotia, 209–10; by Lieutenant Colonel Archibald Campbell, 131–32; among the Patriots, 24, 25, 146, 157, 170, 174, 297n40

radical democracy, 231, 241; in America, 255–56; incarnating Sharp's vision, 231; in Sierra Leone, 231, 233, 240–41

Ramsey, David, 92, 129, 165, 204–5

Randal, Prince, 103

Randolph, Edmund, 254

Randolph, Peyton, 17, 265n14

Ranney, William, 160

Rawdon, Lord, 157, 181, 289n26

Rawls, John, 14; and democratic contractarianism, 14; and original position as a theory of the antislavery judgments during the Revolution, xv, 278n56; and veil of ignorance, 278n56

Raynal, Abbe, 256; *Histoire des deux indes* (*History of Two Indias*), 256

Rediker, Marcus, ix, 11; and revolutionary seamen ,11
Reed, Joseph, 62, 63
Refugee Town, Sandy Hook, NJ, 143, 144
refugees (loyalists), 150
Reid (captain), 179
"Remember the Maine," 268n77
Remington, Jabez, 105
Rennalds, 5–6, 262n19
Report on American Manuscripts, 301n6
"Return of Loyalists leaving New York," 197, 305n93, n94, n96
Return of the Number of Men, Women and Children . . . Victualled at New York . . . between 14th & 21st November, 1779, 289n33, 289n35
Return of Negroes, Royal Artillery Department, 28 April 1780, Charlestown, 126
revolutionary crowds (integrated), 46, 66; and Paul Cuffe, 112
revolutions: of black and brown people to the South, vii; in Europe, vii; political, *vs.* social, viii, 260n2. *See also* two revolutions
Reynolds (Rennalds), 5–6
Rhode Island, 95, 161, 284n12; Abolition Society of, 253
Rhode Island Assembly discussions of bondage, 1774–75, 62, 91; and demand for postwar return of black Loyalists, 203; and resolution to purchase and free blacks in First Rhode Island Regiment, 99–100; and retreat from its resolution, 101
Rhode Island Gazette 102
Rhodes, Martin, xv
rich and poor, 279n63
Richard, Betty, 147
Richard, Jacob, 147
Richard, John, 147
Richards, Dick, 306n107
Richerson, Richard, 224
Richmond, VA, 257

Riddell, John, 8
rights of a British subject, 215, 233, 234, 242
rights of man, 73, 80, 241, 242
Rising Sun Tavern, 113
River St. John, Canada, 197
Roaney, Mr., 171
Robert, 249, 318n28
Roberts, Esther, 200
Roberts, Diana, 200
Roberts, Geo, 307n113
Roberts, Hannah, 307n113
Robins (quartermaster), 157
Robinson, Donald, 299n84
Robinson, James, 241
Robinson, Mingo, 101
Robinson, Sylvester, 101
Roebuck (ship), 31, 32, 36
Roeper, Martha Laurens, 93–94
Roger, Abby, 223
Rogers, Henry, 191
Rome, 53, 74
Romeyn, Dirck, 147, 148
Rose, 204
Rose (ship), 179
Rousseau, Jean Jacques, 66, 84; and the abolition of slavery 66, 74–75, 76; and citizenship, 168; and dangers of oligarchy, 75–76, 279n63; *Discours sur les origins de l'inegalite*, 74–75, 81, 246; *Du contrat social*, 73, 246, 295n5; and egalitarian republic, 278n57; and general will, 81, 278n45; influence on the Amis des noirs and the abolitionist movement, 246–47; and the right, 73–74; John Laurens as an American follower of, 73–79, 277n43; on law-giving and appeals to divinity, 295n5; and the security of Odysseus in the cave of Cyclops, 74; and will of all, 74, 76, 78, 278n45
Royal, John P., 31
Royal Armed Boat Company. 149
Royal Artillery. 182

Seventy-First Highlanders, 267n56

Seventy-Sixth Regiment, 204

Shakespeare, 73

shame, 196

Sharp, Granville, x, 224, 225, 263n33, 312n63; *Declaration of the People's Natural Right to a Share in the Legislature*, 216; and democracy in Sierra Leone, 218, 224, 231; As democratic theorist of American liberty, 216–17, 312n62; and forty-hour work week, 219; and inspiring British abolitionist movement, 312nn60–61; and the link of abolitionism to American independence and democracy in Britain, xi, 6, 216, 277n44; and natural equity, 215, 216, 229; and old English system of mutual frankpledge, 218; *Short Sketch of Temporary Regulations*, 218; and Society for Effecting the Abolition of the Slave Trade (London), 244–45, 247, 252; and Somerset 8, 9; and tithingmen and hundreders, 218–19, 231; vision of, 225, 313n63

Sharp, Henry, 141

Sharp, Horatio, 4

Shaw, Robert Gould, 280n96

Shays, Daniel, 256–57, 299n84, 319n56

Shays's Rebellion, 257, 260n6

Shelburne, 197, 198, 204, 209, 212, 214, 221, 235

Shelton, Clough, 170

Shepherd, Elisha, 142

Shepherd, Mary and Priscilla 308n134

Shrewsbury, 293n134

Sidney, 78

Sierra Leone, viii–ix, 141, 217, 229–42, 312n51; "black" as democratic and for self-determination, 231, 232; democratic versus "nationalist" revolt, xiii, 230, 240–41, 257; Henry Beverhout and democratic demands, 235; historians' misinterpretation of black democracy, 231, 235; numbers involved in emigration from Nova Scotia to, 208–9, 313n83,

313n86; the "obnoxious arrogance of the rulers," 231; "white" as authoritarian, dictatorial, exploitative, racist, 231. *See also* radical democracy; Sharp, Granville; Peters, Thomas

Sierra Leone Company, 218; and antiradical ideology, 232; *Orders and Regulations*, 230; promises to prospective black settlers from Canada, 220–21; racist autocracy of, 230

Silas, 248–49

Silva, 187

Silvia, 307n117

Simonsbury, John, 306n107

Sinclair, Matthew, 239

Slain, Simon, 126

slave action against owners as the British approached, 138–39

slave communication of information along hundreds of miles, 120, 270n119

"slave dealers and their abettors," 247–48, 252

slave escape to the crown, 35; and resistance of families, 201–2

slave rebellions, 3, 35, 45, 254, 262n21, 293n139; Bermuda, Granada, St. Croix, Dutch Guyana, British Honduras, Montserrat, St. Thomas, Tobago, 4–5; Caribbean, 2, 3, 4, 28, 47, 59; and Colonel Tye, 142; Perth Amboy, New Jersey, St. Andrew's Parish, South Carolina, Norfolk, Virginia, Dorchester County, Maryland, Boston, Ulster County, New York, 11; St. Bartholomew's Parish, South Carolina, 6, 12; and South Carolina patriotism, 37; Williamsburgh, VA, 17

slavery as torture, rape, murder, exploitation, degradation and the breaking up of families, 172

slave trade: and black celebration of congressional ban of in Boston, 111; as the crime of murder, 273n14

Sleek, Fryday, 313n82